D0212785

THE CHRONICLE OF BATTLE ABBEY

THE CHRONICLE OF BATTLE ABBEY

EDITED AND TRANSLATED
BY
ELEANOR SEARLE

OXFORD
AT THE CLARENDON PRESS
1980

Oxford University Press, Walton Street, Oxford OX2 6DP

OXFORD LONDON GLASGOW
NEW YORK TORONTO MELBOURNE WELLINGTON
KUALA LUMPUR SINGAPORE HONG KONG TOKYO
DELHI BOMBAY CALCUTTA MADRAS KARACHI
NAIROBI DAR ES SALAAM CAPE TOWN

Published in the United States by
Oxford University Press, New York

British Library Cataloguing in Publication Data
Battle Abbey
The chronicle of Battle Abbey. – (Oxford medieval texts)
1. Battle Abbey – History
I. Title II. The chronicle of Battle Abbey
III. Searle, Eleanor IV. Series
942.2'52 DA690.B32 78–40257
ISBN 0–19–822238–6

Printed in Great Britain
at the University Press, Oxford
by Eric Buckley
Printer to the University

TO

THE MEMORY OF

V. H. GALBRAITH

PREFACE

THE editor has many debts of gratitude to scholars who have generously given their time and have answered the many questions that arise in the course of such a work. Most particularly I am grateful to Dr. Michael Winterbottom who reviewed the entire Latin text and English translation. His suggested emendations of the text have been acknowledged in the notes below. His many suggestions have been an incalculable help in the translation, and any inaccuracies and inelegancies that remain are my own responsibility. To Professor C. N. L. Brooke I am grateful for his comments on the text and for his constant encouragement and help. I am grateful too to Dr. Diana E. Greenway for the time and care she has given to the work. Professor Richard Rouse generously put at my disposal his great knowledge of codicology and palaeography, and I am deeply grateful for his help. To the President and Fellows of New Hall, Cambridge, I owe many thanks for allowing me to join their congenial number during a summer when this work was in its early stages. I am also indebted to Carol B. Pearson for her invaluable advice and help in making the index. To the Huntington Library I owe the gratitude of one who continually enjoys its scholarly riches and incomparable atmosphere.

University of California, Institute of Technology

CONTENTS

ABBREVIATIONS

Biblical references are to the Vulgate

Benson, *Bishop-Elect*: R. L. Benson, *The Bishop-Elect, a study in medieval ecclesiastical office* (Princeton, 1968)

BL: British Library

Cal.Ch.Rolls: *Calendar of the Charter Rolls 1226–1516*, 6 vols. (HMSO, London, 1903–27)

Carmen: *The Carmen de Hastingae Proelio of Guy bishop of Amiens*, ed. C. Morton and H. Muntz (OMT, 1972)

Constable, *Tithes*: Giles Constable, *Monastic Tithes from their Origins to the Twelfth Century* (Cambridge, 1964)

DB: *Liber Censualis, vocatus Domesday Book*, 4 vols. (Record Commission, London, 1783–1816)

Dialogus: *Dialogus de Scaccario*, ed. Charles Johnson (NMT, 1950)

DNB: *Dictionary of National Biography*, ed. L. Stephen and S. Lee (London, 1885–1901)

Downer, *Leges Henrici Primi*: *Leges Henrici Primi*, ed. L. J. Downer (Oxford, 1972)

Du Boulay, *Canterbury*: F. R. H. Du Boulay, *The Lordship of Canterbury* (London, 1966)

Eadmer, *Hist.Nov.*: Eadmer, *Historia Novorum in Anglia*, ed. M. Rule (RS, 1884)

Econ.H.Rev.: *Economic History Review*

EETS: Early English Text Society

EHR: *English Historical Review*

Gervase of Canterbury: *The Historical Works of Gervase of Canterbury*, ed. W. Stubbs, 2 vols. (RS, 1879–80)

Gratian: *Corpus juris canonici I: Decretum Gratiani*, ed. E. Friedberg (Leipzig, 1879)

HBA: Henry E. Huntington Library, Battle Abbey Collection

Heads: *The Heads of Religious Houses, England and Wales, 940–1216*, ed. D. Knowles, C. N. L. Brooke, V. C. M. London (Cambridge, 1972)

Hist.MSS.Comm.: *Royal Commission on Historical Manuscripts*, Reports and Calendars.

HMSO: Her Majesty's Stationery Office

Lanfranc, *Constitutions*: *The Monastic Constitutions of Lanfranc*, ed. D. Knowles (NMT, 1951)

Le Neve, ed. Greenway: *Fasti Ecclesiae Anglicanae 1066–1300*, ed. J. Le Neve: i, *St. Paul's London*, compiled by Diana E. Greenway (London, 1968), ii, *Monastic Cathedrals (Northern and Southern Provinces)*, compiled by Diana E. Greenway (London, 1971)

Letters of Gilbert Foliot: *The Letters and Charters of Gilbert Foliot . . .*, ed. A. Morey and C. N. L. Brooke (Cambridge, 1967)

Letters of John of Salisbury: *The Letters of John of Salisbury*, i, ed. W. J. Millor and H. E. Butler, revised by C. N. L. Brooke (NMT, 1955); ii, ed. W. J. Millor and C. N. L. Brooke (OMT, 1979)

Malmesbury, *De Gestis*: William of Malmesbury, *De Gestis Regum Anglorum*, 2 vols., ed. W. Stubbs (RS, 1887–9)

Materials: *Materials for the History of Thomas Becket* . . . 7 vols., ed. J. C. Robertson and J B. Sheppard (RS, 1875–85)

Mayr-Harting, *Acta*: *The Acta of the Bishops of Chichester 1075–1207*, ed. H. Mayr-Harting, Canterbury and York Society lvi (1964)

Medieval Miscellany: *A Medieval Miscellany for Doris Mary Stenton*, PR Soc. xxxvi (1962 for 1960)

Milsom, *Legal Framework*: S. F. C. Milsom, *The Legal Framework of English Feudalism* (Cambridge, 1976)

NMT: Nelson's Medieval Texts

OMT: Oxford Medieval Texts

Ord.Vit.: *The Ecclesiastical History of Orderic Vitalis*, ed. Marjorie Chibnall (OMT, 1968–)

PL: *Patrologiae Cursus Completus, series Latina*, ed. J. P. Migne (Paris, 1844–64)

PN Soc.: English Place-Name Society

PR: *Pipe Roll*, edited for the Publications of the Pipe Roll Society, London

PRO: Public Record Office, London

Proc.Brit.Acad.: *Proceedings of the British Academy*

PR Soc.: Pipe Roll Society, London

Ralph de Diceto: *Radulphi de Diceto . . . opera historica*, ed. W. Stubbs (RS), 1876, 2 vols.

Red Book: *Red Book of the Exchequer*, ed. H. Hall, 3 vols. (RS, 1896)

Regesta: *Regesta Regum Anglo-Normannorum 1066–1154*, i, *Regesta Willelmi Conquestoris et Willelmi Rufi 1066–1100*, ed. H. W. C. Davis (Oxford, 1913); ii, *Regesta Henrici Primi 1100–1135*, ed. Charles Johnson and H. A. Cronne (Oxford, 1956); iii, *Regesta Regis Stephani ac Mathildis Imperatricis ac Gaufridi et Henrici Ducum Normannorum 1135–1154*, ed. H. A. Cronne and R. H. C. Davis (Oxford, 1968) (iv *not used*)

Regula: *Regula sancti Benedicti*

Regularis Concordia: *Regularis Concordia*, ed. T. Symons (NMT, 1953)

Religious Houses: D. Knowles and R. N. Hadcock, *Medieval Religious Houses, England and Wales* (2nd edn., London, 1971)

Rog. Howden: *Chronica Rogeri de Houedene*, ed. W. Stubbs, 4 vols. (RS, 1868–71)

RS: Rolls Series

Saltman, *Theobald*: Avrom Saltman, *Theobald, Archbishop of Canterbury* (London, 1956)

Searle, *Lordship*: Eleanor Searle, *Lordship and Community: Battle Abbey and its Banlieu 1066–1538* (Toronto, 1974)

Stubbs, *Charters*: *Select Charters and other illustrations of English Constitutional History from the earliest times to the reign of Edward the First*, ed. W. Stubbs, ninth edition revised by H. W. C. Davis (Oxford, 1913)

TRHS: *Transactions of the Royal Historical Society*

Van Caenegem, *Writs*: R. C. Van Caenegem, *Royal Writs in England from the Conquest to Glanvill*, Selden Society, lxxvii (1958/9)

VCH: *Victoria History of the Counties of England*

VE: *Valor Ecclesiasticus, temp. Henrici VIII auctoritate regia institutus*, ed. J. Caley and J. Hunter (Record Commission, London 1810–34)

Wace: *Le Roman de Rou de Wace*, ed. A. J. Holden, Société des anciens textes français (Paris, 1970)

Walther: Hans Walther, *Proverbia sententiaeque Latinitatis medii aevi: lateinische Sprichwörter und Sentenzen des Mittelalters in alphabetischer Anordnung*, 6 vols. (Göttingen, 1963–9)

Warren, *Henry II*: W. L. Warren, *Henry II* (London, 1973)

West, *Justiciar*: F. J. West, *The Justiciarship in England 1066–1232* (Cambridge, 1966)

Will. Jum.: William of Jumièges, *Gesta Normannorum Ducum*, ed. Jean Marx (Rouen, 1914)

Will. Newburgh: William of Newburgh, *Historia rerum Anglicarum* in vols. i, ii of *Chronicles of the reigns of Stephen, Henry II and Richard I*, ed. R. Howlett, 4 vols. (RS, 1884–9)

Will. Poit.: William of Poitiers, *Histoire de Guillaume le Conquérant*, ed. Raymonde Foreville (Paris, 1952)

INTRODUCTION

(i) *The Historical Context*

THE text printed here and long known as 'the chronicle of Battle abbey' is a roughly chronological account of legal and administrative affairs of Battle abbey, a Benedictine monastery in Sussex, from the foundation of the house in the late eleventh century until the 1180s. It is, at the same time, one of the liveliest narratives of the twelfth century, offering a vivid and almost certainly first-hand account of Henry II's court in the years during which the king's great legal innovations were being created. When, after the dissolution of the monastery, the text was bound into a volume with various annals and 'Brut' histories, it was entered in the list of contents as a 'Cronicon'.[1] Yet the term is something of a misnomer. Our text was not written to recount history, but, as the author tells us in his opening paragraph, to commit to writing pieces of evidence about the abbey's lands, and to explain the background and prosecution of a series of lawsuits, few if any of which could be thought fully settled when he was writing. *The Chronicle of Battle Abbey* is both a narrative cartulary and, at the same time, the casebook of a common lawyer, an old man writing to instruct his successors on how to carry on a number of cases, one, in particular, of the greatest delicacy: the notorious dispute between Abbot Walter de Luci of Battle and Bishop Hilary of Chichester, in which the abbey had won, quite against all expectation, complete immunity from the bishop's jurisdiction.[2]

Battle abbey, as our author tells us, was founded by William the Conqueror on the site of the battle of Hastings. It had been generously endowed with estates, with jurisdictional privileges, and with sweeping exemptions from the harassment of governmental officials, secular, and, probably, ecclesiastical. Our author

[1] The text was bound with others by the time it became part of the Cotton collection in the seventeenth century. For the MS., see below, pp. 23–8.

[2] For the author, see below, pp. 9 ff. It should be noted briefly here that there are two independent sections of the chronicle, probably by two different authors. The first, brief, section is a collection of abbey documents, and hardly a narrative; the main author's text begins on p. 66 below.

carefully includes in his text the written evidence of endowment and privileges, the charters of William I and his successors' confirmations.[1] His problem, however, was not an easy one. On the one hand his abbey claimed unusually great privileges that would require vigorous defence and convincing evidence, precisely because they were great. On the other hand, there was the difficulty that however genuine the oral tradition of the Conqueror's gift of immunities, the abbey's written evidence had been forged in the 1150s. The charters our author cites are extant today and we can see that this is so.[2] The delicate task he undertook was that of recounting the story of how an oral tradition, shared by diocesan and monks, sufficed to ensure the abbey an acceptable degree of independence until an abbot and a bishop quarrelled over the nature of the evidence required to defend anomalous privileges. He tells his tale with much indirection, avoiding both the temptation to present the charters explicitly as genuine, and the admission that they were not. In his roundabout way he puts Battle's forgeries in context, most probably to warn his successors. He has thereby left a document of great value. Forgeries of the twelfth century abound, but usually we can only guess at the forgers' motives. In the Battle chronicle the veil is for a moment lifted, and we can see the living world in which an abbot came to the pass where forgery was his last, best hope of victory.

In 1147 a trained canon lawyer became bishop of Chichester, the diocese in which Battle lay. Expecting his full diocesan rights, he became increasingly impatient at being referred by the monks to stories of William the Conqueror. At last he excommunicated the abbot, Walter de Luci. But this was an abbot with no ordinary connections. He was the brother of the chief justiciar of England, Richard de Luci, the centre of the royal administration. Within a short time the matter came before the royal court, and suddenly charters were at hand. They are the charters our author uses. He

[1] The question of the development of the abbey's jurisdiction and its economic development is analysed by the present author in *Lordship and Community: Battle Abbey and its Banlieu 1066–1538* (Pontifical Institute of Mediaeval Studies, Toronto, 1974). There the chronicle is heavily relied on, and its relation to other evidence is examined.

[2] They are printed and studied by E. Searle, 'Battle Abbey and Exemption: the forged charters', *EHR*, lxxxiii (1968), 449–80. The charters and the chronicle were studied in the context of the entire development of exemption by David Knowles, 'The Growth of Exemption', *Downside Review*, l, N.S. xxxi (1932), 218–25, 431–53.

had, perhaps, little choice but to use them, for they are, with one significant exception, the basic evidence of landholding and secular privileges necessary for the legal affairs of the abbey.[1] Certainly, however, he treats these dangerous charters carefully, pointing out the phrases that were objectionable to a Lambeth gathering before which they were read, and describing the subsequent trial before Henry II in such a way that we are left in no doubt that the outcome was an act of patronage by the king to his justiciar, however much Henry required that charters be in evidence to justify his decision. From the chronicler's narration one can see that he believed in the oral tradition of his abbey. But he knew better than to believe in his abbey's charters, and he did not defend them as he was willing to defend the essential truth of the tradition.

Our author's tale, then, gives us important testimony about the manœuvrings that accompanied the increasingly potent claims to jurisdiction made on behalf of the episcopal office in the twelfth century in England. Few stories are more detailed, and few can be more revealing. At the same time the tale concerns an important change in the nature of acceptable legal evidence, from oral tradition to written record. The significance of the change can hardly be over-emphasized. Our author shows the English Exchequer and the royal courts coming to rely upon the written word before writing itself was widespread. As far as the administrative practices of monasteries were concerned, the change to written record-keeping clearly opened new possibilities in the exploitation of their endowments. The change itself is marked by activity along two lines in particular, and often marred or accelerated by crises such as the quarrel of the abbot of Battle and his diocesan. Ceremonies of donation when lands were acquired had, time out of mind, been designed to be memorable.[2] Now they came to be more and more commonly reinforced by the evidence of charters, even when the donation and the donor were relatively unimportant. When the monks of Battle bought a meadow, they solemnly accepted the 'donor' into confraternity, gave his son a dog—and had a charter written up. Twelfth-century charters frequently

[1] The exception is a charter of William I that did not mention ecclesiastical exemption. Our author was enthusiastic when Abbot Walter's successor chose to make it the foundation of the abbey's claims to secular liberties. See below, pp. 308–12.

[2] For an example, see below, pp. 252–4, Abbot Walter's impressive ceremony to mark his obit gift to his abbey.

express the new confidence in writing and a strong distrust of memory.[1] A 'person about whom there are doubts', the abbot of Battle is told, is required by papal administrative practice, to offer, with his oath, a written document by which he can be more securely bound.[2] We are shown a case being won at common law, but the extant charter that records the settlement includes the agreements, not only of the abbey and its unsuccessful opponent, but of his uncle, mother, brothers, and cousin—all possible claimants, bound for ever by writing.

The second line of activity was the replacement of the repeated tales of the elders concerning material matters and patrons, with less fallible and more indestructible documentation. With these activities was necessarily associated a change of mental habit no less profound than that connected with the making of indexes and with the correlation of easily available, but discordant, texts.[3] For whereas the best defence of rights preserved by oral tradition is stubborn tenacity and perhaps a dramatically demonstrated belief in the efficacy of supernatural aid, the defence of the easily retrieved and documented claim is rationality, argument, and quickness of mind. On the one side of this cultural divide lies collective memory; on the other lies the archive and the cartulary.

Between them lay the age of the charter-forgery and of such a chronicle as that of Battle: a history of the house, recording the story of the endowment of the abbey and of its subsequent care.[4]

[1] *Facsimiles of Early Charters in Oxford Muniment Rooms*, ed. H. E. Salter (Oxford, 1929), no. 6 (1140): 'Quoniam breuis est uita hominis super terram et etas uolubilis rerum gestarum obscurat memoriam, necesse est que predecessorum confirmauerit auctoritas literarum testimonio committere, ne aliquibus causis emergentibus, ea posteritas ualeat informare', and nos. 9, 11, 27. *Facsimiles of Early Charters from Northamptonshire Collections*, ed. F. M. Stenton, Northants. Rec. Soc. iv (London, 1930), no. 56. The *Leges Henrici Primi*, ed. L. J. Downer (Oxford, 1972) expresses the same thought in a reference to Augustine, p. 90: c. 5, 18.

[2] Below, p. 166.

[3] See Richard Rouse, *The Development of Aids to Study in the Thirteenth Century*, forthcoming. David Walker, 'The Organization of Material in Medieval Cartularies', in *The Study of Medieval Records. Essays in Honour of Kathleen Major* (Oxford, 1971), pp. 132–50. For the relation between the making of indexes, references to government archives, and the defence of *quo warranto* suits in the thirteenth century see Searle, *Lordship*, pp. 243–6.

[4] There are many such, particularly among the publications of the Rolls Series. For two further examples, not published there, see F. M. Stenton, *The Early History of the Abbey of Abingdon*, University College of Reading, Studies in Local History (Oxford, 1913) and *Liber Eliensis*, ed. E. O. Blake, Camden Third Ser. xcii (London, 1962). One of the most interesting examples, if one

Neither forgery nor 'house history' were entirely replaced by the archive and the cartulary. But both were at their height during the twelfth century, when challenges from ecclesiastical and secular rulers questioned searchingly the old traditions of monastic houses; when, in Norman England especially, the increasing powers of the royal court made the recovery of properties better pursued by brisk legal action than by a boundary-march with the relics, and not least, when the hide- and wool-trade had sufficiently flourished to make parchment easily available.

This is the historical moment of the 'house history' known as the *Chronicle of Battle Abbey*. Our author was as aware of the danger of forged evidence as he was of the problems of detecting forgery. He had heard Henry II laugh about the problem and tell a litigant that if he could prove his contentions that a certain seal of Henry I was a forgery, a thousand pounds' worth of property would be the royal windfall.[1] Forgery was perhaps usually a step in providing the house with charters required by royal and ecclesiastical courts.[2] But although they must often have stated no more than the monastery's oral tradition, the opportunity to go farther—too far—was very real. The danger that such forgeries constituted to the genuine tradition must have provided an incentive to collect the house's documents into a narrative history rather than a plain cartulary, for, out of context, 'doctored' charters could be very vulnerable. Where there was uncertainty or ambiguity, the best testimony as to a privilege or a possession was often the tale of its donation and of its unwearied defence over the years, written and preserved in a desired version for the future. There is a warning, as well as a plaintive, note to a preface which avers that, since human memory is defective and charity cold, 'it is worthwhile to reduce to writing certain things which may be useful . . . and, by

considers the genre rather widely, is Abbot Suger's *De rebus in administratione sua gestis*.

[1] Below, p. 216.

[2] The general problem of twelfth-century forgeries in Benedictine houses is set out by C. N. L. Brooke in 'Episcopal Charters for Wix Priory', in *A Medieval Miscellany for Doris Mary Stenton*, ed. Patricia M. Barnes and C. F. Slade, PR Soc., N.S. xxxvi (1962), pp. 54–5. For the forgeries of some other houses during the period, see P. Chaplais, 'The Original Charters of Herbert and Gervase, abbots of Westminster (1121–1157)', op. cit., pp. 89 ff., W. Levison, *England and the Continent in the Eighth Century* (Oxford, 1946), Appendices 1, 4, and G. V. Scammell, *Hugh du Puiset, bishop of Durham* (Cambridge, 1956), Appendix 4.

inspection of this little book, may help our brethren, both present and to come, when difficulties arise and they are persecuted by a cruel world'.[1] The warning, if not the pathos, is there too in the preface of the Battle chronicler.

Like many such monastic histories, a central theme of our author's chronicle is the preservation of an oral tradition, one of inadequately conveyed rights faithfully defended, of abbots chivvied into doing their duty towards corporations that would endure when they were gone. Such traditions have often the immediacy of dramatic stories told to willing listeners, and in this they should rank with the *lais* and *chansons* that were their contemporary secular expression. Those who had passed down such traditions must often have been gifted story-tellers, men who had polished their tales over the years to perfection. Such a man is our author, an old lawyer set, at the end of his life, to record his own voice, the voice of the community. He chose to integrate the forged charters into his tale in such a way that he could use and pass down what was valuable in them, yet tell no direct lies concerning them. He surmounts the difficulty with the style of a great story-teller. He neither lies, nor tells the plain truth, about an action that was both a serious crime and a useful bit of work for the abbey. Instead, he tells his story as a series of scenes set largely in the court of Henry II, and in them the politics of patronage is clearly, though delicately, sketched. Like a *trouvère*, our author builds scenes and portrays character, and he relies upon his readers' scepticism and their sensitivity to his language to enable them to see what he is telling them.

The generation that followed understood his warning. For when a new bishop reopened the case in the early thirteenth century, the abbey relied upon only its genuine charters. But by the 1230s a new generation of administrators approached their muniments in a new way. During that decade the chronicle was replaced by a cartulary in which the old charters were fully copied, forged and genuine alike. There is no reason to think that the chronicler's work was relied upon, for the earliest annotations are in a fourteenth-century hand. His oblique warning had, of course, been right. In January, 1234, the forgeries were again brought forward as evidence against the bishop, and Battle's case collapsed for ever.[2]

[1] *Ecclesie de Bernewelle, Liber Memorandorum*, ed. J. Willis Clark (Cambridge, 1907), pp. x, 37.

[2] For the events, see Searle, *Lordship*, pp. 95–9.

If the chronicler was still read, such insinuations as his went unregarded. Perhaps such artistry, half revealing, half concealing the truth, could be appreciated only by men who must have known something of the tale already, as we can know it from examining the charters our author used. Whatever the reason, the limitations of this essentially oral, ironic tradition are all too clear in the failure of the Battle chronicle to keep alive its warning.

(ii) *The Text and its Sources: the Text's Importance*

(*a*) *The Two Chronicles*

The text published here is in fact two separate anonymous chronicles, bound together in BL MS. Cotton Domitian A ii. The first is by far the shorter of the two. It begins with a well known account of the invasion of England by Duke William, to which we shall return; it then records, somewhat haphazardly, a number of documents concerning the abbey's *banlieu*. There is no reason to think that the author intended to do more than this. None of the documents he copied has survived elsewhere, but they can be compared with similar documents of a slightly later period in the region, and with the later documents of Battle abbey. They appear to be accurate, and they are revealing about the settlement of the Weald in the Anglo-Norman period.[1] The second chronicle is the main text. It occupies ff. 22–130. We have no way of knowing whether the two were bound together in the Middle Ages. But their survival and juxtaposition in the Cotton volume give some reason to think that they had been connected earlier. Certainly one preface sufficed for both and succinctly expresses their common purpose. Which chronicler wrote the preface is impossible to tell. It now covers precisely one side of a leaf, and could have been written as a common preface from the beginning. That leaf, with a few following, was recopied in the thirteenth century, leaving no clue as to the scribe who wrote the autograph. The preface mentions an earlier narrative which it is the author's intention now to expand. H. W. C. Davis concluded that the first chronicle is in fact the later, and is a fragment of a revision of the second, main text.[2] This conclusion rests upon the first author's detailed treatment of the abbey's endowment, the local liberty court, and the tenantry.

[1] Searle, *Lordship*, pp. 44–88.

[2] H. W. C. Davis, 'The Chronicle of Battle Abbey', *EHR*, xxix (1914), 427.

Two considerations, however, seem to me to make an opposite conclusion more likely. In the first place, our second, main author seems to be referring to the preface when, after recounting the long lawsuit with the bishop of Chichester, he returns to lawsuits over property, and, as a connecting device, uses the very phraseology of the preface.[1] This argument gains strength from the fact that a correction of the first chronicle was made in what is almost certainly the main hand of the second.[2]

There is no way of telling from internal evidence which chronicler wrote first. Both wrote after 1155, for both use a forged foundation charter shown for the first time, and very likely forged, in that year.[3] The second chronicle can be dated rather more precisely, for it mentions events of the 1180s. The first chronicler gives one clue by which we may date his work, when he speaks of the 'pilgrims' house called the hostel', near the abbey gate. Abbot Odo (1175–1200) is said by the second chronicler to have built such a guest-house. We appear therefore to have contemporaries, both writing in the last third of the twelfth century, doing the same job. Their chronicles were bound together probably because each included valuable information not found in the other. The main sources of both are pointed out in their common preface: the written muniments of the house, particularly its charters, the oral tradition of the house, and personal memory.

(*b*) *The Main Chronicler: the World of the Twelfth-Century Law*

The real importance of the text lies in the tale told by the main chronicler, for his chief source is evidently his own experience. There is no reason to distrust his account of that experience, for he has been shown, again and again, from independent evidence, to be reliable and accurate. His circumstantial story of Henry II devising the *inspeximus* clause and explaining exactly how it would be an improvement upon earlier confirmation formulae, had long been considered, as V. H. Galbraith pointed out, 'too good to be true', until Professor Galbraith happened to find the very charter of which our author was writing.[4] The account of Exchequer's reception of the abbey's claims concerning the Forest Pleas is fully

[1] Below, p. 210. This may imply that he wrote the preface, since it refers to an earlier work, now being enlarged.

[2] On f. 10. Below, pp. 27, 38.

[3] Below, pp. 36, 66, 154.

[4] V. H. Galbraith, 'A New Charter of Henry II to Battle Abbey', *EHR*, lii (1937), 68. Below, pp. 310–12.

substantiated by the published Pipe Rolls.[1] Our author was writing to instruct his successors in legal administration: for them he carefully avoided lying about the abbey's forged charters, but he directed them pointedly to a genuine charter, of which several copies had recently been obtained from the royal Chancery, and which, he advises, should be used in secular suits.[2] He was recording his experiences as part of the legal education of his abbey's future advocates, writing a legal textbook. His stories are very good indeed, but, seen in the context of their function, they are not too good to be true. There is much reason to accept them.

What, then, do we know about our chronicler? He tells us that he witnessed an event in chapter during the abbacy of Warner (1125–38).[3] The last event he mentions occurred some fifty years later, in 1184.[4] His account breaks off at the settlement of a lawsuit in 1176, and there ceased to be a single copyist some time earlier.[5] From the 1150s on, he writes as one who witnessed case after case before the many forms of the *curia regis*, and he relates with such particularity the background upon which the pleading of each case rested that it is reasonable to infer that he was himself the advocate. Further, although few monks are named in his work, one monk, and he alone, is mentioned twice by name, and as an abbey advocate. The monk conducted cases at which our author seems to have been present. He was called Osmund, we are told. Though it goes beyond our evidence to identify Osmund as our author—for that author kept his textbook deliberately anonymous—it is not too much to imagine that he succumbed to temptation so far as to introduce himself, discreetly, to the later reader, in the lawyer, Brother Osmund.

Whatever his name, the chronicler lived during the profound changes in culture and society of which we have spoken in the first part of the introduction; he outlived Henry I and Stephen, and may have died about the time of Henry II's death in 1189.[6] Such a long life, and in such a period, has an interest in itself. The cast

[1] Below, p. 222, and ibid. n. 1.

[2] Below, p. 312.

[3] Below, p. 106.

[4] Below, p. 310. The translation of Walter of Coutances to the archbishopric of Rouen in 1184.

[5] At the foot of f. 83v. Below, p. 208.

[6] The chronicler generally mentions the later careers of ecclesiastics who enter his tale, and his omission of the elevation of Godfrey de Luci to the bishopric of Winchester in 1189 is some reason to imagine that our author himself died between 1184 and 1189.

of mind of a lawyer during a period when the law was rapidly developing, and for which such personal evidence is virtually lacking, has real significance. And we can know a good deal about our author's mind and his education. He tells us that he is making use of oral testimony as well as written. His first precedent at common law goes back to the first decade of the twelfth century. The case has no bearing on any of his later cases, for its importance was in establishing the claim to conduct a private court.[1] Our author does not concern himself with Battle's own court. His work seems to have lain in defending the abbey's interests as a litigant in courts outside its liberty. The memory of his elders concerning the case in Henry I's early years may well have been part of the education of monks destined for legal careers, and entered into his text as a story that would be otherwise forgotten and is not insignificant in the abbey's legal history. Indeed, the garbled story is revealing, particularly of the limitations of oral tradition and of the primitiveness of legal procedure under the Lion of Justice. His real education in the law was pursued in court itself, as a member of the abbot's entourage and then, very likely, as the abbot's advocate, pleading alone.[2] The abbot of his young manhood and active maturity was Walter de Luci, brother of the chief justiciar and himself a pleader before the royal courts. Our author writes as if he had been Abbot Walter's clerk and apprentice, and his successor in advocacy. If so, his career brought him very close to the men whose administrative changes were revolutionizing English land-law, and an acute awareness of legal innovation pervades his work. His method, for example, of setting out a case for his readers is the pleading of *novel disseisin*, as it appears in our earliest records, and as it was worked out during his active career. In several instances, as when dealing with advowsons, royal justices had not yet quite hit upon the forms of action that were to characterize the common law after *c.* 1180. In his accounts of them we are able to see the sorts of cases that were the very difficulties that the final forms of the assizes were meant to solve.[3] His teachers, as was to be the case with common lawyers for so long, were the royal justices at work, and as with any lawyer, his professional education continued

[1] Below, pp. 108–12.

[2] Besides the cases in which Brother Osmund's advocacy is described, and others minutely and coherently described, the legal procedures of Exchequer are described with the detail and accuracy of one who understood them.

[3] e.g. below, pp. 232 ff.

throughout his career. Most dramatic of all teachers was Henry II himself, on the bench and among his councillors, not only presiding, but patiently explaining his legal and administrative innovations to great men, petty knights, and monks alike.[1]

Trained in this way, it is not perhaps surprising that our author is a superb raconteur. Nor is it surprising to find, as we do, that, like common lawyers for so long after him, he was a common law man to the bone. He is dismissive of the ineffective honorial court of the local magnate, the count of Eu;[2] he is deeply impressed with the effectiveness of Henry II's legal administration, and deeply distrustful of the new ecclesiastical courts of papal judges-delegate.[3] Towards the end of his life, he found his old training, and that available in his abbey, unequal to the task of defending its interests in those new courts where they were compelled to plead. And he gives, quite incidentally, an interesting example of another ecclesiastic taking the new road that led to competence in such courts. For it is significant that Walter de Luci in the 1130s had seen his chance for a bishopric as through a monastery and the common-law courts of England; by the 1170s, his nephew's course lay via the schools abroad, no doubt Bologna. Uncle and nephew were both shrewd men, and in fact Godfrey de Luci's road led ultimately to the *cathedra* of Winchester.[4]

Our author's literary education left him with a sound style in which to convey a story that required at times considerable indirection. He writes a complex and rather heavy Latin, but he has a wide vocabulary and a subtle sense of the meaning of words. His style is more classical than that of the generality of contemporary chroniclers. It is hardly, however, to be compared with the Latinity of his epoch's best stylists, men like John of Salisbury. Long sentences tempted him, and occasionally into syntactical obscurity. His piety is simple and his moral world is that of the Rule of St. Benedict, by which he judges the life of his abbey and the two abbots he knew so well. Walter de Luci's wordly wit, abilities, and energy in the abbey's interests our author appreciates

[1] Below, pp. 216, 310–12. [2] Below, p. 212.

[3] Below, pp. 226 ff. For a good summary of the system of appeals to Rome and the direction of those appeals to local judges-delegate in the mid-twelfth century see A. Morey and C. N. L. Brooke, *Gilbert Foliot and his Letters* (Cambridge, 1965), pp. 234–44.

[4] Below, p. 326. The development of canonical thought in the twelfth century towards jurisdictional, and away from the consecrational, aspects of ecclesiastical office is traced by R. L. Benson, *The Bishop-Elect* (Princeton, 1968).

and praises. But with a delicate charity informing his judgement, he shows us, none the less, a hard and haughty man, ruling his monks' spiritual development rather than guiding it. Abbot Odo, who followed Walter, was our author's ideal, and the portrait he draws of Odo, piling incident upon incident with the most minute observation, is surely one of the freshest that remains to us from the epoch. The ageing lawyer had found in Odo the ideal presented to him as a young monk during the distant days of Henry I, and his whole being responded to its unworldly, stubborn sweetness.

To judge from his literary allusions, our author's reading was neither wide nor classical. Most are from the Rule of St. Benedict or from the Bible, and there they are largely confined to Psalms, the more familiar stories, and to proverbs. Besides legal precedent, proverbs and popular maxims are his chief mental baggage, and a rhetoric that can hardly stem from another source than simple monastic sermons is the highest flight of his literary fancy. 'Man proposes; God disposes' is by far his most commonly used proverb, largely to comment on the discomfiture of enemies. He knows little of politics. The subject does not interest him sufficiently to stir his considerable powers of observation. He recounts a jejune and credulous version of the dispute between Henry and Becket, and contents himself with a naïvely one-sided version of Becket's relations with the English bishops, of whom he was inclined to believe the worst.

Two recurrent preoccupations stand out in his narrative, beyond his carefully told tale of his abbot's lawsuit over immunity. The first preoccupation is explicit. It is seisin, the peaceable possession of land. From few other sources do we get quite so vivid a sense of the difficulty of keeping hold of land before the legal work of Henry II, and of the support that Henry's assizes found among landlords who understood their significance.[1] Our author is acutely conscious that the reign of Stephen was exceedingly difficult for all but the violent. He speaks his mind clearly in a number of rightly famous, pithy phrases about that time 'in the midst of iniquity'. But he gives significant evidence of the difficulty of controlling estates in any case, before Henry II's legal work made secure freehold tenure a reality for at least those with good evidence and good

[1] As his abbey's advocate in its lawsuits as under-tenant, he was aware of those abuses of seignorial power to which the assizes were addressed, and he understood the proprietary implications. Cf. Milsom, *Legal Framework*, chap. 2.

lawyers. Such testimony as that of our author is of as great significance for the questions of economic development in the twelfth century as for legal history. Before the availability of the possessory assizes, it is clear, an estate's chief lord might demand from his enfeoffed tenant payments that were variable and that could increase disastrously if the holder invested in his estate and increased its productivity. As the monks of Battle found, after improving a manor they had purchased from a Norman undertenant of Withelard de Baillol and with that lord's confirmation, a lord could even dispossess his improving tenant and keep his chattels, as well as the land, without compensation.[1] From the pleading in the case of Barnhorn manor, we see that, as late as the 1150s or 1160s, an overlord could look upon the chattels of a knightly tenant as his own, and ask to be awarded them whatever the outcome of the land case.[2] Feudal enfeoffment, land tenure secured by the principle of lordship, seems to our author the very opposite of security: it is a chief obstacle to uninterrupted possession. It prevents improvements: lords repossess at will; archdeacons prey upon ecclesiastical estates under their protection; local magnates, relied upon as patrons, give out others' lands to their own followers. For our author, land-law was a tenurial chaos out of which Henry II was beginning to bring the order of secure seisin and fixed payments to the overlord. The hope engendered was clearly heady.

A second preoccupation of our author is not treated directly, for it is not of legal interest to him. Rather, it is conveyed as if it were the air that the court of Henry II breathed: one may call it 'seignorial conciliarism'. His tale of the lawsuit over wreck is evidence, not only for early twelfth-century maritime custom; more important perhaps is Abbot Walter's argument that while kings may change law for their own lifetimes at their own will, such laws will not outlive them, except with the consent of council.[3] The abbey's liberties are thought of, anachronistically, as bestowed by the Conqueror after taking counsel.[4] Henry II, after 1175, refuses to confirm an abbey charter except by counsel.[5] The rhetoric of conciliarism reaches its height as Richard de Luci and Robert, earl of Leicester, argue for the abbey's ecclesiastical immunity before Henry II in 1157. They are depicted as present-

[1] Below, pp. 210–12. [2] Below, p. 216. [3] Below, p. 144.
[4] Below, p. 148. [5] Below, p. 310.

ing to the new Angevin king a historiography of the Norman Conquest as seen by Anglo-Norman nobles of the mid-twelfth century. Richard and Earl Robert had a peculiar right to instruct the young king: they had survived in England through the disrupted reign of Stephen; they, perhaps above all others in the kingdom, had preserved the old royal administration through years of anarchy, and had handed it over, with the considerable gift of their own influential loyalty, to Henry, duke of Normandy and count of Anjou. Their view of the Conquest and of the Anglo-Norman settlement was complete and articulate in 1157, and by good fortune his abbey's own affairs caused our author to write down what they said. It is startlingly 'modern' for the period, and reminds us that the conciliarism of the barons under John and Henry III had roots that went back into the bonds of lordship and to tales of the Conquest. To Richard and Earl Robert, the Conquest was 'your, and our, triumph', undertaken 'by the aid and counsel of our kinsmen'. Together king and nobility 'acquired realm and crown for himself and his successors.' Most significantly, speaking of 'all this gathering of Norman nobles', Richard de Luci can say, 'As for us, it is by virtue of gifts conferred by William and by succeeding to our kin, that we possess great estates and riches', for which reason, he argues, a gathering of nobles can speak with a single voice about the inheritances of king and nobility alike.[1]

A structural necessity of the governing circles of twelfth-century England is reflected in the crucial importance and pervading presence of private alliances in our author's tale. As we see them here they are associations of mutual aid among the ministers in households of magnates, and they are evidently of some degree of formality. Richard de Luci's circle of allies are said to have a pact of friendship with him and his brother.[2] All are from the royal household except the abbot, included by his relationship to one of the allies. The king recognizes the alliance. When he wishes to favour Richard in a legal case, he calls Richard's sworn friends, and no others, to be his councillors.[3] From the household of the archbishop of Canterbury springs another confederation that includes monks of Christ Church, Canterbury. Odo of Battle, formerly of Christ Church, relies upon it in the 1170s and, ultimately, it does not fail him. Its structure is more complicated

[1] Below, pp. 182, 178. [2] Below, p. 160. [3] Below, p. 176.

than what we see of the de Luci connection. The archbishop's household continually supplied bishops for vacant sees, and his clerks received multiple benefices. Such men entered new webs of loyalty, bishop to canon, canon to canon, and conflicts could arise between old and new loyalties. Yet a wide enough circle of friends sworn to mutual aid is shown as an effective protection for the man without a birthright of landed influence.[1] Connection and maintenance have a long history, and, in the twelfth century as in the late Middle Ages, are most clearly seen in the manipulation of justice.

(c) *The First Chronicler and the Battle of Hastings*

For the dramatic foundation story of Battle Abbey, the sources must be sought farther afield, among narrative histories of the Norman Conquest. Both of our chronicles begin with an account of William's life, the invasion and the battle of Hastings, for of course that battle was the reason for the abbey's foundation. Upon the spot where Harold Godwinsson died, the Conqueror commanded his monks to place the high altar of their church, in a solemn parody of a saint's resting-place, disregarding entirely their protests that it was a most difficult spot for building. Our chronicle's two accounts are essentially the same, that of the main chronicler being a condensed version of the first. That of the first has so frequently been taken to be of value as a primary source for the events of October 1066, and for the tactics of the battle, that something should be said about his sources and the purpose served by the account.

In two details our first author is alone and gives what was probably local tradition. He names the spot on Telham hill where William's men first saw the English: it was at Hedgland, he says, locating it as a tenant-holding of the late twelfth century, just outside Hedgland wood. This seems reasonable, for the holding retained its name for centuries, and the Normans very likely had just emerged from the wood there, and glimpsed for the first time the position of their opponents. Our author's other contribution is less reliable. He claims to identify the ravine or ditch where, in nearly all sources for the invasion, numbers of Norman horsemen are said to have come to a grisly death when their galloping horses pitched over the unseen edge. He describes the ravine and says

[1] Below, pp. 322–24, 328–30.

that it is still called *Malfosse.* But it is not clear that his identification is actually independent, and, significantly enough, he does not record its location. Eventually there was a real *Malfosse* at Battle, whether or not it was the fateful ditch.[1] Charters of the early thirteenth century refer to it as a large field with interior closes held by Battle burgesses. It lay roughly to the north and west of the abbey grounds. By 1250 the name had died out, for the abbey had bought the little closes and had converted the field into cattle pasture.[2] That there are many contenders for the treacherous, bracken-filled ravine of the battle, anyone who has walked the district knows very well, and an authentic tradition might have persisted among local Normans, for it was one of the earliest to have knights settled upon the land. Yet a ditch filled with bodies suggests a *malfosse* of a different sort. It may well have been the site of a mass grave, the knowledge of which had come to light in the hundred years or more following the battle, and had been identified with the no doubt authentic disaster of the narratives of the battle. There had been no kinsfolk to claim the Norman dead, and, in the duke's hurry to consolidate his first victory, a mass grave was surely the best that could be afforded. The field given the name *Malfosse* had been the site of reclamation projects and arable cultivation in the late twelfth century; it can be identified with the one that the chronicler says is, in his day, partly tilled.[3] The bones and accoutrements that would have come to light in such a ditch, as the district was brought under cultivation, would have made the identification with a famous scene irresistible, I think, to monks as impressed with their romantic connections as were those of late twelfth-century Battle.

This I take to be the sum of the first chronicler's independent testimony. His account is no less interesting for that, for it is an Angevin version of what must have been a popular story at the court of Henry II. It can be traced to no single existing source, but it relies upon Norman rather than upon English tradition. Virtually every incident is traceable from William of Poitiers via Norman sources that are, or were used by, Wace and Benoît de Sainte-

[1] A guide to some of the controversies over the geography of the battlefield and itself the most recent addition to the question of the location of the ditch *malfosse* is provided by the Sussex antiquary, C. T. Chevallier, 'Where was Malfosse? The End of the Battle of Hastings', *Sussex Archaeological Collections* ci (1963), 1–13.

[2] Searle, *Lordship*, p. 131.

[3] Below, p. 64.

Maure. Our chronicler also knows Merlin's prophecies, which had become popular with Norman writers, though they figure in neither Wace nor Benoît. Benoît and the Battle chronicler are the only late sources to follow the *Carmen de Hastingae Proelio* in allowing Eustace of Boulogne an important part in the battle.[1] Only Wace and our author have the unlikely tale of the Conqueror rendering his ships useless for flight home.[2]

It remains to consider the very heart of our author's account, the very reason for there being such an account at all. For of course the narration is there in order to assert that not only *on the battlefield*, but *before the battle*, William had vowed to build a monastery there, should God favour him. The abbey is thus raised by implication to being the very thing that had tipped the balance, the fairy-tale promise, or, as one forged charter from Battle has the Conqueror put it, it is 'that which gave me my crown and by means of which my rule flourishes'.[3] The setting of the vow-motif is certainly based upon a *roman de Rou*; possibly a source used also by Wace, quite possibly upon Wace himself. If Wace is the source, it is further corroboration of the 1180s as a *terminus ad quem* for our chronicle, since Wace is thought to have abandoned his work in *c.* 1180.[4] There is indeed reason to think that a copy of Wace's *Roman de Rou* was available for our author's use, for a twelfth-century manuscript of the work still exists that was once in the abbey library.[5] There exists, too, as evidence of the profound effect of Wace on the minds of the contemporary monks, a Battle forgery of *c.* 1200 that is purely Arthurian in flavour, in which William is the king who will remove himself a while, yet come again: the Arthur of Wace rather than of Geoffrey of Monmouth.[6]

Wace's *Roman de Rou* provides a scene the treatment of which suited to perfection our first author's purpose of dramatizing both the abbey's claim to be protected by the Crown, and its romantic importance in the Conquest. Wace includes the common scene, as old as William of Poitiers, of the duke's hauberk being offered to

[1] *Carmen*, ll. 535–40.

[2] Wace, ll. 6593–8.

[3] *Regesta*, i, no. 262: 'sicut illa que michi coronam tribuit et per quam viget decus nostri regiminis', BL Add. Ch. 70980, a Westminster product shown first in 1157. See E. Searle, *EHR*, lxxxiii (1968), 458–9.

[4] There does not seem to be a dependence upon Wace for proverbs. See L. Brosnahan, 'Wace's Use of Proverbs', *Speculum*, xxxix (1964), 444–73.

[5] BL MS. Royal 4.C.xi, ff. 249–78. See T. Duffus Hardy, *Descriptive Catalogue* (RS) ii. 431.

[6] *Regesta*, i, no. 271. HBA charter., vol. 42/1. See Searle, *Lordship*, pp. 104–5.

him wrongly, and, as it seemed, inauspiciously, just as he was being armed for battle. William of Poitiers says that the duke laughed off the incident as mischance and not an evil omen. The story was thereafter differently embroidered by William of Poitiers' followers. Wace is independent in his conclusion to the scene, and he is followed by our chronicler. In it, Wace takes up a theme he had introduced earlier, that of the unreliability of soothsayers. The theme is of some importance in the tale. A soothsayer had predicted to William in Normandy that he would be successful without having to fight the English. The same soothsayer had joined William's army and had been drowned during the Channel crossing. Wace has William ask about him on the landing beach itself, and upon hearing his fate, discourse upon the inanity of such fortune-tellers.[1] Wace reintroduces the theme in his version of the incident of the ill-offered hauberk. William says that many would refuse battle after such an omen, but that he has never believed in omens, nor has he ever liked soothsayers. He trusts in God.[2]

Wace's version was ideal for our author's purpose, and he adopts the words verbatim. All he needed then was the imagination to have the duke speak on in his godly mood, to vow to build a monastery on the spot for those who were about to die, and then to make a hortatory speech to his companions, promising thus to atone for their sin of bloodshed. The companions, our author adds, were greatly heartened by the news. The abbey was thus meant to seem a memento not only for the royal line, but for the Norman barons as well. Artfully, the scene makes Battle abbey, and especially its privileges, not only the effective fairy-tale promise, but a monument to the community of Anglo-Norman magnates, and in some measure even a foretelling of Norman success. For the field was offered to God for the Normans' salvation before the battle: 'a haven for all *as free as the one* I conquer for myself'.[3]

It is likely that the *scriptorium* of Battle came to be involved with tales of the Conquest in the days of Abbot Walter de Luci, when *romans de Rou* were the court-fashion and when Wace was still writing. Abbot Walter's justification for the abbey's privileges lay in the tale of the vow. Furthermore there were hopes in his day that Battle would become a place of pilgrimage. What had he to

[1] Wace, ll. 6535–72.
[2] Ibid., ll. 7499–530.
[3] Below, pp. 36, 66.

offer but the battlefield and a few mementoes of William I?[1] Tales of the lineage of Rollo would be as appropriate for pilgrims to Battle as tales of Roland to those on the pilgrim routes south towards the Pyrenees. Walter and Richard de Luci were themselves Normans, from Lucé, near Lonlay-l'Abbaye, where Walter was first professed a monk. They were no doubt brought up on, and receptive to, tales of great Norman deeds.[2]

It seems likely that another Conquest tale, with a soothsayer-scene similar to Wace's, was at Battle about this time. It is an awkward catch-all of information about the Conquest, now known as the *Brevis Relatio de Origine Willelmi Conquestoris*.[3] The manuscript of this work that is identified with Battle is almost certainly earlier than our text. Indeed, it gives every appearance of having been written in the first half of the century, and its author strongly, though with a strange ambiguity, implies that he is writing in the 1120s. The implication is consistent with his script.[4] It is perhaps the first draft of, or a collection of material for, a tale linking Battle abbey with the Conquest and the Anglo-Norman nobility, emphasizing, as it does, the mission of the house to pray for the dead conquerors. Neither of our chroniclers is its author; both are far better artists and more elegant Latinists. Neither would seem to have borrowed from it. The incident of the hauberk is their only common material. The *Brevis Relatio* does not elaborate the scene as do Wace and our chroniclers, nor does it link the incident with a vow to found the abbey. The accounts are no doubt related, the *Brevis Relatio* being perhaps a collection of Conquest

[1] Below, pp. 90, 256. The main author does not even seem to know whose relics were in the amulets left to the abbey by William I. Below, p. 90. There were never important relics at Battle.

[2] See R. H. C. Davis, *The Normans and their Myth* (London, 1976). In the fifteenth century another forgery was to be seen at Battle: the 'Battle Abbey Roll', a list of the surnames of the Conqueror's companions. BL Royal roll 14.B.i, written in an elaborate form in 1436.

[3] *Scriptores Rerum Gestarum Willelmi Conquestoris*, ed. J. A. Giles (London, 1845), pp. 1–23. It is a collation of a BL MS. Sloane, a thirteenth-century text not from Battle, and Bodleian MS e. Museo 93 (SC 3632), a twelfth-century text that belonged to Battle abbey. N. R. Ker, *Medieval Libraries of Great Britain*, 2nd edn. (London, 1964), p. 384.

[4] I am particularly grateful to Professor Richard Rouse for giving me the benefit of his opinion on the manuscript and its palaeography. To Catherine Morton I am much indebted too for her opinion, which corroborates that of Professor Rouse. There can be little doubt that the scribe is employing a script widely used between 1125 and 1160. It has not yet been established that he really was writing in the 1120s.

'facts', of which a number must have been available in mid-century, to be grist for the mills of Wace and the other contenders for Angevin patronage. The most reasonable conclusion must be that there were at Battle a number of attempts to modify the *romans de Rou* and contemporary Norman legends in such a way as to make of the abbey a royal peculiar and a site holy to Normans. Certainly the first chronicler of our present text, in his adaptation of the soothsayer scene to include a vow to found an abbey on the battlefield, is artistically the most successful, and it is not surprising that, since artistry seems to have been the chief criterion, it became the official version.

In actuality, of course, no source outside Battle Abbey mentions such a vow, and the story never took in any intelligent contemporaries, for it did not enter the chronicle literature. That the abbey was founded by the Conqueror, and on the scene of the battle, there need be no doubt. Its dedication in 1094 is noticed in virtually all English chronicles. Orderic Vitalis, writing in Normandy in 1125, knew of it as founded by William, 'after he had gone to war, triumphed over his enemies and received a royal crown at London'.[1] This is important testimony. One of the problems for the Battle chronicler is in accounting for the long delay between the 'vow' of 1066 and the actual summoning of the monks from Marmoutier. But there is an excellent moment when William would much more probably have made the gesture of promising an abbey as penance for the bloodshed of the Conquest. In 1070 William was formally recrowned by papal legates, and a penitentiary was issued by papal authority, imposing heavy penances upon the Normans for the killing and the plunder of the Conquest. The new king's own penance was not overtly suggested to him so far as we know, but 1070 or very shortly thereafter is the reasonable time for him not only to found another penitential abbey, like the *abbaye aux hommes* and the *abbaye aux dames*, but to make an offering sure to be popular with those companions on whom he still so strongly relied, and whose observance of their own penances might well benefit from some monastic intercession. Seen from this perspective, it was somewhat less than penitent, perhaps, to insist that the abbey be located on the site of the great victory, and mark the spot where the English king fell. The very name 'Battle' is a piece of Norman insolence. It was all no doubt most satisfying to

[1] *Ord.Vit.* ii. 190–2.

the rich warriors penanced in 1070. If we assign this as the earliest likely date for the vow, we dispose at once of our author's problem of timing and we thereby shift the scene, as has been done concerning the famous 'papal banner', to quite other circumstances, and make of our chronicler a *romancier* at the least.[1]

But we must return once more to the chronicler and his vow-motif, for though the treatment of the vow in our first chronicle looks to be dependent upon Wace, the story of the vow being taken upon the battlefield is itself somewhat early to have been taken from the poet. It first appears in a forged charter presented to Henry II for confirmation in early 1155, and probably forged between the death of Stephen in November 1154 and Lent 1155.[2] The forgery is the one designed to make Battle abbey seem, to the new king, a royal peculiar, and to make it independent of the bishop of Chichester. The months during which it was forged were months of drama for the kingdom, with the old king's death and the coming of the duke of Normandy to claim the crown of England. During these months Henry II was consolidating his power, becoming another Norman duke conquering a realm left him by his kinsman. He was a William come again, to his supporters, and the *clers lisants* must have been brushing up the tales of the earlier duke in hopes of the patronage that in fact their efforts received at the court of Rou's descendants, Henry and Eleanor. At the centre of power, a necessary administrator, one of the young duke's select group of counsellors, and Keeper of the Tower of London, was Richard de Luci, and during these months his brother, the abbot of Battle, remained near him. They were well placed to be entertained by stories recited before the king at the Christmas court, when he was crowned in Westminster abbey, well placed indeed to pick up the fragments of tale, information, and rumour that are the *Brevis Relatio*.

The brothers also had reason at that moment to be on the look-out for a story to extricate Walter from a tight situation. For Walter's quarrel with his diocesan had come to a head, and, just at the moment when Duke Henry arrived to be crowned, the abbot

[1] Catherine Morton, 'Pope Alexander II and the Norman Conquest', *Latomus*, xxxiv (1975), 362–82. The Penitentiary of 1070 is printed there, pp. 381–2. See also C. N. L. Brooke, 'Archbishop Lanfranc, the English Bishops and the Council of London of 1075', *Studia Gratiana*, xii (1967), 36–60.

[2] *Regesta*, i, no. 62: BL Harl. Ch. 83.A.12. Searle, *EHR*, lxxxiii (1968), 454–5, 469. Below, p. 154.

was under threat of excommunication for contumacy. The sentence had been stayed, temporarily, in late 1154 by Richard de Luci's influence. Walter's difficulty, as we have said, lay in the fact that he had no written evidence to justify him in his claim to immunities. In all probability he had only a charter of William I mentioning freedom from secular exactions,[1] and an oral tradition that claimed that the obedience other abbeys owed their bishops by right, Battle showed voluntarily.

What was needed was written evidence for Walter's claim: a charter and a dramatic foundation story that would bring in the king as the abbey's patron. By Lent the charter had been found. It was quick work, but the materials were no doubt to hand at Westminster. Very likely Westminster abbey was the workshop, for the abbey was a centre of forgery and the seal on another of Abbot Walter's forgeries exposes it as a Westminster product.[2] The charter's curious mention of Christ Church, Canterbury, the archbishop's cathedral, raises a further interesting question about these months. The moment must have seemed to others besides Walter de Luci an opportunity to effect a radical revision in obligations to superiors. Battle's charter has William say that Battle will be free of 'subjection to bishops', *like Christ Church, Canterbury*. Now the archbishop's monastic cathedral was anything but free from his domination, and yet in this very year, 1154, it was locked in a struggle with Archbishop Theobald for autonomy. The prior of Christ Church was in the archbishop's prison, or had just been released, along with two of the monks who had been preparing to go to Rome for help against the archbishop. Theobald was trying indeed to quiet the rumours that the monks were planning his assassination.[3] The insertion of Christ Church's name as a royal peculiar can hardly have been a mistake in a charter of so politically aware a man as the abbot of Battle. It can hardly have been other than a collusive attempt to free both houses from subjection to episcopal authority, and as such it was taken by Archbishop Theobald and Bishop Hilary. The memory of the Battle charter was green at Christ Church twenty years later, for

[1] Below, p. 312, and ibid., n. 1.

[2] T. A. M. Bishop and P. Chaplais, *Facsimiles of English Royal Writs to A.D. 1100 presented to V. H. Galbraith* (Oxford, 1957), pp. xxi, xxii. Searle, art. cit. p. 455, n. 2, offers some slight evidence for connecting the 1154/5 charter with Westminster despite the lack of a seal.

[3] Saltman, *Theobald*, pp. 56–64, and no. 37.

when Canterbury was burned in 1174, the monks sent their prior to court to secure charters *based upon those of Battle*. Battle thereby accidentally, as it were, received the prior of Christ Church as its new abbot. He was sent to Battle, into exile, he suspected, as a result of the malice of Becket's successor, Archbishop Richard of Dover (1174–84), who clearly knew very well of the dangerous phrase.[1]

As far as the immediate complicity of the Battle monks in their forgery is concerned, they may never have heard of the charter or the 'vow' until Walter de Luci and his entourage returned after Lent, 1155, for our author pictures the abbot as remaining in London from November 1154 until then. Whereas in earlier and later crises Walter is said to have sought the advice of his abbey counsellors, no word implicates the monks in the decisions and actions of these important months, and, it must be remembered, the quarrel was Walter's, not the abbey's. Our main author writes as if he had been present with his abbot, and leaves the graphic scene of the abbot and bishop of Chichester besieging their king with petition and counter-petition while he was attempting to hear mass.[2] Our main author must have known the whole truth, and, for that very reason, was the man to hand down the story. By the time he wrote, in the 1180s, the foundation story of the vow upon the field of Hastings had been, for some thirty years, incorporated in a confirmed charter; and the monks had adopted and improved upon it, as our first chronicler shows, lavishing upon it the awe and ingenuity of tales of the founding saint at more conventionally established abbeys. It had become the 'natural' commencement of their own story, and a tradition that even the otherwise fastidious main chronicler was willing to foist upon his successors as truth: a lie, as he must have known, but one that would be harmless to their interests in the years to come.

(iii) *The Manuscript*

The Battle Abbey Chronicle is known from a single manuscript. Since at least the mid-seventeenth century it has been bound with several other medieval historical texts into the volume now known

[1] Below, pp. 282–4, 288–90, 296. Richard of Dover had once been a monk at Christ Church.

[2] Below, p. 156.

as BL MS. Cotton Domitian A ii. It is not listed as part of Sir Robert Cotton's collection in the earliest catalogues, those of the 1620s and 1630s, but it is found in the incomplete list made between 1638 and 1654, its contents described as they are today, on the MS. flyleaf, by a seventeenth-century hand.[1] A hurried note below the list of the volume's four texts remarks *et quatuor alia*, perhaps indicating the intention, unfulfilled, to rebind with new inclusions; two shelf-numbers, *xxiii.A* and *xiv.A*, reflect its wanderings before it was permanently shelved as A ii. Earlier the MS. seems to have been briefly in the library of Magdalen College, Oxford, very likely part of the collection given the college in 1614.[2] There the trail goes cold. Between 1538, when the monastery was dissolved, and its muniments, at least, sent to the Augmentations Office, and 1614, its whereabouts have not been traced.

The parchment leaves of the MS. measure about 210 by 140 mm. They were trimmed to that size during or after the seventeenth century, for a remark in an early modern hand on f. 142 has been cut through, along with the medieval marginal annotations. The Battle MS. therefore is unlikely to have been originally much larger than its present size, though since the trimming did not affect the other texts, it is evident that our chronicle was altered to fit into a volume with works slightly smaller than itself. Until the rebinding of 1973 that volume was bound in light brown leather and embossed with the Cotton coat of arms.

The volume contains 144 folios. The earliest of the four texts to be paginated was the Battle Abbey Chronicle, evidently not yet bound with the others; the arabic numerals are in an early modern hand, the two parts of the chronicle numbered separately, in the upper right corner. These numbers were crossed out when the entire volume was paginated, commencing on f. 2, in a late-eighteenth or nineteenth-century hand. It placed its new numbers beside the old

[1] BL Add. MS. 36682 B, f. 211. The earliest Cotton catalogue, of 1621, is BL Harl. MS. 6018. The next, of 1631–8, is BL Add. MS. 36789. Both are relatively complete and do not have Domitian A ii. In 1631–8 the Domitian press of the library had only two shelves.

[2] Bodleian James 11 (SC 3848), pp. 97–114 seem to contain notes made from the MS. when it was at Magdalen College. I am most grateful to Mr. N. R. Ker for the suggestion that it was probably part of the Foxe collection, several MSS. of which went to the Cotton collection soon after they had been given to Magdalen College. The smooth brown leather of the binding (replaced in 1973) may be a further reason to connect it with Foxe's collection, for his books were bound in smooth brown calf.

ones of the Battle chronicle, and wrote a remark in Latin concerning the number of folios at the end of the last text (f. 144^v). The present edition uses the most recent pagination, commencing on f. 1, in the bottom right-hand corner, in a hand that enters the date 1875 at the end of the volume.

There are several texts in the volume, and variations in the quiring. However the medieval quires were identified, the lettering is now in an early modern hand. The letters A–C are missing, but the quiring is, briefly, as follows: $(AB)^{1+8}$; leaves 1–7 are numbered 1–7; leaves 2–8 are lettered A to G in a late medieval or early modern hand; 2 and 8 are a large leaf reused as a bifolium, and 8 is blank. $(C)D^{2+8}$ (ff. 8–17); ff. 8–9 are a bifolium that replaced the original, clearly damaged by damp, for the hand is later than that of the other leaves, and traces of damp damage the following leaves. E^{2+4} (ff. 18–21+two blank leaves not foliated); f. 20 is marked E, evidently the former opening of the quire, while ff. 18–19 perhaps belonged originally to the previous quire. With quire F, the second of the two-part Battle chronicle, greater regularity commences. The quires are lettered: F^{10} (ff. 22–31), G^{10} (ff. 32–41), H^{1+8} (ff. 42–50); J^{10} (ff. 51–60), K^{10} (ff. 61–70), L^{10} (ff. 71–80), M^{10} (ff. 81–90), N^{10} (ff. 91–100), O^{10} (ff. 101–10), P^{10} (ff. 111–20), Q^{10} (ff. 121–30). An unlettered quire follows: $(R)^{12+2}$ (ff. 131–44); ff. 143–4 are additions to the quire; f. 144 is lettered S.[1]

Text 1. (ff. 2–7). *Incipit*, written in the hand of the main scribe: 'Cronica quedam brevis fratris Johannis Somour, ordinis sancti Francisci de conventu ville Brygewalter'.[2] A tabular calendar of a Dionysian cycle of 532 years. The year of Grace is entered in the left-hand column, followed by the dominical letters for leap years and for ordinary years. The next two columns record the date of Easter in the Roman form for each year of the entire cycle, and a final column indicates by the letters *a* and *m* whether Easter falls in April or May. The cycle differs from the usual periodicity of the Dionysian cycle in beginning with the year 1000 rather than with the Incarnation. Thus the calendar's 'annus magnus' is 1001–1532. Two thirds of each leaf is ruled for an annal of events, in the common style of Easter tables. The main scribe has entered not

[1] I am much indebted to Professor C. N. L. Brooke for this description of the quiring, and to Margaret Nickson of the BL for the generous time she gave to looking over the binding and quiring with me.

[2] Bridgwater in Somerset. *Religious Houses*, pp. 222–3.

only events from the cycle that was for him the present, but events of the two earlier cycles as well, taking his material from a Brut history, and filling in early events to the end of the calendar, giving present and future the peculiar resonances and significances of medieval cyclical history. The last entry in what is probably the hand of the main scribe is the death of Sir John Fastolf entered under 1459. At least two other hands made entries, but no contemporary notices occur after that year. The main scribe continued his tabular work on f. 7^v with two calendrical tables and what appears to be an astronomical table for the conversion of the transits of astronomical objects to time.

2. (ff. 8–21^v). The first of the Battle chronicle-cartularies; each is pricked and ruled for twenty-three or twenty-four lines. The bifolium 8–9 is later than the following ff.; the hand, decoration, and arrangement on the page all show that it is thirteenth century, and the fact that the writing begins under, rather than over, the top line, is reason for placing it after 1240.[1] The script is an unexceptional hand of the middle third of the century. The decorations appear to be slightly later. They consist of two identical capital Qs: the first is blue decorated with gold and placed on a reddish ground decorated with silver; the second is red on a blue ground. The descender forms a rectangular design down the left-hand margin and encroaches on the lettering of the text. Within the loops of both letters are centaur-like combinations of deer and man. The second is alone and is shooting an arrow. The first is blowing a pipe and beating a small drum. Outside the letter and across the remainder of the top margin are two other figures: one, a man-lion, plays a violin, while between the players a woman dancer performs a back-bend and gestures expressively. Her hair, padded and netted, is in a style found in manuscripts of the second half of the thirteenth century.[2] The bifolium was evidently a replacement of damaged leaves; damage due to damp is still evident on the original leaf that follows it (f. 10). The thirteenth-century scribe could not make out a number of the words. In the first three lines of f. 9 there is a nonsense word, 'ter.rei', and gaps which infra-red light shows not to be due to erasure.

[1] N. R. Ker, 'From "above top line" to "below top line": a change in scribal practice', *Celtica* v (1950), 13–16.

[2] M. G. Houston, *A Technical History of Costume*, iii, *Medieval Costume in England and France* (London, 1939), 46. Herbert Norris, *Costume and Fashion*, ii (London, 1927), 181.

The remainder of the first chronicle (ff. 10–21^{v}) is written in a script of the late twelfth century, a clear charter hand with tall ascenders on the top line and dangling descenders on the bottom. There are changes in the character of the hand, but they are slight enough to be accounted for by interruption or a change of pen. This section of the Battle work was read by the first scribe of the second, who added a dropped phrase on f. 10.

3. (ff. 22–130). The main Battle chronicle. The work ends abruptly with a complete quire and the writing covers the entire last leaf. In the only irregular quire, signature H, a copyist's error appears: ff. 48 and 49 appear to have been copied in inverted order. No medieval marks notice this, and the various numberings do not call attention to the fact, but a Latin note in an eighteenth-century hand calls attention to the mistake at the top of the f. incorrectly numbered 48. The scribe may well have been copying an exemplar with a similar inversion; it is the most reasonable explanation. Certainly he appears to be copying from an exemplar. Several times he corrects his text, making erasures (f. 74, twice), and making additions, such as words or phrases at the beginnings of lines. Several such additions indicate that the scribe was following the shape of his exemplar, and a number of lines with grotesquely wide spaces between the letters, and misshapen letters that fill a line with few words, leave a similar impression. He felt free however to squeeze charters into the lower margin (e.g. f. 46). A single scribe wrote ff. 22–83, and almost certainly added the phrase in the first chronicle, on f. 10, the only evidence that the first text was, if only slightly, the earlier. Ff. 84–130 are in a hand slightly more modern than that of ff. 22–83, one of the turn of the twelfth to the thirteenth century. The interiors of many capitals are decorated with filigree work, and a few trail down the margin, ending in the tendrils that are a mark of the new century and are never found in the earlier hand.[1] The ink is, for the most part, brown up to f. 81, where it changes to black with an occasional brown section. The capitals are in red, blue, green, and violet. The single illumination, a twelfth-century portrait of a king, clearly William I, is seated in an elaborately decorated letter A, with which the text begins.

Two later medieval annotators added marginal notes, making it easier to find matters of interest. One is a hand of the fourteenth

[1] For example, on ff. 84 and 109^{v}.

century, and the other is a somewhat later, extremely quavering hand that occasionally merely repeats what the earlier annotator had written. One other later addition deserves mention. On f. 18^{v}, where the payment made to the new abbot by the burgesses of Battle is entered, the sum has been erased, and a medieval hand, assiduously, but unsuccessfully, copying a twelfth-century script, has written 'centum' over the erasure of a longer word, obviously for a smaller sum. The fourteenth-century annotator has remarked, 'Nota de novo abbate'.

One final and important judgement about the scribes of the Battle MS. deserves mention and indeed emphasis. None worked on the forged charters that are used so often in the chronicle.[1] Although there are close affinities between the chronicle hands and those of several genuine Battle charters, no Battle charter can be positively identified as the work of one of the chronicle scribes. At any rate, palaeography supports the chronicler's implication that Abbot Walter's forgeries were produced elsewhere than in the *scriptorium* of Battle.

4. (ff. 131–42) a Latin chronicle of English history. It lacks its original beginning, but is evidently a version of the Brut histories, continued to 1292 with the homage of John Balliol to Edward I. The cursive hand appears to be roughly contemporary with the last events.

5. (ff. 142–44^{r}) were written by a hand of approximately the same date that begins on the line following the Latin chronicle. An historical piece in French with Latin quotations. It begins again the history of 'la terre que ore est apele Engleterre' 1,200 years before the Incarnation, and ends in the reign of Edward I. It is essentially a list of kings fitted into the 'prophecies of Merlin'. A final fourteenth-century hand takes over in mid-leaf on f. 144^{r}, and returns very briefly to English–Scottish affairs, ending with the coronation of Edward III.

(iv) *Other Editions and Studies of the Text*

The earliest publication made from our text was that of Dugdale, who published extracts relating to the abbey's possessions and liberties in his *Monasticon Anglicanum*.[2] That edition has so many

[1] Nor in the forgery HBA charter vol. 42/1: *Regesta*, i, no. 271.

[2] *Monasticon*, first edition, i (1655), 310–17.

minor copying errors that, although it supplies a few readings from the damaged f. 10, one cannot infer that the condition of the manuscript was better when Dugdale or his copyist saw it than it is today. Certainly it was not damaged in the fire of 1731 that caused serious losses to the Cotton collection.

The first complete edition, and the only one prior to the present one, was published by the Anglia Christiana Society in 1846, as the *Chronicon Monasterii de Bello*. The editor was the Revd. J. S. Brewer, whose name does not appear in the volume. The transcript of the text was not his; it was one made for the Record Commission 'under the direction of' Henry Petrie.[1] As H. W. C. Davis wrote of the edition, it 'provides us with an accurate text . . . but the edition is bad in every other respect . . .'[2] The Anglia Christiana text was translated by the Sussex antiquarian Mark Antony Lower as *The Chronicle of Battel Abbey*, and published in 1851 by John Russell Smith, London. It is a graceful English text, but one that is often misleadingly inaccurate. Neither the Anglia Christiana edition nor the Lower translation has clarifying notes or informed introductions.

The text was briefly described by Sir Thomas Duffus Hardy in his *Descriptive Catalogue of Materials relating to the History of Great Britain and Ireland* ii (RS 1865), 406–8. This supplies the name of the Anglia Christiana editor. Hardy's description was accurate but brief, and the text was analysed in greater detail by H. W. C. Davis in 1914.[3] In 1932 David Knowles published his important study, 'The Growth of Exemption', analysing further the central problem of the text, the relation of the chronicler to the forgeries he uses.[4] The present editor reconsidered the problem in the light of the extant charters in 'Battle Abbey and exemption: the forged charters' in the *English Historical Review*, lxxxiii (1968), 449–80, where the charters are printed and may be checked against our present chronicle text.

[1] *Chronicon*, ed. Brewer, p. v.
[2] *EHR*, xxix (1914), 426.
[3] Davis, *ibid.*, pp. 426–34.
[4] *Downside Review*, l, N.S. xxxi, 218–25, 431–6, esp. 433–6.

THE CHRONICLE OF BATTLE ABBEY

f. 8 Quoniam de situ et institucione loci nostri, ecclesie scilicet beati Martini de Bello, aliquanta iam memorie commendata, ad posterorum monimentum, nobis in promptu habentur, decreuimus et nos de eadem nunc lacius quedam omissorum recapitulando uel supplendo annotare, ut ea que uerbotenus uel eciam scedulis exarata ab antecessoribus ad subsequencium utilitatem memorie digna discere potuimus, his quoque qui necdum sunt, in libello collecta, transmittamus. Quia enim minus lucide de fundo possessionum lacius diffuso, de terrarum situ, de reddituum censu, de consuetudinum dignitatumue eiusdem ecclesie libertatibus, de uariis ad cautelam uel commodum posterorum accidencium uel placitorum causis hactenus digestum est, nunc licet ad hec insufficientes penitus simus, ad eadem plenius expedienda ab exordio animum arccius accomodare non inutile uisum est.

f. 8v Quoniam igitur dispensacionis nutu quo omnia[a] uoluuntur secularia ex insigni Normannorum ac magni principis Rollonis stemmate piissimus dux Willelmus, pater patrie et limes ducatus et regni merito nominandus, ipso in mundi climate prout Lucifer exortus, cum mira industria, per Dei graciam, propria liberalitate, cum Gallice nobilitatis fauore auctus, principatum proprium hereditario sibi iure a patre relictum feliciter optinuit, post multos et innumeros calamitatum turbines illud potenter tandem ad manum pacificauit.[1] Interea uero et Anglice regnum monarchie eidem duci Willelmo a suo consanguineo rege Edwardo e mundo migrante hereditario iure delegatum relinquitur. Quod cum hostiliter a suo periuro quodam Haraldo[2] inuasum memoratus dux

[a] *MS:* ora, *probably a copying error of the thirteenth-century scribe. See introduction, p.* 26

[1] For the earliest views on the question of William's inheritance of Normandy see *Carmen*, l. 37 and Will. Jum., pp. 111–12. D. C. Douglas, *William the Conqueror* (London, 1964), pp. 31–52, puts the matter in the larger context of Norman ducal politics.

[2] The author is here following his Norman sources in emphasizing the oath of fealty sworn by Harold to Duke William in *c.* 1064. Will. Poit., pp. 102–6, 176,

THE CHRONICLE OF BATTLE ABBEY

We of St. Martin's at Battle have readily available to us a good deal of information about the site and organization of our abbey, preserved for the guidance of future generations in a narrative account. This we have now determined to expand, reworking it and supplying some materials that were left out. In this way, what is worth recording of what we have been able to learn from oral tradition and from documents written by our predecessors for the use of those who followed them, we too may hand down, collected into a book, to our own successors. For up to now there has been no really clear account of our endowment of widely scattered holdings, the location of our lands, the rent-roll, the church's liberties, either of customs or privileges, nor—for the warning or convenience of future generations—of what lay behind various mishaps and lawsuits. Now, unequal as we are to the task, it has been thought advisable that we try our best to explain things, fully and from the beginning.

At the command of the authority that governs the secular world, there arose, like the morning star, the most pious Duke William out of the glorious lineage of the Normans, scion of the house of their mighty prince Rollo. William well deserved to be called father of his country, bulwark of his duchy and kingdom. With marvellous energy and a generous hand, aided by the goodwill of the French nobility, and by the grace of God, he successfully won as his own the dominion left him by his father in hereditary right, and after many, indeed countless mishaps, he finally tamed it to his hand.[1] In the meantime, too, his cousin King Edward at his death left him the realm of England in hereditary right. When the duke found that it had been forcibly seized by his own forsworn vassal Harold,[2] he concentrated his mind and resources on taking

230. Will. Jum., p. 133. Will. Poit., p. 206. Wace follows them. Like them, Orderic Vitalis depicts Harold as 'periurum suum', and he uses the word *inuasio* to describe Harold's assumption of the crown. *Ord.Vit.* ii. 134, 138, 140, 142. For an English view of Harold's predicament when required to make a treaty with the duke see Eadmer, *Hist. Nov.*, pp. 7–8. William of Malmesbury's account more resembles Eadmer's; theirs is a different tradition from that of our author's Norman sources. Malmesbury, *De Gestis*, i. 279–80.

rescisset, ad id ui uel arte obtinendum, suorum consilio et auxilio fultus, animum et uires conuertit. Classe igitur parata ingenti, plerique comites, multi nobiles, multi illustres, multi etiam non sue dictionis proceres uel barones, sed et ex circumiacencium finibus prouinciarum innumeri sese eius comitatui pro sibi innata clemencia adiunxerunt. Dux ergo cum incredibili exercitu, diuino comitante fauore, nauigacionem aggressus, prospere tandem prope
f. 9 castrum Peuenesel dictum applicuit. / . . .[a] exercitu per litoris spacia late . . .[b] exilientes Anglie nonnulli gaudenter ter. rei . . . dere,[c] contigit ducem e naui exire . . .[b] in faciem corruisse, littoreque naso uulnerato aliquantum cruentato, terram protensis primo comprehendisse manibus. Verum cum hinc plerique infausti auspicii fortunam mussitantes pertimescerent, intererat et dapifer ducis, Willelmus filius Osberti cognominatus, uir mire probitatis et prepollens ingenio,[1] qui mox animos nutancium deiectos huiusmodi audacter releuauit oraculo. 'Desinite', inquid, 'uiri, hec in aduersum interpretari, quia profecto hinc prosperitatis datur auspicium. Hic enim Angliam utrisque palmis complexam conquisiuit, propriaque progenie hereditandam suo cruore signans dicauit, hancque ex diuine disposicionis presagio potenter optinere meruit.'[2]

Sicque pro uoto cedentibus causis, dux ibidem non diu moratus haut longe situm qui Hastinges uocatur cum suis adiit portum, ibique oportunum nactus locum ligneum agiliter castellum statuens prouide muniuit.[3] Nauium uero parte maxima dispensatorie iam combusta, ne scilicet repatriandi spe aliqui forsitan negligencius ceptis instarent, dux post modicum rex futurus sollicicius circum-
f. 9v iacencia sibimet subiugare festinabat.[4] Quo agnito / regni invasor Haraldus collecto maturius exercitu ad eum expellendum, vel pocius cum suis omnibus exterminandum, ad locum qui nunc Bellum nuncupatur temerarie festinans uenire non formidauit. Occurrit audacter et dux equitum cuneis circumseptus. Perueniensque

[a] See introd., p. 26 [b] *The line is not completed in the manuscript, indicating a gap or illegibility in the original. Two or three words could be missing* [c] *Again the line is not complete; there is space for a single word. The contraction* d'e *begins the third line. The word* ter. rei *is smudged*

---

[1] William fitz Osbern was the son of the Conqueror's one-time guardian, Osbern, steward of Duke Robert I. He was a cousin and close friend of the duke, who created him earl of Hereford shortly after 1066. Douglas, *William the Conqueror*, p. 90 and Appendix, Table 8.

it by force or cunning, supported by the counsel and aid of his vassals. Accordingly a prodigious fleet was prepared, and a great many counts, many nobles, many famous men, many magnates and barons not from his own domains, and innumerable persons from the regions round about, joined his host out of sympathy for him. Thus the duke, with an unparalleled army and attended by divine favour, set out upon his voyage. At length he landed safely near the town called Pevensey . . . the army extensively along an area of shore . . . some leaping out joyously . . . to England . . . it happened that as the duke was disembarking, he fell on his face; his nose was wounded and some blood fell upon the shore; he first grasped the land with hands outstretched. At this many became very frightened, muttering about the meaning of this unlucky omen. But the duke's steward, William fitz Osbern, a man of admirable probity and very clever,[1] was present, and he quickly raised the drooping spirits of the falterers with a bold prophecy: 'Men', he said, 'do not take this as unlucky; it is really an omen of success. See, he has claimed England, taking possession of it with both hands, and he has consecrated it as the inheritance of his own lineage by marking it with his own blood. By this presage of the divine plan he has effectively been given title to it.'[2]

So, with things going as he wished, the duke spent no long time there, but made his way with his men to a near-by port called Hastings. There he found a suitable place, and with foresight he quickly built a wooden fort.[3] Most of the boats had already been burnt at his order, lest anyone, in his desire to get home, might carry out the undertaking half-heartedly.[4] The duke—so shortly to be a king—now hurried the more anxiously to subjugate the surrounding area. When he heard this, Harold, the usurper of the realm, speedily collected an army, and fearlessly, but rashly, hurried to the place which is now called Battle, to expel, or better, to exterminate him with all his followers. As boldly, the duke came to meet him, surrounded by units of cavalry. Arriving at the hill

[2] *Wace*, ll. 6573–92. Cf. Malmesbury, *De Gestis* ii. 300.

[3] *The Anglo-Saxon Chronicle D* has the events as here (*The Anglo-Saxon Chronicle*, ed. D. Whitelock, with D. Douglas and S. Tucker (New Brunswick, 1965), pp. 142–3) as does the Bayeux Tapestry, which shows the landing at Pevensey, followed by a speedy removal to Hastings. William of Poitiers and William of Jumièges say that the first fort was built at Pevensey. Will. Poit., p. 168. Will. Jum., p. 134. Wace follows them. William of Malmesbury has the army land at Hastings, Malmesbury, ii, 300.

[4] Wace, ll. 6593–8 is the only other early version to have this unlikely detail.

ad locum collis qui Hechelande dicitur, a parte Hastingarum situm, dum sese inuicem armis munire contendunt ac eidem duci lorica ad induendum porrigitur, ex inprouiso inuersa ipsi oblata est. Quod aduertentes qui aderant, dum uti infortunii presagium execrarentur, mox memoratus ducis dapifer solita cunctos constancia compescuit, protestatus et hinc quoque prosperitatis collatum indicium, quod scilicet ea que ante restabant ut proposita securiter illi cessura forent.[1] Sed dux nichil motus, uultu placido loricam induens, digna memorie concionatus dixit, 'Scio, karissimi, quod si sortibus crederem bellum hodie nullatenus introirem. Set ego me in omni negocio creatori meo fiducialiter comittens, nec sortibus credidi, nec umquam sortilegos amaui. Vnde et nunc de eius auxilio securus, ad uestras qui mei gracia hoc initis certamen corroborandas manus ac mentes, uotum facio me in hoc certaminis loco, pro salute cunctorum et hic nominatim occumbencium, ad honorem Dei et sanctorum eius, quo serui Dei adiuuentur, con-
f. 10 gruum cum digna libertate fundaturum /[a] monasterium, quod ita ut michi conquirere potero liberum [?uel obl]atum uniuersis propitiabile fiat asilum.'[2]

Cumque in[ter au]ditores et quidam Maioris Monasterii monachus Willelmus Faber cognominatus adesset, qui quondam ipsius ducis seruiens hinc 'fabri' nomen obtinuit, quod cum sodalibus uenatum aliquando profectus sagittis forte deficientibus, cum quendam fabrum huiuscemodi operis ignarum adissent, ipse malleis arreptis mox sagittam artificioso ingenio compegit; postmodumque uoluntate mutata ad Maius Monasterium, quod tunc quammaxime religionis fama rutilabat, sese contulerat, tunc uero diuulgato ipsius ducis in Angliam aduentu, gratia [?commo]di ecclesie sue cum reliquis exercitui sese immiscuerat.[3] Mox ut uotum audiuit, procedens quatinus, ut ei uoto cederent omnia, idem monasterium in uenerationem beati pontificis Martini nominatim fundaretur suggessit. Cuius cum uotis et dux annuens deuotus ita fieri

[a] *The hand of the chief copyist begins on f. 10. This first folio is in poor condition. See introd., p. 26. Square brackets are used throughout to indicate conjectural additions.*

[1] The chronicler's source is Wace, ll. 7499–530.

[2] See introduction, pp. 17–18. The conviction that the invasion was evil, however much forced upon William to uphold a legitimate claim, is expressed in *Carmen*, ll. 289–90.

[3] For a martial monk with William see *Carmen*, ll. 273–6. Both William and Harold relied on monks as envoys and negotiators. Will. Poit., pp. 172, 174.

called Hedgland, which lies towards Hastings, while they were hurriedly getting one another into armour, a hauberk was held up for the duke to get into, and unaccountably it was offered the wrong way round. Those who were nearby and who had noticed it began to curse it as an omen of bad luck, but the duke's steward, with his usual steadiness, checked them all, proclaiming this too as a sign that meant success: that things that were the wrong way round would turn out safely for him as was predestined.[1] But the duke, pulling his hauberk on untroubled and with a calm expression, said something worth remembering. 'My dearest friends, I know that if I credited omens, I should never go into battle today. But in all my affairs I have committed myself trustingly to my creator. I have not been a believer in omens, and I have never liked soothsayers. I am at this moment too, confident of His aid. And to strengthen the hands and hearts of you who are about to fight for me, I make a vow that on this very battlefield I shall found a monastery for the salvation of all, and especially for those who fall here, to the honour of God and of his saints, where servants of God may be supported: a fitting monastery, with a worthy liberty. Let it be an atonement: a haven for all, as free as the one I conquer for myself.'[2]

Among those who heard the duke was a monk of Marmoutier, one William, named 'the Smith'. He had picked up this name when he was a servitor of the duke in former days. For once when he was hunting with some companions, they ran out of arrows, and the smith they went to happened to be unfamiliar with work of that sort. William immediately took up the man's hammers, and improvising cleverly he fashioned an arrow. Some time afterwards he changed course and made profession at Marmoutier, which in those days was especially famous for the quality of its monastic life. But when news of the duke's invasion of England was spread about, he joined the army with the rest, in the hope of profit for his church.[3] Immediately he heard the vow, he acted to make sure that everything went in accordance with it: he suggested that the monastery be founded specifically in veneration of the blessed Bishop Martin. The devout duke assented to his wishes and good naturedly promised that this should be done. After conditions for

Malmesbury, *De Gestis* ii, 301. Orderic Vitalis was acutely aware of monks with William 'the Smith's' motives following the Conqueror to England, and reserves some of his harshest judgements for them. *Ord.Vit.* ii. 268.

benigne spopondisset, post pacem conditionalem a duce per internuntios tertio oblatam, et ab hostibus refutatam,[1] denuo iuxta Merlini uaticinium, gente Normannica in tunicis ferreis Anglorum aucdacter deiciente supercilium, armis uiriliter decertatum est.[2]

Verum cum Anglis indissolubiliter cum rege suo collem quo
f. 10v nunc ecclesia consistit preoccupantibus / . . .[a] tandem strenuissimus Bolonie [com]es Eustachius clam callida premeditata arte, fugam cum exercitu duce simulante, super Anglos sparsim agiliter insequentes cum manu ualida a tergo irruit, sicque et duce hostes firociter inuadente, ipsis interclusis utrinque prosternuntur innumeri. Dispergitur, deprimitur, labitur, laniatur ac necatur inermis ac pedes misera gens Anglica, regeque suo belli fortuito ictu prostrato, per diuersa dissiliens latebras querit. Innumeris itaque in campo uel potius in fuga prostratis, [oculis][b] cunctorum suprema patebat calamitas. Siquidem [et] inter hostiles gladios miserabile quoddam in proximo spatiose protentum, ex naturali telluris hiatu [uel] forsan ex procellarum concauatione, precipitium uaste patens, licet uti in uastitate dumis uel tribulis obsitum oculis minus preuideretur, innumeros et maxime Normannorum Anglos persequentium[c] suffocauit. Nam dum inscii cum impetu dissilirent ibidem in preceps acti flebiliter contriti necabantur. Quod quidem baratrum sortito ex accidenti uocabulo Malfossed hodieque nuncupatur.[3]

Has inter miserias lugubre patebat spectaculum, arua cadaueribus operiri nec in girum obtutibus aliud quam sanguinis ruborem offerri. Conualles undique defluens cruoris riuus replesse ad instar
f. 11 fluuii / procul uidebatur. Quanta [putas?] illic tunc strages facta est de uictis, cum et de uictoribus decem millium in breui, ut fertur, supputationem excesserit! O quanta humani cruoris inibi effusa

[a] *A hole in the upper-left-hand corner and the generally poor condition of the folio make several words here doubtful* [b] *The damage to the leaf makes several words conjectural. MS*: clis [c] *The preceding three words are squeezed into the margin, and the* et *is interlined. They may be in the hand of the copyist of this folio, but look more like the hand of the scribe who wrote fols. 22 ff See introd., pp. 8, 27.*

---

[1] Wace depicts William sending Harold three messages.

[2] Geoffrey of Monmouth, *Historia*, vii, c. 3: Merlin, prophesying to Vortigern, tells him of the defeat of the red dragon, symbol of the Britons, by the white, symbol of the Germanic peoples, of the long oppression of the Britons, and of

peace had been three times offered through emissaries and each time refused by the enemy,[1] the issue was left to valiant combat; and, according to the prophecy of Merlin, a Norman race in iron tunics boldly cast down the pride of the English.[2]

The English had already occupied the hill where the church now stands, in an impenetrable formation around their king . . . at length, by a cunning and secretly planned manœuvre the duke simulated flight with the army, and when the English were scattered in their precipitate pursuit, the vigorous Eustace, count of Boulogne, attacked them from the rear. Thereupon the duke attacked also, and caught between them, great numbers were destroyed. The unhappy English, defenceless and on foot, were scattered, overwhelmed, and felled; they were butchered and slaughtered! When their king was laid low by a chance blow, the army broke up and fled in different directions to find hiding-places. After innumerable men had been cut down on the field, or rather in flight, a final disaster was revealed to the eyes of all. Lamentably, just where the fighting was going on, and stretching for a considerable distance, an immense ditch yawned. It may have been a natural cleft in the earth or perhaps it had been hollowed out by storms. But in this waste ground it was overgrown with brambles and thistles, and could scarcely be seen in time; and it engulfed great numbers, especially of Normans in pursuit of the English. For, when, all unknowing, they came galloping on, their terrific impetus carried them headlong down into it, and they died tragically, pounded to pieces. This deep pit has been named for the accident, and today it is called *Malfosse*.[3]

The spectacle amid these sufferings was pitiable. The fields were covered with corpses, and all around the only colour to meet the gaze was blood-red. It looked from afar as if rivulets of blood, flowing down from all sides, had filled the valleys, just like a river. How great would you estimate the slaughter of the defeated there,

the eventual destruction of the white dragon; 'populus namque in ligno et tunicis ferreis superveniet, qui vindictam de nequitia ipsius sumet'. Geoffrey of Monmouth, *Historia Regum Britanniae*, ed. A. Griscom (London, 1929), p. 386.

[3] See introduction, pp. 15–16. *Chronique des ducs de Normandie par Benoît*, ii, ed. Carin Fahlin, Bibliotheca Ekmaniana, Universitas Regiae Upsaliensis, 60 (Lund, 1954), ll. 39504–6:

'Une tante tolorose voiz
Ne tanz mortex, orrible criz
Ne furent en jor öiz.'

Cf. Wace, ll. 8079 ff.

est unda ubi infortunati non tantum labebantur sed et necabantur. Quantus armorum fragor, quantus ictuum stridor, quantus morientium clamor, quantus dolor, quanta suspiria, quot gemitus, quot suppreme calamitatis dire uoces personuerunt, digne quis estimabit?[1] Vere stupenda proponitur ac deflenda infelicitatis humane misera conditio. In horum ergo contemplatione succumbente calamo subiungendum iam uidetur quod tandem finito certamine Normannis Anglia cessit cum triumpho. Designato igitur loco quo hostilis temerarie inuasionis cecidit signum, dux ulterius propere progrediens quecumque adire ualebat suo iuri mancipari festinabat. Tandem ergo ad regni metropolim perueniens Lundoniam, rationisque ac pacis confederatione ciuibus oblata ac demum ab his etsi egre suscepta, gaudenter ut heres et dominus excipitur. Denuo autem et regni parte nonnulla sagaciter pacificata, cum fauore procerum ac nobilium regni ad natale Domini intrante anno
f. 11v incarnationis ipsius mlxvii regni insignitus solio, / Anglice monarchie obtinens coronam, digno diademate redimitur.[2]

Quo facto, quia multis et innumeris preoccupatus negotiis regnum in breui unire ac pacificare nullatenus quiuerat, plura diutius necessario omisit que maturius exequenda proposuerat. Per plurimum enim temporis ad municipiorum expugnationem atque ad rebellium subiugandam ceruicositatem sollicitius animum occupauit et uires. Vnde factum est ut quemadmodum a Domino electo et promoto regi, cedentibus pro uoto prosperis, nec compatriatarum hostilis astutia, nec malignorum uersuta machinamenta, nec alienigenarum incursus minaciter propositus obessent, sed ipso ubique in auxilio celesti confiso, hinc regni gloria magnifice roboraretur. Et merito. Erat enim moralitate precipuus, liberalitate munificus, mansuetudine spectabilis, ingenio prepollens, animo constans, armis strenuus, in inchoandis magnanimus, in adquirendis efficacissimus, in regendis pacificus, in legum statutis reformandis ac seruandis studiosus, diuinitatis cultor assiduus, totus ecclesiarum utilitati deditus, et, quod magis mirari

[1] Cf. *Draco Normannicus*, ll. 1470–2 in *Chrons. . . . Stephen, Henry II and Richard I*, ed. R. Howlett (RS), ii. 647.

[2] William was crowned on Christmas Day 1066. Our authors both begin the new year on Christmas Day, and thus the coronation is here placed in 1067. Such a convention was common practice in twelfth-century England. R. L. Poole, *Medieval Reckonings of Time* (London, 1921), pp. 43–4.

when tradition has it that that of the conquerors exceeded ten thousand at the lowest count? Oh, what bloodshed, where the wretches were not only felled but slaughtered as well! What a crashing of weapons, what a whistling of strokes, what shrieks of the dying, what grief, what sighs! How many groans, how many dreadful voices calling out in their last suffering—who will do justice to them?[1] Truly the pitiful condition of human wretchedness is shown us that we be struck aghast and weep. In imagining these things then, our pen begins to waver. Yet it must be added that when the battle was at last over, England yielded to the Normans with the victory. Accordingly, the spot was marked where the standard of the enemy's rash usurpation fell, and the duke marched swiftly on, hurrying to bring under his authority all the areas he could reach. At last he arrived at London, the chief city of the realm. He offered the citizens a peace treaty setting out their mutual relations, and finally, though somewhat unwillingly, they accepted it and received him joyfully as heir and lord. A substantial part of the country was, wisely, again pacified, and with the assent of the magnates and nobles of the realm, on Christmas Day, as the year of the Incarnation 1067 was just coming in, he who had been marked out to rule the realm received the English crown, and had the diadem he deserved set on his head.[2]

When this was over he was still preoccupied with many, indeed countless, matters, being unable to pacify and unify the realm quickly. Necessarily, therefore, he laid aside for some time much that he had intended to do more promptly. For long his thoughts and strength were fully occupied with besieging towns and subjugating stubborn rebels. Thus prosperity ultimately attended the king who had been chosen and advanced by God. Neither the hostile tricks of his fellow countrymen, nor the crafty designs of his enemies, nor the dangerous invasion plans of foreigners hindered him. No, for he everywhere trusted in heavenly aid, and from this source the glory of his reign was marvellously strengthened. And justly so. For he was outstanding in goodness, open-handed in generosity, notable for clemency, admirable in his abilities, constant in spirit, vigorous in arms, great-hearted in his undertakings. He was effective in conquering, pacific in ruling, diligent in reforming and maintaining the laws, a devoted worshipper of God, wholly dedicated to the good of churches, and (what one must most

necesse est, cum tot gentibus imperaret adeo ei fomes uirtutum discretio dominabatur ut, alias inuictus, rationis facili ultroneus
f. 12 suggestione oportune uinceretur. Quocirca et potenter imperii / sui fines adauxit et contra spem omnium suo tempore strenue pacificatum gubernauit, heredibusque suis feliciter possidendum reliquit. Sed hec hactenus.

Nunc uero quia minus necessarie propositi textus exordium protendisse ex accidenti uidemur, iam arctius stilo inchoati opusculi materiam sulcando rimante, libet loci nostri prima rudimenta examussim ut promisimus explanare. Igitur preclarissimo rege Willelmo pluribus, ut meminimus, intento, inter alia et uoti pretaxati efficatiam, etsi animo non omisit, diutius tamen temporis illius preoccupationibus intermisit. Verum conscia interius instante conscientia, exterius quoque, non facile, supradicto monacho Willelmo Fabro horum mentionem studiosius inculcante seposito, tandem eidem monacho, ut optauerat, rex, quia ad manum habebatur, operis fabricam committens precepit quatinus in antefato congressionis loco, accitis secum sue ecclesie aliquibus fratribus, oportunum festinaret fundari monasterium. Quod is alacriter excipiens Maius Monasterium ocius adiit hincque quattuor monachos, scilicet Thedbaldum cognomine Vetulum,[1] Willelmum Coche, Rotbertum de Bolonia, Rotbertum Blancard, uiros personalitate ac religione precipuos, secum in Angliam adduxit. Qui /
f. 12v memoratum belli locum considerantes cum ad tam insignem fabricam minus idoneum, ut uidebatur, arbitrarentur in humiliori non procul loco, uersus eiusdem collis occidentalem plagam, aptum habitandi locum eligentes ibidem ne nil operis agere uiderentur mansiunculas quasdam fabricauerunt. Qui locus, hucusque Herste cognominatus, quandam habet spinam in huius rei monimentum.[2]

Igitur cum inter hec regis animus sollicitus de fabrice prouectu quereret ab isdem fratribus, ei suggestum est quod locus ille ubi ecclesiam fieri decreuerat, uti in colle situs, arenti gleba siccus et

[1] There is precedent in Wace for another identification. The village and castle of Vieilles are in Normandy, in the Beaumont fief. In some manuscripts of the *Roman de Rou* Humphrey de Vieilles, father of Roger de Beaumont, the Conqueror's friend, is called 'de Vetulis'. Wace, *Roman de Rou et des ducs de Normandie*, ed. F. Pluquet (Rouen, 1827), ii. 126, n. 7.

[2] The location of *Herste* is given below, p. 64, in the rental. It lay to the north

admire) though he ruled so many peoples, discretion, the kindler of virtues, so ruled him that, unconquered by men, he was of his own accord conquered in good time by the dictates of reason. Thus he both forcefully widened the boundaries of his dominion and vigorously governed what he had pacified, beyond the dreams of all of his time. And he successfully left it to his heirs. But enough of these matters.

We may seem to have wandered into an unnecessarily long preface to our proposed text, but we shall now examine the materials on which we base this little work with our pen kept more strictly to its furrow, and explain with precision the first circumstances of our abbey, as we promised. The illustrious King William was fully occupied, as we have mentioned, and although he never actually forgot his vow, yet because of the preoccupations of this period, he put off its fulfilment (amongst other things) for a long time. However his conscience was urging him from within, while from without the monk William 'the Smith' kept reminding him assiduously, no easy thing to do. At last, since the monk was nearby, the king committed the building of the abbey to him as he had wished, commanding him to fetch some brothers from his own church and set speedily in hand the establishment of a suitable monastery on the battlefield. Accepting with alacrity, the monk went quickly to Marmoutier and brought with him into England four monks from there: Theobald, nicknamed 'the old',[1] William Coche, Robert of Boulogne, and Robert Blancard, men outstanding in character and piety. They studied the battlefield and decided that it seemed hardly suitable for so outstanding a building. They therefore chose a fit place for settling, a site located not far off, but somewhat lower down, towards the western slope of the ridge. There, lest they seem to be doing nothing, they built themselves some little huts. This place, still called *Herste*, has a low wall as a mark of this.[2]

Accordingly, when the solicitous king inquired meanwhile about the progress of the building, it was intimated to him by these brethren that the place where he had decided to have the church built was on a hill, and so dry of soil, and quite without springs,

and west of the abbey. It was a naturally better site for the construction of the abbey, since it adjoins a wide area of level ground and is well watered. The site of Harold's standard was at the summit of a slope, possibly even a steep one. The ground there required artificial levelling before construction could begin.

aquarum foret indigus, atque ob hoc oportere tanto operi aptiorem locum in proximo si placitum haberetur delegari. Quod cum rex percepisset indignatus refugit ociusque iussit in eodem loco quo hoste prostrato sibi cesserat triumphus basilice fundamenta iacere. Cumque obniti non presumentes aquarum penuria causarentur, uerbum ad hec memoriale magnificus rex protulisse fertur. 'Ego', inquid, 'si Deo annuente uita comes fuerit, eidem loco ita prospiciam ut magis ei uini abundet copia quam aquarum in alia prestanti abbatia.' Denuo quoque illis de loci conquerentibus inoportunitate, eo quod scilicet per uicinia latius uti per
f. 13 siluestre solum / nusquam ad edificium apti lapides repperirentur, rex de thesauro suo ad omnia sufficientiam proponens sumptuum, delegauit etiam naues de proprio quibus a Cadomensi uico lapidum copia ad opus propositum transueheretur. Cumque statutum regis exequentes aliquantam de Normannia lapidum portionem aduexissent interim, ut fertur, matrone cuidam religiose reuelatum est quatinus in designato sibi per uisum loco fodientes, ibidem ad opus premeditatum lapidum inuenirent abundantiam. Non longe itaque a presignato ecclesie ambitu, ut iussum fuerat, querentes, tantam ac talem lapidem reppererunt copiam ut manifeste pateret inibi diuinitus ad predestinatum opus lapidum ab euo reconditum thesaurum.[1]

Iactis ergo tandem fundamentis prestantissimi ut tunc temporis habebatur operis, secundum regis statutum altare maius in eodem loco quo regis Haraldi signum, quod 'standard' uocant, corruisse uisum est, prouide statuunt. Et licet peritissimi non uili commertio asciti operi preessent artifices, tamen exactoribus plus propriis quam Iesu Christi deditis, negligentius cepti [operis][a] fabrica ut specietenus ad hoc magis quam studio intendentum proficiebat. Interim quoque et infra designatum monasterii ambitum sibimet idem fratres insumptuosas quodem quo degerent domunculas /
f. 13v edificant. Sicque interdiu sceuo exemplo in exorsis, die diem recrastinante, et regie opes que ad fabrice accelerationem cedebant pro libitu et dispensantur multaque ex eiusdem regis deuota liberalitate illuc collata indiscrete distrahuntur. Hec ad declarandum magnifici regis studium nos interseruisse nulli sit onerosum,

[a] *Winterbottom*

[1] The medieval quarry appears from rentals to have been immediately east-south-east of the abbey church. HBA folder, Rentals: Battle, 1367. PRO E315/57, a rental of 1433. Both show 'le Quarrere', and it is mentioned below, p. 64.

and that for so great a construction a more likely place nearby should be substituted, if it pleased him. When the king heard this he refused angrily and ordered them to lay the foundations of the church speedily and on the very spot where his enemy had fallen and the victory been won. When, without presuming to oppose him, they gave as their reason the lack of water, tradition has it that this noble king uttered a memorable saying: 'If, God willing, I live', he said, 'I shall so endow that abbey that the supply of wine in it will be more abundant than that of water in any other great abbey.' Again they complained of the unsuitability of the site, this time because for some distance round the ground was heavily wooded and therefore stone fit for building could not be found. The king promised expenses sufficient for everything out of his own treasure. He even sent his own ships to bring across an abundance of stone for the proposed work from the region of Caen. And tradition has it that when, following the king's orders, they had brought some part of the stone from Normandy, it was revealed to a pious lady that if they dug in a place shown her in a vision, they would find there an abundance of stone for the projected work. Accordingly they searched not far from the boundary that had been marked out for the church, and there they found such a supply of good stone that it was quite apparent that the Lord had laid up a hidden treasure of stone there from the beginning of time for the predestined work.[1]

And so at length, the foundations were laid of what was in those days thought an outstanding building, and they prudently erected the high altar as the king had commanded, on the very place where Harold's emblem, which they call a 'standard', was seen to have fallen. Now, as it happened, true experts, attracted by motives other than cheap commercial ones, were set to the work. Yet, because the overseers were more interested in their own riches than in Jesus Christ, the construction, though begun, for a while progressed poorly, since they applied themselves more for appearance's sake than with zeal. In the meantime, even within the designated boundary of the monastery, the brethren built themselves plain little huts where they could live. But that unfortunate example at the outset led to procrastinations day after day, and the royal treasures, which had been sent to speed up the building, were spent at whim, as were many gifts sent by the king in his devout generosity. We trust that no one will find it tiresome that

quia licet, ut supra meminimus, innumeris irretitus negotiis nec locum pre dolore intimo adire nec de eodem que proposuerat huiusmodi forte dilationibus circumuentus exequi ualuerit, tamen, ut in his etiam reuera probari potest, tantam initians suis proposuit sufficientiam ut ipsius quoque deuotio perpetim digna sit memorie.

Preterea sic ut meminimus sese tum rebus habentibus, regi suggestum est quatinus ex his unum qui asciti fuerant fratribus cui ceteri intenderent abbatem inibi preficeret. Electus igitur ad hoc prenominatus Rotbertus Blancard perniciter ecclesiam suam, Maius uidelicet Monasterium, deuotione ductus adiit, atque cum omnium congratulatione regrediens, cum iam occeani prope persulcasset equora Angliam intraturus, diuino quo ignoratur commotis fluctibus iudicio, seuis absorptus gurgitibus regimen propositum, e mundo sublatus, ad alium diuina dispositione pre-
f. 14 destinatum transmisit. Quo comperto et / tandem regiis auribus exposito, communicato itidem consilio, misit predictus Willelmus Faber qui totius loci curam administrabat, et a Maiori Monasterio alterum fratrem ad eiusdem abbatie regimen suscipiendum asciuit, Gausbertum nomine, uirum religionis summe, mansuetudinis ac multiplici uirtutum insignitum dote. Quem ad designatum festinantem locum quattuor ex consodalibus secuti sunt fratres: Iohannes scilicet, Hamelinus, Ainardus, Leffelmus, qui simul cum eo prospere Angliam appulsi ad destinatum hilares locum peruenerunt.

Hinc autem eodem uenerabili uiro Gausberto regie nutu maiestatis circa m lxxvi dominice incarnationis annum in abbatie regimen feliciter promoto, et coram altare sancti Martini de Bello benedicto, et in sedem suam locato, cepit sub eo et ecclesie fabrica et fratrum paulatim numerus proficere. Rex igitur magnificus inchoati operis non indeuotus ad victorie sue perpetuandam memoriam ipsum locum Bellum memoriter per succedentia tempora nominari censuit. Cui in primis leugam circumiacentem penitus ab omni exactione uel subiectione episcoporum et aliarum quarumlibet personarum dominatione ac consuetudine terrene
f. 14ᵛ seruitutis liberam et quietam pro uoto, / sicut et cartarum eius comprobatur testimonio, concessit et dedit,[1] ipsumque locum ut regie signum corone non tam multimoda prediorum, dignitatum,

[1] The chronicler is disingenuous here, but he avoids actually saying that the Conqueror issued the charters. The liberties are a general paraphrase of Battle's forged charters. All are printed by Searle, *EHR*, lxxxiii. 449–80. The exempt league of which the chronicler speaks was the diameter of the abbey's circular *banlieu*, which had a radius of a mile and a half, centred on the abbey.

we have added details that demonstrate the care of the glorious king. For although he was, to his grief, never able to visit the abbey, or to accomplish for it what he had intended, it was because he was taken up with innumerable matters. And perhaps he too was cheated by such procrastinations. But from these details we may be quite sure that he planned from the beginning such a sufficiency for his monks that his devotion is worthy of perpetual remembrance.

As we recall, it was while things were still in this state that it was intimated to the king that he might appoint one of the brothers who had been summoned, as abbot, for the others to obey. Robert Blancard was chosen, and in devotion to his own abbey, Marmoutier, he went quickly there. He was returning, full of everyone's congratulations; he had almost crossed the sea and was about to land in England, when by God's inscrutable judgement the waves were whipped up and he was swallowed into the savage waters. Thus snatched from earth, he left the rule that had been planned for him to another who was predestined to it by the divine plan. When this became known and was finally announced to the king, counsel was taken in the same way as before, and William 'the Smith', who had charge of the management of the whole abbey, sent to Marmoutier to bring another brother to undertake the rule of the abbey. This was Gausbert, a man of the highest sanctity and gentleness, and remarkable for his many virtues. He hurried to the abbey, accompanied by John, Hamelin, Ainard, and Leffelm his brothers. After a prosperous journey into England they arrived in good spirits at their destination.

The venerable Gausbert was, by royal command, happily advanced to the abbacy, blessed before the altar of St. Martin at Battle and installed in 1076. From that time on, under his governance both the construction of the church and the number of brothers began little by little to advance. The noble king, therefore, showed his devotion to the work just beginning and resolved that for the ages to come, the abbey be faithfully called Battle, to preserve the memory of his victory. But first of all he gave it a surrounding league, wholly free and quit, as he had vowed, from all exaction or subjection to bishops and from the domination of whatever other person, and from the custom of earthly service, as is also proved by the evidence of his charters.[1] He intended to enrich the abbey, as the emblem of the crown, in various ways, not

ornamentorum uariarumque opum largitione, quam et religionis carismate fratrumque numerositate, ultra quam exequi morte, prohdolor, preuentus ualuit, multipliciter ditari disposuit.

Leuge uero illius spatia his terrarum, ut in libro regis continetur, componuntur portionibus.[1] Ecclesia itaque de Bello tenet circa se unam leugam. Ipsa tenet Boccham[a] et habet ibi dimidiam hidam. De ista dimidia hida est una uirgata foris extra leugam, et pertinet ad Croherste: quam Walter filius Lamberti excambiauit pro quadam silua que erat infra leugam et hac ratione tenet illam.[2] In Bece quam tenet Osbernus de comite Augi tres uirgatas.[3] In Wasingate[b] dicit liber regis quod ecclesia habet unam uirgatam, sed non habet nisi dimidiam.[4] In Wilminte dicit liber regis quod ecclesia habet sex uirgatas set non habet nisi quinque. In Nirefeld[c] habet sex uirgatas. In Peneherste habet dimidiam hidam. In Hou habet dimidiam hidam. In Philesham habet unam uirgatam. In Cattesfelde habet tres uirgatas. In Bulintune habet duas hidas,
f. 15 una / uirgata minus. In Croherste habet unam uirgatam. In Wiltinges habet unam uirgatam. In Holintune habet unam uirgatam.[5] Summa. Sex hide et dimidia uirgata.[6]

Omnes iste terre sunt infra leugam, sicut dictum est, et de his

[a] *Add interlined in a twelfth-century hand, almost certainly that of the scribe*: id est Uccham [b] *Add interlined in same hand*: id est Botherstegate [c] *Add interlined in same hand:* Nedrefeld

[1] The 'king's book' is of course Domesday Book, the information for which was collected in 1086. Battle's *banlieu* is found in vol. i. 17b. For reasons I have discussed elsewhere, the most probable epoch of the following extent is 1086–1107. Searle, 'Hides, Virgates and Tenant Settlement at Battle Abbey,' *Econ.H. Rev.*, 2nd ser. xvi (1963), 291, and ibid., n. 2. It is one of the many early extracts of Domesday Book. See, for example, the extents of Bury St. Edmunds in D. C. Douglas, *Feudal Documents from the Abbey of Bury St. Edmunds* (British Academy, Records of the Social and Economic History of England and Wales, no. 8, 1932), pp. xlvi–lxxxi, and V. H. Galbraith, 'The Making of Domesday Book', *EHR*, lvii (1942), 161–77, and his *Domesday Book, its place in administrative history* (Oxford, 1974), chap. v, pp. 73–99. Battle abbey's own early survey of its lands differed from that in the 'king's book', and the chronicler is here recording the discrepancies for the use of future administrators.

[2] *DB*, i. 17b; 'in Croherst quam tenet Walterus de comite Ow, habet abbas virgatam terre'. Thus in Hastings Rape title to land was sufficiently secure for an exchange to have been considered safe even before 1086. For other examples see Searle, *Lordship*, pp. 54–6.

[3] *DB*, i. 17b. In the Domesday survey Osbern is shown as holding the remainder of his hide of the count of Eu, but 'pro nichilo', perhaps because its worth was so diminished when it was split from the remainder of the holding.

only with a profusion of estates, dignities, ornaments, and a variety of riches, but also with the gift of a relic and with a multitude of brothers beyond what he had the power to accomplish; he was prevented, alas, by death.

The extent of that *leuga*, as they are entered in the king's book. are arranged in these sections of land:[1] The church of Battle holds one league around itself. It holds Uckham and has there half a hide. Of this half-hide, one virgate lies beyond, outside the *leuga*, and appertains to Crowhurst. Walter fitz Lambert exchanged it for a wood within the *leuga* which on this ground he holds.[2] In *Beche*, which Osbern holds of the count of Eu, three virgates.[3] In Bathurstgate the king's book says that the abbey has a virgate, but it has only a half.[4] In Wilmington the king's book says that the abbey has six virgates, but it has only five. In Netherfield it has six virgates. In Penhurst it has half a hide. In Hooe it has half a hide. In Filsham it has one virgate. In Catsfield it has three virgates. In Bullington it has two hides less one virgate. In Crowhurst it has one virgate. In Wilting it has one virgate. In Hollington it has one virgate.[5] Total: six hides and a half-virgate.[6]

All these lands are within the *leuga*, as has been said, and the leuga

It is evidence, however, that the count had enfeoffed Osbern, as he had Walter, before the creation of Battle's *leuga*. The Conqueror clearly caused a difficulty for the two knights; in arbitrarily creating the circular *banlieu* of Battle abbey, he transferred part of their lands to the overlordship of the monks. From Battle's point of view the solution has been to rearrange the lands of Walter, and to accept the other, Osbern, on the land he previously held. For the family see below, p. 266, and Searle, *Lordship*, pp. 51, 60–1, 185–7.

[4] By the time of the abbey's second survey, a generation or so later, there was one virgate 'between Hedgland and Bathurst'. See below, p. 60.

[5] The description of the eleventh-century *banlieu* is a clear example of the outlying members of manors and hundreds in Domesday Sussex. As their place-names show, the *leuga* lands had once been attached piecemeal to manors and hundreds elsewhere, and were probably colonies within the wealden forest. *VCH Sussex*, i. 358; Searle, *Econ.H.Rev.*, 2nd ser. xvi (1963), 293–4. Certainly Bullington, and perhaps Hooe, however, lay outside the circular boundary, in better land near the shore. Below, p. 62 and Searle, loc. cit., 296–7. The new abbey, it would seem, had been given not only its undeveloped wealden lands, but more immediately productive holdings. It is a typical eleventh-century Sussex great estate. Searle, *Lordship*, pp. 48–50.

[6] This figure is perfectly correct if one assumes an eight-virgate hide, as the chronicler does a few lines further on. This survey and the unusual virgate/hide equation represent an early distribution of geld liability, whereby eight virgates bear the geld of one hide, a low-tax incentive to settlement in this poor and thinly populated area, from which the king and the count of Eu wanted not only revenue, but a settled population to act as a defence force. For the full argument see Searle, *Econ.H.Rev.*, 2nd ser. xvi (1963), 290–300, esp. 297.

terris composita est ipsa leuga quam ecclesia de Bello possidet. Quam etiam rex Willelmus liberam et quietam ab omni consuetudine terrene seruitutis et ab omni subiectione episcoporum et maxime episcoporum Cicestrie, seu aliarum quarumlibet personarum dominatione et oppressione uel exactione sicut supra dictum est, fecit, et carta sua confirmauit.[1]

Octo itaque uirgate unam hidam faciunt. Wista uero quattuor uirgatis constat. Leuga autem Anglica duodecim quarenteines conficitur, quarenteina uero quadraginta perticis. Pertica habet longitudinis sedecim pedes. Acra habet in longitudine quadraginta perticas, et quattuor in latitudine. Quod si habuerit uiginti in longitudine habebit octo in latitudine, et sic per reliqua.[2]

Deforis Bodeherste ad orientem est terminus leuge iuxta ter-
f. 15v ram Rotberti Bouis et transit / iuxta terram Rogerii Moin usque ad Hecilande, et includit Hecilande, iuxta terram Willelmi filii Rotberti filii Widonis et terram de Croherste ad meridiem. Inde transit iuxta terram de Cattesfelde et per Puchehole usque ad Westbece iuxta terram de Bodeham ad occidentem. Deinde pertransit iuxta terram de Itintune usque ad aquilonem. Inde est terminus iuxta terram de Wetlingetuna et terram de Wicham et iuxta Setlescumbe et sic reuertitur ad primum terminum, scilicet deforis Bodeherste ad orientem.[3]

Igitur leuga circumiacente in predicti loci proprietatem hoc modo redacta,[4] et iam ecclesie etiam proficiente fabrica, accitis hominibus quampluribus ex comprouintialibus quidem multis, ex transmarinis etiam partibus nonnullis, ceperunt fratres qui fabrice operam dabant circa ambitum eiusdem loci certis dimensionibus mansiones singulis distribuere que hactenus ut tunc

[1] The phrases come from three charters forged *c.* 1155–7, and inserted among the abbey's genuine early documents. They are printed in *EHR*, lxxxiii (1968), 473–5, 477.

[2] This account of land measurements is from a very early document, one certainly made before the active settlement under Abbot Ralph. See Searle, *Econ.H.Rev.*, 2nd ser. xvi (1963), 290–300, and below, pp. 60, 128, 130.

was put together out of these lands, and the church of Battle is in possession of it. King William made it free and quit of all earthly service and of all subjection to bishops—and most especially to the bishops of Chichester—and free from the domination of all other persons whatsoever, and of their oppressions and exactions, as aforesaid, and by his charter he confirmed this.[1]

Eight virgates make one hide. A wist is four virgates. An English league is made up of twelve quarentenes: a quarentene is forty perches. A perch is sixteen feet in length. An acre is forty perches in length and four in width. But if it is twenty in length, it is eight in width, and so on.[2]

The boundary line of the *leuga* is just outside Bathurst to the east, next to the land of Robert le Bœuf, and it runs with the land of Roger Moin up to and including Hedgland; it runs with the land of William, son of Robert son of Guy, and the land of Crowhurst to the south. From there it runs with the land of Catsfield and past *Puchehole* to *Westbece*, bordering the land of *Bodeham* to the west. From this point it runs adjacent to the land of Itinton to the north. From there the boundary borders the land of Whatlington and the land of Wickham, and borders Sedlescombe, and thus it comes back to the first boundary mark, namely just east of Bathurst.[3]

The surrounding *leuga* having been in this way brought into the possession of the abbey,[4] and the building of the church by now making headway, a great number of men were recruited, many from neighbouring districts and even some from across the channel. The brethren who were in charge of the building began to apportion to individuals house-sites of definite dimensions near the boundary of its site. These, with their customary rent and service, can be seen

[3] This description appears to be of the boundary as it was established in the reign of Henry I. See below, p. 128. Robert le Bœuf was a neighbour of the monks during the abbacy of Walter de Luci (1139–71). See below, p. 254. Roger Moin is no doubt the Roger de Mein of *c.* 1180 who witnessed a charter dealing with lands held by the le Bœuf family, *Hist.MSS.Comm.: De L'Isle and Dudley*, i. 36. Shortly before 1210 a William de Moyun held, for the service of two knights, land in the honour of Eu, that is, in Hastings rape where Battle lay. *Red Book*, ii. 554. The *leuga* boundaries having been stabilized *c.* 1115, they here appear as they were *c.* 1170–1200. The lands of Robert le Bœuf and part of *Bodeham* were purchased in the first half of the thirteenth century. Searle, *Lordship*, pp. 159–60.

[4] Chronicler 1 must, in the otherwise curious phrase, 'hoc modo redacta', be alluding to the survey of Henry I. Yet he seems unaware of the date of that survey, for he sets the establishment of the *leuga* boundaries in the eleventh century. The second chronicler knew better. See below, p. 128.

ordinate sunt cum consuetudinali censu uel seruitio subsistentes manere uidentur.[1] Mansurarum uero hic modus est:

1, Prima itaque mansura constat contigua porte curie, iuxta
f. 16 domum peregrinorum que hospitalis / uocatur ex parte aquilonis,[2] que Brihtwini qui fuerat Bedel extitit. 2, Secunda Reinberti de Bece.[3] Quarum utraque septem denarios ad festum sancti Michaelis annuatim persoluit et ad prata de Bodeham colligenda unum hominem inueniet uno die tantum,[4] similiter et ad molendinum restaurandum et unam summam brasii faciet. 3, Post istas est mansura Wulmeri que similiter vii denarios predicto termino persoluit et opera predicta faciet. 4,[a] Mansura Malgari fabri, vii denarios similiter et opera. 5[ta], Elurici Dot, vii denarios et opera. 6, Willelmi corduanarii, vii denarios et opera. 7, Eduardi Gotcild, vii denarios et opera. 8, Radulphi Ducgi, vii denarios. 9, Gileberti textoris, vii denarios et opera. 10, Deringi Pionii, vii denarios et opera. 11, Legarde, vii denarios et opera. 12, Elfuini Trewe, vii denarios et opera. 13, Godieue, vii denarios et opera. 14, Goduini filii Colsuein, vi denarios et opera. 15, Goduini coci, vi denarios et opera. 16, Eduardi purgatoris,[5] vii denarios et opera. 17, Rotberti molendinarii, vii denarios et opera. 18, Rotberti de Hauena,[6] vii denarios et opera. 19, Selaf bouarii, vii denarios et opera. 20, Wulurici aurifabri, viii[b] denarios et opera. 21, Willelmi Pinel, vii denarios et opera. 22, Lamberti sutoris, vii denarios et opera. 23, Ordrici porcarii, vii denarios et opera. 24, Sevugel Cochec, v
f. 16v denarios / ad festum sancti Michaelis et opera; 25,[c] et v denarios ad festum sancti Thome de alia mansura iuxta se, et opera.[7] 26, mansura Blacheni bubulci[d] vii denarios et opera. 27, Willelmi

[a] *Interlined above* mansura [b] *The third digit is added above the number in the scribe's own hand* [c] *The messuage-numbers from here on are frequently in the margin, rather than preceding the entry* [d] *Add interlined in same hand*: bubulci

---

[1] The messuages bordered the monastery on two sides, and extended up a High Street away from the gate of the abbey to a market-place at the far end of the street. For an analysis of the personal names of the burgesses by district see Searle, *Lordship*, pp. 71–6, and ibid. Appendix 12. The earliest immigrants to the town can be seen in the twenty-one *bordarii* listed in Domesday. *DB*, i. 17b. In an extant chirograph of the late eleventh or early twelfth century there appear, among the abbot's witnesses, several men who can plausibly be identified with tenants in the following rental: Hugo *decanus* (Hugo *secretarius*, no. 88), Wluric brad 'de familia abbatis' (Wluric *aurifaber*, no. 20), Malgar (Malgar *faber*, no. 4), and Aegeluuinus (Aeluuin *secretarius*, no. 97). *Hist.MSS.Comm.*, Third Report (1872), 223. For this and for the reasons given in the following notes, the rental

to have remained to this day just as they were then arranged.[1] The messuages are thus:

1: The first messuage stands near to the gate of the courtyard, next to the pilgrim's house called the hostel, to its north side.[2] It became Brihtwin's, who was the beadle. 2: The second: of Reinbert de *Beche*.[3] Each of these pays 7*d.* annually at Michaelmas, and shall find one man for one day only, for the haymaking at Bodiam,[4] and similarly for repairing the mill. Each shall also make one seam of malt. 3: After these is the messuage of Wulmer, which similarly pays 7*d.* at the same term and shall do the same work. 4: The messuage of Malgar the smith, 7*d.* similarly and work. 5: That of Eluric Dot, 7*d.* and work. 6: William the cordwainer's, 7*d.* and work. 7: Edward Gotcild's, 7*d.* and work. 8: Ralph Ducgi's, 7*d.* 9: Gilbert the weaver's, 7*d.* and work. 10: Dering Pionius', 7*d.* and work. 11: Legarda's, 7*d.* and work. 12: Elfwin Trewe's, 7*d.* and work. 13: Godieva's, 7*d.* and work. 14: Godwin's, son of Colswein, 6*d.* and work. 15: Godwin the cook's, 6*d.* and work. 16: Edward the purger's,[5] 7*d.* and work. 17: Robert the miller's, 7*d.* and work. 18: Robert of Havena's,[6] 7*d.* and work. 19: Selaf the oxherd's, 7*d.* and work. 20: Wuluric the goldsmith's, 8*d.* and work. 21: William Pinel's, 7*d.* and work. 22: Lambert the cobbler's, 7*d.* and work 23: Ordric the pigman's, 7*d.* and work. 24 and 25: Sevugel Cochec's, 5*d.* at Michaelmas and work, plus 5*d.* at St. Thomas'[7] for another messuage next door, and work. 26: the messuage of Blacheni the ploughman's, 7*d.* and work. 27: William Grei's, 7*d.*

may be assigned a date between *c.* 1102 and 1107. It does, as our author says, show the town with its earliest inhabitants.

[2] The chronicler is locating the first messuage on his old rental, with reference to the hostel, built on land between the gate of the abbey courtyard and the first of the town messuages after 1175. See below, p. 306.

[3] Reinbert de *Beche* was almost certainly the tenant of the *Beche* wists mentioned above in the early *leuga* survey, at which time Osbern held *Beche* of the count of Eu. With several other tenants of this rental, Reinbert *serviens abbatis* witnessed a charter in which Anselm de Fraelville gave *Breggeselle*, *Dudilonde*, and the tithes of Glasseye to Abbot Ralph (1107–24). HBA charter, vol. 42/1530, and below, p. 121.

[4] The abbey acquired a meadow at Bodiam in the 1090s. See below, p. 86.

[5] The term may have one of at least three meanings. It may have the legal sense of compurgator, a witness to compurgation or ordeal; it may have the medical sense, the administrator of cathartics and emetics; or the metallurgical one of a refiner.

[6] Possibly Havant in Hampshire.

[7] The feast of St. Thomas the Apostle on 21 Dec. or St. Thomas the Martyr on 29 Dec., if this is a later change in the rental.

Grei, vii denarios et opera. 28, Rotberti filii Siflet,[1] vii denarios et opera. 29, Sewardi Gris, vi denarios et opera. 30, Elurici dispensatoris, vii denarios et opera. 31, Wulfuini Hert, cum terra circa mansuram, xi denarios et opera.[2]

32. 33. Iuxta ecclesiam sancte Marie de parrochia,[3] a parte occidentali est mansura Lefui Nuc, que supradicto termino, sancti scilicet Michaelis, vii denarios persoluit et opera. 34, Post illam est mansura Gileberti extranei que cum terra sibi pertinente libera est et quieta, excepta decima terre sue quam reddit, et duobus seruitiis per annum, uno Cantuarie, alio Lundonie.[4] 35, Elurici de Dengemareis libera est et quieta, tantummodo summonitionem facit de terra eiusdem Elurici in Dengemareis quando seruitium suum facere debet.[5] 36, Benedicti dapiferi libera est omnino et quieta. 37, Mauricii, vii denarios et opera. 38, Edrici qui signa fundebat,[6] vii denarios et opera. 39, Gunnild, vii denarios et opera. 40, Burnulfi carpentarii, vii denarios. 41, Eilrici cild, vii denarios et opera. 42, Eilnodi sutoris, vii denarios et opera. 43, Francenfant, vii denarios et opera. 44, Elduini coci, due, xiii denarios et opera, 45. 46, Emme, vii denarios et opera. 47, Elstrildis nonne, vi denarios et
f. 17 opera. 48, Petri pistoris, vii denarios et opera. / 49, 50, Sewini II[e], xiii denarios et opera. 51, Rotberti de Cirisi, xv denarios et opera.[a] 52, Maðelgari Ruffi, vii denarios et opera. 53, Siwardi Stigerop, vii denarios et opera. 54, Golduini, vii denarios et opera. 55, Eduini fabri, vii denarios et opera. 56, 57, Seuugel, II[e], x denarios et opera.[b] 58, Gotselmi, vii denarios et opera. 59, Russelli, vii denarios et opera. 60, Lamberti, viii denarios et opera. 61, Ailrici pistoris, xii denarios et opera. 62, Eilnodi filii Fareman, viii denarios et opera. 63, Gileberti clerici, vii denarios et opera.

[a] *Add interlined in same hand*: et opera [b] *Add interlined in same hand*: et opera. *A space between* x *and* denarios *suggests that other digits were intended*

[1] The name is most probably the OE. Siflaed, spelled by a scribe more used to French than to the fast-disappearing OE. names.

[2] The rental-maker has been listing the messuages running north on the west side of the High Street to the site of the market-place. He now returns to the abbey to list thirty-three messuages across the High Street from the first group. Only when he has completed the High Street section of the town will he return, at number 66, to the boundary he has here reached at messuage 31.

[3] Clearly the rental from which the chronicler is working showed an untenanted thirty-second messuage here. By the chronicler's day the parish church stood on the site. The second chronicler says that the monks themselves, by common consent, had had the church built for the town. It was certainly there

and work. 28: Robert's, the son of Siflet,[1] 7*d.* and work. 29: Siward Gris', 6*d.* and work. 30: Eluric the steward's, 7*d.* and work. 31: Wulfwin Hert's, with the land around his messuage, 11*d.* and work.[2]

Next to the parish church of St. Mary (32),[3] to its west is 33: the messuage of Lefui Nuc, which pays 7*d.* at the same term, namely Michaelmas, and work. 34: After it comes the messuage of Gilbert the stranger, which along with the land appertaining to it is free and quit, except for the tithe of its land, which it pays, and for two services annually, one at Canterbury, the other at London.[4] 35: Eluric of Dengemarsh's is free and quit, save only that it makes summons of Eluric's land in Dengemarsh when it has to do service.[5] 36: Benedict the steward's is wholly free and quit. 37: Maurice's, 7*d.* and work. 38: That of Edric who was casting the bells, 7*d.* and work.[6] 39: Gunnild's, 7*d.* and work. 40: Burnulf the carpenter's, 7*d.* 41: Eilric cild's, 7*d.* and work. 42: Eilnoð the cobbler's, 7*d.* and work. 43: Francenfant, 7*d.* and work.[7] 44, 45: Elduin the cook's, two, 13*d.* and work. 46: Emma's, 7*d.* and work. 47: Elstrildis the nun's, 6*d.* and work. 48: Peter the baker's, 7*d.* and work. 49, 50: Sewin's two, 13*d.* and work. 51: Robert de Cirisi's, 15*d.* and work. 52: Maðelgar Ruffus', 7*d.* and work. 53: Siward Stigerop's, 7*d.* and work. 54: Golduin's, 7*d.* and work. 55: Edwin the smith's, 7*d.* and work. 56, 57: Sevugel's two, 10*d.* and work. 58: Gotselin's, 7*d.* and work. 59: Russell's, 7*d.* and work. 60: Lambert's, 8*d.* and work. 61: Ailric the baker's, 12*d.* and work. 62: Eilnoð's, the son of Fareman, 8*d.* and work. 63: Gilbert the

already, but it was new, by the commencement of the abbacy of Ralph of Caen (1107–24), under whom its position was regularized by the bishop. See below, pp. 124–6. Since the decision to build it is pointedly credited to the initiative of the monks themselves, it was most probably taken during the only years in which they lived without either abbot or *custos*, that is, after the death of Abbot Henry in June 1102 and before the appointment of Ralph in 1107.

[4] Gilbert was dead, as were some of his heirs after him, when the chronicle was written. See below, p. 64.

[5] Dengemarsh was a part of Battle's great manor of Wye in Kent. It lay on Dungeness, and perhaps at this period it owed riding-service for warning of hostile ships, as did some Sussex shore manors. It is perhaps even more likely that all Dengemarsh land owed service on dikes and ditches. At any rate, no service was owed at a later date from Dengemarsh, save the villagers' liability for the latter, local duty. The *trinoda necessitas* applied to none of Battle's holdings.

[6] The abbey church was dedicated in 1095. Below, p. 96. The tense of *fundebat* may suggest that Edric was still working on the abbey bells when the rental was made, that the original rental from which the chronicler is working used the present tense, and that the chronicler is indicating this.

[7] I am indebted to Dr. Cecily Clark for this reading.

64, Lefuini pistoris, xiii denarios et opera. 65, Herodis, xi denarios et opera.

Ex alia parte uie.[1] 66, Orgari, xiiii denarios et opera. 67, Chebel, vii denarios et opera. 68, Deringi, vii denarios et opera. 69, Leffelmi, vii denarios et opera. 70, Benwoldi Gest, vii denarios et opera. 71, Wulfrici porcarii, v denarios et opera. 72, Emme, vii denarios et opera. 73, Slote, vii denarios et opera. 74, Gosfridi coci, vii denarios et opera. 75, Godefridi, v denarios et opera. 76, Lefuini Hunger,[a] vii denarios et opera. 77, Eduini Cniht, v denarios et opera. 78, Goldstani, vii denarios et opera. 79, Wulbaldi Winnoc,[b] vii denarios et opera. 80, Brembel,[2] vi denarios et opera. 81, Rotberti Barate, vi denarios et opera. 82, Lefflet Lounge, iii denarios. 83, Edilde Tipe, v denarios et opera.[c] 84, 85, Goldingi v denarios et opera,[c] et de alia iuxta se, v denarios, et inde non facit brasium, nec inuenit hominem ad prata, nec ad molendinum. 86, Elurici Curlebasse, vii denarios et opera. /

f. 17v A parte orientali ecclesie Sancte Marie.[3] 87, mansura Wulfuini Scot, vii denarios et opera. 88, Hugonis Secretarii, vii denarios et opera. 89, Hunfredi presbiteri, vii denarios et opera. 90, Pagani Peche, vii denarios et opera. 91, Durandi, vii denarios[d] et opera.

Ex alia parte uie.[4] 92, Iuliot Lupi, vii denarios et opera. 93, Elfuini Abbat, vii denarios et opera. 94, Siwardi Crulli, v denarios et opera. 95, Seuugel cannarii . . . et opera.[e] 96, Brictrici ortolani, vii denarios et opera. 97, Elwini secretarii, v denarios et opera. 98, Chenewardi, v denarios et opera. 99, Balduini sutoris, v denarios et opera. 100, Osberti Pechet, viii denarios et opera. 101, Cocardi, v denarios et opera.

Ex alia parte uie iuxta murum monachorum.[5] 102, Mansura Elfuini Hachet ad festum sancti Thome, vii denarios et opera. 103, Eilnoð Hece, vii denarios et opera. 104, Blachemanni de

[a] *Add interlined in same hand*: Hunger [b] *Add interlined in same hand*: Winnoc [c] *Add interlined in same hand*: et opera [d] *Add interlined in same hand*: denarios [e] *Space left empty after* cannarii

[1] With thirty-one messuages on the west side of the High Street, and thirty-four on the opposite side—two being across from the abbey, before the road turns north—the rental-maker has come to a fork in the Battle ridge. He now turns west, where messuages had been allocated on what is now the Netherfield Road. The eastern fork, along the present Whatlington Lane, evidently was not settled at the time of this rental. So fast did the town grow in the thirteenth century that by 1240 the messuages along Whatlington Lane formed one of the

clerk's, *7d.* and work. 64: Lefwin the baker's, *13d.* and work. 65: Herod's, *11d.* and work.

Across the road.[1] 66: Orgar's, *14d.* and work. 67: Chebel, *7d.* and work. 68: Dering's *7d.* and work. 69: Leffelm's, *7d.* and work. 70: Benwold Gest's, *7d.* and work. 71: Wulfric the pigman's, *5d.* and work. 72: Emma's, *7d.* and work. 73: Slota's, *7d.* and work. 74: Geoffrey the cook's, *7d.* and work. 75: Godfrey's, *5d.* and work. 76: Lefwin Hunger's, *7d.* and work. 77: Edwin Knight's, *5d.* and work. 78: Goldstan's, *7d.* and work. 79: Wulbald Winnoc's, *7d.* and work. 80: Brembel,[2] *6d.* and work. 81: Robert Barate's, *6d.* and work. 82: Lefflet Lounge's, *3d.* 83: Edilda Tipa's, *5d.* and work. 84, 85: Golding's, *5d.* and work, and for another next to it, *5d.*, and for it he does not make malt, nor find a man for the meadow, nor for the mill. 86: Eluric Curlebasse's, *7d.* and work.

On the east side of the church of St. Mary's.[3] 87: the messuage of Wulfwin Scot, *7d.* and work. 88: Hugh the sacristan's, *7d.* and work. 89: Humphrey the priest's, *7d.* and work. 90: Pagan Peche's, *7d.* and work. 91: Durand's, *7d.* and work.

On the other side of the road.[4] 92: Juliot Lupus', *7d.* and work. 93: Elfuin Abbat's, *7d.* and work. 94: Siward Crull's, *5d.* and work. 95: Sevugel the reed-cutter's, . . . and work. 96: Brictric the gardener's, *7d.* and work. 97: Elwin the sacristan's *5d.* and work. 98: Cheneward's, *5d.* and work. 99: Baldwin the cobbler's, *5d.* and work. 100: Osbert Pechet's, *8d.* and work. 101: Cocard's, *5d.* and work.

On the other side of the road, next to the monks' wall.[5] 102: The messuage of Elfwin Hachet, *7d.* at the feast of St Thomas, and work. 103: Eilnoð Heca's, *7d.* and work. 104: Blacheman of

three town *borghs*, and the court-house, as well as the market-place, had been located at the fork, that is, at the opposite end of the town from the abbey. Searle, *Lordship*, pp. 121, 141–2 and ibid., n. 31.

[2] In the rental of 1240 there is an area of several cottages, called *Brembelegh*, on the north side of the Netherfield Road. PRO E315/18, ff. 20–8^{v}.

[3] The rental returns again to the High Street area opposite the abbey, to list the messuages lying east of no. 32, probably to about the point where Marley Lane and the Battle–Hastings road meet. Here, near the abbey, live rather more abbey servants and a higher proportion of men with French names than in other sections of the vill.

[4] The east side of the Battle–Hastings road, which has turned south. This is the Battle ridge road up which the Normans marched from Hastings in 1066.

[5] The rental returns once more to the starting-point, the abbey, to list the messuages across the road from the parish church and to follow the ridge as it turns south, on the west side of the Battle–Hastings road.

Bodeherstegate, vii denarios et opera. 105, Reinberti Genester,[1] vii denarios et opera. 106, Elurici Corueiser, vii denarios et opera. 107, Brictrici Barhe, vii denarios et opera. 108, Elfuini Turpin, vii denarios et opera. 109, Rogeri Braceur, vii denarios et opera. 110, Walteri Ruffi, vii denarios et opera. 111, Hunfredi Genester, vii denarios et opera. 112, Goduini Gisard, vii denarios et opera. 113,
f. 18 Siwardi Crulli, v denarios et opera. 114, Brunieve, viii / denarios et opera. 115, Wulfuini carpentarii, viii denarios et opera.

His itaque certis dimensionibus mansionum uilla de Bello ordinata hactenus constare uidetur. Omnes igitur ut supradiximus debent una die inuenire de unaquaque domo hominem ad prata, et ad molendinum refaciendum, et habebit unusquisque panem et dimidium, et companagium, et brasium facient, si necesse fuerit, unusquisque summam unam. Minister uero curie cum equo proprio monachorum singulis singulas deferre debet summas domibus, et hominibus tradere. Homines autem, cum brasium preparatum fuerit, curie reddere cum mensura debent,[2] et eo die unusquisque duos panes cum bono companagio habere debet. Similiter ad prata uel ad molendinum si amplius quam iustum est ire necesse fuerit, non cogantur, sed rogati, si possunt, eant. Qui uero aliquo preoccupatus negotio ire nequiuerit, non inde causetur, nec in forisfacturam ducatur. Eo etiam tenore de brasio faciendo constitutionis ratio tenenda est. /

f. 18v Homines autem ipsius uille, ob eiusdem loci premaximam excellencie dignitatem, burgenses uocantur. Qui cum ab iure consuetudinario in aliquo deuiauerint, et forisfactura rei in placitum ducti fuerint, uentilata causa coram abbate aut monachis, seu ministris illorum, conuicti, consuetudine regali de quinquaginta solidis pro emendatione persoluendis in misericordia presidentis uadimonium dabunt.[3] Veniente autem abbate nouiter ad regimen abbatie, pro libertatibus suis burgenses eiusdem loci abbati centum[a] solidos persoluent.[4]

Hactenus de his que ad uillam pertinent perstrinximus. Nunc

[a] *Added over the erasure of a longer word*: centum

---

[1] *Genesta*, or *genista*, the plant broom, used for dyeing; Reinbald and Humphrey, the tenant of no. 111, may have cut or worked the plant. But the form of their names (unlike *cannarius*, for example) makes it as likely that they are nicknames, as with the name Plantagenet. It may have been a not uncommon French nickname.

Bathurstgate's, 7*d.* and work. 105: Reinbald Genester's,[1] 7*d.* and work. 106: Eluric the leather-worker's, 7*d.* and work. 107: Brictric Barhe's, 7*d.* and work. 108: Elfwin Turpin's, 7*d.* and work. 109: Roger the brewer's, 7*d.* and work. 110: Walter Ruffus' 7*d.* and work. 111: Humphrey Genester's, 7*d.* and work. 112: Godwin Gisard's, 7*d.* and work. 113: Siward Crull's, 5*d.* and work. 114: Brunieva's, 8*d.* and work. 115: Wulfwin the carpenter's, 8*d.* and work.

The town of Battle, laid out with these fixed measurements of the house-plots, can be seen to have stayed just the same to this day. As we have mentioned, each house must provide for one day a man to mow and to repair the mill, and each will get a loaf and a half of bread and something to go with it. And they shall make malt if it be necessary, one seam each. However, a household servant, using the monks' own horse, has to carry one seam to each house and deliver them to the men. When the malt is ready the men have to render it to the household in the proper amount,[2] and on that day each should have two loaves with a good accompanying dish. In the same spirit, if it should be necessary to go to the meadows or the mill more often than is just, they may not be forced, but, when requested, they should go if they are able. But if a man is already occupied with some business and cannot go, he should not be impleaded on that account, nor should he pay a forfeiture. The malt-making regulation too should be taken in this spirit.

Now the men of this town, on account of the outstanding dignity of this pre-eminent place, are called burgesses. And supposing they should violate customary right in anything and be impleaded in a suit involving forfeiture, once the case has been aired before the abbot or the monks or their agents, if they are plainly guilty they shall give a gage at the mercy of the president of the court by the royal custom of paying fifty shillings as punishment.[3] When a new abbot enters upon the rule of the abbey, the burgesses of the town shall pay to the abbot one hundred shillings for their liberties.[4]

So far we have touched upon matters that pertain to the town.

[2] That is, the men must return the amount of malt that should be produced from one seam of corn.

[3] F. Pollock and F. W. Maitland, *A History of English Law* . . . ii. (2nd edn., Cambridge, 1898), 513. Downer, *Leges Henrici Primi*, c. 34.4: at the time of judgement, a *vadium* or security was given in support of one's intention to carry out or challenge the judgement. For the twelfth-century legal meaning of *convictum* see Downer, ibid., Appendix v, pp. 439–41.

[4] See Introduction, p. 28.

ad ea que sunt extra uillam infra leugam describenda ueniamus. Nec causetur quisquam, quod aliter quam in libro regis continetur nos terras et terminos eiusdem leuge descripserimus. Antiquitus enim terre eiusdem leuge quemadmodum in prefato regis libro descripte sunt diuidebantur, nunc autem succedentibus abbatibus prout eis melius uisum est ab eisdem diuise sunt. Diuiditur igitur leuga per wistas, que aliis in locis uirgate uocantur.[1]

In Vccheham sunt tres wiste in dominio.[2] Item in Vccheham
f. 19 sunt quatuor wiste et dimidia, quarum / possessores de unaquaque singulis annis tres solidos persoluent et quarta ebdomada tota omne opus quid eis iniungitur perficient. Sabbato uero cum equo suo quo eis iniungitur pergent.[3] Inter Hechelande et Bodeherste est una wista, cum simili opere et denariis. In Telleham habentur septem wiste, que simili modo ut supradicte opera omnia facient. Vna autem ex his est libera ab his operibus, quia quotienscumque possessor eius summonitus fuerit, cum equo suo ubicumque iniunctum sibi fuerit, cum monacho uel cum aliquo qualicumque perget. Similiter pro hoc seruitio de redditu denariorum liber est. Prebendam de curia equo suo iens habebit et rediens. Similiter conredium habebit et ferra ad equum suum. Quod si equus suus in uia mortuus fuerit, monachi restaurabunt ei. In La Stene est una wista, que denarios prefatos reddit, et opera facit. In Richelherste sunt quinque wiste, que opera et denarios predictos persoluunt. In Puchehole est una wista, simili opere et denariis supradictis constans. In Beche tres wiste sunt, possessor quarum semper debet per dimidium annum in promptu habere equum ad /
f. 19v summonitionem abbatis, talem quem abbas aut unus ex monachis suis possit honorifice equitare, et quotiens necesse fuerit ibit cum equo suo quo ei iniunctum fuerit ad ferra et clauos atque expensam abbatis et monachorum. Pro hoc seruitio liber erit de redditu denariorum. Et si predictum seruitium non fecerit, decem solidos annuatim pro prefata terra persoluet. In Dunintune tres wiste iacent, que redditus denariorum et opera supradicta persoluunt.

[1] The chronicler is about to copy a third survey of the *leuga* lands, the earlier two having been the Domesday extract (above, p. 48) and the boundaries established during the abbacy of Ralph of Caen (1107–24) (above, p. 50). This survey too is evidently one of the chronicler's own time, the late twelfth century. It will be seen that not only have abbots reapportioned the lands around the abbey, but that development had been rapid, and is continuing at the time he

Now let us describe the *leuga* outside the town. And let no one object that our description of the lands and boundaries of the *leuga* differs from that in the king's book. For in the old days the lands of the *leuga* were apportioned as they are described in the king's book. However, succeeding abbots have reapportioned them as they thought best. Accordingly, the *leuga* is divided into wists, which in other places are called virgates.[1]

In Uckham are three wists in demesne.[2] Likewise in Uckham are four and a half wists, the holders of which shall pay three shillings annually for each, and every fourth week they shall perform all work imposed upon them. On Saturday they are to go with their own horses where they are told.[3] Between Hedgland and Bathurst is one wist, with similar work and money-rent. In Telham are seven wists which shall perform all the work in a similar way. However, one of these is free from these works, since as often as its possessor be summoned, he is to go with his own horse wherever he be commanded, with a monk or someone else. For this service he is free of money-rent. He will have fodder from the household for his horse, going and returning. And he too shall have his provisions, and iron for horseshoes. And if his horse should die on the road the monks will give him another. In *La Stene* is one wist, which renders the money and does labour-service. In *Richelherste* are five wists, which pay the work and money. In *Puchehole* is one wist, with the same work and money. In *Beche* there are three wists, the holder of which must for half the year always have ready at the abbot's summons a horse of a quality that the abbot or one of his monks might ride with honour. And as often as it may be necessary, he will go with his horse where he shall be told, the iron and nails and other costs being paid by the abbot and monks. For this service he will be free of money-rent. And if he should not perform the service, he shall pay ten shillings annually for the land. In Donnington lie three wists, which pay money-rent and the service as above.

is writing. One indicator is the new hidation. Four virgates now owe the geld of one hide, instead of eight owing for one hide as was true earlier.

[2] Uckham was in the north-east quarter of the *leuga*. This extent begins, as does the Domesday extract, with Uckham, there called Boccham or Vochehant. The boundary description of 1107–24 ends with Uckham, there called Wickham. All the descriptions proceed clockwise around the circular boundary.

[3] The next customal was taken in 1251–2, and its specific, detailed terms make a striking and significant contrast with the vague ones here. Searle, *Lordship*, pp. 167–72.

Preter hec tres boscos leuga includit: Hechelande scilicet, Bodeherste, et Petlee, quartumque qui Duniford uocatur. Tria etiam pomaria ibi sunt, unum contiguum curie a parte australi, aliud iuxta domum que uocatur hospitalis, tertium iuxta ecclesiam Sancte Marie a parte aquilonali, ubi etiam ortus monachorum esse solet.[1] Tria etiam molendina habet ecclesia in dominio: duo infra leugam, scilicet unum subtus Loxebeche et aliud inferius in ualle; tertium uero partim infra leugam, partim est extra, in parte australi ecclesie in loco qui uocatur Piperinge-ea,[a] que terra extra leugam excambiata est a domino de Cattesfelde pro quodam prato paruulo qui est in Bulintune iuxta Buleworeheðe.[2] /

f. 20 Hactenus de his. Nunc de terris que sunt infra leugam in dominio dicendum est. In Petlee est una wista in dominio, quam quidam qui uocabatur Oter olim possedit. Ista enim quadraginta viii acris constat.[3] In Catecumbe sunt quinque acre, que iacent prope Wetlingetune. Inter Petlee et Vccheham iacent quadraginta ii acre, et usque ad uiam que uadit de Bello ad Wetlingetune. In Vccheham sunt tres wiste, cum prato qui uocatur Hamwisse.[b] Bodeherstegate usque ad uiam iuxta Hechilande[c] iacet, campus permaximus incultus. In Hechilande[c] sunt due wiste. Santlache[c] usque ad domum infirmorum habentur xxx[ta] acre et una, qui locus Dune uocatur. Ex alia parte uie, ubi olim pars aliqua uinee fuit, et in Celuetege, que sunt ex australi parte ecclesie, computantur xxxvi acre. In terra de Chapenore, que est iuxta illas, quindecim acre sunt, exceptis xii acris quas ecclesia sancte Marie habet.[4] Inter Bodeherste et Hechilande, et inter domum infirmorum et Chapenore,
f. 20v et usque ad terram de Telleham / xxxvii acre supputantur. Est

[a] Piperinge-ea: *The word appears to be meant as a single word, but its last two letters are separated from the rest by the long ascender of the* p *in the line above. The final* e *has a cedilla. The place-name was later spelled Peperingeye*
[b] Hãwisse [c] *h*: supra

[1] Throughout the Middle Ages the Little Park, often called *la Plasshet* (a garden surrounded by a plashed hedge) lay here, at a short walk from the abbey precincts. Little Park Farm lies there today. The *esse solet* of the chronicler is somewhat ambiguous, seeming to reflect an unsureness about the permanence of the monks' garden. It is possible that during a vacancy, for example that of 1171–5, the monks bestowed upon themselves a pleasant garden the location of which a subsequent abbot might think unwise. The answer would be an appeal to established custom: *esse solet.* Whatever its twelfth-century status, the garden became the possession, not of the monks, but of the abbots.

[2] See above, p. 48. Bulverhythe is on the coast between Bexhill and Hastings.

Besides these, the *leuga* includes three woods, namely Hedgland, Bathurst and Petley, and a fourth which is called *Duniford*. There are also three orchards: one just south of the courtyard; another next to the house which is called the hostel; the third just to the north of St. Mary's church where the monks' garden also is.[1] The church also has three mills in demesne: two within the *leuga*, namely one below Loxbeech, the other farther down the valley. A third, partly within and partly outside the *leuga*, lies south of the abbey in the place called Peppering Eye; the part outside the *leuga* was obtained by an exchange with the lord of Catsfield for a certain tiny meadow which is in Bullington near Bulverhythe.[2]

So much for this. Now we must speak about the lands that are in demesne in the *leuga*. In Petley is one wist in demesne, which a man called Oter formerly held. This is forty-eight acres in size.[3] In *Catecumbe* are five acres, which lie near Whatlington. Between Petley and Uckham lie forty-two acres, reaching to the road that runs from Battle to Whatlington. In Uckham are three wists, with the meadow called *Hamwisse*. Bathurstgate lies right up to the road next to Hedgland, an enormous, untilled field. In Hedgland are two wists. In Sandlake, reaching as far as the infirmary, are thirty-one acres; the place is called *Dune*. On the other side of the road, where formerly part was used as a vineyard, and in *Celvetege* (these are south of the church) are an estimated thirty-six acres. In the land of *Chapenore*, which is next to them, there are fifteen acres, leaving out twelve acres held by the church of St. Mary's.[4] Between Bathurst and Hedgland, and between the infirmary and *Chapenore*, and as far as the land of Telham, are reckoned

The mills and their ponds are located along the stream in the Great Park in the south-west quarter of the *leuga*.

[3] The usual *leuga* wist was a customary holding of thirty-two acres in all extents, rentals, and customals. The chronicler is here pointing out the exceptional size of Oter's former holding. It should be noted that Oter's wist and Smewin's wist (below, p. 254) are unequivocal instances of the absorption of tenant-holdings into demesne. One can reasonably infer that the other demesne lands described as wists were also once tenant land. The monks of Battle thus seem to have created their demesne not only by clearing forest, but by the engrossment of working peasant homesteads.

[4] *Chapenore* retained its identity throughout the Middle Ages. It lay behind the Sandlake messuages, next to the abbey precincts. The location of the old vineyard and the other lands adjacent to the abbey indicate that the infirmary lay in isolation at a considerable distance from the abbey and well beyond the last houses of the town. The demesne lands, from *Dune* to 'the Quarry', were in Sandlake tithing.

terra quedam que iacet inter pomarium quod est contiguum curie, et uiuarium quod est a parte australi, que uocatur Quarrere, et sunt ibi iiii acre. Ex alia parte uie[1] iuxta pomarium quod est coniunctum domui que uocatur hospitalis, sunt due acre in Herste. Ibi iuxta illas est mansura cum duabus acris sibi pertinentibus, ubi lauantur uestes monachorum, ubi etiam tres alie acre sunt. Ibi etiam a parte occidentali sunt octo acre. Iuxta illas uersus austrum simili modo octo acre de dominio sunt. In Loxebece due wiste habentur. In parte occidentali uille, decem acre optime iacent, quarum alique culte habundant frumento. In Bretherste xi acre
f. 21 sunt. In Plesseiz xv acris terra constat.[2] / Ibi etiam iuxta illas in aquilonali parte sunt xviii acre.

Preter hec sunt quedam terre que libero censu se defendunt, et sunt sine opere, hoc modo: In Vccheham est i acra que reddit iiii denarios. Iuxta uillam in parte orientali sunt xi acre, que sunt de feudo de Vccheham, et reddunt xi denarios. Que terra uocatur terra Coci. Post illas iacent v acre, usque iuxta Santlache, que similiter v denarios reddunt. Ibi est et i acra ubi domus que Gilthalle uocatur stat. Iuxta Strellewelle sunt iiii acre, quas Gilebertus extraneus tenuit et heredes eius post illum, que terra uocatur terra Wrenci, que etiam libera est, pro seruitio quod debet facere cum equo suo quo iussus fuerit illius possessor, sicut supradictum est.[3]/

f. 21v Due etiam gilthalle sunt in eadem uilla: una ut supradiximus in Santlache, que uocatur Gilda sancti Martini. Alia uero est in parte occidentali uille, qui locus uocatur Clauerham. Tertia autem est extra uillam iuxta uiuarium quod est subtus Quarrere, ad opus rusticorum qui sunt extra uillam. His igitur abbas certis temporibus ad ceruisiam faciendam inuenire debet quantum aliquis illorum, et habebit pauperem suum qui in loco illius sedebit in unaquaque, et cum aliis bibet. Cereos autem per homines particulatim collectos, maiores gildarum super maius altare sancti Martini offerre debent. Si casu forisfactura aliqua in ipso ambitu gildarum quanto tempore

[1] The extent, which has been following the same clockwise direction as the boundary descriptions, now lists the demesne lying to the west of the town and from *Herste* to Loxbeech, along the lane bordering the monks' Great Park. This is the area where the first monks built their huts, and where their wall remained in the chronicler's day.

thirty-seven acres. There is a certain piece of land, lying between the orchard next to the courtyard and the fish-pond to the south, which is called 'the Quarry', and there are four acres there. On the other side of the road,[1] next to the orchard adjoining the house called the hostel, are two acres in *Herste*. There, next to them, is a messuage with two acres appurtenant to it where the monks' clothes are washed, and where there are three other acres. Also there to the west are eight acres. Next to those, towards the south, there are similarly eight acres of demesne. In Loxbeech there are two wists. On the west side of the town lie ten of the best acres, some of which are cultivated and yield a good wheat harvest. In *Bretherste* are eleven acres. In *Plesseiz* are fifteen acres.[2] There also, just north of them, are eighteen acres.

Besides these there are certain lands that owe free rent and are without labour-dues, on these terms: In Uckham there is one acre that pays 4*d.* Just east of the town are eleven acres that are of the fief of Uckham and they pay 11*d.* These lands are called 'Cook's land'. Beyond these lie five acres reaching nearly to Sandlake, which similarly pay 5*d.* There, there is also an acre where the house called the Guildhall stands. Next to Strellewelle are four acres which Gilbert the stranger held and his heirs after him. This land is called 'Wrenc's land', and it is also free, for the service that its holder must do: riding where ordered on his own horse, as said above.[3]

There are also two guildhalls in the town, one as we have mentioned above, in Sandlake, called the Guild of St. Martin. The other is in the west part of the town, the part called Claverham. However, there is also a third, outside the town near the fish-pond that is below 'the Quarry', for the use of the peasants who are outside the town. At specified times the abbot must provide these with as much as any of the men towards making the ale, but he will choose a poor man who will sit in his place in each, and drink with the others. The leaders of the guilds must offer candles collected from each of the men, upon the high altar of St. Martin. If by chance any forfeiture should result at the time when the guild drinks, if it happens within the precinct of the guilds, it shall be

[2] See p. 62, n. 1.

[3] This service was quitclaimed by Abbot Ralph of Coventry (1235–61) to a Humphrey Beaufiz in return for his quitclaim of his town messuage, perhaps no. 34 above. HBA charter, vol. 34/693.

gilda[a] biberit euenerit, ipsorum erit. Si uero extra, abbatis est. Pro mortuis abbas nichil cum aliis dabit.[b]

f. 22 *Incipit liber de situ ecclesie Belli et de possessionibus sibi a Rege Willelmo et ab aliis quibuslibet datis*

Anno ab incarnatione Domini m lxvi, dux Normannorum nobilissimus Willelmus cum manu ualida pugnatorum in Angliam transnauigauit ut regnum Anglie sibi a suo consanguineo rege Edwardo dimissum de manu Haraldi, qui illud tirannica fraude inuaserat, abstraheret,[c] sibique illud iure hereditario possidendum obtineret. Hoc audito Haraldus cum exercitu contra illum aduenit, duce strenuissimo Willelmo audacter itidem ei cum exercitu ad locum qui nunc Bellum uocatur occurrente. Dux igitur deuotus in procinctu bellico iam armatus, conuocatis baronibus et militibus suis, uniuersos exhortatione sua et spe promissionum fiducialiter monet pugne insistere, atque ad eorum corda roboranda coram eis cum fauore omnium uotum Deo fecit
f. 22v ut si diuina pietas illi / uictoriam de suis aduersariis concederet,
eundem Deo locum sicut sibi conquirere posset liberum et quietum omnino offerret: ibique cenobium, quo Dei serui congregarentur pro omnium illorumque nominatim qui in eodem bello occumberent salute construeret; qui locus refugii et auxilii omnibus esset, quatinus iugi bonorum operum instantia commissa illic effusi cruoris redimerentur. His animosiores effecti pugnam constanter ineunt, Deoque auctore tandem pridie idus Octobris, hoste prostrato exercituque fugato, triumpho potiuntur. Tirannide itaque hostili undique prostrata, in brevi eciam tota pene Anglia pacificata, eodem anno dux armipotens, regio diademate insignitus, apud Lundoniam mirifice, ut nobilem decebat, coram regni primoribus in regem totius Anglie eleuatur, atque a uiro uenerabili Aldredo Eboracensi archiepiscopo sacra unctione linitus coronatur, electo ad archipresulatum Cantuarie Stigando regi contraire conante.[d]

Rex itaque collate sibi gratie non ingratus, memor fuit Dei et in bono proposito delectatus est, opereque uotum gestiens prelibatum efficere, in predicto certaminis loco tante uictorie condi-
f. 23 gnum precepit fabricari monasterium. Et quia illud / in honorem

[a] *Winterbottom. MS*: Gildam [b] *Two folios between 21v and 22 are blank. The hand of the second scribe begins on f. 22. See introduction, pp. 27–28*
[c] h: *interlined* [d] *Winterbottom. MS*: conanti

the men's. But if it happens outside, it is the abbot's. For the dead the abbot gives nothing when the others do.

Here begins the book concerning the site of the church of Battle and the possessions given it by King William and others

In the year 1066, the most noble William, duke of the Normans, sailed with a mighty army against England, so that he might wrest the realm of England, left him by his kinsman King Edward, out of the grasp of the deceitful usurper Harold, and so that he might win and hold it as his rightful inheritance. When Harold learned of the landing, he marched against him with his army. The energetic duke courageously faced him with his army at the place today called Battle. Now when the devout duke was armed in martial array, he called together his barons and knights and roused them all to fight faithfully in the battle, by his exhortation and by their hope in his promises. And in order to strengthen their hearts, he made, before them and with the approval of all, a vow to God, that if the divine mercy granted him victory over his enemies, he would offer up that place to God, as wholly free and quit as he might be able to conquer it for himself. And there he would build a monastery, where servants of God might be brought together for the salvation of all, and especially of those who should fall in that battle. It would be a place of sanctuary and help to all, paying back for the blood shed there by an unending chain of good works. His speech made the men more courageous; they entered the fight determinedly, and at last, as God had planned, on 14 October, they won the victory: the duke's enemy lay fallen and his army fled. With this, the usurpation of his enemy collapsed everywhere and within a short time nearly all of England was pacified. In that very year the martial duke was crowned and, magnificently, as became his nobility, he was elevated at London before the magnates of the realm, to be king of all England. He was anointed with the holy oil and crowned by the venerable Ealdred, archbishop of York, since the archbishop elect of Canterbury, Stigand, was trying to oppose the king.

The king was not ungrateful for the favour shown him; he was mindful of God and delighted in a worthy plan. So it was that acting to carry out his vow, he commanded that a monastery worthy of such a victory be built on the battlefield. And because he had

sancte Trinitatis, et beate Marie, necnon et beati Martini confessoris Christi, sanxerat consecrandum, eiusdem sancti Martini quosdam acciuit de Maiori Monasterio monachos qui operi preessent religionisque monachice fundamenta iacerent, ut simul cum ecclesie fabrica religionis ibidem norma proficeret, eisque ad opus accelerandum, peccuniarum expensas pronichilo ducens, thesauraria sua pandi faciebat quotiens uoluissent. Sed filii alieni non tam Iesu Christi quam que sua sunt querentes[1] negligentius operi insistebant. Ecclesie igitur structura in dies proficiente, cum eam deuotus rex magnis opibus et regiis dignitatibus mirifice ditare disponeret eo quod ibidem Tonantis gratia uictoriam et regnum sibi suisque heredibus obtinuisset ob uictorie eiusdem memoriam perpetuandam, ipsum locum Bellum appellari uoluit; statuitque conuentum ad minus lx monachorum ibidem congregari, proponens eandem ecclesiam cum dedicari faceret in tantum ditare ut conuentus eiusdem omni tempore numero septies uiginti monachorum existeret.[2] Sed homo proponit, Deus autem disponit.[3]
f. 23v Nam id perficere, proh dolor, / morte que regi eque imperat ut mendico preuentus nequiuit. Tamen sue dilectionis memoriam suis monachis reliquit, constituens in primo monachis eiusdem ecclesie ad cotidianos usus panem regie mense aptum, qui 'simenel' uulgo uocatur, habere pondere lx solidorum et in Quadragesima de quartario maiorem ut elemosine pars sibi cederet.[4] Huic ergo ecclesie sancti Martini de Bello hanc in primis regali auctoritate dignitatem concessit et dedit ut habeat curiam suam per omnia et regiam libertatem et consuetudinem in omnibus possessionibus suis tractandi de suis rebus et negotiis et iustitiam per se tenendam et ut sit libera et quieta in perpetuum ab omni subiectione et exactione episcoporum et ab omni calumnia Maioris Monasterii et quarumlibet personarum dominatione, sicut ecclesia Christi Cantuarie.[5] Et si quis latro uel homicida uel aliquo crimine reus timore mortis fugiens ad hanc ecclesiam confugerit, in nullo

[1] Ps. 18: 45. Cf. Ps. 144: 7.

[2] The chronicler is no doubt right that William I postponed decisions about Battle's final size and endowment. See V. H. Galbraith, 'Monastic Foundation Charters of the Eleventh and Twelfth Centuries', *Cambridge Hist. Jl.* iv (1932–4), 214–22.

[3] Cf. Prov. 16: 9, the chronicler's favourite proverb, repeated frequently.

[4] 'Simnel' was made from fine wheat-flour, the word being derived from the Latin *simila*, a wheat flour of the finest quality. It derives through OF. *simenel* and thence into ME., and therefore is little help in identifying a monk's 'vernacular' in the late twelfth century.

ordained that it be consecrated to the honour of the Holy Trinity and to the blessed Mary and also to the blessed Martin, confessor of Christ, he brought some of St. Martin's monks from Marmoutier to oversee the work and to lay the foundations of the religious life, so that a monastic rule might make progress there side by side with the material fabric of the church. To speed the work for them, he ordered his treasuries to be opened to them as often as they wished, counting the expenditure of money as nothing. But 'foreign sons', seeking not so much the things of Jesus Christ as their own profit,[1] worked carelessly. Still, the church-structure was rising steadily and since the devout king proposed to endow it splendidly with great wealth and with royal privileges, he resolved that the abbey should be called Battle, to preserve the memory of his victory, because there by the grace of God the Thunderer he had won a victory and a kingdom for himself and his heirs. And he ordained that it should have a convent of at least sixty monks, proposing that, when he should have it dedicated, he would so endow the church that it would have for ever one hundred and forty monks.[2] But 'man proposes, God disposes'.[3] For he was not, alas, allowed to carry this out, prevented by death, which rules kings and beggars alike. None the less he left his monks a remembrance of his esteem, ordaining first of all that the monks of the church should have for daily use a bread fit for the royal table. It is called 'simnel' in the vernacular; it was to have a weight of 60*s*., and in Lent the weight was to be increased by a fourth, so that part might go for alms for him.[4] From the beginning and with royal authority he granted and conveyed to this abbey this privilege: that it might have its court for all pleas, and a royal liberty, and the custom of managing its own affairs and its own business within all its estates; and its judgements enforced by itself; and that it should be free and quit for ever from all subjection to and exaction of bishops, and from any claim of Marmoutier, and from the domination of whatever persons, like Christ Church, Canterbury.[5] And if any thief or homicide or a defendant on any charge, fleeing in fear of death, should take refuge in this church, he must by no

[5] The chronicler does not say that the Conqueror issued charters to this effect, and in this he perhaps dissociates himself from the forged charters that were certainly in the monastery when he was writing. *Regesta* i, no. 62. BL Harleian charter 83 A 12; HBA cartulary, vol. 29, f. 13. Christ Church, Canterbury, the archbishop's monastic cathedral, was not in fact an exempt house.

ledatur, sed liber omnino dimittatur. Abbati quoque per totum regnum Anglie latronem uel furem aut alio crimine damnatum a supplicio liberare liceat si forte superuenerit.[1] Thesaurus etiam inuentus in terris eiusdem ecclesie totus illius sit, similiter et
f. 24 murdre / si acciderit, et omnes homines illius ubique a theloneo liberi sint, et omni consuetudine terrene seruitutis, sicut carte ipsius testantur.

Dedit autem eidem ecclesie in possessionem eternam leugam circumiacentem, liberam et quietam in perpetuum ab omni geldo et scoto et hidagiis et denegelgis, et opere pontium et castellorum et parcorum, et clausuris et exercitibus, et omnibus placitis et auxiliis et querelis et siris et hundredis et lestagiis; cum saca et socna et thol et theam et infangenetheof et warpeni et hamsocne et forstal et blodwite et cildwite et latrocinio et omni consuetudine terrene seruitutis et ab omni exactione et subiectione episcoporum Cicestrie et quarumlibet personarum dominatione, ita ut nullius, preter abbatis et monachorum eius, ditioni subiaceat. Nec in ipsa uel in aliqua eiusdem ecclesie possessione quisquam placitari, aut uenari, uel quodlibet negotium exercere sine permissione presumat super forisfacturam regiam. Nec etiam si casu quicquam captum fuerit efferatur, sed ecclesie sit.[2]

Interea nonnullis illuc religionis desiderio confluentibus, quampluribus etiam liberos suos in Dei instruendos seruitio offerentibus,
f. 24v ecclesie utilitati / per singula intendens rex, ex his quos a Maiori Monasterio acciuerat quendam monachum, equidem strenuum et religioni maxime deditum, Gausbertum nomine, predicte ecclesie abbatem prefecit; ea tamen conditione, ut nullatenus ipse uel successorum eius aliquis Maiori Monasterio subiaceret; sed ut religionem ibidem adhuc nouellam sua prudentia ad perfectum perduceret, atque post ipsum omni tempore quem sibi concors congregatio fratrum regulariter elegerit, de eadem congregatione ecclesie Belli, cum regis uoluntate abbas succederet.

Gausberto itaque electo, cum ad eum benedicendum episcopus Cicestrensis Stigandus nullatenus assentiret, nisi Cicestriam

[1] The charter containing this privilege is a forgery of *c.* 1166–7. It was prepared to meet the invasions into the abbey's liberty of Henry II's new justices of the forest. See below, p. 220. By it Abbot Walter de Luci (1139–71) freed his lands from the financial exactions of the new justices, and seems to have given himself a personal privilege which enabled him to protect his men from the physical penalties of conviction as well.

[2] The chronicler has incorporated both forged charters and genuine early

means be harmed, but should be released wholly free. Besides this, the abbot may release from punishment a thief, robber, or one condemned for any crime if he happens upon such a man anywhere throughout the length of the realm of England.[1] Also, all treasure found on the church's lands should belong to it, and similarly, if it chance, the *murdrum* fine. And all its men should be free everywhere from toll and from every custom of earthly service, as his charters bear witness.

Moreover, he gave the church the league surrounding it in perpetual possession, free and quit in perpetuity from all geld and scot and hidages and Danegelds and work on bridges, castles, and parks; and from enclosures and fyrd-service; and from all pleas and aids and complaints, and from shires and hundreds and lastages; with sac and soc and toll and *theam*, and *infangenetheof*, and warpenny and *hamsocne* and *forstal* and bloodwite, and childwite and larceny, and all custom of earthly service, and from all exaction to and subjection to the bishops of Chichester, and from the domination of all persons whatsoever, in such a way that it need submit to the authority of no one save the abbot and monks. Nor should anyone presume to pursue a plea, or to hunt or to transact any business in it or in any possession of the church without permission, on pain of royal forfeiture. And if anything should be taken accidentally, it is not to be carried off: it is to remain with the church.[2]

In the mean time a number of men had flocked there longing for the religious life and a great many had offered their children for instruction in the service of God. The king, who in every way kept the church's good in mind, therefore appointed as abbot one of the monks he had brought from Marmoutier, the energetic and deeply religious Gausbert. The appointment was made on the condition that by no means should he or any of his successors submit themselves to Marmoutier, but that by his own good sense he should guide towards perfection the religious life as yet so new there, and after him for all time, whomever of their number the brethren might agree upon electing according to their rule should succeed as abbot, with the king's consent.

These were the terms upon which Gausbert was chosen, but Bishop Stigand of Chichester would not agree to bless him unless

writs. *Regesta*, i, nos. 58, 59, 260, 261; ii, no. 1348. For the development of Battle's franchise in the Anglo-Norman period see Searle, *Lordship*, pp. 197 ff.

benedicendus adiret, regem hac de causa prouidus abbas caute adiuit; causam exposuit, quid agendum foret inquisiuit. Quo cognito, indignatus rex episcopo interminatus precepit quatinus abbatem in ecclesia sancti Martini de Bello omni remota calumnia benediceret, eo etiam modo ut illic ipse uel suorum aliquis eodem die ex consuetudine nec hospitaretur nec cibum quidem sumeret, in testimonium uidelicet libertatis eiusdem ecclesie. Factum est ergo, et abbate Gausberto ante altare sancti Martini de Bello
f. 25 benedicto / atque in locum suum ab episcopo collocato, memoriale ad posteros transiit, ecclesiam de Bello ab omni exactione et subiectione episcoporum Cicestrie liberam esse sicut dominicam regis capellam, nec in ea uel in omni possessione eius quisquam aliquid calumniari possit, nisi gratis et caritatiue impendatur.[1]

Abbati etiam, cum curiam adiret, liberationem habere constituit. Hospitia quoque apud Lundoniam et Wintoniam delegauit.[2]

Abbate igitur Gausberto, et regie maiestatis reuerentia et propria prudentia, plurimum coram regni primoribus honoris locum optinente, episcopi tamen Cicestrie sepius infestatione uexabatur. Ipsum nempe sinodum apud Cicestriam adire summonebat, abbatiam quasi ad suam diocesim pertinentem plurimis calumniis opprimere querebat ut scilicet in ea uel in his que illius erant sibi aut ecclesie sue aditus dominandi aliquis pateret. Quod precauens abbas hec iterum regie intulit aule. Cuius rei causa coram regis
f. 25v curia uentilata, statutum est in communi ut de eadem ecclesia / et leuga circumiacente se episcopus non intromitteret, sed abbas ecclesie sue et leuge circumiacentis iudex sit et dominus, ut serui Dei secularibus curis expediti soli Deo et saluti omnium intenderent, et sue ecclesie cum predicta leuga et seculari et ecclesiastico more preessent, episcopo hec et reliqua que predicta sunt cum regali auctoritate confirmante.[3] Firma igitur pacis concordia inter

[1] The chronicler is thus claiming that from the beginning the Conqueror exempted his abbey from rendering its bishop the normal episcopal rights to hospitality. He does not say that the king issued a charter to this effect. Indeed, quite the contrary: the precedent, preserved by oral tradition, is seen as the foundation of the exemption. It is no wonder then that the bishop 'often harassed' the first abbot with demands for his other customary rights, as the chronicler says below.

[2] No unimpeachable evidence remains concerning livery and lodging of the abbot, but although this seems early, such arrangements were common under Henry I and were necessary for favoured magnates. *Regesta* i, no. 60.

[3] A forged charter is printed by Searle, *E.H.R.*, lxxxiii (1968), 473–4. It is *Regesta*, i, no. 262. See below, p. 196, and, for the earlier quarrel, pp. 148 ff. The chronicler there implies that Abbot Walter de Luci referred to a charter. It

he would go to Chichester for the blessing. The prudent abbot went immediately to the king about the disagreement, explained the case, and asked what he should do. The king was outraged when he heard of it: he ordered the bishop, under threat, to bless the abbot in the church of St. Martin at Battle, with every claim set aside; and indeed neither the bishop nor any of his household might take hospitality or even food there that day as a customary right, in testimony to the liberty of the church. The matter was done just so. The fact of Abbot Gausbert's having been blessed before the altar of St. Martin of Battle, and by the bishop, has been handed down as testimony that the church of Battle is free from all exaction of, and submission to, the bishops of Chichester like a private chapel of the king, and neither in it nor in any of its possessions may anyone claim anything, save it be given freely and in charity.[1]

Also he fixed an allowance for the abbot to have when he should attend court. He also assigned lodgings at London and Winchester.[2]

Abbot Gausbert, although he acquired a high place of honour before the magnates of the realm, both because of his reverence for the king's majesty and on account of his own wisdom, was none the less often harassed by the persecution of the bishop of Chichester. He certainly kept summoning the abbot to attend synod at Chichester; he kept seeking to oppress the abbey with a great many claims as if it belonged to his diocese, plainly in order that some possibility might open whereby he or his church might have lordship over it and its possessions. To guard against this, the abbot again took the matter to the royal court. The quarrel over this was aired before the king's court and it was ordained by a general judgement that the bishop should not intrude himself upon the church and the surrounding *leuga*, but that the abbot should be judge and lord over his own church and *leuga*, so that the servants of God, unencumbered with wordly cares, might be intent upon God alone and upon the salvation of all, and might have charge of their own church with the surrounding *leuga* in both the secular and the ecclesiastical spheres. This, and the other terms already mentioned, the bishop confirmed, backed by the royal authority.[3]

clearly purported to have been issued on this occasion, but in fact the charter is most probably a forgery meant to deal with the bishop's objection that the abbey possessed no charters containing attestations of his predecessors. The chronicler is here retelling the story that provided the setting of Abbot Walter's forgery, but he is emphasizing the oral tradition of a court decision rather than the issue of a charter.

ipsos uiros uenerabiles ex tunc permanente, hoc etiam sua auctoritate episcopus confirmauit ut si prouincia illa episcopali sententia pro aliqua re interdicta fuerit, ecclesia sancti Martini de Bello non cessabit, sed si infra factam interdictionem aliquis predicte ecclesie frater aut soror morte preuentus in prouincia sepeliri non possit, requisita memorata ecclesia sancti Martini licentiam sepeliendi absque omni calumnia episcopali habeat, nisi forte is qui sepeliendus est interdictionis fuerit causa. Et si forisfacture christianitatis quolibet modo infra leugam contigerint, coram abbate definiende referantur. Habeatque ecclesia sancti Martini emendationem forisfacture, penitentiam uero reatus sui rei ab episcopo percipiant.[1] /

f. 26 Verum quoniam tunc temporis adhuc licitum erat quemque suas decimas quo uel cui uellet attribuere, quamplurimi ex uicinis eidem loco suas decimas iure perpetuo possidendas delegabant. Vnde illas episcopali auctoritate confirmatas ecclesia de Bello hucusque possidet.[2]

Eo itaque tempore in ecclesia sancti Martini de Bello omnibus in tota leuga commanentibus et extra eam etiam quamplurimis ad eandem parrochiam pertinentibus seruitium fiebat. Eratque clericus quidam capellanus qui in curia monachorum degens cum suo clerico quod necesse habebat inde sumebat. Et de his que ad christianitatem pertinebant sub abbatis imperio parrochianis ministrabat; cuncte oblationes et decime et beneficia ecclesie ipsi absque calumnia manebant.

Preterea ipso abbate Gausberto deuotionis gratia Maius Monasterium unde scilicet monachus erat uisitante, eiusdem ecclesie conuentus cum abbate suo moliebantur ut ecclesie Belli quocumque pacto dominarentur: hoc efficere conantes ut abbas eidem
f. 26^{v} ecclesie de Bello in capitulo Maioris Monasterii ordinaretur, / qui ut subditus quotiens mandaretur eos adiret. Abbas itaque Gausbertus hec prenoscens cum in Angliam redisset et hac de causa ut Maius Monasterium adiret iterum iterumque mandatum excepisset, non consensit sed curiam petens regiis auribus huius rei

[1] The chronicler is copying directly, as the present tense would indicate. The charter he seems to be using has survived only in a later, interpolated form. There is no reason to doubt that the bishop granted these privileges. For a

Accordingly, a solid pact of peace endured between those venerable men from that time on, and the bishop even confirmed on his own authority that if that diocese were laid under interdict by episcopal sentence for some reason, the church of St. Martin of Battle will not close. And if within the interdict period any brother or sister of the church should die and cannot be buried in the diocese, the said church of St. Martin, having been sought, shall have a burial licence without any episcopal claim, save if by chance the man to be buried should have been the cause of the interdict. And if for some reason there should be ecclesiastical penalties for offences against Christianity within the *leuga*, they shall be referred to the abbot for determination. And the church of St. Martin should have the payment of the forfeiture, but the bishop shall set the penance for the guilty person's fault.[1]

In those days people were still allowed to assign their tithes where or to whom they wished, and a great many men of the district made over their tithes to the abbey to be held in perpetual right. These were confirmed by episcopal authority, and are still held by the abbey.[2]

At that epoch services were held in the church of St. Martin of Battle for everyone dwelling in the whole *leuga* and even for many outside who belonged to the same parish. A clerk-chaplain, with his own clerk, used to live in the monks' household, and was provided there with his necessities. He ministered as a priest to the parishioners under the direction of the abbot, to whom without counter-claim the gifts and tithes and profits of the church belonged.

Another precedent: On the occasion of a devout visit by Abbot Gausbert to Marmoutier where he had been a monk, the convent of that church and their abbot plotted to obtain lordship over the church of Battle by whatever means. What they tried to accomplish was that the abbot of Battle be ordained in the chapter of Marmoutier. He would then owe it allegiance and would have to attend upon them whenever commanded. But Abbot Gausbert was already aware of this implication, and after he had returned to England, when he was again and again commanded to go to Marmoutier on this pretext, he refused. Instead, he went to court

correlation of this passage with the forged charter see *EHR*, lxxxiii (1968), 478–80 and ibid., 465–7.

[2] See Constable, *Tithes*, pp. 99–136, esp. p. 126.

querimoniam innotuit. Quamobrem commotus rex omnes qui secum aderant Maioris Monasterii monachos remittere precepit ipsique interminatus, 'Per splendorem Dei!' inquit, hoc enim assueuerat iuramento, 'si hac de causa mare transieris aut illuc ulterius ieris, in perpetuum Angliam, ad abbatie mee custodiam, non repedabis.' Quo iussa implente huius modi calumnia quieuit confirmante rege ut ab omni subiectione Maioris Monasterii, ut predictum est, ecclesia de Bello libera in perpetuum permaneat.[1]

In uilla uero de Bello et per totam leugam retenta in ecclesie dominio utiliori, ut uisum est, terre parte,[a] quamplurimi ex comprouincialibus, et nonnulli etiam ex transmarinis partibus asciti, abbatis et monachorum distributione sibi mansiones iam parabant, qui cum terre debito censu, alias quidem liberi, ecclesie diuersa ex more seruitia extunc persoluere soliti sunt.[2] /

f. 27 Dedit etiam idem inclitus Rex Willelmus eidem ecclesie de Bello in Cantia regale manerium quod uocatur Wi cum omnibus appenditiis suis, septem swulingarum, id est hidarum, ex sua dominica corona cum omnibus libertatibus et regalibus consuetudinibus ita liberum et quietum sicut ipse liberius et quietius tenuit uel ut rex dare potuit, scilicet ab omni geldo et scoto et reliquis que suprascripta sunt et ab omni consuetudine terrene seruitutis. Quod cum ecclesie eidem conferret, uerbum memoriale et merito recolendum ipse ter predicandus princeps dixisse memoratur. Siquidem quibusdam tante largitatis causa mirantibus, 'Ego', ait, 'istud corpori meo aufero et anime mee confero. Qua de re,' inquit, 'si corpus illud libere et quiete tenere preualuit, multo dignius est ut anima que melior pars hominis est hoc si fieri potest liberius atque quietius possideat.'[3]

Huius itaque manerii ab antiquitate hec pre ceteris dignitas semper extitit, ut cum suo hundredo uiginti duobus hundredis et

[a] *Add in marg.*: Nota contra eos qui dicunt quod fuit ibidem uilla que uocabatur Sothope

[1] See above, pp. 68–9, and ibid., n. 5. To this chronicler such an oral tradition is of value in strengthening the case for exemption, and again, he avoids the claim of written documentation. The persistence of Marmoutier later (below, pp. 112–14) is some evidence that the confirmation was oral, but it is also evidence that

and laid his complaint before the king. The king, annoyed, ordered all the Marmoutier monks who were with him to take themselves off. He even threatened the abbot: 'By the splendour of God', he said, for this was the expression he used in oath-taking, 'if you cross the sea for this cause, or if you even go there again from now on, you will never come back to England to the guardianship of my abbey!' So, in this way, simply by obeying these commands, the abbot put an end to the claims, and the king confirmed that the church of Battle should remain free in perpetuity from all subjection to Marmoutier, as was said above.[1]

In the town of Battle, and throughout the whole *leuga*, the part of the land that was the more useful, as it seemed, having been kept in hand for the church's demesne, a great many settlers were induced to come from the counties round about, and even a number from across the sea. Already they were building themselves houses on the sites laid out by the abbot and monks. Along with rent due from the land, these men from then on have habitually performed various services for the church by custom, though they are free in other respects.[2]

Out of the crown demesne, the illustrious King William also gave Battle abbey the royal manor called Wye in Kent, with all its members, seven sulings (that is, hides) with all liberties and royal customs, as free and quit as he held it at its most free and quit, and as free as he could give it as king: namely from all geld and scot and the rest which have been recorded above, and from all customs of earthly service. And tradition has it that when he conferred it upon the church, this praiseworthy prince uttered a saying worth remembering and reflecting upon. To those who were wondering at such generosity, he said, 'I take it away from my body and give it to my soul. Since this is so,' he went on, 'if the body has been able to hold it freely and quit, it is more appropriate by far that the soul, which is the better part of man, should possess it if possible more freely and more quit.'[3]

From ancient times this dignity above the rest has belonged to this manor: that with its own hundred, it rules over twenty-two

William I had indeed spoken to this effect, for Marmoutier seems not to have been at that time receiving the obedience due a mother-house. For the oath used by William see also Wace, ll. 6573 ff. and earlier, *Ord.Vit.* ii. 318.

[2] Cf. above, p. 51.

[3] *Regesta*, i, no. 62.

dimidio ad socnam illius pertinentibus preesset.[1] De quibus
f. 27v omnibus quotiens ad comitatus / uel ad alias consuetudinales collectiones conuenire debent, uicecomes de Chent preposito de Wi uel ministro eius loco et termino designato litteris suis sigillatis mandare debet et ipse deinde consuetudinaliter summonere.[2] Quibus collectis, de omnibus placitis et forisfacturis predictorum hundredorum prepositus de Wi uel minister eius uadimonia accipiet et duos denarios similiter. Hundredum uero de Wi liberum est et quietum propter istam summonitionem ab omni consuetudine et sicut olim regi, ita nunc ecclesie sancti Martini de Bello proprium permanet. Consuetudinaliter autem per totam Angliam mos antiquitus pro lege inoleuerat comites prouinciarum tertium denarium sibi optinere. Inde enim comites dicebantur. Vnde quia tunc episcopo Baiocensi Odoni, fratri scilicet suo, rex Cantie comitatum totum dederat liberum et concesserat, iccirco ecclesie sue de Bello duos quos ipse habebat in dominio suo denarios dedit, tertio ab episcopo cui comitatus cesserat retento. Succedente uero tempore, postquam predictus episcopus propriis infortuniis subactus comitatum predictum amisit, idem tertius
f. 28 denarius in redditibus / regiis computatus remansit.[3]

In Dengemareis, quod est unum membrum de Wi, concessit et dedit idem nobilis rex Willelmus omnes maritimas consuetudines quas illic habuit. Quod si piscis qui uocatur 'craspeis' illic appulerit abbatis et monachorum sit totus.[4] Et si in terra uicinorum infra terminos scilicet de Horsmede usque Withiburne quod pertinet ad socnam de Wi aduenerit, duas partes illius cum lingua dedit ecclesie de Bello, et ut abbas et monachi illud tam libere semper habeant et possideant, sicut ipse liberius possidere potuit. Eodem modo et werec quod illic contigerit habere concessit.[5]

In his uero quammaxime quanti pendebat rex utilitates ecclesie de Bello propalabatur, dum quotiens edicta regalia uicecomitibus siue iusticiariis uel ministris eorum Cantie constitutis de eiusdem

[1] *DB*, i. 11b. The royal commissioners were unsure whether the abbey actually had this dignity, for they note: 'si abbas habuisset sacas et socas, £20 plus appreciaretur', though they confirm that 'twenty-two and a half hundreds appurtain to the sake and soke of this manor'. By 1275 the abbot had lost all but two of the Wye hundreds. H. M. Cam, 'Early Groups of Hundreds', *Historical Essays in Honour of James Tait* (Manchester, 1933), pp. 22–3.

[2] This is a very early, and unusually clear statement of the franchise of return of writs. It represents beyond all doubt the operation of that franchise *c.* 1200, for a sheriff's writ of that date from Kent is extant, endorsed, 'transcribatur

and a half hundreds appurtenant to its soke.[1] Whenever they all must come to shires or to other customary assemblies, the sheriff of Kent should notify the bailiff of Wye or his deputy by his own sealed letters with the place and term specified, and it is the custom that the bailiff must then issue the summonses.[2] When they have been assembled, the bailiff of Wye or his deputy is to receive the securities for all pleas and forfeitures of the hundreds, and the two pennies similarly. In fact the hundred of Wye is free and quit, by reason of this summons, from every custom, and is now the property of the church of Battle as it formerly was of the king. On the other hand, by long usage a custom had grown into law throughout England that the earls of the counties took for themselves the third penny. Indeed, it is for this reason that they were called counts. Thus, because the king had at that time granted and conceded the whole county of Kent free to the bishop of Bayeux, Odo, his brother, he therefore gave his church of Battle the two pennies which he had in demesne, while the third was retained by the bishop to whom he had entrusted the county. But later when the bishop was overwhelmed by his own misfortunes, he lost the county, and since then the third penny has been accounted for among the royal revenues.[3]

In Dengemarsh, which is a member of Wye, the same noble King William conceded and gave all maritime customs he had there. If the fish called 'craspeis'[4] should be beached there, it should belong wholly to the abbot and monks. And if it appears on the land of their neighbours within the boundaries from *Horsmede* to *Withiburne* which belongs to the soke of Wye, he gave the church of Battle two-thirds of it with the tongue. And he granted that the abbot and monks should for ever have and hold the manor as freely as he had been able to possess it. And on the same terms he conceded the right of wreck if it should happen there.[5]

In these things indeed it was made evident how greatly the king valued the interests of the church of Battle. Whenever royal commands concerning the affairs of the abbey were sent to the sheriffs or justiciars assigned to Kent, or to their deputies, the

ballivo Wi hundredi'. M. T. Clanchy, 'The Franchise of Return of Writs', *TRHS* 5th Ser. vol. 17 (1967), 60.

[3] The chronicler is reminding his readers that the abbey has a claim to the third penny taken by the royal administration.

[4] Most probably the whale or porpoise. *Regesta*, i, no. 62 grants the privilege.

[5] *Regesta*, i, no. 62.

ecclesie negotiis destinarentur, hoc precipue regii continebant apices, ut omnes de manerio de Wi libertates regiasque consuetudines illibatas obseruarent ut ecclesia et monachi sui de Bello, sicut ipse rex melius potuit, ea omnia in pace manentes absque inquietudine possiderent. /

f. 28v Item dedit unum manerium in Sudsexia quod uocatur Alsistona cum omnibus appenditiis suis, quadraginta iii hidarum et dimidium, quod antea in dominium suum idem rex redegerat, cum omnibus libertatibus et regalibus consuetudinibus predictis.[1] Aliud etiam manerium in Surreia simili modo predicte ecclesie sue de Bello, Limnesfeld nomine, cum suis appenditiis, xxv hidarum, ex sua dominica corona contulit cum omnibus libertatibus et regalibus consuetudinibus suprascriptis.[2] Hou uero nomine in Essexia manerium aliud cum omnibus que sibi adiacebant pacto eodem predicte ecclesie dedit et confirmauit. Hoc itaque trium hidarum et trium uirgarum diuisione dimensum est.[3]

Bristwoldintuna autem decem hidarum ex corona sua idem piissimus rex sue ecclesie in Bearrocsira situm pro anima sua obtulit et carta sua cum predictis libertatibus et regalibus consuetudinibus confirmauit.[4] Craumareis quoque, v^{que} hidarum, quod est in Oxenefordsira, eadem regali auctoritate qua suprascripta
f. 29 eidem ecclesie sue de Bello concessit et dedit. / Ecclesiam etiam in uilla de Radingis ex dominio suo cum possessionibus et terris et decimis illi pertinentibus predicte ecclesie sue concessit et dedit.[5] Sub lege quoque eadem dedit eidem ecclesie memoratus rex in Devenesira ecclesiam quandam dominii sui de villa de Culuntuna cum prebendis quinque ad eandem pertinentibus.[6]

Verum quoniam in eiusdem prouincie eximia ciuitate Exoniensi, magni nominis et fame ab antiquitate pro miraculorum ibidem frequentia, sancti Olaui regis et martyris exstabat capella, illam quoque rex merito preconandus uti cum deuotione munificus, sue ecclesie liberam possidendam delegauit cum terra quadam Sirefordia et Cheneberia et aliis terris uel decimis ad eandem

[1] Cf. *DB*, i. 17b. Domesday Book shows Alciston as held formerly for fifty hides and in 1086 for 44½ hides.

[2] *DB*, i. 34a. It was twenty-five hides *TRE*, but 'modo non se defendit postquam abbas recepit'.

[3] *DB*, ii. 20a: in Barstable hundred. Battle is there shown as holding not only Hutton but *Hersa* in Hinckford hundred, valued at one hide. The smaller

royal writs particularly contained this: that they should respect all the liberties of the manor of Wye and its royal customs undiminished, so that the church and his monks of Battle might possess them all in peace, without molestation, as well as the king himself had been able to possess them.

The king gave also a manor called Alciston, in Sussex, along with all its appurtenances, forty-three and a half hides, which up to then he had retained in his demesne, with all liberties and royal customs.[1] Also on similar terms he conferred upon his church of Battle, out of his crown demesne, another manor, in Surrey: Limpsfield, with its members, twenty-five hides, with all the same liberties and royal customs.[2] And he gave and confirmed to the church on the same terms, another manor, Hutton in Essex, with all that belonged to it. And this was given an assessment of three hides and three virgates.[3]

Moreover, for his soul this same devout king gave his church out of his crown demesne, Brightwalton, a manor of ten hides situated in Berkshire, and he confirmed this by his charter with the aforesaid liberties and royal customs.[4] Also he gave his church Crowmarsh, a manor of five hides, in Oxfordshire, with the same royal authority. He also gave his church of Battle out of his own demesne, a church in the town of Reading, with its appurtenant possessions and lands and tithes.[5] Also on the same terms the king gave this church a certain church of his demesne in the town of Cullompton in Devon, with five prebends pertaining to it.[6]

A chapel of St. Olaf, king and martyr, lay in Exeter, an excellent town of the same shire, of ancient and great renown on account of the frequent occurrence there of miracles. The king, rightly to be proclaimed both bountiful and devout, gave this also to his church to be held as free, with a certain land, *Sireford* and *Chenebury*, and

holding shown in *DB* lay on the far side of the county from Hutton and seems to have slipped entirely from the abbey's grasp and memory. It may be Heard's Farm today, but it has not been so identified. P. H. Reaney, *The Place-Names of Essex*, PN Soc. xii (1935), 427.

[4] *DB*, i. 59b. Brightwalton is there said to have gelded for fifteen hides before Harold Godwinsson received it. It was thereupon assessed at ten hides and in 1086 was assessed 'pro nichilo'.

[5] *DB*, i. 157a. No beneficial hidation is recorded for the manor of Crowmarsh, nor is the abbot credited with a church in Reading in Domesday.

[6] *DB*, i. 104 a. The church at Cullompton is shown as assessed at one hide. In 1535 Cullompton is shown as a manor with a *valor* of £27 1*s.* 7*d.* Tithes amounted to another £31. *VE* ii. 313.

pertinentibus.[1] Ad que omnia recipienda illuc ab ecclesie Belli conuentu quidam frater Gunterus uir strenuus primo directus est. Qui ibidem paululum remoratus cum cure sibi iniuncte utiliter operam daret, reuocatus et pro summe religionis industria Torneie abbas effectus est.[2] Ad predictarum uero curam ecclesiarum alius
f. 29v quidam monachus cum efficacia magnanimus, / Cono nomine, adiuncto etiam sibi quodam fratre nomine Rotberto destinatus, mox, quemadmodum intimum decebat ecclesie filium, ad augendum et extollendum sibi locum commissum utiliter in posterum prospiciens, animum conuertit. Peccunias siquidem reddituum uel oblationum seu etiam cum reliquiarum, quo idem insignitur locus, circumlatione predicationum, uel aliunde pro posse adunatas, terrarum uel ecclesiarum siue decimarum adquisitione cis citraque urbem Exoniensem ecclesie loco scilicet sibi commisso perpetuabat indeque Tonantis gratia fauorem quoque compatriotarum quammaximum obtinebat. Cumque et infra urbem quoque nonnullas mansiones uel terras emptione seu deuotorum largitione iam possideret, deliberauit tandem uir sagax ingenio, eo quod eadem sancti Olavi ecclesia modica foret, monasterium in honorem sancti Nicholai confessoris Christi ad fratrum habitationem accommodum penes eandem fabricare. Quo cum superstitis regis[a] licentia et auctoritate, animum spe in Deo quammaxime magnanimum inopia non angustante, mirifice inchoato pro posse diatim proficiebat. Paulatim ergo opere ad effectum tendente et eodem
f. 30 iam aliquantum loco habi/tabili existente, accitis aliquot ab ecclesia Belli fratribus, cepit ibidem regulariter diuinum celebrari officium; ad eorundem fratrum stipendia cum omnibus ad ecclesiam sancti Olavi pertinentibus, ecclesia quoque predicta de Coluntuna, ubi prius habitauerant monachi, cum quinque terris prebendarum, scilicet Uppetona, Colebroche, Hinelande, Wevre, Esse, et omnibus ad eam pertinentibus ab abbate et conuentu ecclesie sancti Martini de Bello eidem ecclesie sancti Nicholai delegatis, ea tamen conditione ut pro subiectionis recognitione ecclesie sancti

[a] *Interlined in later hand*: Willelmi conquestoris

---

[1] *DB*, i. 104 a, b. The church of St. Olaf in Exeter is shown as having eight

other lands and tithes pertaining to it.[1] Brother Gunter, an enterprising man, was first sent by the convent of Battle to take possession of all this. He spent a short time there and, since he had carried out the responsibility so capably, he was recalled and for his industry in the Lord's work was appointed abbot of Thorney.[2] Afterwards another monk of noble mind and effective in action, named Cono, was given the responsibility of the churches, and with him was sent as his helper, another brother, Robert. He put his mind straightaway to enlarging and building up the place committed to him, looking effectively towards the future as should a trusted son of the church. He turned to lasting use the moneys from rents, gifts, and even from the sermons that accompanied the travels of the relics for which the place is noted, and that accumulated from other available sources, by acquiring lands and churches and tithes around the city of Exeter for his church. And by the grace of God the Thunderer he also obtained to the highest degree the favour of the men of the district. Since he already had possession of several houses and lands within the city through purchase or the generosity of the devout, this prudent man finally determined that because St. Olaf was a humble church, he would build near it a monastery suitable for housing monks, in honour of St. Nicholas the Confessor of Christ. Poverty could not narrow a soul so greatly enlarged by hope in God, and the work, wonderfully begun with the licence and authority of the king, who was still alive, went ahead daily as quickly as possible. When it was gradually nearing completion, and already the site was fairly habitable, some brothers were sent for from Battle and divine office began to be celebrated there according to the rule. For the support of these brethren the abbot and convent of the church of St. Martin of Battle made over to the church of St. Nicholas, along with everything pertaining to the church of St. Olaf, the church of Cullompton where the monks had earlier lived, with five prebendal lands, namely Upton, Colebrook, *Hinelande*, Weaver, *Esse* and everything else pertaining to it. However, this was done on the condition that as a

houses appertaining to it, but these lands are not mentioned. In 1535 it paid a pension to the priory of St. Nicholas of 8*s*., and had presumably been attached to the new foundation from the time of Brother Cono, who found it, as the reader is about to see, too humble to act as the basis of the expansion he saw possible. See B. F. Cresswell, *Exeter Churches*. Devon Notes and Queries vol. 5, pt. 2 (Exeter, 1908), 128–33.

[2] In 1085. *Heads*, p. 74.

Martini de Bello portio census definita, sexaginta solidi scilicet, persoluerentur.[1]

Hec igitur ab ordine digredientes succincte dixisse sufficiat. Ceterum ut omissis se calamus applicet, magnanimus ecclesie sue prospiciens rex, mercatum in uilla Belli, Dominico die, liberum omnino et quietum, ac ecclesie et monachis absque ullius exactione iure perpetuo ut proprium ad disponendum constituit et regia auctoritate confirmauit.[2] Ecclesiam itaque suam de Bello excellentissimus princeps et merito nominandus rex Willelmus, ut supra texuimus, cum leuga et omnibus maneriis suis uel posses-
f. 30v sionibus ad eam perti/nentibus ab omni consuetudine terrene seruitutis liberam et quietam in perpetuum esse constituit et regia auctoritate confirmauit: scilicet ab omni geldo et scoto et hidagio et denegeldo et sires et hundredis et omnibus placitis et querelis, et omnibus auxiliis et lestagiis et sartis et clausuris, et omnibus operibus castellorum et parcorum et pontium et exercituum, cum saca et socna et thol et theam et infangenetheof et warpeni et hamsocne et forstal et blodwite et cildwite et latrocinio si in terris ecclesie illius acciderit. Quod si murdre inuentum fuerit in aliquo loco super terram illius ecclesie sancti Martini scilicet de Bello, in leuga, in maneriis, uel in membris eorum, nullus se intromittere debet, nisi abbas et monachi eius. Et si thesaurus in prefatis terris ecclesie illius repertus fuerit, ut ecclesie et abbatis atque monachorum sit totus concessit. Warennam etiam in ipsa leuga uel in maneriis ipsius ecclesie ubique constituit. Precepit uero idem nobilis princeps quantinus ecclesia illa cum omnibus terris et possessionibus suis libera sit et secura ab omni dominatione principum et baronum et episcoporum seu aliarum quarumlibet
f. 31 personarum exactione, / et ut homines illius omnes liberi sint et quieti ab omni theloneo, et omnia mercata sua per totum regnum suum ubique absque theloneo faciant, et ne quis eis super hoc molestus sit super forisfacturam regiam.[3] Insuper etiam et hoc

[1] Upton Farm, Colebrook, Henland Farm, and Weaver are all near Cullompton in Hayridge hundred in Devon. J. E. B. Gover, A. Mawer and F. M. Stenton, *The Place-Names of Devon*, ii, PN Soc. ix (1932), 554–73. By the fourteenth century St. Nicholas was paying an annual pension of 20*s.* to Battle. Searle, *Lordship*, p. 252, n. 9. In 1535 it paid Battle an annual pension of £7. *VE* ii. 313.

[2] *Regesta*, i, no. 61; ii, no. 62a, pp. 391–2, no. 1348.

[3] The chronicler is adapting one of several possible charters: e.g. *Regesta*, i,

recognition of its subject status a defined portion of rent, namely sixty shillings, would be paid to the church of St. Martin of Battle.[1]

These matters are something of a digression from the narrative; suffice it to have mentioned them briefly. My pen must apply itself to the story I was originally telling. The great-souled king, watching over his church, authorized a market in the town of Battle, on Sunday, wholly free and quit, and under the sole management of the church and monks, without exaction by any, in perpetual right, and he confirmed it with royal authority.[2] In like manner this most excellent lord William, justly to be entitled king, as we have written above, established his own church with its *leuga* and all its manors and possessions appurtenant to it as free and quit in perpetuity from all custom of earthly service, and he confirmed this with royal authority: namely from all geld and scot and hidage and danegeld and suits to shire-courts and hundreds, and all pleas and quarrels and all aids, and lastages and assarts and enclosures and all works of castles and of parks and of bridges and of armies; with sac and soc, toll and *theam*, and *infangenetheof*, and warpenny and *hamsocne* and *forstal* and bloodwite, and childwite and larceny if it should happen within the lands of the church. And if murder should be discovered anywhere on the land of the church of St. Martin of Battle—in the *leuga*, in the manors or in their members—no one should intrude himself save the abbot and his monks. And if treasure should be found in these lands of the church, he conceded that it should all belong to the church, the abbot, and the monks. He also established the right of warren in the *leuga* and in the manors of the church everywhere. In fact this noble prince commanded that the church with all its lands and possessions be free and safe from all domination of princes and barons and bishops, and from the exactions of other persons whosoever, and that all its men should be free and quit from all toll and do all their marketing, throughout his whole realm without toll, and that no one should harass them about this on pain of forfeiture to the king.[3] Furthermore, he also added this: that if any of his barons or

no. 261 (BL Cott.Ch. xvi. 28) or BL Add. Ch. 70981, or Lincoln's Inn Library MS. Hale B 87, f. 8. The latter is Henry II's confirmation of a charter of William I; see below, p. 312, n. 1. The Cotton charter excludes the phrase 'and warpenny . . . in the lands of the church', and excludes mention of free warren. Henry II's confirmation follows the Cotton charter in these divergences, but it, and the chronicle, exclude stallage, mentioned in the Cotton charter. There seem to have been at least three related charters.

addidit, ut si quis baronum uel hominum suorum illi ecclesie aliquas terras uel possessiones aut de suo aliquid aliquando dederit, eandem per omnia libertatem uel regalem dignitatem, sicut supra diximus, in iisdem sua quoque habeat ecclesia, ut serui Dei undique quieti et liberi deo in pace omnimodis intendant.

Quoniam autem loca circa ecclesiam eandem de Bello nimis erant arentia, et pratorum irriguis minus abundabant, ex abbatis Gausberti monachorumque admonitione quidam miles ex uicinis, Osbernus nomine filius Hugonis, ex suo dominio, concedente domino illius comite Augi Willelmo, cum regis Willelmi confirmatione, triginta acras prati ad mensuram Normannie[1] dimensas in fundo manerii sui uocabulo Bodeham septem fere milariis ab ecclesia eadem distantis, partim largitione pro sua suorumque salute, partim uenditione, acceptis pro munere quinquaginta solidis, in perpetuum possidendas ecclesie Belli liberas ab /
f. 31v heredum suorum et aliorum omnium calumnia uel exactione, et ab omni consuetudine concessit et dedit, cartaque sua confirmauit.[2]

Eo etiam tempore quidam baronum regis, uir magnificus Bernardus cognomento de Nouo Mercato, cuiusdam predicte ecclesie Belli monachi nomine Rogerii apud eum aliquandiu forte commanentis inportuna suggestione, eidem ecclesie sancti Martini apud Walie prouinciam, cum quadam possessione que Vetus Villa dicitur, ecclesiam eidem contiguam sancti Iohannis euangeliste extra munitionem castri sui de Brecchennio sitam, liberam cum omnibus ad eam pertinentibus donauit.[3] Quam predictus frater Rogerius ut nouus ualebat colonus cum summo studio et labore a fundamentis restaurans, associato sibi quodam alio sue ecclesie monacho, magne sagacitatis uiro Waltero nuncupato, ibidem ad habitandum edificia construebat, prece uel munere nonnullas interim a uicinis terrarum uel decimarum possessiones eidem loco adquirens, ac pro posse, utpote in commisso fidelis, sibi creditum talentum possessiuncule multipliciter accumulatum matri sue ecclesie impiger reportare satagens.[4] Procedente uero tempore
f. 32 fratribus ad loci commoda / omnino intendentibus, eiusdem

[1] That is, in acres rather than in virgates.

[2] *Regesta*, ii, no. Xa, p. 408, is represented as the royal confirmation of this gift. A version more likely to be genuine is *Regesta*, ii, no. LXXXIa, p. 412. A badly damaged early donation charter with no mention of count or bishop is probably genuine. HBA charter, vol. 42/1141.

[3] The chronicler is mistaken in assigning Bernard's gift to the reign of the Conqueror. Bernard did not even attack Brycheiniog until late in 1088. About

men should ever give to the church any lands or possessions or anything whatever of their own, his church should hold them too with the same complete liberty and royal dignity, just as we have set them out above, as in its own lands, so that in all places and in all ways the servants of God might quietly and freely serve God in peace.

Because the area around the church was wholly dry, and well-watered meadows were scarce, at the request of Abbot Gausbert and the monks, a certain knight of the neighbourhood, one Osbern, son of Hugh, gave out of his own demesne and with the agreement of his lord William count of Eu and the confirmation of King William, thirty acres of meadow (measured by the Norman measure)[1] from the home-farm of his manor called Bodiam, some seven miles away from the church, partly as a gift for the salvation of himself and his family, partly as a sale, accepting fifty shillings in payment; the meadow is to be held in perpetuity by the church of Battle, free of the claims and exaction of his heirs and all others and free of all custom: and this he confirmed by his charter.[2]

About the same time a certain of the king's barons, a splendid man, Bernard, surnamed 'de Neufmarché', at the passionate entreaty of one Roger, a Battle monk who had by chance been staying with him for some time, gave the church of St. Martin's free, and with all appurtenances, a certain possession called the 'old town' and the church near it, of St. John the Evangelist, situated outside the wall of his castle at Brecon in Wales.[3] Brother Roger set to work as a new colonist, rebuilding it from the very foundations with enormous care and labour. He associated with himself another monk of his abbey, called Walter, a man of great common sense. He constructed living quarters there, and in the mean time by prayer or gift he acquired a few possessions of lands and tithes for the place from the neighbours. Faithful to his commission to the limit of his ability, this indefatigable man strove to return to his mother church many times enlarged the talent of the little possession entrusted to him.[4] Now, as time was going on, and the brethren were devoting themselves wholly to the good of

1091 he had reached Brecon and there in 1093 he killed Rhys ap Tewdwr and defeated the Welsh force. W. Rees has suggested that Bernard's gift was planted upon the site of Rhys's death in conscious imitation of the conqueror of England. W. Rees, 'The Medieval Lordship of Brecon', *Transactions of the Honourable Society of Cymmrodorion* (1915–16), 174, n. 2.

[4] Cf. Matt. 25: 18–28.

Bernardi uxor Agnes nomine forte inualitudine tacta eidem loco ex uiri sui assensu de propria hereditate quandam uillulam extra Waliam in Anglia sitam que Berintona uocatur, liberam omnino et quietam, in possessionem eternam contulit.[1] Sicque paulatim ex ipsius quoque Bernardi largitione in terris, molendinis, ecclesiis, sive decimis eiusdem ecclesie possessionibus auctis, et eodem loco cum suis omnibus, cum regie auctoritatis et prefati Bernardi confirmatione, in ius ecclesie Belli delegato, ab abbate et conuentu eiusdem ecclesie sancti Martini predicto Waltero priore iam constituto, decretum est ibidem ex eiusdem ecclesie monachis Dei seruos ad diuinum regulariter peragendum officium adunatos degere, atque pro recognitione subiectionis, per annum census partem, uiginti scilicet solidos, ecclesie de Bello persoluere.[2]

Ceterum ut ad propositum recurram, illis quoque diebus quidam prepotens baronum regis Willelmus cognomento de Braiosa apud Sudsexie comitatum in rapo de Brembre ipsi ecclesie de Bello in eodem burgo de Brembre octo mansuras et tres alias in Sorham liberas dedit et concessit quietas de dominio suo et super hec
f. 32v unam quoque hidam terre in Sorham / in perpetuum absque calumpnia possidendam, insuper et annuatim centum ambras salis et etiam decem modios uini quos illi abbas Fiscamnensis singulis annis reddebat pro quadam terra quam de illo possidebat Wurmincgeherste nomine prope Langlentune sitam.[3] Pro quodam etiam milite suo Hanselino nomine aliam hidam terre que uocatur Herincgeham eodem modo liberam concessit.[4] Tunc temporis etiam alius quidam illius miles uocabulo Radulfus Theodori filius ex suo dominio, eodem domino suo Willelmo de Braiosa concedente et confirmante, alias centum ambras salis eidem ecclesie contulit.[5] Quidam etiam ex ipsius Willelmi de Braiosa hominibus Tetbertus nomine cum fama bonitatis ac religionis preuentus monachicam anhelaret subire conuersionem se eidem loco deuotus contulit, et ex ipsius domini sui assensu et confirmatione terram

[1] Agnes was the daughter of Osbern fitz Richard, the Domesday tenant in chief who held Berrington near Tenbury in Herefordshire. See J. E. Lloyd, *History of Wales*, ii (London, 1911), 397, n. 135. The manor was assessed at two hides. *DB*, i. 176b. In 1535 it was a grange valued at £7. 3*s*. 4*d*. *VE*, iv. 401.

[2] Brecon paid this pension at least until the fourteenth century. Searle, *Lordship*, p. 252, n. 9. In 1535 it was paying Battle 40*s*. *VE*, iv. 401.

[3] This and the following confirmation cannot be later than the mid-1090s, for William de Briouze died before 1094. *Regesta* i, no. 423. *Langlentune* cannot be located, but is probably a misreading of *DB*'s Cengeltune (Chancton) in Steyning hundred. See below, p. 90, n. 1.

the place, it happened that Agnes, the wife of Bernard, chanced to be taken ill, and gave them out of her inheritance and with the assent of her husband, a certain hamlet situated in England outside Wales, called Berrington, wholly free and quit in eternal possession[1] and thus little by little, by the generosity of Bernard as well, in lands, mills, churches and tithes, the possessions of this church were increased. When, by confirmation of the royal authority and by that of the aforesaid Bernard, the place and all its possessions was recognized as the right of Battle abbey, Walter was made prior by the abbot and convent of Battle abbey. They decided that servants of God from among the monks of that church should join the community to carry on divine office there according to the rule, and that as a recognition of subject status they should pay the church of Battle annually a part of their revenue, namely twenty shillings.[2]

To return to our principal subject. In those days also a powerful man among the king's barons, William, surnamed 'de Briouze', gave to the church of Battle in the county of Sussex and in the rape and borough of Bramber, eight messuages, and three others in Shoreham, free and quit, of his own demesne, and besides these, a hide of land in Shoreham as well, to be held for ever without claim, and besides, one hundred *ambrae* of salt annually, and also ten measures of wine which the abbot of Fécamp paid him each year for a certain land he held from him, Warminghurst near Chancton.[3] And on behalf of a knight of his, named Hanselin, he conceded another hide of land called Erringham, free in the same way.[4] And at the same time another knight of his, called Ralph son of Theodore, out of his own demesne, with the assent and confirmation of his lord William de Briouze, gave another hundred *ambrae* of salt to the church.[5] Further, one of the men of William de Briouze, Tetbert by name, won over by the reports of virtue and sanctity, longed to undertake a monastic conversion. He brought himself, dedicated, to Battle and with the assent and confirmation of his

[4] *DB*, i. 28a. William de Briouze held Erringham himself in 1086. It had been assessed at five hides *TRE* and much reduced by 1086. The chronicler appears here to have the confirmation by an overlord of the gift made by a *militulus*. It confirms somewhat the opinion expressed by Richard De Luci that 'it was not the custom in the past for petty knights to have a seal'. It was his lord's confirmation, not the vassal's grant, that gave security to the transaction. Below, p. 214.

[5] *DB*, i. 29a: Ralph son of Theodore held Cookham of William de Briouze in 1086; the holding had a salt-pan worth 40*d*.

suam, scilicet unam hidam terre apud Langlentune in Heregraue que uocatur hida Wulvrun, secum in possessionem eternam ecclesie eidem liberam attribuit.[1] Que omnia etiam Philippus de Braiosa coram patre suo Willelmo predicto concessit et confirmauit.[2] Secundum uero libertates et regales dignitates eiusdem ecclesie Belli concessit predictus Willelmus burgenses quos dederat posse emere et uendere infra easdem domos libere absque calumpnia et sine theloneo, excepto die fori quo in publicum uenalia deferre solitum est. /

f. 33 Cum itaque longe lateque fama bonitatis ac religionis, ut prefati sumus, Dei seruorum apud Bellum degentium diuulgaretur, caritatisque abundantia uniuersis gratuita summopere accumularetur, ab omnibus idem locus merito magnificabatur. Cumque ecclesie fabrica proficiente eam in proximo munificentissimus rex largiflue ditatam dedicare disposuisset, interim aduerse pulsatus molestia fortune Normanniam transfretauit. Vbi in expeditione forte debilitatus, demum Rotomagum adiit. Verum egritudine in dies ingrauescente, cum iam extremum sibi diem imminere sentiret, ecclesie sue quam in Anglia construxerat non immemor, Willelmo filio suo, quem regni heredem constituit, imperare studuit, quatinus Angliam concitus adiens regni diademate insigniretur, atque ecclesie sue de Bello manerium unum quadraginta librarum, super ea que iam ibidem ex suo dono collata fuerant, conferret. Pallium quoque suum regale mirifice auro et gemmis preciosissimis insignitum, et trecenta numero philacteria decenter auro argentoque fabrefacta, quorum[a] plura catenis aureis uel argenteis appendebantur innumerabilium sanctorum reliquias continentia, cum feretro in modum altaris formato, quo multe erant reliquie,
f. 33v super quod in expeditione missa celebrari consueuerat,[b] / que inter alia multiformia ex predecessorum suorum regum cum regno adquisitione obtinuerat et que in regio hactenus reposita thesaurario conseruabantur, eidem loco ex suo munere conferri precepit, atque ut eandem suam dedicari quantotius honorifice faceret ecclesiam. Quo iussis obtemperante idem rex precellentissimus egritudine

[a] *Winterbottom. MS*: quarum [b] *Added at the foot of the folio in the hand of the third scribe*: cum feretro . . . consueuerat

[1] *DB*, i. 28b: in 1086 Tetbert held one hide in Cengeltune (Chancton, a manor in Washington); it had been held of Earl Godwin by Werun. It paid no geld in 1086, and 'there is nothing there'. It was valued at 11*s*. *Heregrave* is now

lord, brought with him, free and into the eternal possession of the church, his land, namely one hide of land at Chancton in *Heregrave*, which is called *Wulvrun-hide*.[1] All of which Philip de Briouze assented to and confirmed in the presence of his father William.[2] And William conceded, according to the liberties and royal dignities of the church of Battle, that the burgesses he gave might buy and sell within their houses freely, without claim and without toll, except on market-day, when it is customary to transact business in public.

And thus (as we have said already) far and wide spread the fame of the virtue and holiness of God's servants at Battle, for they were heaping up a great hoard of grace freely for everyone. Rightly was the abbey venerated by all. And since the building of the church was making progress, the most generous king had decided that he would soon dedicate it and liberally endow it. But in the mean time, impelled by the malice of ill fortune, he sailed to Normandy. Stricken there accidentally on his expedition, he got finally to Rouen. His sickness grew worse daily, and when he sensed that his last day had come, forgetting not his church which he had built in England, he took care to command his son William, whom he had made heir to his kingdom, that straightway upon going into England he should be crowned with the royal crown and confer upon his church of Battle a manor of forty pounds, beyond those with which it had been endowed already by his own gift. He also ordered that there be conferred on the abbey, as his own offering, his royal cloak, marvellously worked with gold and with the most precious gems, and three hundred amulets well made of gold and silver, many of which hung from gold or silver chains, containing the relics of innumerable saints, with a feretory in the shape of an altar, in which were many relics, on which it was his custom to have mass celebrated when on campaign. These things, among the many other possessions of the kings, his predecessors, he had obtained with the kingdom, and they had been kept up to then in the royal treasury. And he ordered that his son should have his church dedicated with the greatest possible honour and as soon as possible. These orders were obeyed. That most excellent king, his

lost but was identified with Washington until as late as the thirteenth century. A. Mawer and F. M. Stenton, *The Place-Names of Sussex*, i, PN Soc. vi (1929), 198.

[2] *Hist.MSS.Comm.*, *Third Report* (1872), p. 223 (Gage MSS.): two charters of Philip de Briouze confirming his father's gifts to Battle abbey.

ingrauescente anno regni sui xx° i°, diem, proh dolor, v idus Septembris clausit ultimum, atque inde Cadomum delatum corpus terrenum in ecclesia sancti Stephani, quam ipse fundauerat, ante altare terre committitur humatum: cuius spiritui pius redemptor regnum prestet perpetuum.

Verum ut huius consideratione paululum inmoremur, quibus uerbis huius uite miserabilis explicetur ortus nequaquam pensare sufficimus, cum tam plangendus regie etiam magnificentie incumbat occasus. Quis enim tam diram huius preclari omnimodis regis non defleat fortunam, cuius studii precipue erat Deum Deique basilicas honorare, extollere, atque sub legum obseruantia non tam regis nomen quam rectoris equitatem obtinere. Huius industrie cum priuatus adhuc aduentaret Normannorum superciliosa cessit feritas, Anglorum barbarica succubuit subacta seueritas, regnorum
f. 34 diuersorum attonita obtemperabat sullimitas: / et tamen cum his omnibus rationis supereminere moderamine, mortis eum, heu pomo nacta, subigere non exhorruit immanitas. O igitur deflendum misere conditionis discrimen. Hunc siquidem quem magnanimitas comitabatur difficilia inchoandi, robur et efficatia conquirendi, sagacitas possessa pacificandi, generale ut his singulis carentem letiferum substrauit discrimen, ut infimi abiectum,[1] secure regis preclarum penetrans limen. Ceterum miseram deflere non sufficiens conditionem, ab his interim me retorquente stilum, sapienti dum licet innuitur eternum sibi procurare asilum.[2] Ad gloriosi uero Willelmi nomine regis et re retexenda ex insigniis aliqua paucis expediamus omissa. Fecit itaque idem princeps nobilissimus ex proprio domini abbatias quidem tres, delegata singulis prediorum sufficientia, exceptis innumeris possessionibus et beneficiis quas anime sue prospitiens diuersis sanctorum monasteriis cis citraque mare largiflue contulerat seu ab aliis conferri concesserat. Duas quidem apud Cadomum construxit, unam monachorum pro se habilem omnino ac locupletem, in qua defunctus ut prefati sumus tumulatur, aliam quoque sanctimonialium satis spectabilem causa et instinctu regine sue Mathildis, in
f. 34v qua et ipsa / mirifice sepulta quiescit.[3] In Anglia uero tertiam, de

[1] The comparison is a common one in medieval proverbs: e.g. Walther, nos. 15126, 15155, 15151, 15181, 15183.

[2] A medieval commonplace. Cf. *The Anglo-Latin Satirical Poets and Epigrammatists of the Twelfth Century*, ed. T. Wright (RS 1872), ii, no. 224.

sickness growing worse, died, alas, on the ninth of September in the twenty-first year of his reign. His earthly body was carried to Caen and committed to the earth before the high altar in the church of St. Stephen, which he himself had founded—whose soul may the compassionate Redeemer grant a perpetual kingdom.

Let us pause a moment to reflect upon this man. How can we find words to talk about life's miserable rise, haunted as we are by the wretched setting of even regal splendour? Who would not weep for the ill fortune of this pre-eminent king? His concern above all was to honour and magnify God and God's churches and, under the laws, to maintain not so much the name of king as the justice of a guardian. To his energy—when he arrived, still only a private person—the arrogant ferocity of the Normans yielded, the outlandish crudeness of the English surrendered in conquest and the insolence of divers nations gave way confounded. And yet, though he proved superior to all these, moderating them by the rule of reason, death's chaotic malevolence, born—alas—of an apple, did not hesitate to conquer him. Oh, how mournful, then, are the risks of our woeful condition! This was a man whom large-mindedness attended in attempting the difficult, strength and practical skill in conquering, and wisdom in enforcing peace on what he possessed. Yet, as if he lacked all these, as if he were the lowest of the low,[1] the deadly danger that awaits all flung him down, easily finding its way across even a king's splendid threshold. I cannot provide fitting lament for his wretched plight, and I turn my pen to other matters. Meanwhile the wise man is warned to insure himself eternal refuge while he may.[2] To narrate some of the great deeds of the glorious William, in name and fact a king, let us briefly set out some we had omitted. Thus, this most noble prince, from his own demesne built three abbeys, giving each a sufficiency of estates, not even counting the innumerable possessions and benefices which, looking to his soul's benefit, he bounteously conferred upon divers monasteries of the saints on either side of the channel, or agreed might be granted by others. He built two at Caen: one of monks on his own behalf, suitable and richly endowed, and there he was buried as we have already said; the other, a splendid convent of nuns, was built for, and at the request of, his queen Matilda.[3] There she too rests, magnificently entombed. Just so in

[3] St. Stephen's and Holy Trinity, built, like Battle, in expiation of sin, in their cases the sin of marriage forbidden by authority.

qua nunc sermo actitatur, in loco sibi a Deo ut supra relatum est uictorie concesse fundauit, in qua et se humari si in Anglia obisset procul dubio decreuit. Ad quam dedicandam quia, proh dolor, non superfuit, multo minoris precii quam proposuerat eam reliquit. Nam illam dum inchoasset, ex precipuis Anglie ecclesiis eam magnitudine ac diuitiis facere proposuerat. Quod efficere prepeditur, ut prefatum est, morte.[1] Vnde sapienti cuilibet persuadetur bonum, si quod proposuit, id hodie, scilicet dum licet, eo quod ignoret utrum sibi crastinus suffragetur dies, peragere. Prudentius est enim hodiernum bonis concessum occupare diem quam spe dubia bonum recrastinare propositum. Siquidem et de peractis bonis securius gaudemus quam de propositis, que utrum efficere possimus ignoramus. Nonnullis etenim id accidit quod bona quando possunt dum agere differunt, iusto in eos Dei iudicio peccati pena preualente, qua quis quod non expedit agere permittitur, nec uoluntas postmodum suppeditet nec facultas. Verumtamen cum bona uoluntate nil probetur ditius, preclari regis summopere attollenda sunt munificentie studia, quibus tanta ec-
f. 35 clesie sue initians manu prestitit largiflua ut per suc/cedentia inhabitantibus tempora si prospere disponantur probentur fore sufficientia. Ecclesie autem sue quamlibet perpetim eius sit plangenda mors insperata, cui non solum damna damnosa uerum et (quod fari sine merore fas non est) hinc accidere irrestaurabilia, Dei tamen suis famulis prouisione prospiciente, largiflua eius munerum largitione ac auctoritate ut commemorauimus fulta, inter multimoda huius sali, prospere interim, discrimina, hactenus diuina gratia cum heredum illius tuetur ac prouehitur beniuolentia. Ceterum nunc accingamur ad subsequentia.

Flebili igitur regii decessus rumore imperium undique concutiente uir preclarus militiaque strenuus regis filius acceptis a patre mandatis, ut prefati sumus, Anglie dominaturus regno ocius superuenit Willelmus. Qui omnium fauore ut decebat magnifice exceptus apud Lundonias ab archipresule Lanfranco, assistente

[1] There may be something in this statement, evidently a tradition among the Battle monks. Battle was not so endowed that it rivalled the old Anglo-Saxon foundations. It ranked fifteenth in England in material wealth, between Chertsey and the nunnery of Shaftesbury. David Knowles, *The Monastic Order in*

England, he founded a third, with which this narrative deals, on the site of the victory given him by God, as has been related above, in which without doubt he determined to be buried if he should die in England. Alas, because he did not survive to dedicate it, he left it with much less wealth than he had intended. For when he began it, he had planned to make it one of the outstanding abbeys in England in size and wealth. He was prevented from doing this, as we have seen, by death.[1] Every wise man receives a warning to accomplish any good deeds he has planned, today while he may, for he knows not whether tomorrow will be propitious. It is more prudent to fill with good deeds the day allowed today, than for a doubtful hope to postpone a planned good. Thus too we rejoice more surely in good deeds accomplished than in those planned, which we do not know whether we will be able to do. And indeed, for some who procrastinate about doing good deeds while they can, it happens that the just judgement of God against them for sin allows them to accomplish things that do them no service, but robs them afterward of will and means. Yet, since nothing can be valued more highly than a good will, this outstanding king's desire to be generous should be greatly praised, for he launched the inchoate church with such a generous endowment that in time to come, if it is properly taken care of, it should prove a sufficiency for the dwellers here. So, although for his church his unexpected death must for ever be a cause for mourning—for it has caused his church not only most damaging losses, but (one grieves to say) irreparable ones—nevertheless by the foresight of God, His servants have been provided for. Upheld amid the manifold dangers of the deep, reliant meanwhile on the generosity and security of the gifts of which we have been speaking, the abbey has up to the present been protected and promoted by the divine favour and the benevolence of his heirs. But now we must gird ourselves to take up the narrative.

As the rumour of the king's lamentable death flew everywhere, alarming the whole realm, that celebrated man and vigorous fighter, the king's son, William, came swiftly over to govern the realm of England, obeying his father's orders as we have seen above. He was received nobly as was fitting, with the goodwill of all. He was crowned at London by Archbishop Lanfranc, attended by the

England, 2nd edn. (Cambridge, 1963), Appendix vi, p. 702. Searle, *Lordship*, p. 36.

regni nobilitate, in natiuitate Christi, intrante anno incarnationis eiusdem uerbi Dei, m lxxxviii, regni diadema suscepit.[1] Quod adeptus, paterni mandati non inmemor, patris pallium regale et
f. 35^{v} feretrum unde supra meminimus, cum ccc^{tis} philacteriis / sanctorum pignorum excellentia gloriosis, ecclesie beati Martini quantocius delegauit, que simul apud Bellum viii^{uo} Kalendas Nouembris mirifice suscepta sunt. Manerium etiam xl^{ta} librarum eidem ecclesie in Wiltesira uocabulo Bromham ex regia corona in possessionem eternam cum membris omnibus eidem manerio delegatis donauit, et illud cum membris suis ecclesiamque de Bello cum omnibus ad eam pertinentibus ab omni exactione et consuetudine terrene seruitutis secundum patris sui cartas, regia auctoritate secundum quod supra commemorauimus, in libertate et quiete manere constituit et carta sua confirmauit.[2]

Igitur uenerabili abbate Gausberto sollicite omnimodis sibi commisso gregi intendente, perfectionisque fastigium subditis indesinenter uerbo et exemplis proponente, religionis caritatis totiusque bonitatis uirtute hec de qua agitur beati Martini ecclesia multipliciter excellebat. Cumque iam operis fabrice preoptata aduenisset perfectio, rege quibusdam causis obortis eandem prouintiam cum multis optimatibus forte adeunte, ex instinctu eiusdem abbatis, paterni memor edicti, eandem dedicari basilicam decreuit. Cumque statuto die rex, baronum et uulgi innu-
f. 36 mero circum/septus agmine, locum adisset, reuerentissimo quoque Deoque dilecto archipresule Cantuariensi Anselmo superueniente, comitantibusque regem uenerabilibus episcopis, Walchelino Wentano episcopo, Radulfo Cicestrensi episcopo, Osmundo Saresberiensi episcopo, Iohanne Bathensi episcopo, Willelmo Dunelmensi episcopo, Rogero Constantinensi episcopo, Gundulfo Rofensi episcopo, et cleri populique multimodo concursu, eandem ab ipsis in honorem sancte et indiuidue Trinitatis et beate Marie perpetue uirginis, necnon et beati Martini confessoris Christi, dedicari magnifice fecit ecclesiam, instante die iii iduum Februariarum, anno uerbi dei incarnati m x^{o}c v^{o}, ex quo uero ipse rex Anglie monarchiam sumpserat anno viii^{o}.[3]

In dotem uero eidem ecclesie magnificus contulit princeps quasdam ex suo dominio ecclesias in Sudfolchia et Norfolchia et

[1] Cf. above, p. 40, n. 2. William II was in fact crowned in Sept. 1087.

[2] *Regesta*, i, no. 290.

[3] *Regesta*, ii, no. 348a, p. 401. BL Egerton Ch. 2211 is the pretended original, actually a forgery of 1155–7. Searle, *EHR*, lxxxiii (1968), 456–7, 470–1. Mistaken

nobility of the realm, on Christmas Day, at the beginning of the year 1088.[1] After he was crowned, he forgot not his father's command, but as quickly as possible sent the church of St. Martin his father's royal cloak and feretory, which we mentioned above, with three hundred amulets glorious in the excellence of their holy relics, all of which were received at Battle on the twenty-fifth day of October. Also he gave a manor of forty pounds in Wiltshire, called Bromham, out of his royal crown demesne to be one of the church's eternal possessions, with the members belonging to the manor. And he ordered this, with its members, and the church of Battle with everything appertaining to it, to remain free and quit of all exaction and custom of earthly service, in accordance with his father's charters, with royal authority, as we have mentioned above, and confirmed it by his own charter.[2]

Now the venerable Gausbert anxiously exerted himself in every way for the flock committed to him, and ever put before his subjects the height of perfection by word and example: wherefore the church of St. Martin, the subject of my book, excelled mightily by virtue of religion, charity, and all goodness. The building had just reached its longed-for completion when the king with many of his magnates chanced to come to the district on some matters that had arisen. Urged by the abbot, and mindful of his father's command, he ordered that the basilica be dedicated. On the appointed day the king arrived at the abbey, surrounded by a huge crowd of barons and common people. There came also the most reverend and beloved of God, Anselm, archbishop of Canterbury, and, accompanying the king, the venerable bishops Walchelin, bishop of Winchester, Ralph, bishop of Chichester, Osmund, bishop of Salisbury, John, bishop of Bath, William, bishop of Durham, Roger, bishop of Coutances, Gundulf, bishop of Rochester, and a great multitude of clerks and laymen. He caused the church to be dedicated magnificently by them, in honour of the holy and indivisible Trinity, and the blessed Mary, for ever virgin, and also of the blessed Martin, confessor of Christ. This was on 11 February 1095, the eighth year of the king's reign in England.[3]

This magnificent prince endowed the church, out of his own demesne, with some churches in Suffolk and Norfolk and Essex,

about the date of William II's coronation, the chronicler is a year out. The king and Anselm were together in Sussex in 1094. *Anglo-Saxon Chronicle*; C. Clark, *The Peterborough Chronicle* (Oxford, 1970), 2nd edn. *s.a.*

Essexia sitas, in episcopatu uidelicet Londoniensi et Norwicensi.[1] In Essexia, que est in episcopatu Lundoniensi, dedit ecclesiam de Sanford omnino liberam et quietam cum plenari decima et terra ad eam pertinente. In Sudfolchia et Norfolchia, uidelicet in episco-
f. 36v patu Norwicensi, dedit ecclesiam de Exelinges, / ecclesiam de Trilawe, ecclesiam de Middehala, ecclesiam de Nortuna, ecclesiam de Brantham cum capella de Bercholt et Selfelege et Benetlege et Scotlege, ecclesiam de Mendlesham cum Andreestou, ecclesiam de Brandford cum Burstale et Eilbrichtestou, ecclesiam de Eilesham cum capellis: Steuechaie scilicet cum ii partibus decime, et Scipdene cum ii partibus decime, et Brundele similiter, et Banningeham similiter, et cum medietate ecclesie de Inguwerðe et cum feudo quod Briðtricus presbiter tenebat, terram scilicet unius socheman in eodem manerio de Eilesham, ita liberam et quietam possidendam, sicut omnes alias terras suas possidet.[2] Similiter et capelle ecclesie de Brantham suprascripte ii partes decime de dominio domini habent. Has igitur ecclesias, cum terris et decimis et possessionibus atque hominibus illis pertinentibus, idem rex, ut predictum est, liberas et quietas ab omni exactione et consuetudine ecclesie de Bello concessit et dedit precepitque etiam ut clerici qui eas inuestiti tunc tenebant ecclesie Belli statutum annuatim persoluerent censum; illis uero obeuntibus, de eisdem ecclesiis
f. 37 abbas et monachi de Bello secundum quod eis utilius foret / disponerent. His ita cum testamento regie carte dispositis, omnium quoque episcoporum qui affuerunt sub anathematis interminatione confirmauit ut nullius super his molestiam paterentur auctoritas. Quibus omnibus rite completis, necnon et ab episcoporum prenominatorum communi omnium sententia penitentibus omnibus ad eiusdem dedicationis diem anniuersariam aduentantibus diebus xxx[ta] relaxatis, post sufficiens uniuersis oblatum caritatis epulum, letabunde discessum est. Tantopere uero memoratus rex eandem amabat, excolebat, tuebaturque ecclesiam eiusque dignitates et regales consuetudines conseruabat ut quemadmodum patris eius tempore nullus ei adeo aduersari presumeret. Ipse quoque quotiens casu uicinia peteret, ex dilectionis abundantia sepius eam reuisere, fouere, et consolari solitus fuerat.

Tempore itaque uenerabilis abbatis Gausberti, hoc modo sub

[1] PRO Ancient Deeds E. 326/12623: the original charter of the grant. That charter is witnessed by the list of bishops just given, with the sole exception of Archbishop Anselm. *Regesta*, i, no. 348. For Henry I's confirmation see *Regesta*, ii, no. 827. The original charter differs from the chronicler's list in omitting

in the dioceses of London and Norwich.[1] In Essex, which is in the diocese of London, he gave the church of Sampford, wholly free and quit, with its full tithe and the land appurtenant to it. In Suffolk and Norfolk, in the diocese of Norwich, he gave the church of Exning, the church of Thurlow, the church of Mildenhall, the church of Norton, the church of Brantham, with the chapels of Bergholt, Shelley, Bentley and Shotley, the church of Mendlesham with *Andreestou*, the church of Bramford, with Burstall and *Eilbrichtestou*, the church of Aylsham, with its chapels, namely Stiffkey with two thirds of the tithe, and *Scipdene* with two thirds of the tithe, and Brundall and Banningham on the same terms, with half the church of Ingworth and the fief that Briðtric the priest was then holding, namely the land of one sokeman in the manor of Aylsham—to be held as free and quit as it holds all its other lands.[2] And similarly the chapels of the church of Brantham, too, have two thirds of the tithes of the lord's demesne. As has already been pointed out, the king gave the church of Battle these churches with the lands, tithes, possessions, and men pertaining to them, free and quit of all exaction and custom. He also ordered that the clerks who had been invested with them and currently held them should pay annually to the church of Battle a fixed rent, but when they died, the abbot and monks of Battle should do with the churches whatever seemed to them most advantageous. All this was laid down in a royal charter, and the authority of all the bishops present confirmed it under threat of anathema, so that the monks might not be exposed to annoyance from anyone on this account. After all these matters were duly completed, thirty days were pardoned all penitents coming for the anniversary of the dedication, by the common decision of all these bishops. A suitable banquet was then offered to everyone out of love, and the occasion ended most joyfully. Truly, so much did the king love, cherish and defend the church, and maintain its dignities and royal customs that no one would have dared to be its opponent any more than in his father's time, and whenever chance brought him into the neighbourhood, he was often wont, out of the abundance of his affection, to revisit, support and encourage it.

So things were, in the time of the venerable Abbot Gausbert

Brundall, Banningham, half of Ingworth, and the fief of Brictric. These were all dependencies of Aylsham.

[2] Several of these churches later became very important abbey estates; for the appropriation of them and their later *valors* see Searle, *Lordship*, pp. 252, 454.

ipso se rebus habentibus, cum iam religionis summe fundamina ut uir celebs et multimoda adornatus uirtute ad perfectum usque apud eundem locum corroborasset, eodem dedicationis ecclesie anno, iam in illius loci administratione quatuor fere fortunate
f. 37v consummatis lustris, idem tandem debilitate / ad extrema actus, vi kalendas Augusti inter discipulorum manus quos religionis excellentia instituerat, de bonis centupla recepturus spiritum datori reddidit.[1] Quo euentu fratres omnes dira calamitate affecti, cum maximo gemitu et merore corpus patris uenerandi in ecclesia eadem ante crucifixum sepeliere. Hic edificia officinarum postquam edificauit ecclesiam predictam Belli uiuente adhuc magnifico rege Willelmo, et ex suo thesaurario ut erat necessarium administrante, quotquot necessaria fratribus erant construxit, nichil in eis sullime ut moris est plurimis, nichil mirabile fabricans sed humilibus tantum consentiens sequebatur humilia, simulque considerans se non habere in mundo mansionem manentem, inquirebat in celis futuram.[2] Quam ut miles Christi emeritus post fidelis certaminis longa curricula percepturus a Christo, ut predictum est, migrauit a seculo[3].

Monasterium igitur de Bello, primo hoc modo patre orbatum, cum absque abbatis iure existere nequiret, memoratus hac de causa rex Willelmus, magni principis Willelmi filius, a fratribus aditur, abbatis decessus intimatur, electionis proprie auctoritas
f. 38 recitatur, / eidem pastorem ecclesie iuxta canonum statuta ex eadem congregatione substitui obnixe supplicatur.[4] Cumque pro uoto regia suppeditasset responsio, induciarum interim dilatione, eatenus obnubilata regie auctoritatis terrore ecclesieque reuerentia zeli conspiratio regis pluribus intentum occupat animum,[5] atque a sponsionis proposito penitus auellit. Vnde aliquanto euoluto tempore, rex assentantibus fauens ecclesie Christi Cantuarie priorem, Henricum nomine, uirum quidem religione, benignitate, mansuetudine, omnique moralitatis uirtute ac litteratura summum, eidem monasterio ex reuerentissimi Anselmi archiepiscopi

[1] Cf. Matt. 5: 12; Luke 6: 23.

[2] Cf. John 14: 2.

[3] Cf. Eadmer, *Life of St. Anselm*, ed. R. W. Southern (NMT 1962), p. 96.

[4] By the chronicler's time the canonical source would have been Gratian, *Decretum*, C. 18 q. 2 c. 2, 3. Election of the abbot is advised in the Benedictine rule: *Regula* c. 44, 1–2. The tenth-century English *Regularis Concordia*, p. 6, however, stipulates 'cum regis assensu et consilio', and this was certainly the

and under his direction, for he had strengthened the foundations of the highest sanctity well nigh to perfection in the monastery, being himself a man chaste and adorned with manifold virtues. In the very year of the church's dedication, after having completed nearly twenty years in his prosperous administration of the abbey, he weakened, and died on 27 July, in the arms of the disciples whom he had instructed in the perfection of holiness, rendering his soul to its giver, to receive for his good deeds a hundred-fold reward.[1] All the brothers, moved by this terrible calamity, grieving and weeping, buried the body of their reverend father in the church before the crucifix. This abbot, after he had built the church of Battle, while the magnificent King William was yet alive and assisting as was necessary from his own treasury, put up as many household buildings as were needed for the brothers. He constructed in them nothing ostentatious as is the way of many, nothing marvellous, but being at home in spirit only with humble things, he sought the humble, and at the same time reflecting that he had no enduring mansion on earth, he sought a future one in heaven.[2] To it he departed from the world, as I have said, to receive it from Christ as His veteran knight after a long career of faithful service.[3]

Thus the monastery of Battle was bereft of its first father and since it was unable to go on without an abbot's rule, King William, son of the great prince, William, was approached on the subject by the brothers. They informed him of the abbot's death and recited the authority of his own right to elect. He was pressingly prayed to replace the church's shepherd out of its congregation according to the canons.[4] Now the royal answer was satisfactory, but during the delay, a jealous conspiracy, hitherto overclouded by terror of the royal authority and reverence due to the church, occupied the king's anxious mind with many matters.[5] In short, it made him quite forget his intention. So that after some time had elapsed, the king listened to flatterers, and by the advice of the most reverend Archbishop Anselm, he transferred to his monastery as abbot the prior of Christ Church, Canterbury, Henry by name, a man in truth most distinguished in piety, benevolence, gentleness, in

case in Anglo-Norman England. For Henry II's veto of proposed candidates, see below, p. 282.

[5] The conspiracy of Mowbray's rebellion of 1095. A. L. Poole, *From Domesday Book to Magna Carta* (2nd edn. Oxford, 1964), pp. 109–10.

consilio abbatem delegauit. Quo euentu ui plus iusto rationi preualente, inmodice calamitatis eidem loco orta sunt fomenta.

Anno itaque uerbi Dei humanati m xc vi in abbatem domino Henrico electo et in ecclesiam Belli iii° idus Iunii ut decebat excepto, cum sibi omnia abbatis iure uindicans quamplurimos Cantuariensium monachorum, quorum uoluntati et consilio se suumque penitus dediderat studium, accisset secumque detinuisset, quamuis ipse natura bonus foret, tamen eum in aliquo partium
f. 38ᵛ simultatibus haud obuiantem impossibile erat non / deuiare. Vnde et episcopus Cicestrensis Radulfus opportunitatem nactus, eum per quosdam suorum ex industria studens, in ecclesia Belli benedicere renuebat, et hac mora multum temporis differens fatigabat. Abbate uero cum suis fortune incerto segnius renitente, demum suorum quibus fauebat instinctu, sed et archipresulis Anselmi consilio cum contra ecclesie sue iura benedictionem Cicestriam inconsulte petens, renitentibus ecclesie sibi commisse filiis, assecutus fuisset, intestina continuo pullulauit dissensio; necnon et aliis quibusdam occasionum succedentibus querelis, non omnino prudenter nec prospere ut decebat domus Dei dispensabatur utilitas. Ille uero tanto insignitus honore multa pro tempore dissimulans sibi commissam cum summo labore inter fluctuum multimodos naucellam strenue gubernabat scopulos atque ut uir celebs et modestia clarus dei seruitium cantuum ornatu dulcisono,[1] ecclesiamque consuetudinibus ornamentorumque nonnullis apparatibus decentissime honestauit.

His ita se habentibus et ecclesie penitus statu in subtilitatem exposito, prefatum contigit regem Willelmum, in Normannia suis negotiis strenue insistentem, a quodam abbate monasterii quod Flagi dicitur ubi beatus Ieremarus uirtutibus insignis quiescere
f. 39 fertur[2] / inter reliquos sue dapsilitatis appetitores adiri; qui a regia munificentia preciosam ecclesie sue planetam, que usitatius casula

[1] The chronicler is probably referring to the part-music (*organum*) which was being actively developed in the eleventh and early twelfth centuries. While central and northern France seem to have been the centres of musical innovation, Anglo-Norman England was by no means a backwater. A famous MS. of the eleventh century from Winchester contains over one hundred and fifty two-part *organa*, in which the innovative 'contrary motion' can already be found. Canterbury would hardly have been far behind Winchester; Abbot Henry and his companions evidently brought the new music with them. For the development see H. Harman, *Medieval and Early Renaissance Music* (London, 1958). In the

erudition, and in every virtue of character. In this result, force prevailed unduly over reason, and it became the source of an injury beyond measure to this abbey.

Thus in 1096, Henry was elected abbot and received fittingly in the church of Battle on 11 June. But arrogating everything to himself as an abbot's right, he sent for a great number of Canterbury monks to whose will and counsel he had wholly given himself and his endeavour, and he kept them around him. Thus although he himself was good by nature, nevertheless it was impossible for a man who gave way in the face of enmities not in some respect to go astray. Ralph, the bishop of Chichester, busying himself assiduously through certain of his men, lit upon the opportunity. He refused to bless him in the church of Battle, and protracting the matter for a long time, wore him out with this delay. The abbot, along with his men, was doubtful of fortune and struggled but weakly. At length at the instigation of his favourites, but also, it must be said, on the advice of Archbishop Anselm, though against the rights of his own church, he ill advisedly went to ask his blessing at Chichester. Though the monks of the church entrusted to him opposed him, the request was accepted. Unceasing internal dissension grew out of this; and since other quarrels followed, the endowment of God's house was looked after not wholly prudently, nor successfully, as it should have been. He who had been distinguished by such an honour, glossed over many things for a time. Thus did he actively and with great labour pilot the little ship entrusted to him past many rocks amid the waves. As a chaste man, and one known for his correctness of conduct, he most fittingly adorned God's services with settings of ornate harmony,[1] and God's church with customs, and with several splendid ornaments.

Things were going on thus, and the status of the church was wholly exposed to guile, when it happened that King William, pursuing his affairs actively in Normandy, was approached, among the many petitioners for his bounty, by the abbot of the monastery called Fly, where St. Germer, renowned for his powers, is said to be buried.[2] This man begged the royal generosity for a precious 'planeta', more familiarly called a chasuble, for his church, or if by

famous and tragic case of Abbot Thurstan at Glastonbury, a Norman abbot tried to force his English monks to 'learn an alien and novel chant from Flemings and Normans'. *Ord.Vit.* ii. 270 and ibid., n. 1.

[2] St. Germer founded the monastery of Fly in the diocese of Beauvais in the mid-seventh century.

uocatur, uel, si in promptu forte non haberetur, pretium largiri quo compararetur petens instabat.[1] Cui cum a rege terminus quousque Angliam repedaret imponeretur, regemque postmodum Angliam reuersum per monachum suum quendam inde crebrius requisisset, tandem in expeditione Walie eius pertesus importunitate rex eundem monachum, quorundam impulsus consilio, cum litteris preceptoriis regia bulla signatis, ad abbatem ecclesie beati Martini de Bello, unde nunc nostra desudat Minerua, destinauit atque ab eo decem argenti libras Anglice monete absque cunctatione ad hoc opus exigi mandauit. Audito igitur hoc abbas Henricus, mandato legationi nequaquam adquiescens, clam duos fratrum, qui regi et summam loci penuriam et prauum abolendum usum ne in posterum hac de causa inolesceret studiose suggererent, transmisit. Quibus rex nullatenus flexus demum interminando integram predicte pensionem peccunie monacho transmarino persolui precepit. Porro monacho iugiter infesto pro predicta instante
f. 39v pecunia, non sine graui abbas merore, inopia coactus, de / sacrosanctis sanctarum reliquiarum philacteriis unde supra meminimus tantum argenti collegit unde molestissimo exactori satisfecit. Quo adepto, letus quesiuit, inuenit, et congruam ad hoc opus purpuram emit, ecclesieque sue gaudenter non unde sed quid adquisisset computans aduexit. Planeta itaque iam exinde facta, nulloque iudiciorum Dei metu superstite dum quasi bene gesta uiderentur omnia, repente quadam die hora iam tertia, intonante de celis domino, aeris tranquillitas tenebrarum caligini et quasi mortis subacta umbre in horridum choruscationis et tonitrui turbinem uersa concitatur. Interim uero hora diei tertia inchoata dum fratres uersum 'Sagitte potentis acute'[2] modulando recitarent, subito die noctis imitante horrorem, cum celi quoque fragoribus concussa terra tremens euehi sub plantis uideretur, fulguris qui timebatur celo decidit ictus, fratribusque omnibus intermissis que ceperant ad orationem prostratis, mox eiusdem loci monachi duo uitali flatu priuantur. Hinc attonitis omnibus cum causa tam dire animaduersionis negligeretur, iustus iudex non distulit[3] Dominus dilecti sui Martini sanctorumque quorum in eius basilica

[1] *Planeta*, a term for the priest's outermost garment, is still used in liturgical books as synonymous with chasuble. The distinction is generally one of shape. See the *New Catholic Encyclopedia* viii (New York, 1967), s.v. 'Liturgical Art', where the *planeta* shape is illustrated, esp. pp. 876–7.

[2] Ps. 120: 4.

[3] Cf. Pss. 78: 21; 7: 11.

chance there were none at hand, to grant the money to buy one.[1] The king told him to wait until he returned to England, and afterwards, when the king did return, one of the abbot's monks repeatedly asked about it. Finally on the Welsh expedition, sick and tired of his importuning, and influenced by the advice of certain men, the king sent the monk, with letters of command sealed by the royal seal, to the abbot of the church of St. Martin of Battle, where now our Minerva is labouring. He was commanded to pay without delay ten pounds in English silver money for the business. When Abbot Henry heard the command, without at all acquiescing in it, he secretly sent two of the brothers to lay before the king both that the abbey was extremely poor, and that the growth of an improper practice should be checked, so that from this precedent no custom be established in the future. Neither argument at all dissuaded the king; finally with a threat he ordered that the entire amount of the money be turned over to the foreign monk. The troublesome monk went on continually pressing for the money. Deeply grieving but compelled by poverty, the abbot got together enough silver from the holy amulets of the saints' relics, of which we have spoken earlier, to satisfy this most irksome exactor. The man took the money, delighted. He looked for, found, and brought purple cloth suitable for the purpose, and bore it joyfully to his church, counting not how but what he had won. The 'planeta' was already made from it, and no fear of God's judgement lingered as long as everything seemed well done, when suddenly, one day just at the third hour, the Lord thundered from the heavens. A gloom like the shadow of death darkened the day, and the calmness of the weather was violently transformed into a frightful whirlwind of thunder and lightning. Meanwhile the day's third hour had just begun, and the brethren were chanting the verse 'Sharp arrows of the mighty',[2] when suddenly the day took on the terror of night, while the trembling earth, shaken by the thunder of heaven, seemed to heave underfoot. Just then there came, as they had feared, a stroke of lightning from the sky. All the brethren broke off the chant they had begun and threw themselves down in prayer. Suddenly two monks of the abbey were robbed of their life's breath. Everyone was stunned at this, but they took no heed as to the cause of so dreadful a chastisement. Nevertheless our Lord, the just judge, did not cast them off.[3] Rather, the Lord would make plain how seriously He took the plunder of His beloved Martin and of the

continentur pignera expoliationem quanti pendat propalare. Nam
sequenti quoque anno iterum incumbente rediuiua intemperie,
f. 40 cum hec de / qua agitur planeta lineo studiose inuoluta panno inter
duas eiusdem precipuas ecclesie casulas collocata iaceret, protinus celitus uibratus fulguris hanc penetrat ictus, ac lineo panno casulisque que supra subterque iacebant illesis, in illius plicatura uis fulminis ignea immodica effecit foramina, hincque tanti causam mali fore intelligi dedit. Vnde diuina ita [?sanctis][a] proponitur uirtus admiranda, dum babilonice fornacis more qua iustorum tantum comburuntur uincula,[1] in hac solummodo ignis preualuit planeta quam de sanctorum iniuste spoliis denotauit adquisitam. Nec molestum cuiquam uideatur nos paulo aliter quam a quodam qui de hac ante nos planeta mirifice scripsit, narrationem texuisse,[2] quia hec ita contigisse nos ab his qui hec presentes conspexerant, et ab ipso nominatim qui huius exactor peccunie fuerat, monacho Ricardo nomine, qui forte cum ipsius Flagiensis ecclesie abbate Odone adueniens, coram domino abbate Warnerio et pleno Bellice ecclesie capitulo, uenia pro se suaque petita ecclesia, ipso attestante abbate, sub diuini nominis inuocatione, ut audientes didiscimus, ueraci sermone relata descripsimus.

Verum stilo ad ordinem reflexo, cum regis Willelmi magni
Willelmi filii circumquaque uirtutis fama et terror crebresceret,
f. 40v contigit eundem regem in siluam, / quam ipse stabiliens 'nouam'
uocitari uoluit, uenatum forte deuenisse.[3] Quo dum suam studiose exercens delectaretur industriam, occulto Dei quo ignoratur iudicio casu, a quodam milite, regni sui anno xiii, sagitta sauciatus, iiii° nonas Augusti uita defungitur, diuine anno incarnationis m c instante. Rege igitur Willelmo regno cum uita hoc modo decessu carente, patria protinus turbata concitatur, optimatumque nonnullis partium dissensioni animum accommodantibus, superueniens ex Dei dispositione regis defuncti frater Henricus eius corpus Wintoniam honorifice deferri et sepeliri fecit, atque ipse

[a] *The word is contracted* (scis) *but is reasonably clear. The phrase is so syntactically unlikely however, that it may well be a copyist's error. Winterbottom emends to* nobis. *See* Ord.Vit. iii. 244, *for a similar phrase.*

---

[1] Cf. Dan. 3: 20–7.

[2] See Introduction, p. 20. There seem to have been several histories of the abbey at hand in the late twelfth century, but none with such a tale has survived.

[3] The chronicler is incorrect, led astray perhaps by the temptation to impose a moralizing irony on the pattern of events. The royal forests were unpopular

saints whose relics are kept in Martin's church. The year following, again a storm bore down upon them. This 'planeta' (our present topic) was lying wrapped carefully in a linen cloth, arranged between two of the best chasubles of the church, when suddenly a stroke of lightning hurled from heaven pierced it, and whereas the linen cloth and the chasubles which lay above and below were unharmed, the fiery force of the lightning made huge holes in the fold of the 'planeta'. And this He did to make them understand that it was the cause of so much woe. Thus it is [?in the saints] that the divine power is displayed to be marvelled at; for just as in the Babylonish furnace, in which only the chains of the just were consumed,[1] so the fire had power over this 'planeta' only, which it branded as acquired unjustly by the plunder of saints. Now, it should not worry anyone that our story differs slightly from that of one who wrote admirably of this 'planeta' before us.[2] For we heard that these things fell out thus from those who saw them before their eyes, and in particular from that man who had been the exactor of this money, a monk named Richard, who happened to come with his abbot Odo of the church of Fly, and sought our church's forgiveness for himself and his community, before the lord abbot Warner and the full chapter of Battle church, with his abbot as witness and upon an invocation of the divine name. And what I thus learned, I have truthfully recorded.

To turn our pen back to its task: when the fame and terror of the power of King William, son of the great William, were increasing everywhere, it happened that this king by chance went hunting in the forest which, when he established it, he wished to be called 'New'.[3] There it was that, while fully absorbed and delighting in his activity, by a secret and incomprehensible judgement of God, he was accidentally wounded by an arrow shot by a knight, and died on the third of August, 1100, in the thirteenth year of his reign. King William thus lost both life and kingdom; the ungoverned land was immediately disturbed, and some magnates were preparing for war among themselves. But by the providence of God, Henry, brother of the dead king, arrived. He had the body borne honourably to Winchester and saw to the burial, and after but a

with the chronicler as with many landlords. See below, pp. 220–2. He has organized his data so as to see the supposed originator die as a result of his creation. In fact the New Forest had been created by William I and can be seen in *DB*, i. 51 a, b. See also J. H. Round, 'Introduction to the Domesday Survey', *VCH Hants*, i. 411–13, 445–7.

paucis post euolutis diebus ex diuine predestinationis dono totius Anglice sceptrum optinens monarchie, solemni die martirii beati Oswaldi regis instante coram nonnullis regni primoribus regio insignitus diademate apud Westmonasterium, nonas Augusti, coronatur. Quod adeptus culmen, ut uir sollertissime sagacitatis profectui intendens omnium, pacificare omnimodis regnum satagebat eique non repugnans fortuna pro uoto fauebat. Hic itaque ut magni Willelmi natura heres et animo ut sue signum corone summo [studio][a] Belli ecclesiam defendens, ac suarum /
41 auctoritatibus cartarum muniens, extollebat studio.

Abbas igitur Henricus post abbatie sumptum regimen bis trium annorum septemque dierum completo curriculo, anno incarnati uerbi quod erat in principio m cii° egritudine ad extrema perductus, xiiii° kalendas Iulii migrauit a seculo atque ab eiusdem ecclesie fratribus de Bello ut ipse suggesserat coram sede presidentis in eiusdem loci tumulatur capitulo. Quo regie illato aule, confestim clericus quidam illuc ad procurandum dirigitur, ac deinde ad abbatie custodiam regis capellanus alius Viuianus nomine delegatur.[1] Vbi perparuum cum deguisset tempus demum rex cuidam monacho sancti Carileffi Gausfrido nomine, uiro quamuis litterarum inerudito, omni sagacitate et prudentia secularique prouidentia summo, idem monasterium ad regendum contulit. Qui xi kalendas Augusti illuc honorificentissime adueniens, ut domum uidit undique destitutam, quasi prima iaciens fundamina, interius exteriusque cepit qua callebat propalare prudentiam. Sub ipso siquidem in breui procurationum instaurantur promptuaria, ecclesie iura fratrumque respirat honorificentia, prediorum reformatur opulentia. Cumque precipuum ecclesie manerium Wi adisset quod quidam abbatis defuncti seruiens procurauerat Robertus cognomento de Ciltuna inuenissetque
f. 41v illud undique / distractum,[2] cepit causas ab ipso preposito rationemque requirere uillicationis. Qui cum domino suo iam defuncto se inde satisfecisse referret, nec sic ille adquiescens testes exigeret, tandem conuictum in eiusdem manerii curiam compulit.

[a] *Winterbottom*

---

[1] For the recent beginnings of this regalian right see M. Howell, *Regalian Right in Medieval England* (London, 1962), pp. 5–19.

[2] Wye was particularly easily broken up, since like many Kentish manors it was made up of separated and probably enclosed *tenementa*, as well as distant members, such as Dengemarsh, itself already becoming a separate manor in the twelfth century. S. R. Scargill-Bird, *Custumals of Battle Abbey*, Camden Soc.

few days, he received the sceptre of the entire English monarchy by the gift of divine predestination. He was crowned at Westminster on 5 August, the day sanctified by the martyrdom of the blessed Oswald, before some of the chief men of the realm. On the throne he showed himself to be a man of the shrewdest sagacity and devoted to general improvement. He busied himself bringing peace to the realm, and fortune favoured him. He was the heir to the great William in nature and in spirit. He defended the church of Battle as the ensign of his crown, he fortified it with the powers of his charters, with care he exalted its position.

Abbot Henry fell ill, and died on 18 June 1102, six years and seven days after assuming the rule of the abbey. He was buried by the brothers of Battle where he had wished before the president's seat in the chapter house. When news of this was sent to the royal court, a clerk was immediately sent to take charge, and next another chaplain of the king, Vivian by name, was appointed keeper of the abbey.[1] When he had spent but a very short time there, the king gave the custodianship of the monastery to a monk of Saint Calais, Geoffrey by name, a man who was, although not a learned man, yet supremely shrewd, prudent, and wordly wise. Arriving there most respectfully on 22 July, he saw the neglected state of the abbey. At once, as if laying anew the foundations, he began, both inside and out, to show that shrewdness in which he was so practised. Under his guidance, the storerooms were soon stocked with supplies, the rights of the church and the honour of the brothers revived, and the prosperity of the estates renewed. When he visited the church's principal manor, Wye, which a servant of the late abbot, one Robert, surnamed 'de Chilton', had charge of, he found it entirely fragmented.[2] He began to question this manager as to the reasons, and to demand an accounting of his management. The man retorted that he had satisfied his lord, now dead, and would not agree to summoning witnesses therefore. At last the procurator charged him in the court of the manor as one manifestly guilty. However, the manager was there backed by the

N.S. xli (1887), 101–36. H. Muhlfeld, *A Survey of the Manor of Wye* (New York, 1933), esp. pp. xxxiii–xxxiv. For early precedents of the royal writ ordering an accounting see Van Caenegem, *Writs*, 188, 345–6. Robert de Chilton was a landholder at Wingham in Kent. *Cal.Ch.Rolls* i. 316. Chilton was a hamlet in the archbishop's manor of Wingham: Du Boulay, *Canterbury*, p. 125. He was perhaps the Robert de Wi who witnessed a contemporary Battle charter. *Hist.MSS.Comm., Third Report* (1872), p. 223.

Cumque ui nobilium prouincie quos sibi asciuerat equitati parere penitus detrectasset, eum suosque presentes ex regis nomine die denominato precipiendo apud Belli curiam adesse isdem ecclesie procurator summonuit. Quibus nec post multam conflictationem quicquam certi respondentibus in his disceditur.

Die uero denominato cum predicti placitatores, Fulbertus scilicet de Cilleham,[1] Rotbertus Fillel,[2] Haimo filius Vitalis,[3] et Broðer presbiter,[4] aliique barones quamplurimi cum predicto Rotberto ui ac terrore regii nominis Bataliensem adissent curiam;[5] et iam hora tardior noctem minitaret, placitum dominus Gausfridus persuasione etsi egre in primum dominici aduentus diem recrastinauit.[6] Habebat enim quoddam in se memoriale, quatinus agendis exterioribus ad memoriam posterorum non solum seniores fratrum sed et iuniores interesse procuraret, et tardiori id hora tunc[a] fieri ordinis custodia prohibebat.[7]

Itaque post opulentam hospitalitatem curia statuta, circumassi-
f. 42 dentibus sibi fratribus, summonitos Gausfridus / affatur, 'Quoniam, mi seniores carissimi, presenti uos premoniti intulistis curie, utrum rectitudinis hinc exequende et recipiende causa adueneritis sciscitor.' Illi uero cum non ibi sed in suo comitatu omnem rectitudinem se exequi debere insisterent, post plurimam dominus Gausfridus controuersiam intulit, 'Si ergo ut asseritis non nisi in uestro comitatu iustitie subdimini causis, nunquid non regie asciti curie conquesta definiri uetaretis?'

'Nequaquam', inquiunt.

[a] *Add. in marg. by the hand of the original scribe and aligned with the line it begins*: tunc

---

[1] I. J. Sanders, *English Baronies* (Oxford, 1960), p. 111. Fulbert I of Dover, a Domesday tenant of Bishop Odo, was the founder of the 'probable barony' of Chilham. He also held *Hothfeld.* He was one of the witnesses for the abbot of Battle of a charter of the late eleventh or early twelfth century. *Hist.MSS.Comm., Third Report*, p. 223. That charter attests the reacquisition of Battle's manor of Alciston after 'plurima placita et plures contentiones', not unlike those over Wye.

[2] Robert was probably a landholder in Kent. He himself cannot be traced, but a Baldwin Fillol was a knight and landholder in Kent in the early thirteenth century. *Red Book*, ii. 614, 622, 707.

[3] A Kentish landholder. D. C. Douglas, *The Domesday Monachorum of Christ Church, Canterbury* (London, 1944), p. 57. *Regesta*, i, no. 188.

force of the county nobles whom he had brought with him, and he totally refused to come to an equitable agreement. Therefore the procurator of the church summoned him in the king's name, along with his supporters who were present, to appear at the court of Battle on a named day. After much dispute they made no positive reply, and they parted on this note.

On the named day, the pleaders, namely Fulbert of Chilham,[1] Robert Fillel,[2] Haimo fitz Vital,[3] and Broðer, a priest,[4] and a number of other barons came to the Battle court along with the aforesaid Robert, brought by the power and terror of the royal name.[5] Since it was already turning to evening, dom Geoffrey, by conviction, albeit regretfully, put off the case till the first day of the Lord's Advent.[6] For he had a custom worth remembering that, during external business which would set a precedent for the future, he would take care that not only the older brothers, but also the younger should be present,[7] and the observance of the rule prohibited this from being done at so late an hour.

Thus after lavish hospitality, the court was constituted and with the brothers seated around him Geoffrey addressed the men he had summoned, 'My very dear lords, since you have presented yourselves to this court in response to a summons, I ask whether you have come for the purpose of pursuing and accepting justice here.' They urged that they they were bound to be subject to all justice done in their own county court, but not here. After much argument, dom Geoffrey put it to them, 'If therefore, as you assert, you are not bound by pleas of justice except in your county, would you not resist the settlement of the complaint, supposing you were brought before the royal court?'

'Not at all', they replied.

[4] Broðir is an Old Norse personal name. He acted with Fulbert of Chilham as one of the abbot's witnesses to a chirograph concerning the Alciston land plea. See above, p. 110, n. 1. The four 'placitatores' were in all probability the lords to whom Robert de Chilton had let out Wye lands.

[5] The description would apply to a writ. None specifically concerning this case is extant, but Geoffrey could well have been using the general one issued in favour of Battle by Henry I the year before in 1101. *Regesta*, ii, no. 529. He could also show that the general writ had been backed up by one specifically transferring a Kentish case to the abbey court at Battle. Ibid., no. 530. But in the last analysis his power may have rested upon the fact of his being a royal agent.

[6] The text is perhaps corrupt. It would make more sense in context if it read 'in primum adventum diei recrastinavit': '. . . till the dawn of the next day'. The *custos* had had enough trouble getting the Kentish barons to Battle. He could delay the hearing no longer than necessary.

[7] *Regula*, c. 3.

'Ergo presenti', inquit, 'curie que regis extat hac ratione contraire nequibitis.'

Qui cum ui ratiocinatione freti renitentes demum erumpere conarentur, protinus basilice ualuas iussit obserari, obtestans singulos regie maiestati exponendos si non regie exequerentur iura curie. Cumque uiri animositatem regieque districtionis recogitassent equitatem, tandem pauidi cessere tiranni et se illic rectitudinem facere et recipere uelle profitentur. Tunc, domino Gausfrido[a] manerii de Wi annullationem prepositumque impotentem uillicationis reddere rationem exponente, tandem post plurium uerborum rotationem reus coram communi iudicio sistitur Rotbertus. Qui reatum confitens cum ueniam flagitaret, decem argenti libris decemque frumenti adiudicatus modiis,
f. 42v cum gratia / misericorditer absoluitur. Hoc peracto, et domino Gausfrido si quid erga ipsum querimonie presentes haberent sciscitante, cum calumpnie nil a quoquam referretur, curia soluta est. Manerium autem illud ceteraque ad ecclesiam pertinentia studiose restauranda commisse ecclesie sibique commisit fidelibus, ipseque utilitati seruorum Dei curiose undique superintendens, domus fabrice et munitioni murorumque circa ambitum fundationi animum contulit.

Sub isdem diebus warec contigit in Dengemareis, membro de Wi, nauem uidelicet regiis ornamentis et opibus onustam fluctibus iactatam cum illic appulisset confringi. Quam cum infra statutum terminum pro more reparare nequissent, regii accessere exactores, nauem cum opibus ut regiam pecuniam ui optinere conantes. Domino uero Gausfrido obnitente cum suis, tandem coram regiis auribus hac uentilata querimonia, rex morem seruari patrium uolens, ecclesiamque suam offendere cauens, iussit quatinus nec de sua quidem peccunia propria cuiusquam ecclesia pateretur iniuriam, sed quod appulsum fuerat totum ecclesie maneret.[1] Vnde dominus Gausfridus, omnia prout utile decreuit disponens, regales uestes ecclesie seruientibus distribuit, et cetera ad usus ecclesie dispensauit. /

f. 43 Gloriosi igitur regis Henrici uirtutis ac magnificentie fama longe

[a] *MS*: dominus Gausfridus

---

[1] *Regesta*, i, no. 62.

'Well then,' he said, 'you cannot on that ground resist this court, for it is the king's.'

But they trusted to the reasoning of force and attempted to resist by actually walking out, and so he instantly commanded that the doors of the church be locked, vowing that each of them would be reported to the king if they would not subject themselves to the rights of a royal court. When they had thought over the courage of this man and the fairness of the royal distraint, finally the timid bullies subsided and declared that they would both do and receive justice there. Thereupon dom Geoffrey expatiated upon the destruction of the manor of Wye and upon a steward unable to give an account of the estate. At last, after much bandying of words, Robert was declared guilty by the general judgement. He acknowledged the charge and, since he sincerely asked forgiveness, he was mercifully released, after it was adjudged that he pay ten pounds of silver and ten measures of wheat. After this was completed, dom Geoffrey inquired whether the parties had any complaint against him, and when no complaint was brought by anyone, the court was dismissed. However, he committed that manor and the rest of the church's possessions to men faithful to himself and to the church entrusted to him, to be thoroughly restored, while he himself, though closely supervising the prosperity of the servants of God in every aspect, concentrated his attention on the building and buttressing of the house and on putting up a wall around the precincts.

It was in those days that a 'wreck' occurred at Dengemarsh, a member of Wye; that is, a ship with a cargo of royal ornaments and treasures, dashed by the waves, was driven ashore there and damaged. Since its crew was unable to repair it duly within the time fixed, the royal collectors arrived, thinking to take the ship with its riches by force as royal property. Dom Geoffrey with his men resisted, and finally this quarrel was brought to the king's ear. The king, wishing to preserve the custom of his predecessors, and taking care not to vex his his own church, commanded that the church should not be exposed to injury by any man, even where his own money was involved, but that the shipwreck should belong in entirety to the church.[1] Dom Geoffrey therefore, deciding as he thought wisest, distributed the royal clothing to the servants of the church and disbursed the rest for the church's use.

The glorious King Henry's reputation for virtue and magnificence

lateque percrebrescente, inter quamplures ipsius curie appetitores tunc temporis rege in Paschali solemnitate apud Wintoniam coronato, de transmarinis partibus uenerabilis Maioris Monasterii abbas Willelmus honorifice aduenit, hanc maxime ob causam ut quoquo pacto hanc de qua agitur ecclesiam de Bello sibi subiugando ancillaret. Is itaque a regia gratanter magnificentia exceptus, post dies tandem solemnes aduentus sui causam regi per internuntios sagaciter suggerere curauit. Rege itaque inmodice eius uotis pro sui reuerentia et ob id quammaxime quod de tam remotis partibus ultro suam expetisset curiam fauere conante, hinc tamen absque consilio nil definiri deliberauit. Affuit igitur et tunc inter reliquos regni primores in curia, uti a regie aule secretis non exclusus, memoratus uir dominus Gausfridus Bellensis ecclesie procurator. Qui dum hec forte rescisset, cause non segniter per se perque sue fautores prudentie intendens, hinc regis penitus animum prouide perstitit auertere. Cum ergo hac de re abbatis eiusdem legationem rex excepisset, dicentis a patre ipsius rege Willelmo Belli monasterium in subiectionis dominium Maiori Monasterio ab initio fundationis illius collatum, confirmationis munimenta hinc ab ipso prouide regii exigebant consiliarii. Ad hec cum ab-
f. 43v bas tanti uiri donum uerbotenus / collatum absque arbitro posse sufficere, nec super hoc quodlibet confirmationis edictum quemquam hactenus quesisse, quia nec necessarium fore putabant, astrueret, responsum est non fore ratam[a] posse donationem tante rei, ubi scilicet et liberalis auctoritas dignitatum necnon et regie corone extabat signum, si non aut cartarum aut certe testium uiua uoce probata roboraretur. Hac igitur ratione tandem cassata exactoris sollicitudine, hinc spes effectus excluditur.

Verum regia non passa est magnificentia tanti nominis personam suam incassum adisse curiam. Nam primo ei obtulit unum quem uellet monachorum suorum, ab omni Maioris Monasterii exutum subiectione, tunc prefate ecclesie abbatem preficere, seclusa in posterum omni subiectionis calumnia. Quod cum renuisset, in monimentum libertatis ipsius ecclesie de Bello, quatinus hinc in perpetuum omnis Maioris Monasterii obmutesceret querimonia,

[a] *MS*: ratum

was by now spreading far and wide, and among the many petitioners to his court when the king was crowned at Winchester during the Easter celebrations, there came from across the sea the venerable Abbot William of Marmoutier, for this purpose above all, that by hook or by crook he might enslave this church of Battle in subjection to himself. He was received gladly by the royal magnificence and after the feast-days were over he cunningly contrived through intermediaries to intimate to the king the purpose of his coming. The king was much of a mind to favour his prayers out of reverence for him, but most of all because the abbot had of his own accord sought out his court from such a far-off place. Still he decided to settle nothing without counsel. Now there was present then at court, among the rest of the realm's magnates, none other than dom Geoffrey, custodian of Battle, privy as he was to the secrets of the king's court. Immediately he happened to hear of all this he actively concentrated on the case, and both personally and through his patrons he foresightedly persisted in drawing the king's mind wholly away from this step. So that when the king came to receive the representations of the abbot about this matter, and he made a speech about how from the beginning of its foundation the abbey of Battle had been given in subjection to Marmoutier as its lord by the king's father, the councillors, warned ahead of time, demanded of him evidence to confirm this. The abbot countered by saying that the gift of so great a man, given orally, ought to be enough without an eyewitness, and that no one had sought, up to now, any confirmatory proclamation about it at all since they had thought that it would not be necessary. It was answered that the grant of so great a place, conspicuous for both the noble authority of its privileges and as the ensign of the royal crown, could not be authentic if it were not confirmed by the proofs of charters or at least by the oral testimony of witnesses. By this reasoning the solicitation of the petitioner was brought to naught and the hope for its accomplishment was dashed.

But the royal magnificence did not permit a personage of so great a name to visit his court in vain. Thus first he offered to appoint as abbot of the church one of the abbot's monks, whom he might choose, freed from all subjection to Marmoutier, and with its claims to any subjection ended for ever. Since he declined this, in testimony of the liberty of the church of Battle, that from then on for ever all complaint of Marmoutier might be silenced as towards a

sicut a dominica regis capella, ipsi ecclesie Maioris scilicet Monasterii regia contulit magnificentia, in Deuenesira, quoddam manerium quod Torvertuna dicitur et ecclesiam in Wiltesira de manerio de Chosham, sicque huiusce causatio eatenus finem sortita conticuit.[1] His quoque pro uoto definitis dominus Gausfridus cum regie auctoritatis confirmatione domum regressus hec fratribus gratulabunde exposuit, hincque ut ceperat impiger domus dei commodis animo insistebat. /

f. 44 Igitur cum multimodo uirtutum studio inuigilans domum desolatam dominus Gausfridus restaurasset, necdum tertio postquam aduenerat euoluto anno, heu, hinc inmature tollitur, atque nature cedens iuri, xvii kalendas Iunii presenti uite finem fecit. Cuius corpus cum maximo merore in capitulo iuxta abbatem Henricum ad leuam a fratribus humatum quiescit. Itaque tam sagaci ecclesia de Bello uiduata procuratore, in quo paternitatis uerus uiguerat affectus, ad eiusdem ecclesie curam ex regis assensu Torneiensis abbas, unde supra meminimus, dominus aduenit Gunterus, atque per suos domus procuratione disposita ad propriam rediit abbatiam, remanente quodam Radulfo modo ipsius nepote apud Bellicum monasterium tempore aliquanto. Quo postmodum quibusdam simultatibus cum omni predicti abbatis potestate secluso, demum rege propriis preoccupato negotiis, totius Bellice cura domus monachorum dispositioni subacta, multa per aliquantum temporis prouehebatur industria.

Anno uero diuine humanationis m c vii rex Henricus congregato uniuersali concilio, cum multis orbatis ecclesiis pastores secundum canones delegasset,[2] inter reliquas proprie capelle sue de Bello non immemor, quendam suorum consilio asciscens
f. 44v Cadomensem / monachum religione et prudentia sagacissimum Radulfum nomine, qui cum Lanfranco archipresule Angliam adierat et tunc ascitus sub uenerabili pontifice Gundulfo Rofensis ecclesie prioratum strenue administrabat, ipsum predicte prefecit abbatem ecclesie. Qui in die sancti Petri ad Vincula electus, et in

[1] Thorverton, in Hayridge hundred, Devon, and Corsham, in Chippenham hundred, Wilts., may have been given in this way by Henry I, but his charter is not extant. Henry II issued a charter confirming these properties to Marmoutier. W. Dugdale, *Monasticon Anglicanum*, ed. J. Caley, H. Ellis, B. Bandinel (edn. of 1817–30, repr. London, 1846), vii. 1097, gives the charter in full.

[2] Henry I had been out of England since the summer of 1106. Tinchebrai was fought in September of that year and, by Lent 1107, the king was able to return

royal demesne chapel, the royal magnificence conferred upon the church (that is, Marmoutier) a manor in Devonshire, Thorverton, and a church in Wiltshire belonging to the manor of Corsham. Thus, the abbot's end being gained to that extent, the plea was silenced.[1] Matters having been settled as he had hoped, dom Geoffrey returned home with a royal confirmation and explained these things, with rejoicing, to the brethren.

From that time this indefatigable man continued as he had begun, concentrating his mind on the advantage of the house of God. Dom Geoffrey watched over the house with a manifold devotion of his energies and had restored it from its desolation, when, before the third year after his arrival was out, alas, he was taken hence untimely, and complying with the law of nature, he ended this present life on 16 May. His body, buried with the greatest grief by the brothers, rests in the chapter house just to the left of Abbot Henry. Thus was the church of Battle bereft of a guardian so wise, in whom the true goodwill of fatherhood flourished. By the king's assent, Gunter, abbot of Thorney, whom we have mentioned above, took over the care of the church. He divided up the custodianship of the house among his men, and went back to his own abbey. Only his nephew Ralph remained at Battle abbey, and that for but a short time. After some disputes he was removed, together with the power of the said abbot. In the mean time the king was preoccupied by his own business and the care of the whole house fell to the management of the monks, who thus had a great deal of business to deal with for some time.

In the year 1107, King Henry called a general council at which, according to the canons, he assigned shepherds to many fatherless churches.[2] Among the rest he did not forget his own chapel of Battle. On the advice of his councillors he chose a monk of Caen, Ralph by name, a man most perceptive in religion and in practical common sense. He had come to England with Archbishop Lanfranc, had been recruited by the venerable Bishop Gundulf, and was at that time actively administering the priory of Rochester cathedral. This man the king appointed as abbot. Elected on the

to England. Anselm was not well and a council to deal with church affairs could not be convened until late summer. It was opened at the royal palace at Westminster on 1 August. Eadmer, *Hist.Nov.*, pp. 186–7. W. Farrer, 'An Outline Itinerary of King Henry the First', *EHR*, xxxiv (1919), 345. *Regesta*, ii, pp. 67–70 gives some of the writs that resulted from the council, including one for Battle, in which the king confirms his brother's gift of the churches: no. 827.

die festo sancti Laurentii apud Bellum cum decenti receptus honore,[1] cepit continuo et religioni qua feruebat et prudenter interius exteriusque ecclesie utilitati animo inuigilare. Itaque ipso uiro uenerabili superintendente, in tantam honoris magnificentiam eadem excreuerat ecclesia, ut ipsius dispositione per fideles fratrum manus utiliter domus cura procurata, interius exteriusque caritatis exibitione uniuersis existente absque dilatione gratuita, nulli Anglie ecclesiarum religione, bonitate, mansuetudine, caritate, humanitatisque gratia esse probaretur secunda. Hoc domesticus fidei quisque clamabat, hoc uulgi ora uariantia perstrepebant, hinc inuidia, si qua forte pullulabat, gemens succumbebat. Bonorum namque omnium superhabundante copia, tanta hospitalitati impendebantur studia, ut hospites quique uel extranei non tam ad hospitandum quam ad diutius pro uelle manendum ut
f. 45 propria adirent / domicilia. Nec tunc hec quelibet arcebat inopia, disponente eo cui singulare est, omni habenti cor in Deo largifluum adiciendo ut superhabundet sufficiens prestare emolumentum.

Eodem itaque tempore domini nostri regis Henrici industria, qui abbatis uice exterius paterno eandem ecclesiam de Bello fouebat et gubernabat amore, ac abbatis Radulfi sollicitudine ut prelibauimus religioni et doctrine interius insistentis, eodem loco in multa quiete et pace opumque copia in dies proficiente, cepit inter alia sagacitatis studia abbas cum fratribus terras perquirendo emere, et amissas, uel iniuste extractas uel ablatas in eiusdem ecclesie maneriis singulis, placitis et expensis ad augmentum possessionum ipsius ecclesie addendo retrahere. Inter quas a quodam Ingelranno, homine Wiðelardi de Bailol, emerunt tres wistas terre, quas ipse apud Bernehorne tenebat, pro lvii solidis. Quod predictus Wiðelardus concedens et confirmans, et decimam quoque totius peccunie de terra sua de Boccholte quam idem Ingelrannus eidem loco dedit, et insuper eisdem sancti Martini monachis terram que usque hodie dicitur mariscus sancti Martini ex suo dedit et concessit.[2]

f. 45v Quidam etiam uicinorum, Geroldus de Norman/uilla nuncupatus, eidem sancti Martini de Bello ecclesie terram de Glesham,

[1] 1 August and 10 August. The chronicler is perhaps emphasizing the briskness with which Abbot Ralph wound up his other affairs and hastened to his new charge, in contrast to the negligence of Gunter of Thorney.

[2] The king's confirmation is *Regesta*, ii, no. 1061 and p. 330. HBA charter,

day of St. Peter ad Vincula, received with proper honour at Battle on the feast of St. Laurence,[1] he began without delay to put his mind and his good sense to the good of the church, within and without, as well as paying heed to the sanctity with which he glowed. Thus under the administration of this worthy man, this church grew to such a height of honour that through his direction, through the care duly taken of the house by the brethren's faithful hands, through the charity displayed to all, both within and without, with no needless delay, it was agreed to be second to none of the English churches in sanctity, benevolence, clemency, charity, and grace in kindliness. This, each of his family in faith proclaimed, this the changeable crowd clamoured in unison; and this was why ill will, if by chance it raised its head, succumbed with a sigh. For with an overflowing supply of all goods, such devotion was lavished upon hospitality that guests and strangers alike arrived not so much for lodging as to stay as long as they liked, as though in their own homes. Nor did any want restrict these activities in those days, thanks to the provision of Him whose singular characteristic it is to provide sufficient reward to those who have generous hearts in God, adding so that they overflow in abundance.

In those days then, by the activity of our lord king Henry, who cherished the church of Battle from without like an abbot and governed it with paternal love, and by the care of Abbot Ralph, urging holiness and learning within, as we have seen, the abbey and its wealth advanced daily amid profound peace and quiet. Among other shrewd endeavours, the abbot and brothers started to look for lands to buy and to recover lands that had been lost or unjustly withdrawn or stolen in the individual manors of the church, and thus by pleas and investments to enlarge the church's possessions. Among these they bought from one Ingelran, the man of Withelard de Baillol, for fifty-seven shillings, three wists of land at Barnhorn which he then held. Withelard allowed and confirmed the sale, as well as that of the tithe of all money which Ingelran gave the abbey from his land of Buckholt; over and above this, out of his own demesne he gave the monks of St. Martin the land called to this day St. Martin's Marsh.[2]

Another neighbour, Gerald de Normanville, sold the church of St. Martin at Battle the land of Glasseye for twenty marks of silver.

vol. 42/1132 is a charter of Henry, count of Eu (1101–40), confirming the grant of the Barnhorn land and the Buckholt tithes.

acceptis a monachis uiginti marcis argenti, concessit. Eodem etiam tempore quidam Weningus de uicinis dedit eidem ecclesie quandam in proximo ecclesiam de Westefelde dictam cum una wista terre, et iudicio aque ad eam pertinente, cum omnibus consuetudinibus suis, liberam in perpetuum possidendam.[1] Hoc quoque dominus ipsius, Willelmus scilicet filius Wiberti, cum suis concessit, deditque et ipse eidem ecclesie de Bello decimam omnium peccuniarum de terra sua de Bocstepe, absque omni calumnia libera. Et in obitu suo terram x^{cem} solidorum de ipsa terra de Bocstepe ecclesie contulit. Tunc temporis etiam emerunt monachi pro undecim marcis argenti terram uicinam leuge sue, que Dudilande et Bregeselle uocitatur, a milite quodam Anselmo cognomento de Fraelvilla, remota omni in posterum heredum suorum calumnia. Ipse etiam Anselmus eidem loco contulit pro anime sue et suorum salute terram quandam ad salinas faciendas, et unam acram prati, decimamque totam uille sue Glesi uocate, omnia hec concedente Rogero filio eius, accepto pro hac concessione uno cane quem requisiuit.[2]

f. 46 Sub isdem quoque diebus, quia pernecessarium uidebatur, / erga baronum illius prouincie quendam, Willelmum scilicet de Sancto Leodegario, egerunt eiusdem loci monachi cum abbate Radulfo quod ipse eis hereditario iure concessit terram suam Prunhelle dictam, que ultra Winceleseie prope manerium eiusdem ecclesie Dengemareis uocatum sita erat, eo tamen pacto quod ipsi medietatem redditus, scilicet xxiii solidos, ad festum sancti Johannis baptiste et medietatem ad festum sancti Andree apostoli illi persoluerent. Pro hac pactione dedit illi abbas Radulfus equum unum de duabus marcis, et perdonauit ei viii solidos et vi denarios quos ei debebat, ut in perpetuum libere terram eandem ecclesia absque calumnia possideret. Postea quidam heredum eiusdem, Clarenbaldus nomine, xii denarios de eodem redditu ecclesie in elemosinam condonauit. Postmodum quoque pro anima illius Clarenbaldi residui duo solidi similiter condonati sunt, ut x

[1] *DB*, i. 18b. No church is listed under Westfield (Westewelle) there. However, this may be the near-by independent church held by Uluuard, the priest of the manor of Filsham. His church had one virgate and did not belong to the manor of Filsham, as *DB* specifically states. It was therefore relatively easy to

At the same epoch one of the neighbours, Wening, gave the abbey in free and perpetual tenure a near-by church called Westfield, with a wist of land and the ordeal of water appurtenant to it, and with all its customs.[1] This was also agreed to by his lord, William, son of Wibert, and his men; and he himself gave to Battle abbey the tithe of all moneys from his land of Bucksteep, free, without any further claim. And at his death he left the church land worth ten shillings of his own land at Bucksteep. At that epoch too the monks bought for eleven marks of silver a land adjacent to their *leuga*, called *Dudilande* and *Breggeselle*, from a knight, one Anselm, surnamed 'de Fraelville', free of any claim of his heirs thereafter. This Anselm too gave the abbey, for the salvation of the souls of himself and his, land for making salt and an acre of meadow and the whole tithe of his vill called Glasseye. His son Roger granted all this and for his grant he received a dog that he wanted.[2]

Also in those days, since it appeared vitally necessary, the monks and Abbot Ralph treated with a baron of the county, one William de St. Leger, and got him to concede them in hereditary right his land called Broomhill which lay beyond Winchelsea almost at the abbey's manor of Dengemarsh. The agreement was that they would pay him half the rent—twenty-three shillings—at Midsummer, and half on St. Andrew's Day. For this agreement Abbot Ralph gave him a horse worth two marks and pardoned him 8*s*. 6*d*. which he owed him, that the church might hold the land freely for ever, without counter-claim. Afterwards, one of his heirs, Clarenbald, pardoned twelve pence of the rent as alms to the church. Later again, two shillings more were similarly pardoned for Clarenbald's soul, leaving henceforth only ten shillings at Midsummer and

sell. Westfield was held as an appropriated rectory in all extant Battle muniments and was a valuable supplier of corn to the abbey. Searle, *Lordship*, pp. 447, 453–4. Henry I's confirmation is *Regesta*, ii, no. 1805. Bishop Ralph Luffa's confirmation is printed in Mayr-Harting, *Acta*, no. 5.

[2] *Regesta*, ii, no. 1225. HBA charter, vol. 42/1530: Anselm's charter concerning *Breggeselle* and *Dudilonde* and the tithes of Glasseye. Unlike Glasseye, which lay near Winchelsea, some miles from Battle, the holdings *Breggeselle* and *Dudilonde* actually lay within the boundaries of Battle's *banlieu*. They seem to have been two adjacent wists, and so excellent was their land that they are mentioned in abbey muniments throughout the Middle Ages. Searle, *Lordship*, s.v. Their location, as well as the royal writ associating the king with Battle's possession of Anselm's and Roger's 'gift', makes it seem likely that the transaction was actually the recovery of land before a royal court.

inde solidi ad festum sancti Iohannis et x itidem ad festum sancti Andree tantum apud Belli curiam ipsi qui hereditario iure successisset omni remota calumnia persoluerentur. Osbernus etiam filius Isilie quidam ex uicinis eidem ecclesie de Bello duas salinas et terram ad tertiam salinam faciendam apud Riam pro anima sua et pro animabus parentum suorum tam uiuorum quam mortuorum concessit. Emma uxor Osberni de Bodeham terram sex solidorum in ipso manerio de Bodeham, et unum in Normannia, molendinum iuxta Criuil situm, Sanrei nomine, Rotberto comite Augi domino suo concedente et confirmante, coram multis testibus supradicte ecclesie dedit.[a] /[1]

f. 46v Illo itaque tempore cum rex excellentie singularis Henricus pro peccaminum suorum absolutione, proque anima patris sui et matris et uxoris omniumque heredum suorum salute, monasterium construere disposuisset, locum ad hoc requirens habilem, apud Radinges secundum uelle suum hoc fieri posse inuenit. Quia uero eiusdem territorii ecclesia cum suis omnibus a magnifico rege Willelmo sancti Martini ecclesie de Bello ut supra meminimus collata fuerat, rex per omnia eidem deuotus monasterio, pro ipsius ecclesie commertio, quoddam manerium quod Fundintune dicebatur Bellice contulit ecclesie,[2] totumque Radinges in proprium redigens dominium, amplam satis et spectabilem, in beate Matris Misericordie honorem, magnificentissime fundauit basilicam. Abbas uero et fratres ecclesie de Bello locum a rege collatum cum non satis utilem sibi prospexissent, regem hac de causa conquerentes adeunt, qui quoddam eis[b] aliud manerium, Apeldreham uocatum, ad unum miliarium prope Cicestrensem urbem situm, hac de causa donauit. Quod carte sue confirmans testimonio, liberum omnino et quietum ab omni terrene consuetudinis seruicio, ut cetera eiusdem ecclesie, de suo dominio in seruorum

[a] *Add. at foot of folio in a contemporary hand, perhaps that of the scribe*: Emma .. dedit [b] *Add. in left-hand margin in hand of original copyist, and aligned with the line it begins*: eis

another ten shillings on St. Andrew's Day to be paid at Battle court to his successors by hereditary right, with all claims removed. Likewise Osbern, son of Isilia, one of its neighbours, gave Battle church two salt-pans and land for making a third at Rye, for his soul and those of his relatives living and dead. Emma, wife of Osbern of Bodiam gave the church a land of six shillings in the manor of Bodiam, and a mill near Criel in Normandy, called *Sanrei*, with the agreement and confirmation of her lord, Robert, count of Eu and before many witnesses.[1]

During the same epoch the excellent King Henry was disposed to build a monastery for the absolution of his sins and for the souls of his father, mother, and wife, and the salvation of all his heirs. Looking around for a suitable site, he found one at Reading where it might be constructed just as he wished. Because the church of the district, with all its appurtenances, had been given by the magnificent King William to the abbey of St. Martin of Battle as we have noted above, the king, devoted to the monastery in all things, gave Battle church a manor called Funtington in trade for that church. Restoring Reading into his own demesne, he most magnificently founded a church, one worth seeing and appropriately large, in honour of the Blessed Mother of Mercy.[2] But the abbot and brethren of the church of Battle, since they foresaw that the place given them would not be really useful, approached the king with a complaint to this effect. The king therefore gave them another manor, called Appledram, about a mile outside Chichester. Confirming this by the witness of his charter, he transferred it from his own demesne into the legal possession of the servants of God, wholly free and quit from all service of earthly custom like the

[1] Cf. *Regesta*, ii, p. 408. The grant was in fact made before 1093, for it was made during the abbacy of Gausbert, who died in 1095, and with the agreement of Count Robert, dead by 1093. Since Emma is here called the wife, not the widow, of Osbern, it is possible that her charter (perhaps that of an heiress of a very early Norman enfeoffment) is genuine but added mistakenly among those that attest to the activity of Abbot Ralph. See above, p. 86. Criel lies some seven miles from Eu in Normandy. Nothing more is heard of the mill in any abbey muniment.

[2] Hugh of Amiens, prior of Lewes, was appointed the first abbot of Reading in 1123. *Heads*, p. 63. *Regesta*, ii, nos. 1423, 1472, 1549 are charters of the 1120s in favour of Reading.

Dei iura delegauit.[1] Preterea quia idem magnificus rex Henricus /
f. 47 multo, ut prelibauimus, eandem ecclesiam de Bello percolebat affectu, sub isdem ipse diebus gratis illuc ex proprio contulit dono quandam ecclesiam in honorem sancti Petri apostoli fundatam apud Waliam, in ciuitate que Chermerdi dicitur, cum omnibus ad eam pertinentibus, liberam et quietam in perpetuum possidendam. Aliam etiam ecclesiam antiquissimis temporibus in honore sancti Theodori martiris ibidem fundatam predicte ecclesie de Bello donauit. Terram quoque non procul sepositam que Pentewi uocatur, quia necessarium fore uidebatur eo quod optimo habundaret frumento, eidem adauxit, multaque instantia ecclesiam de Bello cum suis pertinentibus percoluit.[2]

Quia uero, ut longe supra meminimus, eiusdem uille de Bello parrochianis in ecclesia beati Martini omnia que ad Christianitatem pertinebant primo antiquitus agebantur, et non multo post tempore eo quod monachis hinc[a] inquietudinis cause, quas absque ordinis uiolatione pati nequibant, oriebantur, communi assensu extra murorum ambitum capellam in beate Dei Genetricis Marie honorem, in qua parrochianis presbiter iuxta modum conditionis
f. 47v ab abbate uel fratribus dispositum deseruiret, extruxerant. / Quamquam uero idem monasterium sancti Martini omni dignitatum uel libertatum ut prefati sumus priuilegio insigniretur, multis tamen modis episcopales maxime ministri occasionum querentes fomitem, dissimulando uel causando, oleum uel crisma aliaque ad Christianitatem pertinentia dilatione subtrahentes, hisque et talibus fratres sepius tedio uexantes, locum ancillari moliebantur. Sed hec considerans abbas Radulfus, prouideque quid expediret cum suis

[a] hinc *interlined in same hand*

---

[1] *Regesta*, ii, no. 1238 (variant version, *Monasticon* (1846), iii. 247). The charter as printed in the *Regesta* from the abbey cartularies is addressed to Ralph, bishop of Chichester (d. 1123) and to William fitz Ansgar (d. 1122). The editors accept it as genuine and assign it to Nov.–Dec. 1120. However, this charter adds that the king has also given '40*s*. which formerly pertained to the manor with the *ferm* of Bosham'. As J. H. Round pointed out in his edition of *Ancient Charters*, the inclusion of this last clause places the charter between 1125 and 1133. PR Soc. x, pp. 27–8. The *Regesta* charter cannot therefore be accepted as genuine. The problem is this: although the chronicle makes no mention of the fact, the king, upon giving Appledram, excluded 40*s*. from it. Later, upon a further exchange for lands in Carmarthen (see below, pp. 134–6), the 40*s*. was restored to Appledram and the farm of Bosham added. Both the subtraction and the subsequent restoration of the 40*s*. were probably to balance the slightly different values of the estates. But the restoration could not have taken place

rest of the church's possessions.[1] Furthermore, since this same magnificent King Henry, as we have seen, cherished the church of Battle with great affection, in those times he gave it freely as his own gift a church founded in honour of the holy apostle Peter in Wales, in a town called Carmarthen, with all its appurtenances, to be held for ever free and quit. He also gave the church of Battle another church founded there in very ancient times in honour of St. Theodore the martyr. To it he added a separate land not far off, called Pentywyn, a necessity since it abounded in wheat, and with much zeal he enriched the church of Battle and its appurtenances.[2]

As we said some time ago, from the first, long ago, all Christian observance was performed for the parishioners of the town of Battle in the church of St. Martin. But it was not long before there arose thence causes of disquiet to the monks, which they could not permit without a violation of their rule. Therefore by common agreement they had erected a chapel outside the walls, in honour of the Blessed Mary, Mother of God, in which a priest might serve the parishioners in a manner laid down by the abbot or the brothers. But although the monastery of St. Martin was marked out by every privilege of dignities and liberties, as we have said, nevertheless the episcopal servants in all manner of ways looked for excuses to foment trouble through misrepresentations and casuistry. Through delays they withdrew the oil and chrism and other things pertaining to the sacraments, and by these and the like vexing the brothers often and wearily, they laboured to enslave the place. But Abbot Ralph, reflecting upon this, and prudently discussing with

before 1129 for reasons given both by Round and the editors of the *Regesta* when considering the charter of that later exchange. They date that charter as probably 1130. *Regesta*, ii, no. 1650.

[2] Sir John Lloyd, *A History of Carmarthenshire* i (Cardiff, 1935), p. 331, points out that the ancient 'clas of Llandeulyddog', had an abbot and community already, but was 'too tribal', and 'too closely identified with native aspirations' to be allowed a continued independent existence by Henry I. The land of Pentywyn, near Llanstephan in the Towy valley, is indeed excellent arable. Our author's identification of Theodore with the Celtic saint Teulyddog is quite without warrant. Sir John Lloyd called it 'a bold endeavour to make respectable the unknown and uncouth Teulyddog'. *A History of Wales*, ii (London, 1911; 3rd edn. 1939), 432, n. 108. Teulyddog was eventually supplanted by St. John the Evangelist, who was first associated with Teulyddog by the Normans, and then replaced the Celtic saint entirely. Ibid. 459. The identification is evidence of the Norman custom of Latinizing the names of Welsh saints, part of the romanization of the Welsh Church. Melville Richards, 'Place and Persons of the Early Welsh Church', *Welsh History Review*, v (1971), 348–9.

tractans, apud uenerabilem Cicestrie presulem Radulfum, qui eundem locum multo semper affectu fouit et extulit, huius rei querimoniam absolui utile iudicauit. Facta igitur huius cause contione, abbate cum monachis aliquibus Cicestriam adeunte, coram pleno eiusdem capitulo hac causa uentilata, ab episcopo confirmatum est communi assensu, ut, sicut ecclesia sancti Martini de Bello, et capella quoque sancte Marie de eadem uilla libera et quieta sit in perpetuum de omnibus consuetudinibus et forisfacturis episcopalibus et de denariis olei et sinodi. Presbiter uero illius capelle synodum ad episcopalia tantum precepta audienda adeat, nec ibidem pro aliqua culpa iudicium subeat. Ad clericorum uero capitulum nullatenus sine abbatis precepto uel licentia eat.
f. 49 Quod si forte presbiter / [a]in grauem ceciderit culpam ipsa propter hoc capella non cessabit, sed alius uice illius secundum abbatis prouisionem sumministrabit, eritque confessio reatus et penitentia presbiteri delinquentis in manu episcopi, et forisfactura sancti Martini. Sinodum quoque adire abbas nec summoneatur, ut supra confirmatum meminimus, nec cogatur. His omnibus a toto Cicestrensi capitulo ita concessis et carta cum episcopali auctoritate confirmatis, in huius rei testimonium datus est ab abbate et monachis monasterii de Bello eidem Cicestrensi ecclesie liber quidam epistolarum beati Ieronimi, coram multis hinc indeque testibus.[1] Nec tamen hoc tantum uenerabili suffecit episcopo Radulfo, sed magis affectum, quia[b] eidem gratuita gratia confederabatur ecclesie de Bello, plenius dilatare proponens, cum forte ultima qua illuc aduenerat uice hiemali festo sancti interesset Martini, coram clericis suis, nominatim Henrico archidiacono, Carlone cantore, Rotberto de Andeuilia, Radulfo caluo, et uicinis multis innumerisque qui confluxerant promiscui sexus et ordinis hominibus, inter sacrosancta missarum sollennia, dignitates et libertates eiusdem ecclesie publica uoce contionatus testificari et auctoritate studuit /
f. 49v confirmare; hoc omnibus manifestans, se nec suorum quemquam successorum debere nec posse ibidem imperandi uel dominandi aut cuiuspiam subiectionis calumniandi causam habere, excepto si

[a] *f. 49 should precede f. 48, and an 18th-cent. hand has noted the fact at the top of f. 48. See above, p. 27* [b] *MS*: qua

[1] The phrases are taken from a charter known only in an interpolated form, with the highly suspicious phrase concerning the abbot tacked on. It was

his men what might be the best course, judged it advantageous that this quarrel be settled before the venerable bishop of Chichester, Ralph, who had always cherished this abbey and shown it great goodwill. Therefore a meeting on the case was called, the abbot and some of the monks went to Chichester, the case was aired before the full chapter of that church, and it was confirmed by the bishop with the general assent: that like the church of St. Martin of Battle, the chapel of St. Mary of that vill would be free and quit for ever of all episcopal customs and forfeitures and from the payments for oil and for synod. The priest of the chapel is to attend synod only to listen to episcopal injunctions, not to submit there to judgement for any fault. He is by no means to attend a chapter of the clerks without the command or permission of the abbot. If by chance the priest shall have fallen into serious fault, the chapel itself will not be suspended but another will minister in his place as the abbot shall provide. The confession of guilt and the penance of the erring priest shall be in the hand of the bishop, the forfeiture shall belong to St. Martin. Also, the abbot may not be summoned to attend synod, an agreement we have mentioned above, nor may he be coerced. All these concessions were made by the whole Chichester chapter, and confirmed by a charter with the bishop's warranty. As evidence of this the abbot and monks of the community of Battle gave the church of Chicester, before many witnesses on both sides, a book of the letters of Jerome.[1] Nor did this alone suffice for the venerable bishop Ralph, but since he was united with the church of Battle in a freely bestowed friendship, he proposed to broadcast his affection more widely. During a visit on the occasion of the feast of St. Martin in winter (it was, as it happened, the last time he came) before his clerks, namely Archdeacon Henry, Charles the precentor, Robert of *Andevilia*, Ralph the bald and innumerably many neighbours of both sexes and of various ranks, during the holy service of mass he took care to bear witness to the privileges and liberties of the church aloud before the assembly, and to confirm them by this episcopal authority. By this he made clear to everyone that neither he nor any of his successors should or could have authority of lordship there, nor had they any claim to its

first shown in 1157 by Abbot Walter de Luci. Below, pp. 148, 190, 196: the bishop had never been shown a charter with this privilege before that year. Searle, *EHR*, lxxxiii (1968), 461–2, and 475–6, where the charter is printed in full, as it is in Mayr-Harting, *Acta*, no. 6. The substance of the charter is not unacceptable and may well be genuine.

qua eis impendantur benigne sola tantum caritatiua exibitione, nec se quicquam ibidem aliter posse aut uelle ex debito requirere, hoc solo contentus quod gratuita impenderetur caritate. Hoc quidem ecclesie Belli episcopale testimonium ne in posterum aboleretur, calamo exarasse utile uisum est.[1]

Quia uero, ut prelibatum est, quedam ex preciosissimis sanctarum reliquiarum philacteriis, intercidentibus causarum infortuniis, argento auroque expoliata extiterant,[2] reliquieque sanctorum quamplurime, ex ipsis uel unde unde adquisite, congrue ut deceret non recondebantur, de quorundam philacteriorum catenis aureis uel argenteis, nequando, ut ante hoc factum est, forte distraerentur, terras emere abbas cum monachis decreuit. Quo facto, ne sanctorum pignera debito carerent domicilio, feretrum quoddam auro argentoque et preciosis gemmis opere mirifico fabrefactum decenter idem abbas et monachi fieri fecerunt. Quo perfecto adueniens illuc predictus uenerabilis Radulfus Cicestren-
f. 48 sis episcopus feretrum benedixit, collocatis / in eodem honorifice scilicet sanctis sanctorum reliquiis, easque ibidem annuatim requirentibus septem dies de penitentia indulsit.

Tunc temporis plerique uicinorum leugam circa ecclesiam de suis terris tenere quedam conquesti, sepius abbatem et monachos calumniando commouebant. Vnde factum est ut, regiis hac querimonia illata auribus, communi consilio leugam funiculo metiri oportuisset. Quo peracto, ecclesie quidem omnia que antea possederat et quedam etiam ex pluribus partibus leuge funiculo dimensionis inclusa cessere, sicque sopita hac querimonia ita eadem usque hodie libere possidet et quiete.[3] Cum igitur omnimodis sub uenerabili abbate Radulfo eadem ecclesia interius exteriusque succresceret, et prosperaretur utilitatibus, nulli ut prelibauimus religione caritatisque exibitione gratuita, preter ceteras uirtutum dotes, habebatur secunda. Verum idem abbas

[1] The witnesses appear genuinely of the epoch *c.* 1120. See Mayr-Harting, *Acta*, pp. 8, 211–12. If any charter confirmed the relationship, it has not survived. More likely, as the chronicler here implies, the bishop preached on mutual charity between diocesan and monastery.

[2] See above, p. 104. The amulets had been the deathbed gift of William I. Above, p. 90.

[3] There is a survey on p. 50 above, where the boundaries of the *leuga* are given in respect of fiefs and holdings contiguous to the *leuga*. But it is later than the one mentioned here, possibly a version of this, brought up to date by Abbot Walter

subjection, save only what might be courteously expended upon them as a gift of charity. Nor in any other case had he the right or desire to ask for anything there as a duty, for he sought only what would be expended as freely given charity. So that this episcopal testimony concerning the church of Battle is not lost sight of in the future, it has seemed useful to have set it down in writing.[1]

As we noted earlier, some of the precious amulets containing holy relics had been despoiled of their silver and gold, thanks to misfortunes that had cropped up.[2] A great many of the relics of the saints that had come in them (or wherever they had been acquired) were housed in a way that was most improper. The abbot and the monks decided to buy land with the gold and silver chains of several amulets, lest one day they should be broken up as had already been done once. When this was done the abbot and monks commissioned a feretory, a wonderful work of gold and silver set with precious jewels, to house the saints' relics properly. When it was finished the venerable Ralph, bishop of Chichester, came and blessed it, respectfully arranging the holy relics of the saints in it. And he gave an indulgence of seven days' penance to those who made a yearly pilgrimage to them.

At that time most of the neighbours, complaining that the *leuga* around the abbey included certain of their own lands, were constantly harassing the abbot and monks with false claims. Finally matters came to the point that complaint was made to the king, and it was the common counsel that the *leuga* should be measured with a line. When that was completed, everything that it had before, and even some lands in a number of places outside the *leuga* boundary included in the line's measurement were conceded to the church: thus ended the quarrels, with the abbey holding them free and quit to the present day.[3] Under Abbot Ralph, the church throve within and without, and was blessed with such practical advantages that, as we have seen, it was held second to none in its religious life, its display of charity, and in all its other virtues. The venerable abbot,

de Luci. *Regesta*, ii, no. 1166 (1109–16) and no. 1185 are contemporary writs ordering such boundary surveys. Other examples are mentioned, ibid., p. xix. And see F. W. Maitland, *Domesday Book and Beyond* (Cambridge, 1897), pp. 432–3. *Regesta*, ii, no. 619 (and p. 308) commands the barons of Hastings Rape to make 'enclosures against the land of the abbot of Battle'; it no doubt initiated or resulted from this incident. The context into which the chronicler puts it (the abbot purchasing lands and being involved in lawsuits obviously attendant upon getting clear 'title') makes the date of 1102, which the *Regesta* editors tentatively assign to the writ, unlikely. A date after 1110 is more probable.

uenerabilis domus Dei delectatus decore ecclesiam ipsam plumbo decenter operire, quod residuum erat murorum in girum construere, curie spatium dilatare, nouis eandem fabricis augustare, domusque statum consuetudinibus precipuis uariisque ornamentis que ad honorem Dei haberi erat necesse omnino per se suosque studuit multipliciter exornare. /

f. 48v Preterea his que foris sunt adeo inuigilans, quam sollicitus animarum procurauerit salutem, lingua uel calamo succumbente, paucis saltem commemorare onerosum non sit. Ad singula enim recitanda nullus sufficeret sermo. Iugiter itaque subditorum prelatus inibi seruiuit moribus, nulli imperauit ut dominus. Infirma aliorum sustinuit; ad fortia prouocauit. Fecit ipse quod docuit; uita doctrinam preuenit. Diuinum ad officium festinandum docebat; artus seniles baculo sustentans iuuenes ipse precedebat. Primus choro aderat, postremus aberat. Fuit ergo uite norma; fuit Martha et Maria, fuit serpens et columba, fuit Noe inter undas.[1] Non sponte coruum amisit; sponte columbam admisit.[2] Rexit munda et immunda, rector prudens ad diuersa. Cham nouit perferre, Sem et Iaphet benedictione donare.[3] Factus est uir agricola, terras habitas instanter coli faciens, non habitas habitis prudenter adiungens, quantitatem adusque pretii librarum per annum plus minus uiginti eas multiplicans.[4] Factus est et spiritualis agricola, uomere doctrine multorum quos scripsit librorum corda terrena excolens, ad boni operis frugem humili quidem
f. 50 stilo, sed sensu / moralitatis fecundo ea uocans.[5] Daniel quoque ciborum parcitate, Iob corporis passione, Bartholomeus genuum flectione, flectens ea sepissime orando que uix flectere poterat incedendo.[6] Diebus singulis psalterium ex ordine totum decantans, uix triduo ante mortem a tali genuum flexione uel psalmorum consuetudine cessans. Non nimia tussis, non uomitus sanguinis, non etas senilis, non pelle tenus attenuatio carnis uirum frangere, non a proposito tante religionis unquam ualuerunt inflectere.

[1] Cf. Gen. 7: 18–24; Luke 10: 38–42; Matt. 10: 16; John 11: 1–45. *Regula*, c. 2.

[2] Cf. Gen. 8: 6–8.

[3] Cf. Gen. 7: 13; 9: 22–3.

[4] Cf. Gen. 9: 20.

[5] For Ralph's writings see R. W. Southern, *St. Anselm and his Biographer* (Cambridge, 1963), pp. 206–9.

[6] The description of St. Bartholomew as often kneeling is from the *Acta Fabulosa* of pseudo-Abdia of Babylon. *Acta Sanctorum*, August, v (Antwerp, 1741), 34c: 'Centies flexis genibus per diem, centies per noctem orat Deum.' Canterbury possessed a relic of St. Bartholomew, sold to Queen Emma by the bishop of Benevento from Bartholomew's shrine there. Eadmer, *Hist.Nov.*,

delighting in the embellishment of God's house, took proper pains with the church's lead-work, built what remained to be finished of the encircling wall, enlarged the courtyard, and surrounded it with new buildings. He took great care, both he and his men, to adorn the abbey in many ways with excellent customs and with various decorations that were necessary for the honour of God.

Moreover, while he was so carefully watching over externals, how zealously he looked after the salvation of souls! Though tongue and pen quail before the task, it would not be burdensome at least to set down a few generalities in remembrance of him: for no account would suffice to tell of his qualities in detail. He was the ruler, yet he was ever at the service of the moral conduct of his subjects; to none did he issue commands as a lord. The weaknesses of others he supported, rousing them to deeds of strength. He practised what he preached; his life outstripped his teaching. He taught that divine service was a thing to hurry to; supporting his old joints by a staff he was there before the young. The first to arrive in choir, he was the last to depart. He was a model for life: he was Martha and Mary, serpent and dove, Noah amid the flood.[1] Unwillingly did he lose the raven; willingly, admit the dove.[2] He ruled the pure and the impure, wise in different fields. He knew how to bear with Ham and to bless Shem and Japhet.[3] He became a man of agriculture, vigourously seeing to it that the tenanted lands were cultivated, and prudently adding vacant lands to those held, and thus increasing their value to around twenty pounds a year.[4] He became a spiritual farmer too, cultivating the earth of the heart with the plough of teaching, in the many books he wrote, calling them to a harvest of good work in a style that was low but fertile in its expression of morality.[5] He was a Daniel in the sparingness of his eating; Job in bodily suffering; Bartholomew in kneeling, often bending his knees in prayer when he could scarcely bend them to walk.[6] Every day he chanted the whole psalter straight through. It was scarcely three days before his death when he finally gave up genuflection and the habit of saying the psalms. Neither a severe cough, nor vomiting of blood, nor old age, nor emaciation (he was skin and bones) could break his courage nor ever deflect him from the course of such piety.

pp. 107–110. Battle's connection with Canterbury may account for the chronicler's knowledge of the legend, though no MS. of the *Acta Fabulosa* has been traced to either house.

Ecce autem post multos agones, post multas corporis passiones, post annos uite sue octoginta iiii^{or}, monachatus autem lx^{ta} et dies xxx^{ta} vi, decem uero annos[a] et septem diesque xx^{ti} ex quo Bellensis effloruit abbas; ecce, inquam, iiii kalendas Septembris, hora diei uespertina, cum iam ad diurni mercedem denarii patrefamilias iubente uocaretur,[1] pater iste pius, dulcis, et humilis, dum lectulo decubans uili cibum perparum gustasset, dum fratrum quibusdam deuote benedixisset, dum aliis ut ad se uenire deberent mandasset, sanguinis repente uomitus plus solito nimius, et uelut in frusta pulmonis longa tussi diruti coactus, eum cum solita tussi
f. 50^{v} uehementer inuasit, uexauit, inuoluit, / exanimauit, fratribus concurrentibus, dolentibus, gementibus, deflentibus, spiritum egredientem in manus creatoris ad quem redibat deuote commendantibus. Quem monachi in ecclesia ipsa de Bello in crucis parte aquilonali ante memoriam apostolorum honeste tradiderunt sepulture.

Rege itaque Henrico tunc temporis in transmarinis partibus occupato, cum iam dicti patris Radulfi obitus auribus esset illatus Rogerii Saresberiensis episcopi, qui tunc per Angliam regia iura administrabat, destinauit illuc cum quodam seruiente regis, Iohanne Belet cognominato, clericum quendam nomine Willelmum de Heli, a quibus abbatia tota et ad eam pertinentia abbreuiata sunt;[2] sicque cure cuiusdam ipsius ecclesie monachi, nomine Eilwardi, tota exterius abbatia ad tempus commissa est. Demum uero quibusdam obortis simultatibus, quibus uix aut nunquam huiusmodi carere possunt mutationes, totius ecclesie cura predicto seruienti regis Iohanni Belet delegatur, qui a festo beati Nicholai presulis usque ad dominicam que Album Pascha dicitur, usque quo scilicet abbas ecclesie eidem electus est, non sui gratia incommodi abbatie totius curam gessit.

Anno itaque incarnationis deifice m c xxv^{o} generale domini
f. 51 regis Henrici per fines totius Anglie / ad purificationem sancte Dei Genitricis Marie[3] diuulgatur edictum, ut quecumque pastoribus uiduate fuissent ecclesie, sibimet prospicientes, regis in transmarinis partibus presentiam ad suscipiendos prelatos per idoneos

[a] *Interlined in later hand*: annos

[1] Cf. Lev. 19: 13; Job 7: 1–2.

[2] Henry was in Normandy from June 1123 to September 1126. W. Farrer, 'An Outline Itinerary of King Henry the First', *EHR*, xxxiv (1919). For Roger of Salisbury's itinerary see E. J. Kealey, *Roger of Salisbury, Viceroy of England* (Berkeley and Los Angeles, 1972), pp. 217–18. John Belet held land in Surrey and was sheriff of Berkshire in 1130. *PR 31 Henry I*, ed. J. Hunter (London,

Yet visualize him: after many torments, after many bodily sufferings, after eighty-four years of life, sixty years and thirty-six days a monk, seventeen years and twenty days a brilliant abbot of Battle. Visualize, I say, the scene on August 29th: it is the evening hour, when the Master of the house begins to summon the labourers to their daily-penny wage.[1] This father, devout, sweet and humble, lying ill on a mean cot, had just tasted a little food, had devoutly blessed some of the brothers and had commanded that others come to him. Suddenly he began to vomit blood much more than before, as if pieces of lung were being ripped out by the long cough. And now that cough came upon him again grievously, shook him, overwhelmed and strangled him. The brothers came running. With grief and moans and weeping they faithfully commended his departing spirit into the hands of the creator to whom it was returning. The monks gave him a fitting burial in the church of Battle, to the north of the cross, before the shrine of the Apostles.

At the time King Henry was busy overseas, and Roger, bishop of Salisbury, who was then administering the royal rights throughout England, was notified of the death of Father Ralph. He sent to Battle a clerk, William of Ely, along with one of the king's servants, John, surnamed Belet, who made a brief survey of the entire abbey and its appurtenances.[2] The whole management of the abbey's external affairs was entrusted for a time to the care of a monk of the church, named Ailward. But at length, quarrels arose, of a kind which such changes of governance are rarely or ever without, and the management of the entire abbey was entrusted to John Belet, the king's servant. He administered the whole—and not to his own disadvantage—from the feast of St. Nicholas to Whit Sunday, when an abbot was elected for the church.

In 1125 a general edict was published through all England at the feast of the Purification of Mary, Holy Mother of God,[3] that all churches without pastors should, in their own interests, send worthy delegates overseas to the king to receive rulers. Following

1833, repr. 1929), pp. 13, 49, 123. In that year he witnessed the charter, *Regesta*, ii, no. 1645. A William of Ely witnessed a charter shortly thereafter. Ibid., no. 1910. William, archdeacon of Ely and nephew of Bishop Hervey of Ely, is called the king's chaplain in 1127. Ibid., no. 1502. See Le Neve, ed. Greenway, ii, p. 50. From what follows it seems that John Belet took the profits of the abbey, as was quite usual during a vacancy, but it does not bear out Kealey's assertion that Belet and William 'seriously depleted the defenseless monastery's revenues'. Kealey, pp. 63–4.

[3] 2 Feb.

adirent legatos. Tunc et huius de qua agitur ecclesie de Bello prior, uir magnificus Hildewardus nomine, cum tribus eiusdem monasterii monachis mare transiens regem adiit, contioneque facta rex consilio usus archiepiscopi Canturie Willelmi, necnon et episcopi Cicestrensis Seifredi, qui tunc ad episcopatum Cicestrie electus fuerat, ecclesie de Bello monachum Cantuariensem quendam Warnerium nomine, uirum modestia, sapientia, ac litteratura summum, abbatem delegauit.[1] Quo in ebdomada post mediam[a] xl stabilimento confirmato, predicto priore maturato reditu cum suis repatriante, sabbato ante Dominicam Palmarum illis[b] domum regressis, mox totius abbatie cura in ius predicti, ad eiusdem regimen electi, locum qui preerant dantibus, redacta est.[2] Paschali ergo imminente tempore cum domino archipresule Willelmo predictus Warnerius Angliam aduenit tertioque post Pasche solempnitatem dominico die, priusquam sui regiminis adisset ecclesiam, benedictione petita, sexta dehinc feria, que dies tunc erat octavo kalendas Maii, in ecclesia sibi commissa de Bello
f. 51v festiue ut decebat susceptus est. / Adeptus ergo culmen regiminis cepit continuo abbas Warnerius prudentie quo callebat studio domum a regiis ministris multimodis dissipatam paulatim restaurare, adquietare, et in pristinum statum promouere. Quia uero illius anni sterilitate magna omnem terram occupauerat egestas, mira probitatis industria importuna oportunis coequans, honorifice ut summi patrisfamilias fidele mancipium commissam disponens domum, inopiam opulentia in breui superauit.[3]

Quia uero, ut supra meminimus, rex prefatus Henricus sua munificentia eidem loco in Walia quandam ecclesiam de Carmerdin cum pertinentibus contulerat, ubi iam fratres ad Deo seruiendum adunati fuerant, episcopus eiusdem prouincie Bernardus, loci illectus amenitate, miro cupidinis ardore quoquomodo eandem ecclesiam in ius proprium moliebatur redigere.[4] Cum igitur hinc frequentius et regie quoque, tam a se quam et a suis oberatis,

[a] *MS*: medium [b] *Interlined in hand of main copyist*: illis

[1] *Regesta*, ii, no. 1424: the king's notification of Seffrid's appointment to the see of Chichester. He was consecrated on 12 Apr. 1125. The blessing of Abbot Warner must have been one of his first acts as bishop. William of Corbeil had been consecrated archbishop in 1123.

[2] A general requirement. Lanfranc, *Constitutions*, p. 72.

[3] Cf. Matt. 25: 21, 23.

instructions, the prior of this church of Battle, a splendid man, Hildeward by name, crossed the sea with three of the monks of the house, to seek out the king. At an assembly the king, on the advice of William, archbishop of Canterbury, and also of Seffrid, newly elected bishop of Chichester, assigned a monk of Canterbury, one Warner, a man excellent in modesty, wisdom and learning, as abbot of Battle.[1] This decision received formal confirmation during the week after mid-Lent. The prior and his monks returned hastily, reaching home on the Sunday before Palm Sunday. Immediately those who were in charge gave up their places, and the care of the whole abbey was made over to the rule of the abbot elect as his right.[2] It was almost Easter when Warner reached England with the Lord Archbishop William, and on the third Sunday after Easter, before he had come to the church under his governance, he asked for the blessing. Six days later, on 24 April, he was received, joyously, as was fitting, in the church of Battle, now entrusted to him. Having been elevated to a high command, Abbot Warner began directly, and with practical judgement, in the exercise of which he was experienced, to restore little by little a house in many ways run down by the royal administrators, to pay off its debts, and to bring it up to its former condition. Since that year there was a crop failure, great want was felt over the whole land. But with a splendid assiduity and uprightness he made disadvantages into advantages. Caring for the house entrusted to him honourably, like the faithful servant of the highest Master of the house, he soon brought plenty in place of poverty.[3]

As we have said, King Henry in his generosity had given this abbey a church in Carmarthen with all its appurtenances. Brothers had already been assigned there for God's service, but the diocesan bishop, Bernard, seduced by the delightfulness of the place, kept trying to make it his own by any available means, displaying an extraordinarily strong greed.[4] Even the king was repeatedly nagged about it by the bishop himself and by those who owed him

[4] Bishop of St. Davids 1115–48. A royal clerk, Bernard was the first Norman appointed to the Welsh church. He vigorously reorganized his diocese, romanizing the ancient Celtic patterns. Battle's loss was part of his reorganization of the Celtic monasteries and their estates, of which J. Conway Davies has said, 'He found them the property of the *clas*; he left them the property of the bishop baron.' James Conway Davies, *Episcopal Acts . . . Relating to Welsh Dioceses 1066–1272*, i, Historical Society of the Church in Wales (Cardiff, 1946), 141, 245, no. D 63. See above, p. 125, n. 2.

pulsarentur aures, tandem in abbatis Warnerii electione huius cause absoluta questione, a rege episcopo idem locus donatur, ecclesieque de Bello quedam terra lxx solidorum, regii uidelicet manerii uocabulo Mienes membrum, quod uocatur Langenhersse, in possessionem eternam libere tenenda, et ab omnibus consue-
f. 52 tudinibus quieta excambiatur. / Quo cum regie maiestatis auctoritate confirmato, et utrinque concesso, mox ad Anglie reditum, redeuntibus domum fratribus, ecclesiam predictam episcopus obtinuit, necnon et abbas predictam possessionem in ecclesie sue iura redegit.[1]

Episcopo autem Seifrido, ut iam meminimus, apud Cicestriam episcopatus gradu sublimato, cum ipsi et abbati predicto mutua uideretur inesse concordia, suorum tamen importunitate abbatem episcopus sinodum suam in ipsa utrorumque recenti promotione adire summonuit. Ad quod dum sano usus consilio a pleno sue ecclesie capitulo quid sibi agendum foret abbas prouidus requisisset, fratres morem hactenus seruatum inferentes ex regia hoc auctoritate ostenderunt quod pro nulla summonitione nec exactione hoc fieri oporteret, sed si sibi per liberum arbitrium illuc uel alias ire placuisset, libere quem uellet absque calumpnia adire ualeret. Quo abbas responso certificatus, episcopum ultroneus adiit; causam dignitatum ecclesie cui preerat exposuit; nec se summonitione coactum aduenisse, sed ne mutua inter eos caritas sua iura hactenus obseruata uiolaret, flagitare se ut ecclesiam suam et se in pace secundum morem pristinum esse sineret, ne deterius
f. 52v quippiam [ex][a] huiusmodi forte / simultatibus oriretur. Quibus pontifex pacificatus, omnem calumpnie nodum dissoluit, ecclesiamque et eundem abbatem oppido diligens, consilio et auxilio studiose prelationis sue tempore fouit.

Restaurationis igitur ecclesie in dies proficiente statu sub predicto abbate, cepit idem summa prudentia et sagacitate usus ad fratrum numerum multiplicandum accommodare studium, domusque Dei salubri delectatus decore et ecclesie partem plumbo operuit et multis ac preclaris ornamentis, non solum in uasis altari

[a] *Winterbottom*

[1] Probably in the parish and village of Langrish, near East Meon, Hants, a manor taken from the bishop of Winchester by William I before 1086. *DB*, i. 38a. However, the hundred of East Meon contained two tithings, either of which may be the member here mentioned. One was Longhurst; the other Langrish.

favours, till at last at the election of Abbot Warner the complaint was settled by the king giving the place to the bishop and compensating the church of Battle with a holding worth seventy shillings from the royal manor of Meon: namely a member called Langrish, to hold for ever free and quit of all customs. When both parties submitted to this and it had been confirmed by the king, they quickly returned to England, the brethren going home. So the bishop got the church and the abbot got the property as the right of his church.[1]

Bishop Seffrid, as we have noted, had been raised to the see of Chichester. Although there seemed to be a mutual friendship between himself and the abbot, nevertheless, at the urging of his people, the bishop summoned the abbot to a synod at a time when both had been but recently promoted. At this the abbot, guided by wise counsel, sensibly asked the full chapter of his church what he should do. The brothers, adducing the custom followed up to that time, declared it to be by royal authority that he should not be coerced by any summons or exaction, but that if by his own free will he should wish to go there or anywhere else, he had the right to approach anyone he liked, without dispute. Taught by this answer, the abbot went voluntarily to the bishop. He pleaded the case of his abbey's privileges: he had not come coerced by the summons. But in order that mutual charity between them should not violate the rights of either, rights respected up till then, he entreated the bishop to leave his church's original customs and himself in peace, lest perchance something more serious should come of rivalries of this sort. The bishop was appeased by this. He ignored the whole tangled dispute, and highly esteeming the church and the abbot, he cherished them during his prelacy with counsel and aid.

Since the task of restoring the church's condition was progressing day by day under this abbot, he undertook, with great prudence and sagacity, to increase the number of brothers. Delighted by wholesome decoration in God's house, he had part of the church worked with lead and he strove to perpetuate his memory, and his devotion, with ornaments both numerous and splendid: not only

VCH Hants, iii. 64–6. For the royal notification see *Regesta*, ii, no. 1649 and p. 368. It is there dated 1129–33, since Bernard, bishop of St. Davids is shown holding the honour of Carmarthen in that year. *PR 31 Hen. I*, 90. This provides a motive for his determination to control directly an old and important monastic centre, but not necessarily a date by which he had obtained it. It was probably *c.* 1130. See above, p. 124, n. 1.

aptis argento uel auro preciosis, sed et in cappis et albis palliisque precipuis sui memoriam et deuotionem perpetuare sategit. Curam etiam uillicationis sibi commisse interius exteriusque uigili strenuitate agens, et religioni ad sui filiorumque salutem ut uirum eruditissimum decebat operam dare, et ecclesie iura uel dignitates dirationando seruare possessionesque restaurans honorificentissime se suaque omnia studebat disponere.

Igitur cum omnimodis accurate omnia tractans honoris delectaretur accumulatione, solebat ad patroni communis beati Martini festum hiemale, pro tante solempnitatis excellentia, episcopum Cicestrensem sepius summonendo mandare. Quadam ergo uice /
f. 53 hoc modo submonitus caritatis gratia, atque adueniens, post peractam ut decebat solempniter festiuitatem, contigit episcopi ministros, iam patrio forte calentes mero,[1] ecclesie cellerarios et seruientes ambitionis quodam euectos coturno obiurgare, et quasi per dominium ultra domus sufficiens stabilimentum, que placita forent, auctoritate sua intemptando extorquere. Sed ecclesie prouide renitentibus ministris, ad aures tandem peruenit pontificis. Quem multa commotum indignatione uenerabilis demum abbas adiit, ratione uirum placare temptauit. Qui furori addens contumaciam abbatis patientia nullatenus mitigari potuit. Cumque et sibimet dominium exercere comminans in ipsa ecclesia ut in sua uelle se diceret, abbas restitit; postque multas obiurgationes uerbum obliuioni non tradendum subintulit: quod scilicet ipsi episcopo nec cuiquam suorum ne alimenta quidem tunc ex consuetudine darentur. Qui cum ad hec exsanguis pene ui hec extorquere comminaretur, abbate econtra uiriliter se tam libere quemadmodum ipse episcopatum suum eandem abbatiam regalem gubernare affirmante, denuo cum utrorumque disceditur obstinatione.
f. 53v Cumque ad dicti probationem episcopus cum / suis in crastinum perendinasset, abbate inflexibiliter sententiam [de][a] exitu ad multorum in posterum utilitatem confirmante, ministrorum ecclesie obsequio destitutus, incibatus horam ibidem transegit episcopus demumque si libuit sibi et suis necessaria procurans aforis comparauit. Verum subsequentem furoris et indignationis ac abolende comminationis noctem cum abbas et sui quiete et

[a] *Winterbottom*

[1] Cf. Isa. 5: 11; Horace, *Epode* 11.

gold and silver vessels for the altar, but copes and albs and rich pallia. Thus he was vigorous about the management of the stewardship entrusted to him, in internals and externals: as became a most learned man, he took pains over the religious life, for the salvation of himself and his sons; he actively preserved the rights and privileges of the church by establishing title to them; and most honourably he expended himself and his all on restoring its possessions.

Now this abbot came to be somewhat dazzled by the great honour he had earned by his care in administration. And thus it was that at the winter feast of the community's patron, St. Martin, on account of the exceptional dignity of such a service, it became his custom often to command the attendance of the bishop of Chichester with a summons. One time when the bishop was summoned in this manner out of charity, and had come, after the feast had been finished in customary manner, as was proper, things fell out thus. Members of the bishop's retinue, men elevated by ambition and perhaps heated with the local wine,[1] pompously reproved the cellarers and servants of the abbey and, as if they were speaking for their lord—a sufficient support outside this house—they tried to extort what they wanted by threats of his authority. When the church's servants prudently withstood them, they complained to the bishop and he was most indignant. The abbot finally went to him and tried to calm him by reason, but he added a stubbornness to his anger that the abbot's patience could not soften. But when the bishop menacingly declared that he meant to exercise lordship over him in this church as in his own, the abbot drew the line. After a good deal of argument, he made a statement that should not be forgotten: namely that neither the bishop nor any of his retinue should be given the food normally given. At these words the bishop went pale, but although he threatened to extort it by force, the abbot courageously maintained that he governed this royal abbey as freely as the bishop his diocese. Finally they parted, with determination on both sides. To put it to the test, the bishop and his men stayed till the next day. On his part, the abbot remained inflexibly firm in his opinion about the outlay, a useful example to many in the future. Deprived of the obedience of the church's officials, the bishop passed an hour there unfed, till at last he had to buy provisions for himself and his retinue out in the market. A night of fury, indignation, and horrible threats followed, though the abbot

pacifice peregissent, mox maturatum diei diluculum impacificatos cum indignatione concepta ad propria transmisit. Per plurimum ergo temporis cum inter episcopum et abbatem nullatenus ira deferbuisset, non hinc aliud emulationis genus quam monimentorum posteris insignia administrauit. Denique rationi episcopo tandem submittente animum, pristinam discordiam multimodo utrique dilectionis carismate postmodum accumulauerunt.

In Normannia igitur memorato rege Henrico existente, tandem
anno regni sui xxxvi°, generali preualente conditione, iiii° nonas
Decembris ultimum huic mundo reliquit uale. Cuius corpus, a loco
qui dicitur Liuns quo obierat, in Angliam translatum, in monasterio
ab eodem in beate Dei Genitricis Marie honorem mirifice
apud Radingas fundato, cum magno honore tumulatum est. /
f. 54 Eodem uero anno qui ab incarnatione domini nostri Ihesu Christi
erat m c xxxv^{tus} non longe post mortem magnifici regis Henrici
successit in regnum Anglie nepos illius Stephanus comes Bolonie,
annitentibusque nonnullis regni primoribus, apud Westmonasterium
xi kalendas Ianuarii, ab archipontifice Cantuarie Willelmo
sacra unctione linitus, regio diademate coronatur. Quo in regno
confirmato cum non absque pestiferis tumultibus, unde nunc
temporis commemorare non est, dissidentibus inter se proceribus,
patrie iura disponerentur, inter reliquos, quibusdam obortis
occasionibus, uenerabilis abbas Warnerius regiam simultate non
satis idonea incurrens offensam, loco cedere quam indignationi,
aliisque quibusdam obortis querelis succumbere utilius iudicauit.
Denique non multo post, apud Westmonasterium ante natale
Domini, quorundam instinctu, et consilio maxime Alberici sancte
Romane ecclesie legati, qui tunc in Anglia erat, sese ultroneus
anno xiiii° ex quo abbatie gubernacula sumpserat ab omni cura
prelationis demisit,[1] sicque suimet dumtaxat curam habens ad
sancti Pancratii religione satis spectabile monasterium in Leuuensi
situm castro secessit, ibique ad usque obitus sui diem religiose /
f. 54^{v} permansit.[2]

Anno uero m c xxx° ix° humanationis deifice inchoante, continuo post natale Domini, memoratus rex Stephanus apud

[1] Alberic, bishop of Ostia, came as papal legate in 1138 and assembled a synod at Westminster in mid-December 1138, to deal with church reform and to elect a new archbishop. The court had moved from Westminster by 8 Jan. 1139.

and his monks passed it quietly and peaceably. When dawn came, it sent them home unplacated, in a passion of indignation. Though for a long time the fury between bishop and abbot would not cool, it led to no consequences save to be a warning for the future. At length the bishop listened to reason, and from then on they both buried their former disagreement under manifold displays of love.

Meanwhile in Normandy, in the thirty-sixth year of his reign, and on 2 December, King Henry died, as all men must. His body was transported from Lyons-la-Forêt to England, and he was buried with great honour in the monastery so splendidly founded by him at Reading in honour of the Blessed Mary, Mother of God. In the same year, 1135, not long after King Henry's death, his nephew Stephen, count of Boulogne, succeeded to the realm of England. After several of the magnates of the kingdom had worked for him, he was anointed and crowned by William, archbishop of Canterbury, at Westminster on 22 January. When he was in control of the realm (though, since the magnates disagreed among themselves, he could not assert his rights in the country without devastating insurrections which this is not the time to recall), various disputes ensued. On certain pretexts the venerable abbot Warner incurred the royal disfavour owing to a discreditable rivalry. Certain other quarrels having arisen, he judged it better to surrender, yielding his position rather than yielding to anger. Finally, not long afterwards at Westminster, before Christmas, at the instigation of some, and especially on the advice of Alberic, legate of the holy Roman church, who was then in England, he voluntarily laid aside all the care of abbacy, in the fourteenth year after he had assumed governance of the abbey.[1] And so, having responsibility for himself alone, he withdrew to St. Pancras at Lewes, a monastery very notable for its religious life, and there he remained devoutly until his death.[2]

At the beginning of the year 1139, immediately after Christmas, at Canterbury, King Stephen, guided by the counsel of his queen

Alberic had left England soon after. *Regesta*, iii, no. 366. There is no reason to think that Warner had been irregularly appointed or had acted subsequently in any way that would have disqualified him in the legate's eyes. Considering the immediate provision of Walter de Luci to the abbacy, Warner was most probably advised to resign so that the king might have a gift of patronage to offer his valued administrator, Richard de Luci, who had, as the chronicler implies, been looking for just such a gift for some time.

[2] A Cluniac priory. *Religious Houses*, pp. 97–100.

Cantuariam, regine sue et predicti Alberici legati necnon et quorundam baronum regni sui usus consilio, abbatiam de Bello cuidam monacho de Lunlegio transmarino, Waltero nomine,[a] fratri cuiusdam baronis regni prepotentis Ricardi cognomento de Luci, commendauit.[1] Hic ergo prudentia multa ac sapientia necnon et eloquentie ornamento litteralique ac seculari argutia pollens, cum abbate sancti Albani cognato suo, Gausfrido nomine, aliquandiu in Anglia manserat, fratrisque sui industria regiam cognitionem et procerum fauorem obtinuerat. Die igitur vi° iduum Ianuarii electus, demum cum honore debito, comitante episcopo Cicestrensi Seifrido, apud ecclesiam Belli ii idus Ianuarii est susceptus. Prelationis ergo consecutus apicem, cepit prudenter ecclesie profectibus intus et extra inuigilare. Et quamuis tunc temporis dissidentibus inter se proceribus regni, tota undique patrie libertas et opulentia, conturbantibus ac distrahentibus maliuolis, qui regia abutebantur simplici mansuetudine, sceuo exemplo pro libitu
f. 55 cederet; ipse tamen et ecclesie thesauros / terrasque ac libertates regalesque consuetudines eidem delegatas, inter tantos turbinum fluctus inuiolabiles seruari uiriliter insistebat. Nec ei summa defuit pietas, dum regem omnino ipsi et sibi commisse ecclesie deuotum et protectorem esse obtinuisset.

Sub isdem itaque diebus tempestate preualente, contigit nauem quandam uariis sumptibus refertam de Rumenel, terra archiepiscopi Cantuarie, super terram ecclesie de Bello in Dengemareis, membro de Wi, confractam, hominibus uix euadentibus, iactari. Sciendum autem est hoc pro lege ab antiquitate per maris littora obseruatum, ut naui fluctibus contrita, si euadentes infra statutum terminum et tempus eam minime reparassent, nauis et quecumque appulsa forent absque calumpnia in dominium terre illius et in werec cederent. Sed supramemoratus rex Henricus hanc abhorrens consuetudinem, tempore suo, per imperii sui spatia, edictum proposuit quatinus si uel unus e naui confracta uiuus euasisset, hec omnia obtineret. Verum quo nouus rex cedit, et noua lex. Nam defuncto eo, regni primores, edicto recenti pessundato, morem antiquitus obseruatum sibimet usurparunt. Vnde
f. 55v factum est ut homines / de Dengemareis secundum maritimas

[a] *Add in marg.*: Nota quod abbas Walterus [? fu]it alienigena

[1] It is probably anachronistic to call Richard de Luci *prepotens* as early as

and the legate Alberic, and also by certain barons of his realm, granted Battle abbey to a foreign monk from Lonlay in Normandy: one Walter, brother of a very powerful baron of the realm, Richard, surnamed 'de Luci'.[1] This Walter was a man esteemed for his great intelligence and wisdom, for the distinction of his eloquence, and for his scholarly and wordly wit. He had for some time been staying in England with his kinsman Geoffrey, abbot of St. Albans and he had attracted the royal attention and the favour of the magnates through the assiduity of his brother. He was chosen on 8 January, but it was not until 12 January that, accompanied by Seffrid, bishop of Chichester, he was received with due honour in the church of Battle. Having become abbot, he began to watch prudently over the interior and exterior progress of the church. At that time the magnates of the realm were in discord among themselves and everywhere the whole liberty and prosperity of the country was thrown into confusion by the malevolent, who abused the ingenuous and gentle king, and whoever liked might follow the evil precedent. Yet the abbot stood manfully firm in the midst of such a storm, to preserve unharmed the treasures of the church, its lands, liberties, and royal customs. Nor did he lack the very greatest piety, whilst, at the same time, he had wholly won the king as a devoted protector for himself and for the church committed to him.

In those days, during a storm, a ship out of Romney, in the territory of the archbishop of Canterbury, fully loaded with various goods, was wrecked upon land of Battle abbey in Dengemarsh, a member of Wye. Its crew barely escaped. Now it should be understood that from antiquity it has been held as law along the sea-coast that in the case of shipwreck, if the survivors have not repaired her within an established boundary and time, the ship and whatever may have been landed falls without challenge under the lordship of that land as 'wreck'. However, King Henry was averse to this custom and promulgated an ordinance for his own time and throughout his empire, that if even one person should escape alive out of the wrecked ship he should have everything. But, new king, new law. For after his death the magnates of the realm did away with the new ordinance and exercised the ancient custom themselves. So it was that the men of Dengemarsh, following the

1139. He was still beginning his long career in royal administration. *Regesta*, iii, p. xxi. West, *Justiciar*, pp. 24–5.

consuetudines et regales dignitates ecclesie Belli predictum werec ui obtinerent. Quo agnito, archiepiscopus curiam adiens coram rege de abbate de Bello, quod in hac re ui et hostilitate usus fuisset, querimoniam fecit. Nec mora, rex abbatem mandans coram se uenire fecit.[1] Quibus a conuentu nobilium apud regiam uentilatis curiam, cum studio et arte Willelmi de Ypra,[2] qui Cantie comitatum tunc possidebat, rex quoque archiepiscopo fauens abbatem ut pacis transgressorem argueret, quod scilicet contra regis Henrici sancita fecisset, post plurimam utrinque controuersiam, tandem sic curia sedatur. Nam abbas, ratione usus premeditata, regem Henricum pro libitu antiqua patrie iura mutare in diebus suis posse testificatus est, sed non nisi communi baronum regni consensu in posterum rata fore. Vnde si id, unde calumniabatur, sue dignitatis compatriote, barones scilicet qui aderant, cum regalis curie assensu concessissent, et ipse libens cederet. Cumque presentes regni primores hec uno ore contradicerent, in communi tandem decretum est, ut eadem soluta curia, abbas regia dignitate hinc suam nactus curiam apud Dengemareis, die denominato, hominibus archiepiscopi aduenientibus, omnem rectitudinem
f. 56 teneret. Sed / in hoc conuentu uerbum memoriale quo magis regius emollitus est animus prouidum dixisse abbatem contigit. Nam cum argueretur, ad regem conuersus intulit: 'Nunquam', inquiens, 'te diutius, o rex, coronam Anglie ferre Deo sit placitum, si tantillam ecclesie nostre libertatem a rege Willelmo et ab aliis antecessoribus tuis regibus datam et obseruatam destruxeris.'

Verum abbate diem constitutum obseruante, ante diem sequentem ex parte archiepiscopi nullus aduenit. Vnde transgressionis iudicio obmutescentes, cum frustrati discessissent, iterum ad regias aures huius rei querimonia ab archiepiscopo delata est. Abbas iterum mandatus aduenit, causisque expositis a communi consessu adiudicatum est, abbatem suam causam dirationasse, nec ab archiepiscopo hinc aliquam calumpniam ulterius pati debere. Atque in his soluta curia, singulis in sua regressis, reuerendus abbas hec omnia

[1] The chronicler is using the phraseology of royal writs, as in Van Caenegem, *Writs*, 422, 488. The phrase is particularly common in the thirteenth century. *Bracton: de Legibus et Consuetudinibus Angliae*, ed. G. E. Woodbine, transl. and revised by S. E. Thorne, ii (Cambridge, Mass., 1968), 201–2, 310, 316, 317, 333, 422, 427.

[2] William of Ypres, illegitimate son of Philip, count of Ypres, was Stephen's confidant, and principal mercenary commander. Like the Battle chronicler, Gervase of Canterbury says that he had custody of Kent. Gervase of Canterbury (RS), ii. 73. He never appears as earl of that county, but he drew revenues from

maritime customs and royal liberties, took this wreck by force for the church of Battle. When he heard this the archbishop went to court and brought before the king a complaint against the abbot of Battle, that he had used force and hostility in this matter. The king at once commanded the abbot to appear before him.[1] The matter was aired at the royal court before a gathering of nobles. The king himself was inclined towards the archbishop and, through the zealous and skilful William of Ypres,[2] who at that time held the county of Kent, he accused the abbot of breaking the peace, since he had acted against a decree of King Henry. After much disputation, the abbot calmed the court with an argument planned ahead of time. For he pointed out that while King Henry could at will change the ancient rights of the country for his own time, that fact should not establish anything for posterity except with the common consent of the barons of the realm. So, if his equals in privilege, namely the barons who were present, would, with the royal assent, give up for themselves the point at issue, he would willingly give it up too. The magnates present unanimously refused to do this and it was finally decreed in common that this hearing be closed and that the abbot should, by royal privilege, convene his own court on the matter at Dengemarsh on a stated day, with the archbishop's men in attendance, and should have complete jurisdiction. Now at this assembly it happened that the abbot uttered with foresight a memorable phrase that much weakened the king's spirit. For when he was accused, he turned directly to the king and said, 'Not for long may you wear the crown of England, O King, so please it God, if you destroy even such a small liberty given our church by King William and respected by your other predecessors.'

The abbot kept to the arranged day, but no one arrived for the archbishop until the next day. Thus losing their say in the settlement of the offence, they went away disappointed, and once more a plaint reached the king from the archbishop. Once more the abbot was summoned and came. The points of difficulty were explained and by general consent it was adjudged that the abbot had proved his case and that he ought not not to be challenged further on this by the archbishop. The hearing was dissolved, and each returned

it till 1156. His presence therefore provides no clue as to the date of the incident. The chronicler dates the incident in the mid-1140s. See following note. For William's career see H. A. Cronne, *The Reign of Stephen* (London, 1970), pp. 147–9.

unde agitur pro libitu disponens, aliquibus sumptibus qui appulsi fuerant archipresulem et suos pacificauit, precipua tamen sibimet et sue ecclesie de Bello retinuit, sicque huius rei querimonia quieuit.

Eo tempore uenerabili uiro Seifrido episcopo succedente in
cathedram Cicestrensem uiro magnifico Hilario,[1] qui Romane
f. 56v curie noticiam ac fauorem / plurimum obtinuerat, cepit memora-
tum Belli monasterium in dignitatibus suis, quorundam emulatione, plurima pati molimina. De quibus, quia non incongruum uidetur, latius per singula dissputandum est.[a] Erit enim presentibus iocundum, futuris utile, summumque dignitatum eiusdem ecclesie sancti Martini de Bello memoriale, atque[b] ad perpetuitatis monimentum contra insurgentium machinas inuidorum scutum inexpugnabile. Nam per plurimum temporis prouidi abbatis Walterii patientia protractum, cum semper insurgentium ars multimoda simili cassaretur arte, tandem cum tanto honore constat determinatum ut utiliter huiusmodi dilatio facta probetur. Siquidem per hanc dilationem et ecclesie dignitas, et cartarum eiusdem ab antecessoribus collata auctoritas, non solum regie curie, sed et nobilium ignobiliumque per totius regni spatia latius solito diuulgata per populos pro miraculo predicatur, hincque et regie auctoritatis terror, et ecclesie libertas corroboratur. Nunc ergo ab exordio pretaxate controuersie modum expediamus. /

f. 57 Opere enim pretium est ad posterorum memoriam litteris commendare, qualiter inter uenerande memorie eundem Hilarium Cicestrie episcopum et predictum uirum Walterum abbatem ecclesie sancti Martini de Bello, controuersia de dignitatibus et libertatibus ecclesiarum suarum diu inter illos habita, ad pacis et dilectionis concordiam perducta sit. Quod legentes ueraci digestum non dubitent calamo, scientes etiam multa propter diuersam sermonum materiam pretermissa, ne tedium inferrent lectoribus.

Anno ab incarnatione Domini m c xlviii° regnante in Anglia Stephano rege piissimo ex clarissimo regis Willelmi magni stemmate orto, anno scilicet xiii° regni ipsius, reuerendus uir quidam Hilarius nomine, moribus honestis artiumque liberalium prefulgens nitore, ecclesie sancte Trinitatis Cicestrie antistes preficitur.

[a] *Written in letters so exaggerated as to occupy the space of one line*: dissputandum est [b] *Written in letters so exaggeratedly extended as to occupy nearly the whole of two lines*: ecclesie . . . memoriale

[1] Seffrid Pelochin was deprived in 1145. Hilary was consecrated in 1147, not in 1148 as the chronicler believes.

home. The abbot, disposing as he wished of all the goods that had caused the trouble, pacified the archbishop and his men with some of the shipwrecked goods, but the important things he kept for himself and for his church of Battle. And so the quarrel over this matter ended.

About this same time the venerable Bishop Seffrid was succeeded in the see of Chichester by the majestic Hilary.[1] He had received much notice and favour in the Roman court, and Battle abbey, through the envy of certain persons, began to suffer many attempts against its privileges. It does not seem out of place that we should treat of them at length and in detail. It will be delightful to the present generation, useful to future generations, a supreme memorial of the privileges of this church of St. Martin at Battle, and, thus put on record for ever, it will act as an invincible shield against the plots of envious assailants. For by the patience of the foresighted Abbot Walter over a very long time, when he continually frustrated the protean cunning of his adversaries by cunning equal to theirs, it has finally been settled with so much honour as to prove that a delaying action like this was useful. For by that prolongation both the rank of the church and the authority of its charters conferred by the king's predecessors were revealed unusually widely, not only to the royal court, but also to the nobles and commons throughout the kingdom, and are preached among the people as miraculous. Through it the terror of royal authority and the liberty of the church have been strengthened. Wherefore we shall unravel this dispute from the beginning.

For it is worth while setting down in writing, for future generations to remember, how a dispute between Hilary, bishop of Chichester, of reverend memory, and Walter, abbot of the church of St. Martin at Battle, concerning the privileges and liberties of their respective churches, after having been kept up for a long time, was brought to harmonious peace and affection. Readers need not doubt that I am telling the truth, though they should understand that much has been omitted owing to the complexity of the subject, to avoid tedium for them.

In the year 1148, in the thirteenth year of the reign in England of the most pious Stephen, of the distinguished line of the great William, a certain reverend man, Hilary by name, of worthy life and with a brilliant reputation in the liberal arts, was made bishop of the church of the Holy Trinity in Chichester. Now when he

Qui cum iura et dignitates ecclesie sue undique perscrutari cepisset, a quibusdam ei intimatum est, ecclesiam sancti Martini que cognominatur de Bello, eo quod ibidem Deus regi Willelmo conquisitori Anglie de inimicis suis uictoriam contulit, eius ditioni subiacere debi-
f. 57v tam / fuisse. Venerande ergo memorie uir cum hec accepisset, Walterum eiusdem loci abbatem super hoc multociens conuenit. Abbate uero resistente nec eidem assentiente, dissensio inter eos permaxima orta est. Modus autem dissensionis inter illos huiusmodi erat.

Episcopus Cicestrie abbatem de Bello ad sinodum suam apud Cicestriam ire, et omnia episcopalia secundum canones[a] persoluere cogebat. Hospitari etiam in eadem abbatia et in maneriis eiusdem, auctoritate episcopali et quasi ex consuetudine, affectabat. Abbatem uero et abbatiam hospitando, queque pro libitu disponendo, suo iuri subdere anhelabat. Hinc etiam hac utebatur auctoritate dicendo abbatem de Bello electum in ecclesia Cicestrensi cum professione canonica benedictionem suam ecclesiastico more consequi debere, indeque illum sibi et sue ecclesie omnino subiectum fore. Abbas uero econtrario non superbie sed patientie et humilitatis utens exemplis, nunc uiua uoce, nunc missis Cicestriam nuntiis, libertatem et dignitatem sue ecclesie opponebat, dicens regem Willelmum, quem diuina prouidentia aduexit in Angliam ut ius sibi debitum adquireret, in procinctu belli eodem in loco cum fauore omnium secum comitantium uotum fecisse, locum scili-
f. 58 cet illum Domino Christo dare tam / liberum quam sibi posset adquirere; clementiaque fauente diuina uictoriam adeptum uotumque soluentem, ecclesiam ibidem in honorem Dei et beati Martini construxisse, pro salute omnium et maxime omnium ibi interfectorum, ita liberam et quietam ab omni exactione terrene seruitutis et ab omni subiectione et oppressione atque dominatione episcoporum sicut est ecclesia Christi Cantuarie.[b][1] Hoc etiam consilio et testimonio Lanfranci archiepiscopi Cantuarie et Stigandi Cicestrie episcopi aliorumque multorum scriptis suis confirmasse, Stigandum necnon Cicestrie episcopum, presente Gausberto primo eiusdem loci abbate et monachis suis, in quantum sui iuris

[a] nes: *add. in marg. in the hand of the scribe* [b] *MS*: Catuarie

commenced to investigate the rights and privileges of his church thoroughly, it was intimated to him by some that the church of St. Martin called 'Battle' since there God gave the victory over his enemies to King William the conqueror of England, should be subject to his authority. When this man of reverend memory had satisfied himself about this, he summoned Abbot Walter to him many times about it. Since the abbot resisted and would not yield to him, a most serious dissension arose between them. It took the following form.

The bishop of Chichester forced the abbot of Battle to attend his synod at Chichester and to pay all episcopal dues according to the canons. He also aimed at being entertained in the abbey and in its manors by episcopal right and as by custom. By lodging and by disposing things as he willed, he was trying to establish rights over abbey and abbot. This was why he also exerted authority in declaring that the abbot elect of Battle must receive his benediction in Chichester cathedral according to ecclesiastical usage and must make a canonical profession. Thus would the abbot be made wholly subject to himself and his church. In contrast, the abbot, following examples not of pride but of patience and humility, kept adducing the liberty and privilege of his church, at times explaining in person, at times by messengers sent to Chichester, saying that King William whom divine providence had brought to England to secure a right due to him had made a vow at that place on the battlefield with the approbation of all his companions, that he would give the place to the Lord Christ, just as free as he himself might win it. And when, by divine favour he had won the victory and could discharge his vow, he built a church there in honour of God and St. Martin, for the salvation of all, and particularly of all killed there, as free and quit from all exaction of earthly service, from all subjection, oppression, and domination of bishops as is Christ Church, Canterbury.[1] And that he had confirmed this in writing, with the counsel and witness of Lanfranc, archbishop of Canterbury, Stigand, bishop of Chichester, and many others. And also that Stigand, bishop of Chichester, in the presence of Gausbert, the first abbot of the abbey and his monks, had confirmed it, as far as

[1] The chronicler is referring to the version enshrined in the foundation stories (above, pp. 36, 68, 72–4) and in the forgery, *Regesta*, i, no. 62. For the reception of the charter in 1155 see below, p. 158.

erat hoc eodem modo litteris suis corroborasse,[1] et ex tunc ad noticiam omnium transisse ecclesiam sancti Martini de Bello ab omni subiectione episcopi Cicestrensis omnino liberam fuisse. Hac igitur ratione tanti uiri calumpniis abbas obuians, flagitabat obnixe, quatinus libertatem, quam ecclesia predicta tantorum uirorum auctoritate hactenus uidebatur possedisse, inuiolabili illibatoque iure tenere licitum foret. Presul uero, his minime adquiescens, crebras abbati simultates ingerebat, interminando quod nisi sinodum peteret, interdictum post unius anni curriculum in sinodo sollempni auctoritate canonica uinculo illum[a]
f. 58v anathematis constringeret. / Fauebat autem ei tunc Romane pastor ecclesie Eugenius, necnon et uenerabilis Teodbaldus Cantuarie archiepiscopus et multi alii, quorum fretus auctoritate abbatem et ecclesiam de Bello sibi et sue ecclesie penitus subiugare sperabat. Verum spe consilioque deceptus inani, rem effectui mancipare non potuit, quia spes in dubio posita plurimos nonnunquam fefellit.[2]

Quodam igitur predicti Stephani piissimi principis tempore, sinodum apud Cicestriam adire abbas summonitus, nec ueniens, interdictus est ab episcopo, eo tamen tenore: quod si infra xl dierum spatium satisfacturus non ueniret, ab officio suo suspensus cessaret. Quod abbas audiens curiam apud sanctum Albanum adiit prepropere atque hec regie intulit aule. Rex itaque, accersito quodam clericorum suorum Rotberto de Cornuuilla nomine, misit ad episcopum, mandans et precipiens quatinus ecclesiam sancti Martini de Bello sicut dominicam regis capellam et regiam coronam ab omni exactione et oppressione liberam et quietam Christo Domino pacifice sineret deseruire.[3] Terminum etiam ei prefixit, quatinus die octauarum sancti Andree ipse et abbas Lundoniam uenirent, ut ibi dissensioni eorundem coram se, episcopis, et baronibus suis presentibus finem imponeret.[4] Die constituta uterque affuit. Multis igitur causis ibidem discussis,

[a] *Interlined in hand of main scribe*: illum

[1] No such charter was shown the bishop until the matter came before Henry II in 1157. Searle, *EHR*, lxxxiii (1968), 458–9. Stigand's supposed confirmation of the liberties he accepted at Battle is paraphrased above, p. 74. The chronicler is here referring to an interpolated version of that charter, which purported to have been made in the presence of Gausbert and his monks. It is printed in Mayr-Harting, *Acta*, p. 71.

was in his right, in the same way in writing.[1] And thus it came to be common knowledge that the church of St. Martin of Battle was wholly free from all subjection to the bishop of Chichester. By this argument the abbot kept opposing the challenges of so great a man. He kept insisting resolutely that the liberty the church could be seen to have possessed up to that moment, by the authority of such great men, it should be allowed to keep unimpaired as an inviolable right. The bishop, far from being satisfied, kept up his quarrel with the abbot, threatening that unless he came to synod before a year was out, an interdict, made in solemn synod and by canonical authority, would bind him with the chain of excommunication. He was in favour with Eugenius, the pope of the Roman church, and also with the venerable Theobald, archbishop of Canterbury, and with many others, by whose authority he hoped wholly to subjugate the abbot and church of Battle to himself and his church. He was deceived by vain hope and counsel, and was not able to achieve his aim: hope fixed on the uncertain has disappointed many.[2]

Upon a time, during the reign of the most pious prince, Stephen, the abbot was summoned to a synod at Chichester. He did not go, and he was interdicted by the bishop in this sense: that if he did not come to make satisfaction within forty days he would be suspended from office. When the abbot heard this he hastened to the court at St. Albans and put the matter before the royal court. The king, summoning one of his clerks, Robert surnamed 'de Cornuvilla', sent him to the bishop commanding that he allow the church of St. Martin of Battle to serve the Lord Christ free and quit of all exaction and oppression, as if a royal chapel or even the royal crown.[3] He set him a date in the week after St. Andrew's Day when he and the abbot were to come to London so that there their dissension might be settled before himself, the bishops, and such barons as would be there.[4] On the day set both attended. After

[2] Cf. 1 Tim. 6: 17.

[3] Robert of Cornuvilla seems to be known from no other English source, but the editors of the *Regesta* suggest an identification with a Robert de 'Corneivilla', canon of St. Martin le Grand. *Regesta*, iii, p. xii.

[4] 7 Dec. 1148. The bishop was pursuing the recovery of other lost episcopal rights as well, at the court. He recovered from the count of Eu the manor of Bexhill in Sussex, seized by the count's predecessor and held by him in 1086. *DB*, i. 18. *Regesta*, iii, no. 183. Bexhill is there incorrectly indentified with Bexley in Kent.

f. 59 abbas regi presentiam suam exhibuit, paratus, / si quis eidem quicquam obicere uellet, iusta rationis equitate pro libertate ecclesie sue resistere. Episcopus uero nonnullis ibidem detentus negotiis, coram rege die eadem uenire distulit. Lectis igitur coram rege cartis et munitionibus de hac eadem re, a rege Willelmo magno subscriptis, rex altiori usus consilio precepit ecclesiam sancti Martini de Bello ab omni subiectione et exactione Cicestrensis episcopi secundum regis Willelmi et aliorum regum predecessorum suorum cartas, liberam omnino existere. In crastinum licentia a rege abbas accepta domum rediit, rege eidem pronuntiante se ecclesie de Bello sicut dominice sue capelle et corone regie in omnibus iusta defensione protectorem fore.

Haut longo postmodum tempore, anno scilicet incarnationis dominice m c liiii° viii kalendas Nouembris, eodem piissimo rege Stephano ex hac luce subtracto, et in ecclesia quam ipse in honorem sancti Saluatoris mundi a fundamentis construxerat apud Feuresham tumulato,[1] episcopus tempus ut sibi uidebatur opportunum nactus quo suam ad libitum prosequeretur causam, predictum abbatem Cicestriam ire summonitum nec uenientem in sinodo solempni excommunicauit.[2] Quod quidam de Ierosolimitanis Fratribus de Templo scilicet ibidem existens cum acce/-
f. 59v pisset, Lundoniam festinanter tetendit, ubi tunc temporis abbas predictus, precepto uenerabilis Cantuarie archiepiscopi Teodbaldi, cum quodam fratre suo ex nobilibus Anglie Ricardo de Luci nomine, aduentum Henrici Normannorum ducis regis futuri expectans morabatur, atque hoc eiusdem Ricardi auribus pandit. Quo audito, Ricardus, cum predicto abbate fratre suo locutus, hec ut erant archiepiscopo referre non distulit. Communicato itaque consilio misit idem uenerabilis pater quendam ex clericis suis Salomonem nomine ad episcopum, mandans ei quod abbate secum detento domini sui futuri Henrici ducis Lundonias expectabat aduentum. Vnde mandando uolebat quatinus sententiam quam super abbatem posuerat relaxaret, donec in unum conuenirent. Antistes uero Cicestrie domini sui legati annuens uoluntati sententiam relaxauit.

Adueniente itaque domino nostro Henrico duce, atque apud Westmonasterium anno incarnationis dominice eodem, xiiii° kalendas Ianuarii in regem eleuato, et a uenerabili Teodbaldo Cantuariensi archiepiscopo et totius Anglie primate necnon et apostolice sedis legato ibidem coronato, totius Anglie primoribus ad eum confluentibus, iuste consilio eorum omnia disponebat.

many cases had been discussed, the abbot presented himself to the king, prepared, if anyone should argue against him, to fight for the liberty of his church calmly and reasonably. But the bishop, occupied with other business there, failed to appear that day before the king. Thus when the charters and the supporting evidence containing the assent of the great King William were read out, the king, guided by noble advice, commanded that the church of St. Martin of Battle should remain wholly free from all subjection and exaction of the bishop of Chichester in accordance with the charters of King William and his other royal predecessors. The following day the abbot was given leave to return home, the king promising him that he himself would be in all things the protector of Battle abbey, defending it rightly as he would his own private chapel and royal crown.

Not long after, in fact on 25 October 1154, this most pious King Stephen died and was buried in the church he himself had founded in honour of St. Salvator in Faversham.[1] To the bishop the moment seemed to present a golden opportunity to settle the matter in his own favour. In solemn synod he excommunicated the abbot for not obeying the summons to Chichester.[2] A Templar happened to be present, and when he heard this he hurried to London, where the abbot was then staying at the order of Theobald, the venerable archbishop of Canterbury. He was with his brother Richard de Luci, one of the English nobles, awaiting the arrival of Duke Henry of Normandy, the future king. The Templar took his news to Richard, who, after talking it over with his brother, referred it immediately to the archbishop. The venerable father took his advice, and sent one of his clerks, a man named Salomon, to the bishop, to inform him that the abbot was in his own retinue awaiting the arrival in London of his future lord, Duke Henry. For this reason he must order him to relax the sentence against the abbot until they could all have a meeting. The bishop of Chichester bowed to the will of his lord the legate and relaxed the sentence.

Our lord, Duke Henry, arrived and on 19 December in the same year, at Westminster he was enthroned and crowned by the venerable Theobald, archbishop of Canterbury, primate of all England and legate of the apostolic see. The magnates of all England flocked to him and he set everything in order justly, with their counsel. By

[1] Founded in 1148. *Religious Houses*, pp. 54, 65.

[2] Cf. Gratian, C. 11 q. 3 c. 43.

f. 60 Ecclesiis etiam possessiones et dignitates ab ante/cessoribus suis concessas sua auctoritate confirmauit. Et in sequenti Quadragesima congregauit generale concilium apud Lundoniam, et renouauit pacem et leges et consuetudines per Angliam ab antiquis temporibus constitutas. Ibi quoque nonnulli ex episcopis et abbatibus cartas et priuilegia ecclesiarum suarum presentis regis scripto et sigillo confirmauerunt. Inter quos predictus abbas de Bello, regis Willelmi et aliorum regum cartis et scriptis per ordinem ostensis, ut in scripto et sigillo eiusdem principis confirmarentur obtinuit. Quod episcopus Cicestrensis cum accepisset, citato gradu archiepiscopum adiit, eique abbatem de Bello cartas contra dignitates Cantuariensis ecclesie et sue etiam ecclesie Cicestrie scilicet possedisse, et ut in presentis regis sigillo confirmarentur obtinuisse intimauit. Obsecrare igitur ut hoc communi prohiberent sententia, ne alii per Angliam abbates quasi quoddam priuilegium hoc contra episcopos suos sibi uindicarent, si predictus abbas contra illos preualuisse uideretur. His archiepiscopus auditis, nimiumque credulus effectus, sponsione affirmauit certissima se nunquam his suum prebere assensum, quo aliquo hec pro uoto abbatis fine terminari potuissent. Factum est autem.

In crastinum rege et archiepiscopo in unum conuenientibus, archiepiscopus super his sermonem intulit, dicens regem pati non
f. 60v debere Cantuariensem ecclesiam, matrem uidelicet / totius Anglie et per quam idem rex diademate insignitus fuisset, necnon et Cicestrensem ecclesiam eiusdem uidelicet suffraganeam, libertates et dignitates ab antiquis temporibus possessas pro ecclesia de Bello non tante auctoritatis et dignitatis annullari. Acceperat namque abbatem illius loci cartas contra dignitates et libertates ecclesiarum predictarum possedisse. Flagitare itaque ut hec regali omnino annullaret auctoritate, aut carta abbatis regio careret sigillo, donec suo correcta consilio ecclesia Canturie necnon et Cicestrie ius suum non amisisse gauderent. Rex igitur tanti uiri, utpote sui patris spiritualis et a quo diademate regali haut longe ante fuerat insignitus, annuens uoluntati, cancellario accito regio prohibuit cartam abbatis de Bello regali sigillo confirmari.

Quid multa? Per uulgi ora dispersa abbatis auribus hec propere fama intulit.[a] Redeunte itaque luce abbas curiam adiit sed

[a] quid . . . intulit: *The words do not quite fit into the space, and the scribe has begun his second line in the left-hand margin. The writing is slightly larger than that usual in this section*

his authority he confirmed the churches in the possessions and privileges conferred by his predecessors. The following Lent he convened a general council in London and renewed the peace and restored the laws and customs established from ancient times throughout England. There too a number of bishops and abbots had the charters and privileges of their churches confirmed by the writ and seal of the present king. Among them the abbot of Battle displayed in order the charters and writs of King William and of other kings, and secured the promise that they would be confirmed by the writ and seal of the prince. When the bishop of Chichester heard of this he went at once to the archbishop and put it to him that the abbot of Battle possessed charters contrary to the privileges of Canterbury and of his own church of Chichester, and that he had been promised that they would be confirmed by the seal of the present king. He therefore implored that they combine to prevent this, for if the abbot were seen to prevail against them, then other abbots throughout England might claim this against their bishops as though it were some kind of privilege. The archbishop, hearing this and being all too ready to believe it, promised firmly that he would never give his assent to anything that would enable the abbot to have his way in this. As indeed it turned out.

The following day when the king and the archbishop were in conference, the archbishop turned the conversation to the matter, saying that the king ought not to allow the church of Canterbury, the mother of all England and the authority by which the king himself had been crowned, or the church of Chichester, its suffragan, to be despoiled of liberties and privileges held from ancient times, merely for Battle, a church of no such authority or rank. He understood, he said, that the abbot possessed charters opposed to the privileges and liberties of the aforesaid churches. He earnestly asked that he might nullify this with the royal authority, or that the abbot's charter go without the royal seal until it had been revised by his advice so that the churches of Canterbury and Chichester might rejoice that they had not lost their rights. The king assented to the wish of such a great man, his spiritual father and the one who had crowned him so recently. Calling the chancellor to him he forbade the charter of the abbot of Battle to be confirmed by the royal seal.

Why go into detail? A widespread rumour about this quickly reached the abbot. When day came the abbot went to court, but he

rege uenatum eunte nil die eadem proficiens, ad hospicium suum reuersus est. Sequenti luce summo mane abbas iterum Westmonasterium petiit, ibique, coram altare quo rex missam erat auditurus opperiens, multis mente modis uoluebat quid super hac re facturus esset. Adueniente rege ut missam audiret, post misse introitum abbas regem conueniens, 'Domine', inquit, 'uestra pre-
f. 61 ceperat excellentia cartam ecclesie nostre / sigillo confirmari regio, sed qua de causa repulsam passa sit ignoro. Iubeat igitur clementia uestra ut uerbum regium fixo stet gradu, nec pro cuiusquam inuidia pessumdari uideatur.' Accito itaque cancellario precepit rex ut carta abbatis sigilli sui confirmaretur impressione.

Necdum uerba compleuerat, et ecce, episcopus festinato gradu, illud ut erat mente suspicatus, accurrens, regem tali affatur colloquio. 'Domine mi, meminisse decet clementiam uestram unde nudiustertius uenerabilis Cantuarie archiepiscopus et ego querimoniam coram uobis deposuimus de abbate scilicet de Bello qui contra dignitates nostrarum ecclesiarum cartas querit, ut que hactenus iure canonico uidentur possedisse, eius calliditate preualente lugeant se amisisse. Prohibeat itaque regia dignitas uestra ut hoc nullatenus aliqua confirmetur auctoritate, ne alii huius exemplo contra episcopos suos insurgere uideantur.'

Rex uero precepit cartam abbatis regio confirmari sigillo, et deinde episcopum et abbatem simulque cancellarium coram archiepiscopo conuenire, lectaque carta abbatis, illis audientibus, si qua corrigenda essent eorum consilio corrigerentur, sicque in pace cum carta sua abbas domum rediret. Quod si sententia discordante discessissent, carta abbatis in capella regis a cancellario
f. 61v custodiretur / donec sententia regis quid inde fieret discerneret. Percantato itaque misse canone usque ad 'Pax Domini', episcopus ut moris est pace a sacerdote accepta regi detulit, et deinde abbati multis plurimum mirantibus porrexit.[1]

Episcopo igitur et abbate simulque cancellario multisque aliis coram archiepiscopo apud Lametham conuenientibus, lectaque

[1] The mass had been sung through to the priest's greeting before communion, 'Pax domini sit semper vobiscum', at which point in the early church the kiss of peace was given. This is an early reference to an object being passed round (a cross, one of the sacred vessels, or a special 'pax-board') instead of the physical kiss, a change that had become general by the thirteenth century. *New Catholic Encyclopedia*, vol. ix, s.v. Mass, Roman. See below, pp. 200–2. The abbot and

could get nothing that day since the king had gone hunting. He returned to his lodging. The following day at dawn the abbot again made his way to Westminster and there, while he waited at the altar where the king was to hear mass, he turned over in his mind many approaches to what might be done about the problem. The king arrived to hear mass, and after the introit, the abbot addressed him. 'Lord, your excellency ordered the charter of my church to be sealed with the royal seal. For some reason I do not understand, that order has been countermanded. But may your clemency command that the royal word be steadfast and not seem to be overruled by anyone's envy!' Calling the chancellor to him the king ordered that the abbot's charter be confirmed by the impression of his seal.

The words were scarcely out of his mouth when, behold, the bishop came up at a near run, full of suspicions, and addressed this speech to the king: 'My lord, surely your clemency remembers that the day before yesterday the venerable archbishop of Canterbury and I laid a complaint before you. It was about the abbot of Battle who is trying to secure charters opposing the privileges of our churches, that they may mourn the loss of what they can be seen to have possessed up to now as a canonical right, if his craftiness prevails. May your royal dignity forbid it to be confirmed with any authority, lest others follow his example and rise against their bishops!'

But the king ordered that the abbot's charter be confirmed by the royal seal, and that the bishop and the abbot, with the chancellor, should meet on the matter before the archbishop. There the abbot's charter could be read openly to them, and if there were things that required correction they were to be corrected by their counsel, and so the abbot could return home in peace with his charter. But if they parted without reaching agreement, the abbot's charter should be taken into the chancellor's custody in the king's chapel until the king could decide what was to be done about it. When the mass had been sung through to the 'Pax Domini', the bishop, as is the custom, took the pax from the priest. He offered it to the king and then, to the amazement of many, held it out to the abbot.[1]

The bishop, the abbot, the chancellor, and many others met before the archbishop at Lambeth. During the reading of the

the bishop had between them taken up nearly the entire mass, pressing petition and counter-petition upon the king.

carta magni Willelmi regis, exemplo cuius omnes alie carte regum sequentium confirmate sunt, ubi uentum est ad quoddam uerbum quod in eadem continetur carta, 'quod ecclesia scilicet de Bello libera sit omnino ab omni subiectione episcoporum sicut ecclesia Christi Cantuarie',[1] clamor undique attollitur, quibusdam asserentibus hoc contra canonum instituta extitisse, aliis dicentibus hoc contra dignitates Cantuariensis ecclesie fuisse, nonnullis nimium clamantibus hoc uerbum peremptorium esse, multis etiam hoc aliter obiurgando interpretantibus, hinc inde confusa perstrepebat sententia. Carta perlecta, cum neminem predecessorum suorum episcoporum prefatus Cicestrie episcopus Hilarius in subscriptis eiusdem carte inueniret testibus, precellentissimam huius uerbi dignitatem sacrorum canonum in perpetuum auctoritate damnandam, et presentium simul iudicum confirmatione censuit delendam. Huius sententiam concors etiam archiepiscopi conclamatio prosecuta est. Abbate uero quamuis rationabiliter resistente, non tamen
f. 62 illorum quieuit commotio.[a] / Cancellarius autem, audiens illos inter se discrepantes, retulit cartam abbatis inde discedens in capellam regis, eamque ibi seruandam iuxta regis preceptum tradidit. Abbas uero, amicorum suorum usus consilio, ad propria reuersus est, nil de Dei desperans auxilio. Episcopus letus et hilaris effectus est, sperabat enim abbatem ecclesiamque de Bello carte sue omnino confirmatione priuari. Verum ut scriptura testatur, 'Homo proponit, Deus autem disponit';[2] non passus est Christus ecclesiam suam antiquis suis et iustis carere priuilegiis, sed sua preueniente misericordia tempore ei opportuno in melius restituit.

Eodem itaque anno in tempore Paschali quidam ex Anglie nobilibus Hugo de Mortuo Mare cognomine, uir pollens uiribus, sed multo maxime ingenio ualidus, prediues opibus, militari negotio strenuus, regem utpote adolescentem eiusque industriam indignationi habens, castris suis munitis eiusdem imperiis se suaque summitti refutabat. Ea uero postquam regi enuntiata sunt, congregata militum multitudine non modica, ipsum Hugonem in quodam castro suo Bregge nomine obsedit, ualloque et castris undique circumdedit, omnemque illi egrediendi spem omine mutato

[a] Carta . . . commotio: *Written in the larger script of f. 60v. The final words have had to be squeezed into the bottom margin*

---

[1] See above, pp. 22, 68. The phrase would have been particularly offensive to the archbishop's entourage, implying as it does that the monks of his own

charter of the great King William (from a transcript of which all the other charters of the kings who succeeded him had been confirmed), when they reached a particular phrase in the charter—'that the church of Battle be wholly free from all subjection of bishops, like Christ Church, Canterbury'[1]—a shout went up from all sides. Some declared it to be contrary to the canons, others said that it was contrary to the privileges of the church of Canterbury. A few called out out that this phrase was too drastic, and many reproachfully interpreted it in another sense. They made a great noise with their divergent views. When the charter had been read through, Bishop Hilary of Chichester found that none of his predecessors were put down as witnesses to the charter. He moved that the extraordinary privilege in this phrase be condemned in perpetuity by the authority of the holy canons, and that it be deleted by a unanimous resolution of the judges present. The archbishop associated himself with this suggestion with a shout of assent. Although the abbot opposed it in a reasonable manner, their shouting did not die down. However, the chancellor, noting that there was disagreement among them, took the abbot's charter with him when he returned to the king's chapel, and handed it over there to be kept according to the king's instructions. Following his friends' advice, the abbot returned to his abbey, doubting not God's help. The bishop was happy and cheerful, for he expected that the abbot and church of Battle would be wholly denied the confirmation of their charter. But, as is written, 'Man proposes, God disposes.'[2] Christ did not suffer His church to be bereft of its ancient and just privileges, but at an appropriate time, by His watchful mercy, He renewed them stronger than before.

At Easter that year one of the nobles of England, Hugh de Mortimer, a powerful man, but more than that, exceedingly able, rich, and vigorous in warfare, estimating the king to be a mere boy, and indignant at his activity, fortified his castles and refused to submit himself and his to the king's orders. When this was announced to the king, he gathered a sizeable force of knights and besieged Hugh in his castle of Bridgnorth. He completely encircled it with a ditch and rampart, and with the situation neatly

cathedral were very likely also preparing to claim an uncustomary freedom from the archbishop. The archbishop and monks had been quarrelling since *c.* 1150. For the affair see Saltman, *Theobald*, pp. 56–64 and no. 37.

[2] Cf. Prov. 16: 9.

interclusit. Abbas autem tempus ut sibi et amicis suis uisum est f. 62v opportunum nactus, regem ibi adiit, et, ut in / tali decet negotio, muneribus suis honorauit, atque super carta sua eidem sermonem intulit. Acceptoque a rege responso super hoc optimo, ad quasdam terras suas iuxta regionem illam sitas ad tempus perendinaturus secessit.[1] Haut multo postmodum tempore rex ipsum Hugonem ad deditionem coegit, mandans per Angliam uniuersam archiepiscopos, episcopos et abbatum plurimos, comites et barones uniuersos, quarto die precedente festum sancti Benedicti estiui temporis ibidem conuenire.[2] Quibus congregatis, pax inter regem et Hugonem facta est.

Tertia die post pacem factam affuit et abbas. Consilio igitur fratris sui Ricardi de Luci et aliorum amicorum suorum, abbas regem in crastinum adiit atque super carta sua illum interpellatus est. Rex cum quibusdam secreti sui consciis consilio communicato, Deo fauente et beato Martino Christi confessore qui nunquam in se sperantes deserit auxiliante, coadiuuantibus etiam terreni consilii patronis, comite scilicet Cornubie Raginaldo, et Ricardo de Humez regis tribuno, qui cum Ricardo de Luci et abbate Waltero amicitie federe coniuncti erant, reddidit rex cartam predictam abbati, et per illum ecclesie de Bello, que est signum corone regie Anglie, eam misit, letantibus omnibus abbatis et ecclesie de f. 63 Bello amicis, inmensoque gaudio tripudian/tibus, inimicis uero eorum undique perfusis merore et confusis. Valedicens igitur regi abbas et gratias agens, a curia cum carta sua recessit, et iuxta statuta dierum itinera ad Bellum reuersus est.[3] Ibique carta coram fratribus eiusdem ecclesie perlecta, exposuit eis omnia que sibi contigerant, gaudentibus omnibus et Deum maximo cordis affectu super hoc glorificantibus.

In sequenti natiuitatis Domini festo tenuit idem excellentissimus rex concilium suum apud Westmonasterium, et dispositis omnibus suis propter quedam negotia sua transnauigauit in Normanniam. In illo eodemque anno, die decollationis sancti Iohannis Baptiste, pro quibusdam causis et negotiis ecclesie de Bello transfretauit abbas mare, iuitque ad regem.[4] Inueniensque

[1] Battle's cell of St. John, Brecon, held land at Berrington, near Tenbury in Herefordshire, a relatively short distance from Bridgnorth.

[2] 7 July 1155. Gervase of Canterbury (RS) i. 162. Will. Newburgh, i. 105. For a reconstruction of Henry's situation and Hugh's calculation about his weakness see Warren, *Henry II*, pp. 57–61. Bridgnorth was a royal castle, held by Hugh, who refused to give it up.

reversed he shut off all hope of Hugh's getting out. To the abbot and his friends this seemed an opportune moment. He went to the king and, as seemed proper in such a matter, showed his respect with gifts, and spoke with him about his charter. He received a handsome response from the king and then withdrew to some lands of his in the area for several days.[1] Shortly thereafter the king forced Hugh to surrender. He sent throughout England to the archbishops, bishops, and many abbots, and to all earls and barons, to come to a meeting on the fourth day before the feast of St. Benedict in summer.[2] When they had assembled, peace was made between the king and Hugh.

On the third day after peace was made, the abbot too arrived. On the advice of his brother Richard de Luci and other friends, the abbot went to the king the next morning and spoke to him about his charter. The king asked the advice of certain confidants. God was propitious and the blessed Martin, confessor of Christ, who never deserts those who have faith in him, lent aid. Patrons too assisted with earthly counsel: namely, Reginald earl of Cornwall and Richard du Hommet, the king's constable, who were both joined to Richard de Luci and Abbot Walter in a pact of friendship. So the king returned the charter to the abbot and through him he sent it to the church of Battle, which is the emblem of the English crown. All the friends of the abbot and the church of Battle were glad and rejoiced greatly, while everywhere their enemies were covered with shame and confusion. The abbot bade the king farewell, gave him thanks, left the court carrying his charter, and returned straight to Battle in full-day stages.[3] Once there he had the charter read carefully to the brothers of the church and he explained to them everything that had happened to him. All rejoiced and from the bottom of their hearts they praised God for it.

The Christmas following, the most excellent king held his council at Westminster and, when all the business was disposed of, he sailed to Normandy about his affairs. In that year, on 29 August, the abbot crossed the sea and sought out the king about some litigation and business of the church of Battle.[4] He found him at

[3] The phrase *iuxta statuta dierum itinera* emphasizes the abbot's deliberate speed. It is also evidence that (for purposes of assembling a host, for example) a particular distance along royal roads could be anticipated, and indeed prescribed, as a day's stage.

[4] Since the chronicler begins the year with Christmas, August 1156 is 'in that year'.

illum apud Salmurum, locutusque cum eo, consilio regine Anglie et Ricardi de Luci fratris sui qui cum rege ibi aderant, omnibus pro uoto rite perfectis, reuersus est in Angliam. Hoc nonnulli ex ecclesiasticis personis Anglie male acceperunt, putantes ipsum abbatem insidiose, quo eos exosos faceret, opera eorum fallacia regi annuntiasse. Verum hoc postmodum patuit omnibus esse falsissimum. Hac de causa episcopus etiam Cicestrie reputans se ipsius abbatis intimatione erga regem non bene acceptum fore,
f. 63v necnon et pro aliis / suis negotiis, circa festum sancti Martini hiemale transiuit ad regem et cum eo moratus est, donec rex reuerteretur in Angliam.[1]

In prima ebdomada Quadragesime sequentis uenerunt duo decani episcopi Cicestrie, Ansgerus scilicet Lewensis, et Thomas Hastingensis, Bellum, adducentes secum quinque presbiteros, locutique cum abbate obtulerunt ei litteras domini pape[a] Adriani, instantes ut responsum eius super his festinato gradu archidiacono Cicestrie Henrico referrent. Abbas autem in secretiori loco litteris inspectis et perlectis, accito priore eiusdem loci et fratribus nonnullis, consilioque communicato in omnibus secundum tenorem litterarum se respondit obediturum, saluo honore ipsius domini pape, et fidelitate simul et honore domini sui regis Anglie, et persone sue, et ordinis sui, saluo etiam iure ecclesie sue. Hoc accepto alia eidem intulerunt, dicentes Iohannem Cicestrensis ecclesie decanum, et Henricum archidiaconum, et Rogerum thesaurarium eiusdem ecclesie, ex parte domini pape, mandando summonuisse, quatinus Cicestriam dominica que est 'Letare Ierusalem'[2] conueniret, ibi auditurus precepta ipsius domini pape; sicque discesserunt. Abbas uero ut semper de Dei, et beate Marie Virginis, necnon et beati Martini confessoris Christi confisus
f. 64 auxilio, cum archiepiscopo Cantuarie et / quibusdam secreti sui consciis consilio communicato, die statuta Cicestriam uenit.

Intransque capitulum ubi omnes congregati fuerant, assurgentibus sibi omnibus et in sede honorifice collocantibus, residentibus quoque circa se uniuersis atque reticentibus, sic demum abbas ora

[a] *The word has been scratched out*

---

[1] Nov. 1156. Hilary stayed with the court until its return in April 1157. R. W. Eyton, *Court, Household and Itinerary of King Henry II* (London, Dorchester, 1878), p. 20. On the basis of our chronicler's statement, Mayr-

Saumur and spoke with him as advised by the queen of England and his brother Richard de Luci, who was with the king there. He achieved everything he wished and returned to England. Now some English ecclesiastics took this badly, thinking that, to discredit them, the abbot had deceitfully denounced their stratagems to the king. But afterwards this was revealed to all to be most false. On its account however the bishop of Chichester thought that after the abbot's intimations to the king he would not be well received. He also had other business of his own, and about the time of the feast of St. Martin in winter he crossed to the king himself and stayed with him until the king's return to England.[1]

In the first week of the following Lent there arrived at Battle two deans of the bishop of Chichester—Ansgar of Lewes and Thomas of Hastings—bringing with them five priests. They spoke with the abbot and showed him a letter of Pope Adrian instructing that they bring his answer to it as soon as possible to Henry, archdeacon of Chichester. The abbot took the letter to a more private room, inspected it, and read it through. He sent for the abbey's prior and several brothers and after consultation with them he replied that he would obey in all respects as the letter required, saving the honour of the lord pope, his fealty to and the honour of his own lord king, his own person, and his order, and saving the rights of his church. Having heard this they brought up other things, saying that John, dean of Chichester, Henry the archdeacon, and Roger the cathedral treasurer had summoned him on the part of the lord pope to appear at Chichester on the Sunday 'Letare Ierusalem',[2] there to hear the pope's commands. Thereupon they left. The abbot, trusting as always in the aid of God and the Blessed Virgin Mary and of the blessed Martin, confessor of Christ, after consultation with the archbishop of Canterbury and some of his confidants, went to Chichester on the day fixed.

On his entrance into the chapter house where all were gathered, everyone rose and seated him honourably. When they had reseated themselves around him and only when their talk had subsided, did

Harting suggests that the letter of John of Salisbury to Bishop Hilary concerning a situation about which the archbishop was worried, referred to the case of Battle abbey which follows. H. Mayr-Harting, 'Hilary, Bishop of Chichester, and Henry II', *EHR*, lxxviii (1963), 223. C. N. L. Brooke dates the letter as ? 1156–7. *Letters of John of Salisbury*, i. 79. The reference to Christ Church in the abbot's charter would certainly be reason enough for the archbishop's concern.

[2] The fourth Sunday in Lent.

resoluit. 'Nuper, domini et fratres,[a] quidam ex uestris ad nos uenientes litteras domini pape[b] nobis pretulerunt, summonentes etiam ex ipsius domini pape[b] auctoritate quatinus huc hac die presenti conueniremus, eiusdem uenerabilis domini audituri precepta. Assumus ob reuerentiam et honorem tante excellentie patris, in omnibus, saluo eiusdem patris honore, et fidelitate simul et honore domini nostri regis Anglie et persone nostre atque ordinis nostri, saluo etiam iure ecclesie nostre, parati eiusdem parere preceptis.'

His eiusdem ecclesie decanus auditis prohibuit ne aliquis ei nisi prius consilio communicato responsum redderet.[1] Conuocansque maioris auctoritatis fratres secreto eorumque usus consilio, rediit, et his abbatem uerbis affatur: 'Nimirum, uenerande domine abbas, ut se res habet, precepto domini pape[b] summonitus huc aduenistis. Nunc igitur restat quatinus nobis litteras domini pape[b] uobis directas ostendatis, ut per illas que nobis precepta sunt ordine
f. 64v competenti / uestre dilectioni pandamus. Eritque [uestrum][c], ratione dictante, his que uobis earum auctoritate obiecta fuerint demisso uultu obedire aut supercilio erecto contraire.'

Abbas uero litteras secum neque detulisse neque quemquam se super hoc conuenisse perhibebat. Tunc quidam ex clericis decano contrascriptum litterarum obtulit, iussusque in auditu omnium perlegit. 'Adrianus episcopus, seruus seruorum Dei, dilecto filio Gauterio abbati de Bello, salutem et apostolicam benedictionem. Recte a suis subditis illi obedientia denegabitur qui suo prelato debitam recusat obedientiam exhibere. Peruenit ad nos quod uenerabili fratri nostro, Y. Cicestrensi episcopo, cui professionem fecisti, debitam obedientiam subtrahas et ipsius contradicas obedire mandatis. Quod quam pernitiosum sit, et omni rationi contrarium, si primi hominis penam ad memoriam reduceres, posses de facili inuenirę. Ideoque per presentia tibi scripta mandamus quatinus ei tanquam episcopo tuo et patri, atque commisse sibi ecclesie, studeas fideliter obedire. Alioquin, scire te uolumus quod sententiam quam in te idem frater noster propter hoc canonice promulgauerit, nos auctore Deo ratam habebimus. Data Rome, apud Sanctum Petrum, kalendis Martii.'[2] /

[a] *Add in marg.*: Nota prudenciam abbatis [b] *The word has been scratched out* [c] *Winterbottom*

---

[1] The dean was John of Greenford, later bishop of Chichester. See H. Mayr-Harting, *The Bishops of Chichester 1075–1207, Biographical Notes and Problems* (Chichester, 1963), pp. 12–14.

[2] P. Jaffé, *Regesta Pontificum Romanorum* . . . eds. W. Wattenbach, S. Loewen-

the abbot begin to speak. 'Lords and brothers', he said, 'a while ago you sent us emissaries. They brought us a letter of the lord pope and they summoned us on the lord pope's authority to come here today to hear the commands of that venerable lord. We are here out of reverence and honour for so excellent a father, prepared to obey all his commands, saving the honour of the holy father, and the fealty and honour of our lord the king of England and of our own person and our order, and saving the rights of our church.'

When he heard this, the dean of the cathedral forbade anyone to reply before there had been a consultation.[1] He called a private meeting of the brothers of greater authority and, having taken their advice, he returned and addressed the abbot. 'To be sure, reverend lord abbot, as the case stands, you have come here at the command of the pope. It now remains for you to show us the letter sent you by the pope, so that by means of it we may explain to your reverence in a proper order the commands sent to us. And it will be as your reason dictates whether you humbly obey what you are charged on their authority, or whether you haughtily resist.'

The abbot asserted that he had not brought the letter with him, and that no one had told him to do so. Then one of the clerks brought the dean the copy of the letter, and at his command read it aloud to all: 'Bishop Adrian, servant of the servants of God, to his beloved son Walter, abbot of Battle, greetings and apostolic blessing. Rightly will obedience be denied by his inferiors to one who refuses to show a due obedience to his own superior. We have been informed that you have withdrawn the obedience you owe to our venerable brother Y., bishop of Chichester, to whom you made profession, and that you object to obeying his mandates. You would quickly realize how pernicious this is and how contrary to all reason if you recalled the punishment of the first man. Therefore by this present letter we command you to apply yourself to obeying him faithfully as your father and bishop, and the church entrusted to him. Otherwise, we would have you know that we will consider valid, with God as warrantor, the sentence canonically pronounced against you for this by our brother. Given in Rome at St. Peter's, 1 March.'[2]

feld, F. Kaltenbrunner (Leipzig, 1885–8), ii, no. 10002. There dated 1 Mar. 1155. This date implies that Bishop Hilary proceeded against the abbot about the time of the Lambeth meeting at which Walter's exemption charter was condemned. Above, p. 158. This was two years before Walter was summoned to Chichester.

f. 65 Epistola perlecta, 'Audistis', inquit decanus, 'domine abbas, quo ordine dominus papa[a] uos hortatur ut prelatis uestris obedientiam exibeatis et quam maxime huic ecclesie Cicestrie et tuo episcopo Hilario. Notare namque decet prudentiam uestram qua de causa dominus papa[a] tuo episcopo interposuit. A fundamentis itaque ecclesia de Bello constructa, primus eidem abbas electus iussa canonum secutus est, atque in hac sancta ecclesia cum professione benedictionem suam canonice consecutus est. Deinde omnes eius substituti, quorum nomina haut in memoriam habemus, cum quibus uos etiam, Waltere, quem hic residere et moderamina illius ecclesie tenere perspicimus, idem fecisse nulli dubium est. Quia uero in aliquibus prudentia uestra a uia obedientie huic ecclesie professe declinauit, postulat hec sancta ecclesia et nos qui huius sancte ecclesie filii sumus quatinus uos ut filius matrem uestram hanc scilicet ecclesiam de uobis certificetis, ut in omnibus, sicut canonicum est, eidem canonicam deinceps obedientiam omni ambiguitate detersa exibeatis. Reuera etenim, reuerende pater, ut optime nouit caritas uestra, canones sacri personam huiusmodi ambiguam aut testibus legalibus, uel sacramentis ecclesiasticis, seu etiam scedula eiusdem corroborata sigillo, sanxerunt/
f. 65v astringi.[1]

'Nempe dominus noster episcopus Hilarius, suscepto huius sancte matris uestre ecclesie regimine, iuxta canonum instituta, uos cum quadam parrochie sue persona alia, semel, iterumque et tertio, sinodum adire apud Cicestriam summonitos nec uenientes, interdixit. Verum persona alia supplici uoce ueniam petens obtinuit, uobis modo in sententia permanente post unius anni curriculum in sinodo sancta uinculum anathematis impositum est, quo uos etiam usque in hodiernum astrictum tenemus. Quamobrem hec sancta ecclesia, uobis ut filio condolens, postulat ut his nunc relictis, nobis fratribus uestris scilicet audientibus, que sibi iure debetis profiteri non differatis. Et quia, ut superius protulimus, uno ex tribus uinculo persona ambigua more ecclesiastico est astringenda, ob honorem et dignitatem ecclesie et persone uestre prouidimus[b] excellentissimum esse et congruum quatinus scedulam paruissimam uestre professionis modum continentem sub quadam renouatione ecclesie huic et nobis perscribatis et sigilli uestri impressione sub quorundam testimonio confirmetis, quo omni deinceps ambiguitate detersa, ecclesia presens ut filium uos diligendo foueat, et in omnibus consilium et auxilium prebeat, sic

[a] *The word has been scratched out* [b] *Add. in marg. in hand of scribe*: mus

When the letter had been read through, the dean said, 'Lord abbot, you have heard the manner in which the pope exhorts you to show obedience to your superiors, above all to this church of Chichester and to Hilary your bishop. It behoves your prudence to note on what provocation the pope has interposed on behalf of your bishop. After the foundation of the church of Battle the first abbot chosen for it followed the commands of the canons: he sought blessing and made his profession in this holy church canonically. We do not clearly recollect the names of all his successors, but there is no doubt that they all did the same, as you did too, Walter, whom we see seated here, abbot of that church. Now in certain respects your prudence has deserted the path of obedience vowed to this church. Therefore this church and we her sons require that, like a son, you show your mother, this church, a guarantee of your canonical obedience henceforward in all matters, and with all doubt wiped away. For truly, reverend father, as your reverence well knows, the holy canons ordain that a person about whom there are doubts of this kind be bound either by lawful witnesses, or by ecclesiastical oaths, or by a charter authenticated by his seal.[1]

'Our lord, Bishop Hilary, upon assuming the governance of this your holy mother church, in accordance with the canons, summoned you and another person of this, his diocese, to attend synod at Chichester. When he had done this three times and you did not come he laid an interdict upon you. The other person humbly sought pardon and obtained it. But you remained obdurate. After a year, the chain of excommunication was fastened upon you in holy synod, and to this day we regard you as so bound. Wherefore this holy church, grieving over you as a son, demands that now you leave your ways and, in the hearing of us, your brothers, no longer delay acknowledging what you owe by right. As we have said, by ecclesiastical usage a dubious person is to be bound by one of three chains. On account of the honour and rank of your church and of your person, we have thought that the best and most fitting plan would be that you should write out for this church and for us, just a very small document, containing the mode of your profession, somewhat rectified, and confirm it before witnesses with the impression of your seal. In that way all future doubt will be wiped out, this church can cherish you as a beloved son, and give you all aid and counsel. There will be peace between us, you will be restored

[1] Gratian, C. 2 q. 8; cf. C. 3 q. 9 c. 3; C. 4 q. 2.

f. 66 itaque pace communicata, gremio sancte ecclesie resti/tutus, hilari cordis affectu redeatis ad propria. Nos uero in his quibus uestra fraternitas erga uenerabilem nostrum episcopum Hilarium deliquisse cognoscitur, mediatores interpositi indignationem illius erga uos et iram pace coniuncta dei annuente gratia sedabimus. Prouideat igitur dilectio uestra quatinus tam magne auctoritatis atque nobilitatis persona perfectarum scientiarum utatur consilio, nobisque modesto super his atque accepto sermone respondeat. Neque in dubio sit, quin eloquiis dulcissimis a uobis propalatis humilitas nostra benigne faueat, ampullosis uero et sesquipedalibus uiriliter contradicat, quamuis ingenuam uestri generis magnanimitatem non superbie tipo extolli sed patientie atque rationis uirtute sciamus deuinci.'[1]

His itaque huiuscemodi sermone a decano habitis, omnibus hoc iustum fore atque his se fauere acclamantibus, tandem silentio imposito abbas hoc modo et hac ratione responsionem obiectis subintulit. 'Orationis uestre, patres dilectissimi, oppositam propositionem dulci sermone prolatam in secreto cordis mei perpendens cubili, magnifice libertatis famosique nominis ecclesie de Bello occurrit excellentia, animumque per diuersa nutantem nimium
f. 66v perturbat / horum improuidentia. Namque uobis ut patribus et fratribus dulcissimis affatu digno et dulcifluo respondere paraui, et omnimodis uestre satisfacere caritati. Verum inopinatis stupefactus sermonibus de alio cogor transire ad aliud, uerens tamen ne modum excedere cogat respondendi necessitas. Neque ut quidam gladium melle litum proferam,[2] sed uerissimis innixus assertionibus, uobis satisfaciam. Sepenumero enim fama diuulgante quam maxima celsitudo libertatis et dignitatis Bellensis ecclesie a magnifico rege Willelmo constructe extiterit, optime nouit caritas uestra. Quod si de primo eiusdem loci abbate Gausberto nomine agere uoluerit dilectio uestra, haut incognitum habemus eundem in eadem ecclesia de Bello auctoritate et dignitate regia, simulque Lanfranci Cantuariensis archiepiscopi assensu, a Stigando huius ecclesie tunc antistite benedictionem suam absque professione consecutum. Henricus eius substitutus, et alii successores eius predecessores

[1] This may refer to his family or to his Norman origins. Walter had been born and brought up in Normandy. Even earlier, the distinction could be made among the Anglo-Normans, between themselves and men of Norman *gens*. Downer, *Leges Henrici Primi*, pp. 43–4.

to the bosom of Holy Church and can return to your abbey without anxiety in your heart. Concerning incidents in which you are known to have failed in your brotherly duty towards our venerable lord Bishop Hilary we shall act as mediators. God willing we shall moderate his anger against you and make peace between you. Let your reverence realize that a person of your great authority, nobility, and most polished learning should accept advice, and give us a modest and satisfactory answer. Be in no doubt that our humility will listen with favour and kindliness to soft speech from you, but we will manfully refute everything polysyllabic and bombastic. Still, we know that the natural high-mindedness of your people is not given to vain shows of pride, but bows before the force of patience and reason.'[1]

When the dean finished speaking to this effect, everyone acclaimed it as just, and said that they agreed. At length they were brought to order and the abbot answered the charges. 'Dearest fathers, your argument against me was couched in honeyed words. Yet as I pondered it in the recesses of my heart, the splendour of the great liberty and of the famous name of the church of Battle rose before me. I had not foreseen this attack and it disturbs beyond measure a soul faltering beneath its divers burdens. For I was prepared to answer you fittingly and gently as my dearest fathers and brothers, and to satisfy your reverences completely. Stunned by these unexpected words, I am forced to change the manner of my approach, though I fear that the necessity of replying will force me to overstep. Still, unlike some I shall not hold out a sword smeared with honey;[2] I shall hope to satisfy you with plain truth. Since it is famous, your charity is well acquainted with the exceedingly extensive liberty and privileges of Battle, a church built by the great King William. Would your reverence like to look at the case of Gausbert, first abbot of the abbey? We understand that the fact is well known, that Stigand, then bishop of Chichester, blessed him without profession, in Battle church, by royal authority and privilege, and with the assent of Lanfranc, archbishop of Canterbury. If it can be proved that his successor Henry and my other predecessors acted

[2] A knightly variant of the proverb, 'Beware of honey that must be licked from a thorn.' Other variants use the nettle, but as far as I am aware, this is the only known use of the sword. Richard Morris, *Old English Homilies of the Twelfth and Thirteenth Centuries*, EETS, xxxiv (London, 1868), 185. Cf. *Hali Meidenhad*, EETS, xviii (London, 1866), p. 9.

mei, si quid contra libertatem et dignitatem eiusdem ecclesie, [aliter] ac iustum foret, egisse probantur, nichil mea interest. Ego uero minimus omnium nil contra iura et dignitates ecclesie nostre, sed
f. 67 saluo iure eiusdem ecclesie et dignitate omnia / peregisse me recolo. Si uero in aliquibus contra ius et dignitatem ecclesie eiusdem aut ignorantia aut animo festinato deliqui, licet mihi male acta in melius equitatis ratione dictante reformare. "Prudentis est enim", ut quidam ait, "in aduersis lapsum corrigere, in prosperis moderationem tenere."[1] Vnde et ego in negotiis ecclesie nostre moderationem et discretionis modum[a] ubique tenens, in melius si qua a me uel a predecessoribus meis contra eandem ecclesiam acta sunt reformare satagam. Verum si quid contra ecclesiam hanc conuictus a quoquam deliquisse extiterim, omnimodis, saluo ut supradiximus honore domini pape,[b] et honore atque fidelitate domini nostri regis Anglie, et persone nostre et ordinis nostri, saluo etiam iure ecclesie nostre, quo debeam et quo ordine satisfaciam. Vinculo anathematis me constrictum a uenerabili episcopo uestro asseritis. Hoc itaque nec per episcopum uestrum neque per aliquem alium mihi hucusque insinuatum esse probatur. Quod si hoc ueritati innititur, miror prudentiam tante discretionis uiri, miror etiam in hoc sententiam eiusdem tam precipitem, cum nil contra predictarum statuta ecclesiarum egisse me a quoquam probari possibile sit. Quod si quis contra hoc ausu temerario niti uoluerit, procedat in publicum, dicat, audiat, sicque res omni dubio remoto limitem ueritatis attingat.'/

f. 67v Nullo igitur ex assistentibus rationem contra reddente, sed omnibus simul reclamantibus, abbas orationem suam prosequitur: 'Scedulam quam uobis perscribendam exigitis neque domini pape[b] litteris hoc nobis designatum constat, nec ratio nobis aliqua ut perscribatur occurrit. Quia uero ratione dictante paceque dilectionis uestre omnia concludi uellem, rogo quatinus inducie nobis dentur, quo dominum nostrum regem in transmarinis constitutum partibus, cuius capella dominica et signum corone regie ecclesia nostra esse dinoscitur, adire possimus, eius preceptum super hoc audituri, simulque consilio ipsius episcopi Hilarii, cui dominus papa,[b] non uobis, ut debitam exibeamus obedientiam precepit, uti liceat, ut omnia sano consilio compleantur. Neque enim ea que

[a] *Winterbottom. MS*: nodum [b] *The word is scratched out*

[1] 'Hegesippus', *de Bello Judaico*, iv. 2. *Hegesippi qui dicitur Historiae Libri V*,

otherwise than justly against the rights and privileges of our church, it is of no matter to me. I, the least of them all, consider that I have in no way acted against the rights and privileges of our church, for in everything I have specified "saving the rights and privileges of the church". If out of ignorance or impetuousness I have in any way acted against the rights and privileges of that church, it is my right to reform what was ill done. For as the saying goes, "in misfortune the wise man corrects his mistake; in prosperity he holds to moderation".[1] Wherefore I too, ever upholding moderation and discretion in my abbey's affairs, should busy myself to reform any acts done by myself or my predecessors against this church's interests. If I should be proved guilty of any failure in duty towards this cathedral, let me amend it properly, saving, as I have said, the honour of the lord pope, the honour and fealty of my lord the king of England, myself and my order, and saving the rights of my church. You assert that your venerable bishop bound me with the chain of excommunication. But you do not demonstrate that I have been notified about it either by your bishop or by anyone else up to now. If this is the case, I wonder at the good sense of a man so discreet. Indeed I wonder at a decision so precipitate, for it is impossible for anyone to demonstrate that I have acted contrary to the statutes of the aforesaid churches in any way. Should anyone have the audacity to wish to disprove this, let him come forward. Let him speak and listen, and in this way the whole truth can come out, without any shadow of doubt.'

None of those sitting round made any reasoned answer. Everyone was objecting at the same time. So the abbot continued his oration. 'As to your demand for a written document, this does not accord with the instructions in the letter of the lord pope to me, nor does any reason for writing one occur to me. Since I should wish everything to be concluded reasonably and to your reverence's satisfaction, I pray that a delay be granted me to go to our lord king across the sea, for my church is known to be his demesne chapel and the emblem of the royal crown. I would hear his command concerning this, and at the same time would take counsel with Bishop Hilary, to whom, and not to you, the lord pope commanded that I show due obedience. With their sound advice

ed. V. Ussani, *Corpus Scriptorum Ecclesiasticorum Latinorum*, lxvi (Vienna, 1932), 241.

uobis et ecclesie huic a nobis persolui debentur pessumdari cupio, nec nostram ex libera ancillam effici preopto. Dominus etiam rex ne super his absque eiusdem permissione quicquam ausu temerario aggredi temptaremus prohibere curauit.'

Omnibus igitur inducias dare abnuentibus, quibusdam uero asserentibus dominum regem quatinus ecclesia de Bello Cicestrensi ecclesie ius debitum persolueret illis audientibus precepisse, et iccirco inducias dare minime debere, res diutius protracta fine potiri nequiuit. Abbas uero in hoc ut sibi inducias darent quo
f. 68 regem super illud conueniret / perstitit, simulque commemorabat se de his absque consilio et licentia fratrum suorum monachorum de Bello quicquam minime acturum fore. Dicebat enim se mortalem esse et moriturum, ecclesiam uero de Bello se defuncto permansuram, ideoque[a] absque eiusdem consilio et licentia se nil acturum, inducias dari fore necessarium.

Illis autem multis modis contradicentibus multisque sententiis hoc etiam diiudicantibus, abbate in sententia induciarum dandarum persistente, decanus silentio imposito abbatem ita conuenit. 'Domine', inquit, 'abbas, congregatio hec scedulam a uobis propter ambiguitatem superius uobis indictam perscribi et in ecclesia hac in memoriam conseruandam exigit, quo, omni deinceps ambiguitate detersa, huic sancte ecclesie que iure a uestra fraternitate et a successoribus uestris debentur impendantur. Nos itaque ecclesia sumus, episcopo decedente permanebimus, et hac de causa hoc a uobis exigimus.'

Abbate ergo renitente nec eisdem assentiente, cum diu persisterent nec quicquam proficerent, decanus abbatem fixo in sententia sua persistere gradu, simul etiam in nil proficiendo diem ex maxima expensum parte perspiciens, tandem murmure sedato, his uerbis conclusit: 'Dominus', inquit, 'noster, episcopus noster,
f. 68ᵛ pastor noster, pater noster Hilarius, / persona litteris et moribus egregia, honesta, religiosa, nobis discipulis suis tanquam filiis hanc formam uerborum, mare transiens, tradidit, hac forma instruxit, premuniuit, precepit, quatinus uos, reuerende pater et abbas, hac aggrederemur, circumueniremus, quo nobis et ecclesie huic scedulam quam a uestra paternitate exigimus perscriberetis. Nos uero, ut tanti patris decet filios, preceptis insistentes, hoc a uobis exigimus. Quia igitur uestre non placet Minerue ut nobis quod exigimus perficiatur, nos hoc in medium relinquimus, et patri

[a] *Interlined in same hand*: que

everything may be settled. I do not wish to abrogate what is due to you and this church from me. But neither do I desire that my church be reduced to slavery from freedom. And our lord king has expressly forbidden me to meddle rashly in these matters without his permission.'

They were all unwilling to allow the delay. Some of them even claimed to have heard the lord king command the church of Battle to pay its rightful due to the church of Chichester: for that reason they ought not grant a delay, but settle the protracted dispute. But the abbot insisted that they give him the delay to consult the king about the matter, and he reminded them too that he would do nothing in the affair without the counsel and permission of his brothers the monks of Battle. For, he said, he was mortal and would die, but the church of Battle would be there when he was gone. Therefore he would not act without its counsel and permission, and it was necessary that delay be granted.

They offered many arguments against this, and offered many judgements upon it, but the abbot held to his determination that he be given a delay. The dean called for silence therefore, and addressed the abbot thus, 'Lord abbot, because (as was charged) your words are not to be relied upon, this congregation demands that you have a document written, to be preserved henceforth as unambiguous evidence in this church, so that what you and your successors owe this church by right will be paid. We are the church. We will remain after the bishop has gone. That is why we demand this of you.'

But the abbot would not be persuaded, though they persisted long and profitlessly. At last the dean, seeing that the abbot was unmovable and that a large part of the day had been spent without achieving anything, called for silence again and summed up with these words, 'Our lord, our bishop, our shepherd, our father Hilary, a man famous for his life and learning, a man honourable and scrupulous, entrusted to us his disciples, as to his sons, this form of words when he went overseas. He equipped and fortified us with this formula, commanding us to use it to attach and catch you, reverend father and abbot, so that you would have to write out for us and our church the document we demand of you. We remain faithful to his commands, as becomes the sons of such a father, and we demand it of you. But since it displeases your wisdom to comply with our demand, we will leave the matter unfinished. We

nostro omnia litteris nostris et nuntio renuntiabimus, expectantes super hoc eius rescriptionem.'

Hoc dicto, singulis dissono, non absque strepitu, murmure hinc mussitantibus, excutiuntur sedibus, sicque[a] soluta concione suis quique agendis operam accommodauere. Abbas coram altare sancte Trinitatis ibidem facta oratione et sancte Crucis munitus signaculo cum suis ad propria reuersus est. Reputans igitur et in se abbas recogitans[b] quod de his nisi regali determinatione finis non haberetur, per nuntium omnia Ricardo de Luci fratri suo exposuit. Qui omnia ut acceperat, regi intimare curauit. Rex uero accito episcopo precepit quatinus abbatem de Bello ut suum capellanum in pace ab omnibus querelis esse permitteret, donec in Angliam
f. 69 rediret. / Factum est autem.

Post Pascha citato gradu rex ad mare properans nauemque ascendens, flante austro secundo, in portu Hamtonie appulit indeque uersus Lundoniam iter arripuit. Quod abbas cum accepisset, paratis que necessaria erant, eidem apud quoddam castrum fratris sui Ricardi de Luci in Essexia situm, Angra nomine, occurrit.[1] Congratulantibus itaque ad inuicem, quod Deo fauente prospere rex reuersus extiterat, inter multam confabulationem rex eidem precepit abbati quatinus die Pentecostes proximi apud sanctum Edmundum ubi tunc corona sua regia insigniri debebat, ita premunitus et instructus his que sibi forent necessaria ueniret, ut quod sibi et ecclesie sue iustum foret, contra episcopum Cicestrie Hilarium cui etiam ibidem super his tunc terminum prefixerat, ratione dictante, dirationare preualuisset. Hoc audito abbas ad quoddam manerium suum haud longe a predicto castro situm secessit, Hou nomine, opperiens ibi diem sibi prescriptum./

f. 69v Anno igitur ab incarnatione dominica m c lvii°, anno scilicet iii° regni Henrici predicti regis iunioris, Henrici magni ex filia nepotis, mense ii° ex quo de transmarinis partibus, ubi anno precedente transierat, idem rex repatriauit et quo exercitum duxit in Waliam, die Pentecosten quem tunc die festi sancti Dunstani anni reuolutio in orbem celebrandum reduxerat, idem memorandus princeps apud sanctum Edmundum diademate insignitus regali, multis ibidem conuenientibus, archiepiscopo scilicet Cantuarie,

[a] sedibus sicque: *Written in the same hand in left-hand margin properly aligned with text.* Singulis . . . accommodauere *in ink different from rest of f*
[b] cogitans: *Written in the same hand in left-hand margin properly aligned with text*

shall report everything to our father by letter and messenger, and shall await his answer.'

When he had finished, they were all obliged to rise, but they whispered about it in a confused murmur that rose to a din. Still, the assembly broke up and everyone went back to minding his own business. The abbot prayed there before the altar of the Holy Trinity, armed himself by the sign of the holy cross, and returned home with his retinue. Thinking the matter over and reflecting privately that the affair would never end except by a royal decision, the abbot sent a messenger to explain it all to his brother Richard de Luci. Immediately Richard heard of the whole affair, he let the king know about it. The king called the bishop to him and ordered that the abbot of Battle, as his own chaplain, should be left in peace from all complaints until he himself returned to England. This was done.

After Easter the king galloped to the coast, took ship, and with a following southerly wind soon landed at Southampton and from there went to London. When the abbot heard the news, he prepared what was necessary and joined the king at Ongar, a castle of his brother Richard de Luci, in Essex.[1] They greeted one another, rejoicing that with God's blessing the king had had a prosperous home-coming. In the course of a long conversation the king commanded the abbot to come on Pentecost next to St. Edmund's, where he would hold a crown-wearing. The abbot was to be fortified and provided with the necessary evidence to establish a title to a just and reasonable claim for himself and his church in relation to Hilary, bishop of Chichester, to whom he had also assigned a hearing then. The abbot listened and then went to Hutton, a manor of his not far from the castle, to await the prescribed day.

In 1157, in the third year of the reign of King Henry the Younger, daughter's son to the great Henry, in the second month after his return from across the sea where he had gone in the preceding year, and in the year during which he led an army into Wales, on the day of Pentecost, which that year fell on the feast of St. Dunstan, that memorable prince wore his royal crown at St. Edmund's, before a great multitude—the archbishop of Canterbury,

[1] Chipping Ongar, the *caput* of Richard's honour, granted him by Henry in 1153–4, only a few years earlier. J. H. Round, 'The Honour of Ongar', *Transactions of the Essex Archaeological Society*, N.S. vii (1900) 142–52.

episcopis, abbatibus, comitibus, baronibus, et populi multitudine, diem ut decebat festiue transegit.[1] Inter hos igitur uenerabiles etiam, ut predictum est, Hilarius Cicestrensis episcopus et Walterus abbas de Bello propter controuersiam predictam libertatum et dignitatum ecclesiarum suarum diu inter illos habitam sedandam ab eodem magnifico principe, dato eis ibidem die peremptorio, conuocati sunt. Quia uero rex aliis ibidem occupatus negotiis illorum causam tunc determinare nequiuit, terminum eis apud Colecestriam prefixit, quia illuc a sancto Edmundo recedens uenturus erat. Die Iouis proximo, omnes ibidem et etiam numero plures adueniunt.

In crastinum, die scilicet Veneris, abbas cum Ricardo de Luci fratre suo regem adiit, iussusque a rege in capitulum monachorum/
f. 70 ibidem Deo seruientium secessit, expectans eius aduentum. Rex uero missa audita capitulum intrauit, precipiens ut nullus nisi quem ipse uocaret ex nomine ingrederetur. Acciuit itaque Thomam cancellarium; comitem Legacestrie, Rotbertum; Ricardum de Humez, tribunum; Ricardum de Luci; Warinum filium Geroldi; Nicholaum de Sigillo. Affuit cum eis quidam in arte medicine peritus, Radulfus nomine. Affuit et Henricus de Essexia regis tribunus, iam ante a rege ad abbatem in capitulum missus.[2] Superuenit etiam frater eiusdem regis iunior Willelmus nomine, et cum aliis iuxta illum resedit.[3]

His itaque ibi cum domino rege residentibus, abbate etiam cum tribus monachis suis considente, Ricardus de Luci ita exorsus est: 'Domine mi rex, uestra summonuisse dignata est excellentia quatinus abbas de Bello frater meus huc ueniret, ut querela inter illum et Cicestrensem episcopum de dignitatibus et libertatibus ecclesiarum suarum diu habita coram uobis fine potiretur. Adest abbas cum cartis et priuilegiis suis.'

Tunc iussit rex abbati cartas ecclesie sue palam proferre. Legit

[1] On 19 May 1157 Henry held a council at Bury St. Edmunds at which probably the main business was dealing with the instability in the eastern counties. Robert de Torigny, ed. R. Howlett, *Chronicles of the Reigns of Stephen, Henry II and Richard I* (RS), iv. 192–3. Warren, *Henry II*, pp. 67–8.

[2] A group of Henry II's important household administrators. Thomas Becket was chancellor after Jan. 1155. Robert, earl of Leicester (1120–90) was justiciar, with Richard de Luci. For his career see West, *Justiciar*, pp. 35–7. Warin

bishops, abbots, earls, barons, and a crowd of common people—and, as was fitting, spent the day in festival.[1] Now among the rest, as we have said, the worshipful Hilary, bishop of Chichester, and the worshipful Walter, abbot of Battle, were assigned a day by that splendid prince's peremptory summons for the settlement of their old controversy over the privileges and dignities of their churches. Because he was occupied with other affairs, it was impossible for him to settle their case then, but he arranged for their appearance at Colchester, to which he would be going when he left St. Edmund's. The following Thursday, all and even a larger number, arrived there.

The next day, Friday, the abbot went to the king accompanied by his brother Richard de Luci. At the king's command he withdrew into the chapter house of the monks serving God there, to wait for him. As soon as he had heard mass, the king came along, commanding that no one should enter except anyone he called by name. He sent for Thomas the chancellor, Robert, earl of Leicester, the constable Richard du Hommet, Richard de Luci, Warin fitzGerold and Nicholas de Sigillo. With them was one skilled in the art of medicine, Ralph by name, and also Henry of Essex, the king's constable, whom the king had sent beforehand to the abbot in the chapter house.[2] The king's younger brother William also came and sat beside him among the others.[3]

When all had been seated there with the lord king, and the abbot and three of his monks were seated with them too, Richard de Luci began thus, 'My lord king, your excellency has deigned to summon here my brother, the abbot of Battle, so that the protracted quarrel between him and the bishop of Chichester over the privileges and exemptions of their churches may be settled before you. The abbot is here with his charters of exemption.'

Then the king commanded the abbot to show publicly the charters of his church. Thomas the chancellor read the charter of

fitzGerold's activities both in the household and at the Exchequer are prominent in the early pipe-rolls. He was the king's chamberlain until his retirement in 1158. J. E. A. Jolliffe, *Angevin Kingship* (London, 1955), pp. 143, 233. For Henry of Essex see below, p. 190, n. 1. Ralph de Beaumont (d. 1170) was a physician in the royal household, and is regularly mentioned in the pipe-rolls as a holder of royal land in Northamptonshire. *Gesta Henrici Secundi* (RS), i. 4. Cf. J. Lally, 'Court and Household of King Henry II' (Liverpool Ph.D., 1969), pp. 336–7. Nicholas is probably Nicholas de Hampton, keeper of the seal. *Regesta*, iii, p. xi.

[3] The third son of the Empress Matilda and Geoffrey of Anjou, born in August 1136.

itaque Thomas cancellarius cartam regis Willelmi magni coram illis.[1] Qua perlecta, rex in manus eandem accipiens, atque undique circumspiciens, magno extollere dignatus est fauore, benedicens f. 70v animé illius / regis incliti qui affectu tam magnifico ecclesiam illam a se constructam dilexit, et eam tam magnis libertatibus et dignitatibus premuniuit. Iterum legit cancellarius aliam eiusdem regis Willelmi cartam super negotio abbatis proprio.[2] Quam similiter rex in manus accipiens atque circumspiciens, iussit eam cum aliis diligenter reponi et magna diligentia custodiri. Contestabatur etiam quod si quandoque Deo inspirante abbatiam fundaret, nullius nisi Bellensis ecclesie libertates et dignitates sue prescribi ecclesie. Aliorum etiam regum, Willelmi scilicet regis iunioris, et Henrici regis cartis, et carta simul suo confirmata sigillo inspectis,[3] iussit simili modo reponi et diligenti custodia seruari.

Tunc cancellarius abbatem intuens, 'Domine', inquit, 'abbas, episcopus Cicestrensis ratione, ut multis uidetur, contra uos utitur premaxima, obiciens uos in ecclesia Cicestrie professionem fecisse. Quocirca uestre dilectioni prouidendum est.' Abbas uero se nil contra dignitatem et libertatem ecclesie sue egisse testatus est. Rex autem cancellarium respiciens, 'Professio', ait, 'non est contra dignitates ecclesiarum. Non enim qui professionem faciunt nisi quod debent promittunt.'

Ricardus de Luci hec audiens iterum sic cepit. 'Domine, celsitudo uestra libertates audiuit et dignitates a nobili rege Willelmo / f. 71 ecclesie sue quam cognominauit[a] de Bello eo quod ibi Deus uictoriam sibi de inimicis suis contulit traditas, quas etiam ecclesia eadem que est capella uestra et signum regie corone uestre hucusque inuiolabili iure seruauit. Magna itaque dignitate ecclesia illa a uobis et a nobis omnibus Normannis, dico, extollenda est, quia ibi ille nobilissimus rex Willelmus Dei gratia parentumque nostrorum adquisiuit auxilio, unde uos, domine rex, coronam regni Anglici hoc tempore iure hereditario possidetis nosque omnes opulentia maxima ditati sumus. Rogamus igitur clementiam uestram quatinus predictam ecclesiam cum dignitatibus et libertatibus suis

[a] cognomina: *Written above line in a similar hand, perhaps copying the letters*

[1] Almost certainly BL Add. Ch. 70980, forged to answer the objection of the bishop to the earlier forgery, that it had not the attestation of a bishop of Chichester. See above, p. 158, and below, pp. 196–8, where the bishop declared that this was a charter he had never heard of. Searle, *EHR*, lxxxiii (1968), 458–9. The charter is printed there, pp. 473–4.

the great King William before them.[1] When he had finished, the king took it in his hand and looked it over thoroughly. He deigned to approve it highly, praising the spirit of the famous king who lavished such affection upon the church built by himself, and who fortified it with such great liberties and privileges. Next the chancellor read another charter of King William's concerning the abbot's private affairs.[2] The king took this too in his hand and examined it, and ordered it to be put back carefully with the others and to be looked after with great care. He even swore that if he were ever inspired by God to found an abbey, he would have for it none but the liberties and privileges of Battle abbey. He also inspected the charters of other kings: of King William the Younger and of King Henry, and at the same time the charter confirmed by his own seal.[3] He ordered them to be similarly replaced and kept carefully.

Then the chancellor, turning to the abbot, said, 'Lord abbot, the bishop of Chichester has brought a powerful argument, as it seems to many, against you, pointing out that you made profession in the church of Chichester. Your worship must therefore answer this.' The abbot declared that he had done nothing against the privileges and exemption of his church. The king looked at the chancellor and said, 'Profession is not against the privileges of churches. For those who make profession do not promise anything beyond what they ought.'

Hearing this, Richard de Luci began again, 'Lord, your highness has heard the exemptions and privileges given by the noble King William to his church which he named Battle because there God gave him the victory over his enemies. Up to the very present this church—your chapel and emblem of your royal crown—has preserved these by inviolable right. I say that this church should be elevated to the highest rank by you and by all us Normans. For there the most noble King William, by God's grace, and with the aid of our kin, won that by which you hold the crown of England at this very moment in hereditary right, and by which we all have been enriched with great wealth. We therefore pray your clemency to protect this church and its privileges and exemptions with the

[2] This cannot be positively identified. BL Add. Ch. 70980 has a personal privilege. But a later, interpolated version, *Regesta*, i, no. 262, may be what is referred to.

[3] BL Harl. Ch. 83 A 12, which Thomas Becket was to have kept in his custody after the inconclusive hearing at Lambeth several years earlier. Above, p. 158.

uestre auctoritatis dextera protegat, et eam omnino cum suis omnibus sicut semper in antecessorum uestrorum fuisse temporibus dinoscitur liberam esse precipiat. Quod si uestre hoc non placet auctoritati, uoce peto supplici quatinus abbatem, fratrem meum scilicet, a loco amoueatis, ne illius tempore, que ecclesia predicta antecessorum suorum tempore inuiolabili iure uisa est possedisse, lugeat se[a] amisisse.'

His comite Rotberto Legacestrie atque etiam ut rex eandem ecclesiam sicut suam coronam et parentum eorumdem adquisitionem seruaret cum aliis conclamante, rex affirmabat se nullo modo
f. 71v his animum suum prebere, quo predicta ecclesia / libertates et dignitates suas suis temporibus uideretur perdidisse, se cum episcopo locuturum, et omnia in pace dispositurum. Sic igitur surgens ad alia negotia sua tetendit perficienda.

Die itaque Martis post octauas Pentecostes rex mane capitulum monachorum intrauit, comitantibus secum archiepiscopis Teodbaldo Cantuariensi, Rogero Eboracensi, episcopis etiam Ricardo Lundonensi, Rotberto Exoniensi, Rotberto Lincolniensi, abbatibus Siluestro ecclesie sancti Augustini Cantuarie, Gausfrido Holmensi;[1] Thoma cancellario regis, comitibus etiam Rotberto Legacestrie, Patricio Saresberie; baronibus etiam nonnullis, Henrico de Essexia, Raginaldo de Warenna, Ricardo de Luci, Warino filio Geroldi, aliisque nonnullis, populique insuper multitudine non modica. Assunt etiam et episcopus Cicestrensis Hilarius, abbasque Bellensis Walterus. Ventilato igitur negotio ibidem quod inter uenerabilem Theodbaldum Cantuariensem archiepiscopum et Siluestrum ecclesie sancti Augustini que sita est extra muros civitatis Cantuarie abbatem erat, de professione scilicet eiusdem abbatis ecclesie Christi Cantuarie facienda,[2] reticentibus omnibus, Ricardus de Luci surgens et in medio stans, omnibus intenta aure audientibus, regem his uerbis alloquitur.

'A magnifica excellentie uestre gloria, domine mi[b] rex, uirtuti cuius fortuna coniuncta est, uenerabili fratri meo Waltero rectori
f. 72 ecclesie uestre de Bello, in / huius loci consistorio, contra reuerende auctoritatis episcopum Cicestrie Hilarium pro dignitatum et libertatum ecclesiarum suarum controuersia sedanda diu inter illos

[a] Se *interlined after* lugeat *in same hand* [b] *Originally* mro, *probably an error for* nostro. *The* o *has been erased and the* r *turned into a long* i, *an unusual letter for the scribe to use*

hand of your authority and to command that it, with all its possessions, be free, just as always in the times of your predecessors it is known to have been free. If it does not please your authority to do so, I humbly pray that you remove the abbot my brother from office, so that the church may not have the grief of having lost in his time what it is known to have possessed as an inviolable right in the days of his predecessors.'

At this Robert, earl of Leicester, and others began calling out that the king should preserve that church as if it were his own crown, and the property won by their kinsmen. The king vowed that he would in no way lend himself to anything by which the church might be seen to have lost its exemptions in his time. He would speak with the bishop and settle everything peacefully. With this he rose and strode out to settle other business.

On Tuesday after the octave of Pentecost, in the morning, the king entered the monks' chapter house, accompanied by the archbishops, Theobald of Canterbury and Roger of York; the bishops Richard of London, Robert of Exeter, Robert of Lincoln; the abbots Silvester of St. Augustine's, Canterbury, 'Geoffrey' of Hulme,[1] Thomas, the king's chancellor; the earls Robert of Leicester, and Patrick of Salisbury. There were barons as well: Henry of Essex, Reginald de Warenne, Richard de Luci, Warin fitz-Gerold and several others, and a large number of ordinary people besides. Hilary, bishop of Chichester, and Walter, abbot of Battle, were also present. First a case was aired there between the venerable Theobald, archbishop of Canterbury and Silvester, abbot of St. Augustine's church outside the walls of Canterbury, concerning the abbot's profession to Christ Church, Canterbury.[2] Afterwards, when silence had fallen, Richard de Luci rose and walked to the centre of the room. Everyone listened intently as he addressed the king thus.

'My lord king, in whom fortune matched herself with virtue! The splendid glory of your excellence has set today, in this court, for my worshipful brother Walter, ruler of your church of Battle, to appear against Hilary, bishop of Chichester, of holy authority, in a settlement of their long-protracted disagreement over the

[1] *Recte* William. See *Heads*, p. 68.

[2] Bishop Hilary acted as one of the mediators in the dispute between the archbishop and Abbot Silvester. The charter is dated 11 July 1157. Mayr-Harting, *Acta*, pp. 88–9.

habita hodierna lux adueniendi constituta est. Iussis itaque uestris obtemperans in presentia adest uestra, in omnibus saluo honore uestro et iure ecclesie uestre sibi commisse si quis eidem quicquam obicere uoluerit paratus satisfacere. Verum illa ecclesia uestra de Bello a nobilissimo rege Willelmo ob uictoriam a Deo in eodem loco in inimicis suis sibi prestitam a fundamentis edificata, magnis est dignitatibus atque libertatibus premunita, quas usque hodie intemerato iure tenuisse comprobatur. Magnificis igitur a uobis, domine rex, et a nobis omnibus Normannis scilicet ecclesia illa extollenda est preconiis, quia ibidem inclitus rex ille Willelmus, nutu Dei consilioque et auxilio parentum nostrorum, inimicos suos regnum Anglie et coronam iniuste ab eodem auferre conantes deuicit, sibique et successoribus suis regnum coronamque Anglie adquisiuit; ex cuius consanguinitatis propinquitate iure hereditario uos in eiusdem solio omnis regni[a] populus nunc regnare congaudet, nosque eiusdem collati beneficii dono, et ex parentum nostrorum successione, possessionum et diuitiarum copiam possidemus. Quo-
f. 72v circa domine, regum excellentissime, / omnis hec Normannorum nobilium uotis supplicat intimis coadunatio quatinus locum illum ut uestri et nostri signum triumphi in propria dignitate et libertate contra omnes sibi aduersantes, et quammaxime aduersus Anglorum insidias, uestra regalis protegat seueritas, ut nullus eidem nocendi pateat introitus.

'Si quidem uestre placitum hoc non fuerit uoluntati, iubeat fratrem meum loci illius abbatem illis parcere locis, atque amici alterius futuri cedere loco. Satius enim est illum, amisso pastoralis cure officio, priuatum monachum et pauperem uitam libere transcurrisse, quam celsa sede residentem, et quorundam calliditate iugo indebito seruitutis oppressum, libertates et dignitates predicte ecclesie hactenus a predecessoribus suis intemerate predecessorum uestrorum auctoritate conseruatas, ut signi regie corone uestre et adquisitionis sue, omnis Normannorum nobilitas eiusdem temporibus lugeat amisisse.'[b]

His dictis, eo residente, abbas surrexit atque his uerbis locutus est: 'Domine mi, sicut Ricardus frater meus hic patenti ratione ostendit, huc iussu uestro adueni. Si quis quicquam contra nos uel contra dignitates et libertates ecclesie de Bello opponere uoluerit, uestro consilio, cuius ecclesia predicta dominica capella est et

[a] *Winterbottom. MS. adds* regni *before* solio [b] *Winterbottom. MS.* lugeat se amisisse. Se *is interlined by same hand*

privileges and liberties of their churches. He comes into your presence obedient to your commands and prepared to make satisfaction in every way to any who would reproach him, saving your honour and the rights of your church, which is entrusted to him. This your church of Battle, built from its foundations by the most noble King William in commemoration of the victory over his enemies given him there by God, was fortified with great privileges and liberties. These are acknowledged to have been held inviolate until today. This church should be famously praised by you, lord king, and by all us Normans, for it was there that the famous King William, by the will of God, and by the aid and counsel of our kinsmen, defeated his enemies who had thought to steal his realm of England and his crown. There he acquired realm and crown for himself and for his successors. By the closeness of your relationship, through right of inheritance, the whole people of this realm rejoice that you now reign from his throne. As for us, it is by virtue of gifts conferred by William, and by succeeding to our kin, that we possess great estates and riches. Wherefore, my lord, most excellent of kings, all this gathering of Norman nobles asks with fervent prayers that your royal severity maintain that abbey, as the emblem of your and our triumph, in its proper privileges and exemptions against all its enemies, and above all against the stratagems of the English! Let there be no breach in its defences!

'But if this is not in accordance with your will, order my brother its abbot to leave the place and give way to some other who will be a friend. It is better for him to lay down the duty of pastoral care and to pass his life freely as a poor and private monk than to sit in the high seat, oppressed by a wrongful yoke of slavery through the cunning of certain persons. Better that, than that the whole Norman nobility should grieve that he has lost in his time liberties and privileges maintained inviolate until now by his predecessors, through the authority of your predecessors, as the emblem of your royal crown and their enrichment.'

When he had spoken, he sat down and the abbot rose and made this speech: 'My lord, as my brother Richard has shown clearly in his argument, I have come at your bidding. If anyone wishes to raise anything against us or against the privileges and liberties of the church of Battle, we shall answer as you counsel, for that church

f. 73 signum corone uestre regie, / obiectis respondebimus. Verumtamen dignum est ut carte ecclesie illius a nobili rege Willelmo in fundamento ipsius ecclesie conscripte, et a successoribus suis et a uobis etiam confirmate, in presentia uestra et omnium hic uobiscum consistentium primitus si iubetis audiantur.'

Tunc idem abbas tradidit cartam regis Willelmi magni domino regi, iussusque ab eodem quidam ex clericis in auditu omnium perlegit. Qua perlecta, Thomas regis cancellarius episcopum Cicestrensem respiciens dixit, 'Domine episcope, audiuit caritas uestra que hic coram domino rege omnibus audientibus acta sunt. Nunc igitur si quid contra hec uestre placuerit prudentie respondere, licitum est. Ad uos enim, ut nobis uidetur, respicit parabola hec.'

Tunc episcopus surgens ita exorsus est, 'Non studio sane ut multorum moris esse dinoscitur per orbem uagandi, sed amore et honore uestri, domine mi rex, huiusce[modi][a] inscius oppositionis, in his regni uestri partibus cum aliis presentibus conueni. Quocirca si uobis et abbati aliisque hic uobis coram positis dulci complaceret affectu, saluo iure ecclesie nostre Cicestrensis et ecclesie de Bello pacis compositio inter me et predictum abbatem uobis mediantibus fieri foret possibile. Etenim huc tali ordine adueni. Quod si hoc
f. 73v uestro non insedisse animo cognouerim, ingruente / necessitate pro me et pro ecclesia Cicestrensi mihi commissa ut huiusmodi impremunitus oppositionis et ignarus satisfaciam.'

Renuentibus quibusdam pacis fieri compositionem, dicentibus etiam rem illam diu inter illos habitam fine digno debere concludi nec inposterum prolongari, episcopus uoce eleuata reticentibus omnibus dixit, 'Quia pax compositionis inter nos uobis impedientibus fieri non potest, ego que ecclesie mee Cicestrensis iuris sunt et rem inter nos hactenus habitam, patenti ratione domino regi omnibusque hic consistentibus pandam.' Hac igitur usus ratione, hoc modo incepit: 'Iesus Christus, domine mi rex', et repetens, 'Christus Iesus dominus noster', tertioque reiterans, 'audite', inquid, 'omnes, et intelligite. Iesus Christus dominus noster binas mansiones potestatesque binas in huius seculi dispositione constituit: unam scilicet spiritualem, alteram materialem. Spiritualis illa est, de qua dominus noster Iesus Christus in primo pastore nostro Petro

[a] modi *has been added between the lines in the hand of a fourteenth-century annotator*

is your demesne chapel and emblem of your crown. However, it is fitting, if you should command it, that the charters of that church, drafted by the noble King William when he founded it, and by his successors, and also confirmed by you, be first of all heard in the presence of yourself and of all assembled here with you.'

Then the abbot gave the charter of the great King William to the lord king, and at his order one of the clerks read it aloud to all. When he had read it through, Thomas, the king's chancellor, fixing his eye on the bishop, said, 'Lord bishop, your charity has heard what has been done here before the king and in everyone's hearing. Now if your prudence would wish to say anything in rejoinder, it is permitted. Your turn has come, I think.'

Then the bishop got up and spoke. 'My lord king, I have come into these parts of your realm with the others present, not, as is known to be the way of many, from a desire to wander the earth, but out of love and honour for you, all unaware of this kind of antagonism. Therefore if there is a spirit of goodwill here among you and the abbot and this assembly, it should be possible through your mediation to reach an agreement between this abbot and myself, saving the rights of our church of Chichester and of the church of Battle. Indeed I have come here for that purpose. But if I find that this is not your settled intention, I shall have no choice but to compromise for myself and the church of Chichester entrusted to me, neither forewarned nor forearmed as I am against such opposition.'

There were those who rejected a peace compromise, saying that this quarrel which had gone on so long between them should be brought to a proper finish and not handed on to another generation. The bishop silenced all by raising his voice and proclaiming, 'If you are unwilling to let this be settled between us by a peace compromise, then let me explain to the king and to all sitting here exactly what are the rights of my church of Chichester, and what our dispute up to now has been.' Having adopted this line, he began as follows, 'Jesus Christ, my lord king', and he repeated, 'Jesus Christ, our lord', and then he said it a third time, 'Hear, all, and understand! Jesus Christ our lord has established two abodes and two powers for the governance of this world: one is the spiritual, the other the material. The spiritual is that to which our lord Jesus Christ referred when He said to our first shepherd, the

scilicet apostolo omnibus discipulis suis eorumque successoribus pronuntiauit dicens, "Tu es Petrus, et super hanc petram edificabo ecclesiam meam."[1] Vnde, ut caritas uestra nouit, ab eiusdem temporis nouitate in ecclesia Dei mos inoleuit quatinus pastores ecclesie sancte, eiusdem beati apostolorum principis Petri uicarii existentes, ecclesie Dei sancte digna gubernatione presiderent. /
f. 74 Hinc nobis ecclesie Dei presidentibus in illis beatis apostolis a domino Iesu Christo dictum est, "Qui uos audit, me audit."[2] Hinc etenim ecclesia Romana, eiusdem apostolorum principis apostolatu insignita, tantam tamque magnificam per totius mundi latitudinem optinuit principatus dignitatem, ut nullus episcopus, nulla persona ecclesiastica absque eius iudicio uel permissione a sede ecclesiastica deponi possit.'

Ad hec rex protensis manibus, 'Verissimum est', ait, 'episcopum non posse deponi, sed ita, manibus pulsus protensis, poterit expelli.' Arridentibus uniuersis, episcopus iterum sic cepit, 'Sicut iam dixi iterum iam dico, hoc modo statum ecclesie ab antiquis temporibus constitutum fuisse. Neque ulli persone laicali, immo etiam nec regi cuiquam, ecclesiis quibusque dignitates uel libertates ecclesiasticas dare licet, uel ab iisdem attributas eisdem, nisi eiusdem patris permissione uel confirmatione, ratas fore non posse iure Romano ecclesiastica probat auctoritas.'

Tunc rex ira commotus, ...[a] 'contra dignitatum regalium auctoritates mihi a Deo concessas calliditate arguta niti precogitas. Vnde tibi fide et sacramento mihi astricto precipio quatinus de uerbis presumptoriis corone et dignitati regie contrariis equitati
f. 74v rectitudinis subiaceas. Presentes uero archiepiscopos / scilicet et episcopos ut de te iustitiam mihi rectitudinis impendant, saluo iure regie corone mihi a summa maiestate concesse, obsecro. Agis enim, ut patet, contra dignitates regales atque libertates ab antiquitatis iure mihi concessas a maiestate regali demere elaboras.' Murmure itaque in populo contra episcopum concitato, uix sedari potuit.

Tunc cancellarius: 'Haut dignum est a cordis uestri excidisse memoria, presul uenerande, cuius excellentiam . . . tis enim in dominum nostrum regem, cui fidei sacramentum uos fecisse nulli dubium est.[b] Vnde prudentie uestre prouidendum est.'

[a] *An erasure of a third of one line and two-thirds of the next. They are illegible even under ultraviolet light* [b] *One line has been erased, and the words* Haut dignum, cuius excellentiam, *and* uos fecisse *have been squeezed into the margin, appropriately aligned with the text, by the scribe's own hand.* Nulli dubium est: *written over erasure.* *See above, p. 27*

apostle Peter, and through him, to all his disciples and successors, "You are Peter, and upon this rock shall I build my church."[1] Whence, as your charity knows, from those first beginnings of His epoch a custom has grown up in God's church that the shepherds of Holy Church, the vicars of the blessed Peter, prince of the apostles, should worthily superintend the governance of the holy church of God. Hence it was to us, the superintendents of the church of God, that the lord Jesus Christ spoke when He said to the blessed apostles, "Who hears you, hears me."[2] As a result the church of Rome, marked out by the apostolate of the prince of the apostles, has achieved so great and so marvellous a pre-eminence world-wide, that no bishop, no ecclesiastical person at all, may be deposed from his ecclesiastical seat without its judgement and permission.'

'Very true', said the king, 'a bishop may not be deposed.' And he made a gesture of pushing with his hands. 'But, see, with a good push he could be ejected.' Everyone broke out laughing. But the bishop began again, 'As I have said already, so I say again, this has been the constitution of the church from antiquity. It is impossible for any layman, indeed even for a king, to give ecclesiastical privileges and exemptions to churches. And ecclesiastical authority shows that it is impossible for those arrogated to them by laymen to be valid except by the permission and confirmation of the holy father, by the laws of Rome.'

The king became angry. . . . 'you are plotting to attack the royal prerogatives given to me by God, with your crafty arguments. Well, by your fealty and your binding oath to me, I command that you undergo just legal judgement for presumptuous words against my crown and royal prerogative. I ask the archbishops and bishops present to give me justice against you, saving the rights of the royal crown given me by the Highest Majesty. Your actions clearly show that you are trying your best to diminish the royal prerogatives and ancient liberties granted to me by right.' This stirred up such a murmur against the bishop that it could hardly be silenced.

Then the chancellor said, 'It is not at all worthy of you, venerable bishop, to have forgotten . . . . . . towards our lord the king, to whom you have, no one doubts, taken an oath of fealty. You should therefore be prudent, your prudence.'

[1] Matt. 16: 18.
[2] Luke 10: 16.

Episcopus uidens se ab omnibus maiestate regia offensa circumuentum, tandem murmure sedato, orationem suam hoc modo prosequitur, 'Domine mi,[a] si quid ex ore meo uestre regali intempestiuum maiestati constat fore prolatum, Deum celi uestramque regalem testor dignitatem, nil me contra uos uel contra uestre dignitatis excellentiam uersuta calliditate protulisse. Ego enim uestram omnimodis preoptaui paternitatem, extuli excellentiam, magnificaui dignitatem, uos ut dominum precordiali affectu semper dilexi carissimum. Nichil igitur in me mali uestra rogo regalis celsitudo suspicetur neque hoc suggerenti cuiquam facile credat.
f. 75 Nil enim a uestra potestate / minui cupio, quam semper et dilexi et pro uiribus meis magnificaui. Ad honorem igitur et decus uestre celsitudinis omnia protuli.'

Ad hec rex, 'Procul hic honor', inquit, 'atque decus hoc a nobis et a nostris amoueantur, hecque prophanationis propulsentur abolitione, quibus ea que antecessorum meorum regum auctoritate et hereditario iure, Dei cooperante gratia, mihi concessa sunt, blandis atque fallacibus, ut omnibus patet, annullari cupis sermonibus.'

Tunc episcopus, 'Omnia, domine mi, que hic uobis audientibus a me studiose prolata sunt, pace uestra omniumque hic ut proposueram consistentium me ratus sum perorasse. Quia uero a me incepta non placent, omissis his rem propositam paucis expediam. A piissimo rege Stephano ecclesie Cicestrie antistes datus, Cantuariam profectus sum, a uenerabili Teodbaldo eiusdem loci archiepiscopo, ut canonicum est, sacrandus. Ibi affuit et abbas de Bello, sciens hoc iustum esse et canonicum, ad sacrationem scilicet sui episcopi in cuius diocesi manere dinoscitur conuenire. Fecit igitur quod debuit. Reuersus uero ad sedem meam Cicestrie, ibidem abbas idem conuenit, et cum aliis festiue indutus in sede propria ab eo-
f. 75v dem, sicut ubique consuetudinis habetur, / sum collocatus. Idem etiam in illo eodemque anno summonitus Cicestriam petiit, festiueque indutus in sinodo cum aliis precepta consuetudinesque sinodi consedit auditurus. Haut longo postmodum tempore, ut canonicum est, parrochiam meam circuiens Bellum deueni, atque ab eodem abbate et omnibus fratribus loci eiusdem honorifice indutus, sicut loci illius proprius et specialis episcopus, processionaliter receptus sum. Inde cum eodem capitulum intrans, uerbum Dei loci illius fratribus sicut filiis seminaui, et ut patrem decet

[a] Domine mi: *written over erasure*

The bishop saw that since the king was offended everyone was against him. Finally the noise subsided and he began again. 'My lord, if I have been tactless towards your royal majesty, I declare before God in heaven and your royal dignity that I meant no crafty attack upon you or your royal prerogative. I have desired your fatherly care in all things; I have exalted your excellence; I have made much of your privileges; from the bottom of my heart I have always loved you as my dearest lord. I pray your royal highness, do not suspect any evil in me, and do not easily believe anyone who would suggest it. I wish nothing to be taken from your royal power, which I have always cherished and praised with all my heart. I meant everything for the honour and glory of your highness.'

'May those kinds of honour and glory be far removed from me and mine', said the king. 'Let them be warded off by the withdrawal of this profanation. By it, as everyone is aware, your fawning, lying words are meant to destroy the prerogative that by God's grace has been handed down to me from the kings, my ancestors, in hereditary right.'

'My lord', the bishop answered, 'I thought that I could have explained fully all the points I have so carefully brought up in your hearing, with the goodwill of yourself and the court. However, since my beginning displeases you, let me lay that aside and proceed to a brief statement of my main theme. When I was presented to the see of Chichester by the most pious King Stephen, I went to Canterbury to be consecrated by the venerable archbishop Theobald, as is canonical. There too came the abbot of Battle, for he knew that it was just and canonical to be present at the consecration of his bishop, in whose diocese he was known to reside. He therefore acted as he ought. I returned to my see of Chichester. The abbot came there as well. Ceremonially clad, I was by him amongst others set in my proper place, as is everywhere regarded as customary. That same year he was summoned and came to Chichester. In his ceremonial robes, he took his seat in the synod with the others to hear the decrees and customs of the synod. Not long after, in visiting my diocese as is canonical, I arrived at Battle. There I was received in my ceremonial robes by the abbot and all the brothers in procession as their own, and only, bishop. I entered the chapter house thus with him. I preached the word of God to the brothers as to sons, and as a father ought I strengthened those

filios in fide catholica confirmaui. Hinc ad hospicium deductus, honorifice ut decebat sicut suo episcopo que necessaria erant impendit, atque inde recedentem muneribus me suis decenter ditauit.'[a]

His Henricus de Essexia regis tribunus[1] respondit, 'Bene uoluntateque benigna ab illo acta a uobis sinistra remuneratione sunt accepta. Malum enim pro bonis uobis collatis nunc illi rependere uultis. Atque utinam tali quisquam remuneratione acceptus uobis in posterum haut prebeat hospicium.'

Episcopus autem: 'Extunc', inquit, 'domine mi carissime, nescio quo idem usus consilio a sinodo se subtraxit, summonitusque ipse uenire renuens, priorem ecclesie sue cum quibusdam fratribus suis
f. 76 ad sinodum destinauit. / Pro amore illius nichil in hoc mali estimans semel iterumque atque tertio hec patiens, grato animo accepi. Hec itaque omnia inter nos, ut audistis, pacifice acta sunt, donec episcopo Lundoniensi mortuo,[2] nescio quo aut inuidie uel superbie spiritu idem inflatus, rectis oculis me intueri non poterat. Sperabat enim me sibi fortuitu, ut credo, in illo nocuisse negotio, quod omnino probare non poterit.'

Ad hec Henricus de Essexia, 'Si de episcopatu Lundonie agere . . . dilectio[b] uestra uoluerit, profecto omnibus notum est, abbatem istum illius honoris ambitione quicquam contra Deum uel sacrum ordinem illum simoniace aliquo tempore agere noluisse. Quod si, ut nonnulli, peccunia mediante in sede illa collocari affectaret, omnes pro certo repulsam passi intronizari pre omnibus meruisset.'[3] His Ricardus de Luci subiunxit: 'Absit hoc ab eo, ut intercessore tali tam sacrum tamque magnificum ordinem adipiscatur. Nullum enim mortalium nobis nouimus in hoc opere fore uerendum.'

Submurmurantibus nonnullis, episcopus spiritum resumens orationem inceptam prosequitur. 'Res igitur, domine mi,[c] ex tunc

[a] *In marg., aligned with text, by scribe*: Ditauit [b] *Word missing between* agere *and* dilectio [c] *All but the first letter of* domine mi *are written over an erasure*

---

[1] Henry of Essex, disgraced for alleged cowardice in 1163, was a valued servant of Henry II in the 1150s. See *Letters of Gilbert Foliot*, p. 215 and refs.

sons in the Catholic faith. He led me thence to the guest-house and respectfully supplied all my wants, as was fitting towards his bishop. When I left, he fittingly loaded me with gifts.'

To this Henry of Essex, the king's constable,[1] said, 'His good deeds and his goodwill have received a nasty reward from you. You now wish to repay him with evil for the good given to you. I hope that from now on anyone who has received such thanks from you will offer you no hospitality.'

The bishop continued, 'Fom that time, my dearest lord, following I know not what advice, he has withdrawn from synod. When summoned he refuses to come, and has sent to the synod the prior of his church with some of his brothers instead. Out of love for him, and seeing nothing malicious in it, I endured it once, twice, thrice, with equanimity. All these things were managed peaceably between us, as you have heard, until the bishop of London died.[2] After that he became filled with—I don't know what—a spirit of envy or pride, and could not look at me straight in the eyes. He feared, I think, that I had by chance harmed him in that affair, although he will not be able to prove it.'

At this Henry of Essex broke in: 'Had your holiness wished to act . . . concerning the bishopric of London, everyone very well knows that the abbot, in striving for that honour, was unwilling to do anything at any time simoniacally against God and that holy order. If, like some, he had striven to be preferred to that see by means of money, he before anyone else would have deserved to be enthroned.'[3] Richard de Luci added, 'Far be it from him to reach so sacred and glorious a rank by such a mediator. We know no man whom we need to fear in connection with that affair.'

A number of people were muttering about this, and the bishop, taking heart again, took up his address, 'My lord, from that time

there. As well as being constable, he was a baron of the Exchequer and sheriff of Bedfordshire, and heard pleas alone and in the company of Becket and the earl of Leicester. W. L. Warren calls him, along with Richard de Luci, Thomas Becket, Simon fitzPeter, Richard du Hommet and Robert, earl of Leicester, one of the 'senior ministers of the Crown'. Warren, *Henry II*, pp. 264, 284–5. See *PR 2–3–4 Henry II*, ed. J. Hunter (London, 1844; PR Soc. repr. 1930), index s.v. Essex, Henry of.

[2] Robert de Sigillo, bishop of London, d. 29 Sept. 1150. Le Neve, ed. Greenway, i. 2.

[3] Richard de Belmeis was elected 1152. Le Neve ed. Greenway i. 2. It was generally known that he had paid King Stephen £500 for the office. Saltman, *Theobald*, p. 118 and refs. there.

inter nos in dubio posita est, nec quisquam nostrum ab opere incepto declinare uoluit. Tunc quidam ad me uenientes intimauerunt
f. 76v abbatem hac de causa / sinodum petere noluisse, quod cartis et priulegiis sue utens ecclesie earum extollebatur auctoritate, dicendo se canonicam Cicestrensi ecclesie minime exhibere obedientiam debere. Quod postquam accepi, nolens ecclesiam meam antiquis suis et iustis meis temporibus minui dignitatibus, abbatem cum quadam parrochie mee persona alia sinodum apud Cicestriam petere tempore constituto summonitum nec uenientem interdixi, eo tamen tenore quod si infra quadraginta dierum spatium satisfacturus non ueniret, ab officio suo suspensus cessaret. Verum persona alia supplici uoce ueniam petens obtinuit, abbate in sententia permanente. Quod abbas ut audiuit regem Stephanum adiit, atque illi super hoc questum intulit. Rex uero quendam ex clericis suis Rotbertum de Cornuuilla nomine ad me misit, mandans quod die octauarum sancti Andree Lundonias coram eo uenirem, et quod abbas etiam ibidem conuenire deberet, atque ibi consilio archiepiscopi Cantuarie et baronum suorum pacis fedus inter nos poneret. Die constituta coram rege affui. Ibi itaque nec abbas neque quisquam pro eo, ut tunc omnibus patuit, contra me aduenit. Ita igitur ad propria reuersus sum, abbate in sententia permanente. Post illius anni curriculum, in sinodo sollemni secundum canonum
f. 77 statuta illum / excommunicaui. Abbas uero, hoc accepto, archiepiscopo retulit. Archiepiscopus autem, ipsius abbatis precibus, litteris suis mihi mandauit quatinus sententiam relaxarem donec in unum conueniremus. Ipse enim inter nos omnia bene disponeret. Pro honore ipsius domini archiepiscopi sententiam ad tempus relaxaui.'

Tunc Henricus de Essexia: 'Rege Stephano defuncto, si hoc ueritati innititur, uos id fecisse constans est quo uiuente nunquam ausu temerario uos probatur hoc presumsisse. Non enim expediret uobis. Quid nunc dominus noster facturus sit suo iuri et potestati committitur.'

Ita episcopus subintulit, 'Tunc res inter nos habita est, nec aliquo tempore abbas ad satisfactionem uenisse comprobatur. Postquam dominus noster Iesus Christus, domine rex, uos in regni huius solio collocauit, quod mihi pre omnibus gratissimum fore constat, abbas nec mihi ut suo episcopo que debebat exhibuit, nec mee ecclesie, Cicestrie scilicet, immo etiam me ubique uitando spernebat atque uerbis turpissimis ubique pro posse suo diffamabat. Accidit autem quod idem cartas ecclesie sue in sigilli uestri

the issue has been in doubt between us, and neither of us has wished to back off, once it had begun. Then people came to me and intimated that the abbot refused to attend synod for this reason, that, guided by the charters and privileges of his church, he was being exalted by their authority, to the point of saying that he need not show canonical obedience to the church of Chichester. When I heard this, I was unwilling that in my time my church should lose any of its ancient and just privileges. I summoned the abbot, along with another person of my diocese, to Chichester at an appointed time. When he did not come, I interdicted him, with the stipulation that if he should not come within the limit of forty days to make satisfaction, he would be suspended from office. The other person, humbly seeking forgiveness, obtained it, but the abbot's sentence went into effect. When he heard this he went to King Stephen and complained of it. The king sent one of his clerks, Robert de Cornuvilla, to me with an order to come before him on the octave of St. Andrew in London. The abbot was to come there as well, and, with the counsel of the archbishop of Canterbury and his barons, he would work out a compromise between us. On the day set I came before the king. But neither the abbot nor an advocate in his place appeared against me, as everyone then knew. I therefore returned to my see and the abbot's sentence remained. A year later, in a solemn synod and according to the statutes of the canons, I excommunicated him. When the abbot learned this, he returned to the archbishop, who at his entreaties ordered me by letter to relax the sentence until we could all meet. He would make peace between us. For the honour of the lord archbishop I relaxed the sentence for the time being.'

Henry of Essex said, 'If this is true, it establishes that after King Stephen's death you did something you would never have dared to do had he been living, for it would not have been to your interest. What our lord may do here now is up to his right and his power.'

The bishop continued, 'Since then we have been in dispute, and it is acknowledged that at no time has the abbot come to make amends. After the lord Jesus Christ placed you upon the throne of this realm—for which above all others I am most grateful—the abbot did not act as he should have to me as his bishop, or to my church of Chichester. On the contrary he has despised me, avoiding me everywhere; he has everywhere maligned me to the best of his ability in the most shameful words. However, it happened that he

renouatione confirmari disponeret. Peruenit itaque ad aures meas in eiusdem cartis contra ecclesie mee Cicestrie dignitates et etiam
f. 77v contra Cantuarie ecclesie, matris uidelicet totius Anglie, / aliqua contineri. Quod archiepiscopo, sicut illi cui omnes nos professionem fecisse nulli dubium est, et cui etiam et ecclesie Cantuariensi canonicam per omnia debemus obedientiam, intimare curaui. Archiepiscopus uero uos inde conuenit. Ego etiam pro me et pro ecclesia mea Cicestrie querimoniam coram uobis deposui. Precepit igitur clementia uestra quatinus coram archiepiscopo ego et abbas cum cancellario uestro domino Thoma conueniremus, ibique lecta abbatis carta consilio archiepiscopi ea que corrigenda erant, ea scilicet que contra dignitates predictarum ecclesiarum Cantuarie scilicet et Cicestrie existebant, correcta, unusquisque, que sui iuris esse uidentur, adquisisse gauderet. Conuenimus ibi. Lecta igitur coram assistentibus carta abbatis, ea que contra dignitates Cantuariensis ecclesie et Cicestrensis erant iusta consideratione peremptoria esse precepta sunt. Abbas ira commotus multis me ibidem et maximis aggressus est iniuriis. Nec solum dumtaxat tunc, sed anno etiam presenti Cicestriam ueniens capitulum nostrum cum nimia nimis arrogantia intrauit, atque multis et innumerabilibus modis in presentia conuentus mei minando atque spernendo me diiudicauit. Hac itaque ratione et hoc modo, domine mi carissime, rerum series inter nos hactenus habita est. Peto igitur excellentiam uestram quatinus antiquam et iustam canonum institutionem inter
f. 78 nos ratam per omnia esse / atque hec more ecclesiastico determinare precipiat.'

Tunc rex: 'Mirum et mirandum nimium hic audiuimus, cartas scilicet predecessorum meorum regum, iusta dignitate corone Anglie et magnorum uirorum testimonio confirmatas, a uobis, domine episcope, peremptorias esse iudicatas. Absit hoc, absit a regni mei excellentia, ut quod ratione dictante consilioque archiepiscoporum et episcoporum atque baronum meorum a me fuerit decretum a uobis et a uestri similibus damnandum esse iudicetur.'

Tunc abbas: 'Ab antiquis temporibus, regnante Willelmo rege nobilissimo, omnia hec, ut a senioribus ecclesie nostre accepimus, coram eodem domino nostro rege, Lanfranco Cantuariensi archiepiscopo et aliis quampluribus episcopis presentibus, Stigando etiam

intended to have the charters of his church confirmed by your seal. I heard that there were things in his charters against the privileges of my church of Chichester and also against those of the church of Canterbury, the mother of all England. This I was at pains to make known to the archbishop, as the superior to whom there is no doubt we have all made profession, and to whom and to the church of Canterbury we owe canonical obedience in all things. The archbishop consulted you about it. And I too, for myself and my church of Chichester, have brought my complaint before you. Your clemency therefore ordered that the abbot and I, together with the lord Thomas, should meet before the archbishop, that the abbot's charter be read there and with the counsel of the archbishop those things that required emendation—namely what was against the privileges of the churches of Canterbury and Chichester—should be corrected. Each, then, might rejoice at having gained what is seen to be his by right. We met there. The abbot's charter was read before those assembled and those phrases in it that were against the privileges of Canterbury and Chichester were quite properly ruled to be too drastic. The abbot angrily heaped insults upon me there. And not only then: this very year he came to Chichester and entered our chapter house with arrogance beyond measure, and in the presence of my chapter with innumerable threats and insults he condemned me. Thus, my dearest lord, there has been a succession of provocations up to the very present. Wherefore I beseech your excellency to command that the ancient and just procedure of the canons be fulfilled between us and that we settle it in the manner of the church.'

The king answered, 'We have heard something of a marvel here, something to be exceedingly wondered at: that charters of the kings my predecessors, confirmed by the just prerogative of the crown of England and by the witness of great men, have been adjudged too drastic by you, lord bishop. May it not come to this! May the splendour of my reign never see a time when things I decree, using my reason and by the counsel of my archbishops, bishops and barons, are to be judged condemned by you and your ilk.'

The abbot spoke. 'The elders of my abbey have informed me that all these matters were settled in olden times, during the reign of the most noble King William. It was settled before the lord king himself, and with him were Lanfranc, archbishop of Canterbury, and many bishops, among them Stigand, then bishop of Chichester,

tunc Cicestrie episcopo in presentia eiusdem regis consistente, qui Gausbertum ecclesie de Bello abbatem primum super his infestabat, summonendo illum ut sinodum apud Cicestriam peteret, et alia omnia episcopalia persolueret, determinata sunt. Vnde et cartam ipsius domini regis super hoc negotio propriam, Lanfranci Cantuariensis archiepiscopi et aliorum nonnullorum episcoporum sed et etiam ipsius Stigandi Cicestrensis episcopi testimonio confirmatam, presentem habemus.' Hec dicens, tradidit cartam regi, atque eam unus ex clericis eius nutu omnibus audientibus /
f. 78v perlegit. Hec itaque inter alia in illa continebantur carta, quod ecclesia scilicet de Bello libera sit omnino a subiectione Cicestrensis episcopi, neque ad sinodum abbas summoneatur, nisi ipse pro aliqua re sponte ire uoluerit.[1] His perlectis, episcopus se cartam illam nunquam uidisse uel audisse affirmabat, neque abbatem sibi aliquo pacto eam pandere uoluisse.

Abbate nonnulla contra obiciente, rex eidem ut taceret precepit. 'Non enim', inquit, 'hoc amodo uestre diracionandum incumbit prudentie sed me uti proprium atque regale tueri decet negotium. Quapropter uestra interim sileat fraternitas, nobis hoc euidenti ratione atque regali protectione uti proprium determinantibus. Ad nos itaque huiusmodi spectat negotii diffinitio.'

Multis igitur super his hinc indeque habitis, tandem silentio inposito Ricardus de Luci surgens regem uoce supplici exorauit quatinus abbati de Bello fratri suo super his respondendi consilium cum amicis suis secretius habere liceret. Rege his annuente, aduocans Rogerum Eboracensem archiepiscopum, Thomam cancellarium regis, Iohannem thesaurarium Eboracensis ecclesie, Rotbertum comitem Legacestrie, Patricium comitem Saresberie, Henricum de Essexia, Raginaldum de Warennia, Warinum filium Geroldi, et aliorum nonnullorum baronum et militum multi-
f. 79 tudinem non modicam, cum fratre suo / abbate, omnibus his sibi coherentibus, in unam capituli partem secessit, atque super his eorum sententiam perquirere cepit. Rex missam interim auditurus ecclesiam adiit, iterumque post missam ibidem rediens in sede sua resedit. Ricardus de Luci cum abbate et omnibus sibi iunctis consilio communicato rediit, impositoque responsionis sermone

[1] This is the second forgery produced by Abbot Walter. It answers Bishop Hilary's earlier objection. BL Add. Ch. 70980. An interpolated version of the

who had been harassing Gausbert, the first abbot of Battle, by summoning him to synod at Chichester and to pay all the other episcopal dues. I have here at hand the king's own charter about the affair, confirmed by the attestation of Lanfranc, archbishop of Canterbury, and several other bishops, including even Stigand, bishop of Chichester.' Saying this he handed a charter to the king and at his nod one of the clerks read it to the whole assembly. These among other things were contained in the charter: that the church of Battle should be wholly free of subjection to the bishop of Chichester. Nor might the abbot be summoned to synod, although he might for some reason go there voluntarily.[1] When it was read through, the bishop swore that he had never seen nor heard that charter, nor had the abbot seen fit to make it known to him in any form.

The abbot had begun to argue when the king ordered him to be quiet. 'From now on it is not necessary for your prudence to establish your claim. It is I who must defend it as my own personal and royal business. So be silent a while, my brother, for I shall settle this reasonably and with royal protection as my own. The decision in such a matter therefore is mine.'

Many things were said on this side and that, but when silence had been imposed, Richard de Luci, rising, prayed the king in humble voice to allow his brother the abbot of Battle to take private counsel with his friends about a reply to the accusations. The king agreed. Richard called Roger, archbishop of York, Thomas, the king's chancellor, John, treasurer of the church of York, Robert, earl of Leicester, Patrick, earl of Salisbury, Henry of Essex, Reginald de Warenne, Warin fitzGerold, several other barons and a whole flock of knights, together with his brother the abbot. All these men were his allies and he went aside with them into a part of the chapter house and began to ask their opinions. In the mean time the king went to the church to hear mass. When it was over he returned and again took his seat. Richard de Luci, having consulted, returned with the abbot and his party.

early thirteenth century is *Regesta* i, no. 262. Both are printed by Searle, *EHR*, lxxxiii (1968), 473–4, and are discussed ibid. 458–9, 465. It is there suggested that Westminster, a centre for forgery, had supplied the charter and its forged seal, for Westminster had made its seal matrix available to several monasteries besides Battle. T. A. M. Bishop and Pierre Chaplais, *Facsimiles of English Royal Writs to A.D. 1100, presented to V. H. Galbraith* (Oxford, 1957), pp. xxi, xxii. See also Pierre Chaplais, in *Medieval Miscellany*, PR Soc., N.S. xxxvi (1962 for 1960), 89–99.

Thome cancellario regis, omnibus audientibus, facunda oratione hoc modo idem responsum reddidit heros.

'Diu, pater reuerende Hilari, questionis a uestra prudentia habite seriem retexentes, certa equitatis ratione, certis etiam procerum presentium suffragiis, nonnulla referre decreuimus. Inprimis igitur uenerabilis abbas Gauterus grates uestre prudentie quammaximas refert,[a] quod pro beneficiis uobis ab eodem collatis, illum in tanta tamque, ut hic nunc constat, curia magnifica, presentibus etiam tantis tamque uiris nobilibus, magnifica laude extollitis. Quod si illis temporibus in tanta tamque curia excellenti sibi hoc tam maxime laudis extollentia inputandum speraret, profecto ut fatetur beneficium amplificaret. Verum inde quammaximo dolore conficitur, quod pro beneficio ab eo benigna animi deuotione uobis collato, ut omnibus hic presentibus patens est, uice uersa ueneficia
f. 79v illi omni mentis annisu rependere satagitis. / Nunc igitur contra sibi obiecta hoc modo responsum refert. Si Cantuariam petens in sacratione uestra presens extitisse et post apud Cicestriam uobis obuius in sede uestra sollempniter uos collocasse, necnon et in sinodo uestra resedisse cum ceteris comprobatur, dignitate et libertate ecclesie sue de Bello, teste etiam carta sua hic perlecta, utrumlibet sibi aut fecisse licet horum uel minime egisse. Neque enim uinculo aliquo a uobis, ut hec rigore ecclesiastico persoluere debeat, constrictus est, quippe cum uestre non subiaceat ditioni, immo teste carta sua predicta liber est ab omni subiectione uestra. Archiepiscopum etiam dominum nostrum Cantuariensem scilicet contestatur, hoc se ipso precipiente perfecisse.'

Ad hec archiepiscopus: 'Verum est, illum me precipiente hec effectui mancipasse.'

'Quod parrochiam uestram', cancellarius inquit, 'ut consuetudinis habetur circumiens Bellum petistis, atque a fratribus loci illius abbate presente processionaliter susceptus extitistis indeque capitulum illorum intrans uerbum Dei illis seminastis, omnibus ultra citraque mare existentibus ecclesiis consuetudinarium esse dinoscitur, episcopo Hiberniensi uel etiam Hispalensi, uel cuilibet alii, hunc dignitatis et caritatis honorem, absque ulla consuetudinis
f. 80 exactione, gratis impendere licitum fore. / De episcopatu uero Lundonie hoc uestre abbas intimare procurat prudentie, quod nec

[a] Diu . . . refert: *The writing is larger than that usual in this section, and runs into the margin*

Thomas the king's chancellor had been chosen to reply. With everyone listening, that hero delivered his oration in his eloquent style.

'Reverend father Hilary, we have decided at the behest of certain nobles here to go back over a few points, and in the sure light of justice to unravel the knot of this dispute so long kept up by your prudence. In the first place the venerable Abbot Walter thanks your prudence exceedingly for having so highly praised him in so great and so magnificent a court as this, and in the presence of such great and such noble men, for the kindnesses shown you by him. If in those days he had thought he might be so highly praised for it before so great and so excellent a court, he would certainly, he confesses, have increased his favour. Yet he is grieved that though the feeling which prompted him to do you this service was one of kindly devotion, as is clear to all here, yet you try, with all your powers, to repay his benevolence with malevolence. Now therefore he replies to the charges against him thus. What if he was at Canterbury and present at your consecration, and afterwards, encountering you at Chichester, he ceremonially conducted you to your seat and also sat in your synod along with the others? By the privilege and exemption of his church of Battle, as the charter read here witnesses, it was entirely up to him whether he did either of these things, or did not do them. He is not bound by anything that would force him by ecclesiastical sanctions to render you these services, for he is not subject to your authority. Indeed as his charter attests, he is free from all subjection to you. He also calls to witness our lord archbishop of Canterbury that it was done at his command.'

'It is true', the archbishop said. 'It was at my command that he agreed to do them.'

The chancellor said, 'Now visiting your diocese on circuit as is customary, you arrived at Battle and you were received by the brothers in procession and in the presence of their abbot. Then, entering their chapter house, you preached the word of God to them. In all churches everywhere, here and across the sea, it is known to be the custom that this honour, this symbol of respect and affection, is properly bestowed upon a bishop, be he Irish or even Spanish or whatever. It is gratis and is no precedent for a custom. About the bishopric of London, the abbot hastens to inform your prudence of this: that neither by look nor act nor even gesture did

uultu, neque actu, nec etiam nutu aliquo uobis quicquam pro illo eodemque episcopatu Lundonie, scilicet significationis contrarie, ingessit, quippe cum in illius dispositione negotii nil contra se a uobis mali suspicatus fuerit. Sed ut quodam in loco dictum est, conscius ipse sibi omnia putat contraria sibi;[1] pro re quidem a uobis gesta remordente fortuitu conscientia, illum simplici uultu gradientem nunquam recto uos lumine sperabatis intueri potuisse.[2]

'Quod illum sinodum apud Cicestriam petere summonitum nec uenientem interdictum a uobis insinuastis, et ob hanc causam regem Stephanum per Rotbertum de Cornuuilla clericum suum uobis coram illo [? ad] hec determinanda diem prefixisse, uosque ibidem nullo ex parte abbatis uobis obuio conuenisse, sicque inde recessisse, abbas e contrario refert, se scilicet coram rege Stephano die statuta, presentibus episcopis Wintoniensi scilicet et Heliensi necnon et abbate Westmonasterii, et etiam baronibus nonnullis, in capella eiusdem regis iuxta Turrem Lundonie sita conuenisse, atque ibi a uenerabili Wintonie episcopo cartis et scriptis sue
f. 80v ecclesie perlectis, rege sibi suggerente, / se capelle sue, abbatie scilicet de Bello, ubique protectorem fore, uosque super hoc conuenire, atque omnia inter uos pacificare, ad propria ipso precipiente reuersus est. Ad sinodum uero summonitione aliqua nisi spontanee ire uoluerit, teste carta sua hic perlecta et more antiquitatis in ecclesia sua hactenus conseruato, compelli non poterit.[3] Vnde, ut uerum fatear, ire ad sinodum uel non ire eiusdem iuris et spontanee uoluntatis esse comprobatur, quippe cum uestre, ut omnibus patet, non subiaceat ditioni, sed liber omnino ab uniuersa uestra existat subiectione.

'Illum a uobis exommunicatum perhibetis. Hoc illi omnibusque suis mirandum uidetur, quia tempore regis Stephani nil huiusmodi super illum presumptione temeraria uos constat egisse. Quid ergo huius nunc domini nostri regis tempore a uobis actum sit incognitum habet, presertim cum primo regni sui anno, ipso domino nostro rege in ecclesia sancti Petri Westmonasterii, uobis utrisque cum aliis multis presentibus, missam audiente, ubi uentum est ad "Pax Domini", uos, ut moris habetur, pace a sacerdote accepta
f. 81 domino regi attulistis, atque abbati uobis statu / propinquiori

[1] See Walther, no. 3122: *Dion. Cato* 1, 17, 2: 'Conscius ipse sibi de se putat omnia dici.' Cf. Ovid, *Fasti*, 1. 4. 311.

[2] Becket refers to the bishop's words, above, p. 190.

he inflict upon you anything that had a hostile meaning. For he suspected no ill will against himself from you in the settlement of that affair. But as is said somewhere, the conspirator thinks everyone is against him.[1] Your conscience was by chance troubling you over something you had done, and you expected that this man, though he goes his way with an open countenance, could never look you straight in the eyes.[2]

'You tell the story that you summoned him to synod at Chichester and interdicted him when he did not come, that it was for this that King Stephen, through Robert de Cornuvilla his clerk, set a day for settling it before him, that no one came to oppose you on the part of the abbot, and that you therefore left. The abbot on the contrary declares that on the stated day he came before King Stephen in the presence of the bishops of Winchester and Ely and of the abbot of Westminster and several barons, in the king's royal chapel at the tower of London. And there the charters and written accounts of his abbey were read by the venerable bishop of Winchester. The king added that he would be the protector anywhere of his own chapel, the abbey of Battle, and that you should meet and make peace between you. At his order the abbot returned home. Unless he wishes to go voluntarily to synod, he cannot be forced by any summons, as his charter read here attests, and in accordance with ancient usage observed in his church to the present day.[3] Wherefore, to say truly, to go to synod or not to go is proven to be a matter of his right and of his free will. For, as all can see, he is not subject to your jurisdiction, but is wholly free from any subjection to you.

'You assert that he was excommunicated by you. This seems very strange to him and all his friends, for it is quite certain that you did not dare to do such a presumptuous thing to him in the time of King Stephen. What you may have done in the time of this our present lord king he knows nothing of. After all, in the first year of his reign, when our lord king was one day hearing mass at St. Peter's church, Westminster, and both of you were present among many others, when the "Pax Domini" was reached, you received the pax from the priest and took it as is the custom to the king. And afterwards you bestowed the kiss of peace upon the

[3] The forgery BL Add. Ch. 70980 reads, 'ad sinodum vero abbas ire non summoneatur neque compellatur nisi propria voluntate pro aliquo negotio ire voluerit.'

iuncto postmodum eiusdem pacis osculum non ut excommunicato, sed ut filio ecclesie et christiano tribuistis.'

Ad hec episcopus, 'Si in hoc aut animo inscienti uel nonnullis ut multociens prouenit cogitationibus occupatum temerarie constat me deliquisse mea culpa, peccatum meum domino meo archiepiscopo confessus, penitentia mihi ab eodem iniuncta delictum illud diluam.'

'In cartis ecclesie sue de Bello', cancellarius inquit, 'que capella regis propria omnibus esse patens est, contra Cantuariensis ecclesie uel etiam uestre Cicestrensis scilicet dignitates, nil noui insitum, omnibus quammaxime preclarissimum est. Ab inclito enim rege Willelmo eadem ecclesia constructa maximis et preclaris dignitatibus Lanfranco Cantuariensi archiepiscopo, aliisque episcopis, abbatibus, baronibus nonnullis, iuxta corone Anglie dignitatem, cum rege suo confirmantibus ecclesia predicta confirmata est, quas etiam usque hodie inuiolabili iure tenuisse comprobatur. Quas etiam, precepto domini regis, coram domino nostro archiepiscopo Cantuariensi, non uobis pessima ingerendo, sed ratione uigenti easdem a uobis peremptorias iudicatas defendendo ut regales nobis audientibus retinere cupiebat. In capitulo uestro Cicestrensi eun-
f. 81v dem hoc anno absentibus / uobis superbe intrasse, et uos multis modis ibidem diiudicasse opponitis. Quod euidenti ratione non superbe ut asseritis, sed coactus et pacifice se hoc egisse demonstrat. Duo namque decani uestri, Lewensis scilicet et Hastingensis, cum v sacerdotibus in testimonium, in Quadragesime initio Bellum uenientes, litteras domini pape Adriani a uobis, ut rei ueritas est, perquisitas abbati pretulerunt, summonentes eum etiam ex parte ipsius pape, ut dominica que dicitur "Letare Ierusalem" Cicestriam ueniret, ibi auditurus eiusdem domini pape precepta. Quia uero domino nostro rege in transmarinis partibus tunc constituto illum super hoc adire nequibat, cum domino nostro Cantuariensi archiepiscopo et quibusdam amicis suis consilio communicato, Cicestriam die statuta petiit atque in capitulum, domini pape auditurus precepta, presentibus illis duobus decanis et supradictis quinque sacerdotibus intrauit. Ibi etiam illi duo decani, que abbati apud Bellum pretulerant, et que illis abbas retulerat, uiua testificati sunt uoce. Ibi clerici uestri contra auctoritatem regie dignitatis quedam ab eo exigebant. Abbas uero, ut inducias sibi quo dominum nostrum regem adire, atque eius super hoc consilium et uoluntatem audire posset darent petiit, sed ipsis
f. 82 renuentibus easdem inpetrare nequiuit. / Verum etiam insuper hoc

abbot, immediately following you in precedence, not as an excommunicate, but as a Christian and a son of the church.'

To this the bishop said, 'If I have sinned in this, through absent-mindedness or preoccupation, as often happens, I shall confess my sin to my lord archbishop and will remove my guilt by the penance he will assign me.'

The chancellor said, 'In the charters of his church of Battle, which, as is clear to everyone, is the king's own chapel, no novelty has been inserted contrary to the privileges of Canterbury, or your church of Chichester either. That is abundantly clear to everyone. That church, built by the famous King William, was strengthened by great and outstanding privileges. Lanfranc, archbishop of Canterbury, and other bishops, abbots, several barons, along with the king himself, by the prerogative of the English crown, assured them to the church. These, it is established, it has possessed up to the present by inviolable right. These are what he was trying to preserve, when summoned by the lord king into the presence of our lord archbishop of Canterbury. He is not doing this to do you any evil, but very reasonably to defend as royal what you in our hearing have judged too drastic. You allege that this year in your absence he entered your chapter house at Chichester haughtily and there demeaned you in many ways. But with plain reason he points out that he did not act haughtily as you assert, but peaceably and under compulsion. For two of your deans, Lewes and Hastings, along with five priests as witnesses, went to Battle at the beginning of Lent. They served upon the abbot a letter procured by you (for this is the truth of the matter) from Pope Adrian, summoning him on the pope's behalf to go to Chichester on the Sunday "Letare Ierusalem", to hear the commands of the lord pope. Since our lord the king was on the continent he could not approach him about this but, after consulting our lord the archbishop of Canterbury and various of his friends, he went to Chichester on the day assigned and in the presence of the two deans and the five priests he entered the chapter house to hear the pope's commands. There the two deans testified orally as to what they had served upon the abbot at Battle and what the abbot had replied. There your clerks kept demanding from him things that were against the royal prerogative. The abbot prayed that they give him a delay so that he might go to our lord king and hear his advice and his wishes in the matter. They refused and he was unable to get his delay. Indeed, further, they

a illis uobis inpositum, neque aliud quam illis preceptum extiterat agere potuisse testati sunt. Hoc modo abbas inde recedens, omnia domino regi ut erant per nuntium suum significauit. Dominus uero noster rex uobis utrisque, dico, super his diem presentem constituit.'

Tunc rex uultu mutato episcopum respiciens dixit, 'Nunquidnam litteras has, ut hic recitatum est, perquisistis? Super fidem et sacramentum quod mihi debetis, ut ueraci hoc mihi proferatis sermone precipio.'

Episcopus uero: 'Super fidem et sacramentum quod uobis feci ut domino, has litteras nec per me, neque per alium quemlibet me sciente, excellentia uestra nouerit esse perquisitas. Verum abbas, quendam ex clericis suis Romam nuper mittens, me ibidem in curia Romana multum nimiumque diffamauit. Ego autem in illa curia omnibus notus sum, et cuius honestatis uel moralitatis sim omnibus ibidem commanentibus haut incognitum est. Per illum enim ibidem me infamari inpossibile est. Fortuitu ergo per illum litteras illas sibi perquisiuit.'

Tunc rex, 'Mirum et nimium stupendum uideretur, abbatem uidelicet contra se et suam ecclesiam hec, si ita res habet, perquirere uoluisse.'

His cancellarius subiecit: 'Si alio modo quam a uobis, ut hic re-
f. 82v latum est, has litteras perquisitas probare / uoluerit dilectio uestra, abbas en presens est, litteras in manu tenens. Legantur littere, uideatur quorsum illarum uergat intentio, sicque rei ueritas comprobabitur.'

Archiepiscopus autem audiens episcopum litteras ab eodem perquisitas[a] coram omnibus denegasse, sciens omnia ut erant, et quod littere ab eodem episcopo perquisite fuissent, signo crucis pre nimia admiratione se signauit. Tunc cancellarius: 'Non solum dumtaxat de his litteris dominus noster rex ueritatem scire proposuit, uerum etiam si alias quaslibet litteras uos, aut alium quemlibet per uos, in presens uel in posterum abbati aut ecclesie de Bello nociuas noueritis possedisse, ut in medium proferatis precepit.' Episcopus uero neque litteras illas presentes, nec alias quaslibet ipse uel alius quislibet per ipsum, abbati uel ecclesie de Bello tunc aut in posterum nociuas iure iurando affirmabat, mirantibus omnibus, habuisse. His tali modo coram domino rege habitis, archiepiscopus Cantuarie regi dixit: 'Precipiat excellentia uestra nos super his quid faciendum sit consilio retractare, atque ordine iudiciario consuetudinis ecclesiastice determinare.'

'Non ita', inquit rex, 'hec per uos determinari precipiam, uerum

[a] sitas. *Add. in marg. in scribe's hand. The word is broken between two lines and he had evidently forgotten to finish it*

swore that this was your order to them and that they were not able to act except as you had ordered. This was the position when the abbot left, and he explained everything to the king by messenger. And our lord king set today for you both, I say, on the matter.'

Then the king's face changed and, looking at the bishop he said, 'This letter that was mentioned: did you ask for it? By your oath of fealty to me, I order you to tell me the truth about this.'

The bishop said, 'By the oath of fealty which I took to you as my lord, may your excellency know that this letter was not asked for by myself, or by anyone to my knowledge. But the abbot lately sent one of his clerks to Rome and he slandered me terribly there at the Roman court. However, I am known to everyone at that court and it is not at all unknown to everyone there what kind of honesty and morality I am made of. So it is impossible for me to be brought into disrepute by him there. Perhaps therefore he may have asked for this letter himself through him.'

The king said, 'Well, it would seem remarkable to me, not to say astonishing, if the abbot wanted to ask like this for something detrimental to himself and his church.'

At this the chancellor interjected, 'If you should wish to prove that these letters were sought in another way than by yourself, as has been suggested, the abbot is present, holding the letter in his hand. Let the letter be read so we can see the drift of its meaning; then we shall get to the truth.'

The archbishop, hearing the bishop deny before all the letter he had asked for, and knowing the whole story as it was, that the letter had been asked for by him, crossed himself in his great surprise. The chancellor turned to the bishop, 'Our lord the king intends to know the truth not only about this letter. He commands that if you know that you have, or anyone in your name has, any other letter that is, or might in the future be, harmful to the abbot or the church of Battle, you are to admit it in the presence of all.' With everyone most astonished, the bishop swore on his oath that he had not had the present letter nor had he, or any agent, had any others which might be harmful to the abbot or the church of Battle then or in the future. Things having reached this stage before the king, the archbishop of Canterbury said to him, 'May your excellency command us to reconsider what should be done about this and settle it by the judicial method of church custom.'

'No', said the king, 'I shall not command it to be settled that way

ego uobis comitantibus, consilio super his habito, fine recto concludam.'/

f. 83 Hec dicens, surrexit et in cimiterium monachorum, omnibus secum preter episcopum et abbatem comitantibus, secessit. Consilio igitur communicato, misit rex pro episcopo. Qui ueniens atque cum aliis residens, multis super his cum eodem habitis, tandemque termino finali conclusis, rege precipiente, Henricus de Essexia abbatem cum monachis suis adduxit. Quo cum aliis residente, rege innuente, episcopus omnibus audientibus sic locutus est:

'Ego Cicestrensis presul ecclesie, o rex excellentissime, ecclesiam de Bello sicut uestram dominicam et propriam capellam, in qua et super quam nil iuris habere iuste possum uel debeo, ab omnibus rebus uel calumpniis a me illi hactenus oppositis quietam et omnino clamo liberam. Abbatem etiam absoluens sicut illum cui uinculum anathematis iniuste imposui, quia nec potui iuste nec debui, a quo etiam, dignitate sua et sue ecclesie precellente, nil nisi interueniente caritatis gratia exigi potuisse uel debuisse me protestor, atque a die hodierno in perpetuum ab omnibus episcopalibus exactionibus et consuetudinibus simili modo proclamo liberum.'

Ad hec rex, 'Non coactus[a] sed uoluntarie hoc te fecisse et protulisse constans est?'

f. 83v Episcopus: 'Verum est, me hoc uoluntarie / iusta ratione cogente fecisse necnon et protulisse.'

Tunc archiepiscopus: 'Iusta, domine rex, his determinatione conclusis, omnes uestram una deprecamur clementiam quatinus si qua contra uestre celsitudinis indebita dignitatem inprudenti uidetur episcopus protulisse sermone, nobis flagitantibus pacis osculo prelibato uestra indulgere illi dignetur clementia.'

'Non solum', rex inquit, 'semel tantummodo pacis osculum, sed, omnia illi si qua sunt indulgens, centies uestris precibus atque ipsius dilectione flexus tribuam.' Assurgensque atque amplexus episcopum deosculatus est.

Archiepiscopus: 'Nunc igitur episcopus et abbas ut amici se deosculando, pacis fedus inter se uestra confirmatione retinentes, in posterum in pace permaneant.' Tunc episcopus et abbas regis

[a] *Sic MS. Recte* coactum?

by you. I shall put a proper finish to it, in your company and having taken counsel about it.'

As he spoke he got up and walked out into the monks' cemetery accompanied by everyone except the bishop and the abbot. When he had talked it over, he sent for the bishop. He went and sat down with the others and they talked a long while with him. Finally things were brought to an end. By the king's order Henry of Essex summoned the abbot and his monks. When he was seated with the rest, the king nodded and the bishop made this statement in everyone's hearing:

'Oh most excellent king, I, bishop of Chichester do quitclaim and wholly acknowledge as free from all claims and charges upheld by me until today, the church of Battle, as your own demesne chapel in which and over which I neither should nor justly can have any rights. I absolve the abbot as one on whom I placed the chain of anathema unjustly, which I neither could nor should have done in justice. On account of his own high rank and that of his church, I declare that I could not and should not have demanded anything save out of his voluntary charity. Similarly I proclaim him free from today and for all time from all episcopal exactions and customs.'

The king then said, 'Is it correct that you have done and said this not under compulsion, but voluntarily?'

The bishop said, 'It is true. I have done and said this voluntarily, on the compulsion of right reason.'

The archbishop said, 'Lord king, now that the affair has been settled justly, we all, as one, pray your clemency for the bishop. Though he may seem to have said some imprudent and unwarranted things against the prerogative of your highness, may your clemency deign to answer our prayers and offer him your kiss of peace and your forgiveness.'

The king said, 'Moved by your prayers and by love of him, I would give him the kiss of peace not once only, but a hundred times, forgiving him all, if there is anything to forgive.' Getting up, he embraced the bishop and kissed him.

The archbishop said, 'Now let the bishop and the abbot kiss as friends and, keeping the pact of peace between them that you have confirmed, let them stay at peace in the future.' Then the bishop and the abbot at the king's command exchanged kisses while the

precepto se deosculantes, archiepiscopo signo[a] crucis super illos faciente, pacis et dilectionis federe iuncti, concordes effecti sunt.[1]

Archiepiscopus: 'Adhuc quiddam restat, quod in hac scilicet pacis et dilectionis concordia uenerabilis frater abbatis Ricardus de Luci episcopo iungatur.' Qui ilico, rege precipiente, utpote uir modestie atque prudentie uirtute insignis episcopo pacis osculum, oblitis occasionibus omnibus, prelibauit. His itaque rite perfectis, omnibus de pacis dilectione inter illos hoc modo confirmata
f. 84 con/gaudentibus,[b] rex ad alia negotia sua inde recedens tetendit perficienda. Abbas uero ad propria rege concedente reuersus est, dominum Iesum Christum, et beatissimam Mariam matrem eiusdem, necnon et beatum Christi confessorem Martinum, qui nunquam deserit sperantes in se, cum suis collaudans, et gaudio magno pro uoto suo exultans adepto.

Hoc igitur fine et termino finali res ista diu in dubio posita, in presentia domini nostri regis Henrici secundi, presente etiam Theobaldo Cantuariensi archiepiscopo, Rogero Eboracensi archiepiscopo, Ricardo Lundoniensi episcopo, Roberto Lincolniensi episcopo, Roberto Exoniensi episcopo, Siluestro abbate sancti Augustini Cantuarie, Gausfrido abbate Holmensi,[2] Thoma cancellario regis, Roberto comite Legacestrie, Patricio comite Saresberie, Henrico de Essexia, regis tribuno, Ricardo de Luci, Raginaldo de Warenna, Guarino filio Geroldi, presente quoque ipso Cicestrensi episcopo Hilario, et eodem abbate prenominato Waltero, et aliis tam clericis quam laicis multis, v kalendas Iunii apud Colecestriam determinata est.[3]

Ad exprimendam uiri uenerabilis abbatis Walteri quam pro commisse sibi ecclesie libertate tuenda exercuit instantem sollicitudinem, sufficiat hactenus ista dixisse. In quibus quot corporis
f. 84v uexationes, quot ani/mi anxietates priusquam hoc fine concluderentur, quot etiam expensarum dispendia sustinuerit, nemo est qui facile possit explicare. Licet igitur plurimum fatigatus, licet

[a] *Sic MS. Recte* signum? [b] *A new hand begins with the new fol., and writes the remainder of the text*

[1] Much later, during his own quarrel with the king, Becket referred to this case in very different terms. He was writing to Pope Alexander both to defend himself against the accusation that he himself had helped Henry to enlarge his prerogative claims over the church, and to shock the pope with the extent of Henry's claims. Since he evidently felt he had to bring up the case of Battle abbey, it must have been an open and long-remembered scandal. Becket's words to the pope do not have the ring of genuinely outraged honesty, when they

archbishop made the sign of the cross over them. And thus, joined in a bond of peace and love, they were made friends.[1]

The archbishop said, 'One thing yet remains. Let the abbot's venerable brother Richard de Luci be joined to the bishop in this alliance of peace and love.' Instantly, at the king's command, Richard, a man remarkable for his correctness of conduct and his prudence, offered the bishop the kiss of peace, all quarrels forgotten. These ceremonies over, everyone congratulated them on the alliance thus confirmed between them, and the king left to finish his other business. With the king's consent the abbot returned home with his entourage, praising the lord Jesus Christ and His most blessed mother Mary, and St. Martin, Christ's confessor, who never deserts them who trust in him, and exulting with great joy that he had achieved what he had wished.

This issue, so long in doubt, was finally settled on 28 May at Colchester in the presence of our lord King Henry II and with these witnesses: Theobald, archbishop of Canterbury, Roger, archbishop of York, Richard, bishop of London, Robert, bishop of Lincoln, Robert, bishop of Exeter, Silvester, abbot of St. Augustine's, Canterbury, 'Geoffrey', abbot of Hulme,[2] Thomas the king's chancellor, Robert, earl of Leicester, Patrick, earl of Salisbury, Henry of Essex, the king's constable, Richard de Luci, Reginald de Warenne, Warin fitzGerold. Hilary, bishop of Chichester and Abbot Walter were also present, as were many others, both clerks and laymen.[3]

Let it suffice to have said this much, in order to portray the zealous care exercised by the venerable Abbot Walter in protecting the exemption of the abbey entrusted to him. In the course of it, no one can easily relate how many bodily vexations and mental anxieties he sustained before it could be brought to such an end, or how much expense he went to. He was much harassed, and not a

are compared with the words attributed to him by our author in this work that would be kept private within Battle abbey: 'Sed et episcopus Cicestrensis quid profecit adversus abbatem de Bello, qui, privilegiis apostolicis fretus, cum ea nominasset in curia, et abbatem denuntiasset excommunicatum, eidem incontinenti coram omnibus communicare compulsus est sine omni absolutione, et eum recipere in osculo pacis? Sic enim placuit regi et curiae quae ei in nullo contradicere audebat; et hoc, sanctissime pater, contigit, tempore vestri decessoris et nostri.' *Materials*, vii. 242–3, no. 643. Becket's outline of the case substantiates that of our author, who would, one may suppose, have been more than surprised at Becket's later tone.

[2] See above, p. 181, n. 1.

[3] The charter, with these witnesses, is printed also in Saltman, *Theobald*, no. 11, pp. 243–4.

plurima corporis sui parte inualidus, non tamen proprie imbecillitati, non expensis parcere uoluit, quin commisse sibi ecclesie utilitati et promotioni omnimodis inuigilaret. Voti itaque sui, in libertatis sue ac dignitatis conseruata integritate, compos effectus, nichilque sibi iam in hac parte ueritus, aggreditur male dispersa reuocare, et hostilitatis tempore alienata iuri ecclesiastico mancipare. Ex quibus quoniam exemplificandi gratia quedam posteris mandare decreuimus, ut res amplius possit elucescere, necesse est retroacta tempora breuiter replicare.

Dum adhuc Anglorum gubernacula teneret inclitus rex Henricus, nobilissimi regis Willelmi Anglice monarchie conquisitoris et ecclesie sancti Martini de Bello fundatoris filius, felicis memorie abbas Radulfus, qui tunc temporis eidem ecclesie preerat, a quodam Ingelranno cognomento Beccheneridere, homine Wiðelardi de Baillol, ipso Wiðelardo consentiente ut suprascriptum est, tres wistas terre in Bernehorne dato pretio comparauit.[1] Addidit autem gratis de proprio idem Wiðelardus quandam partem terre in marisco prefatis tribus wistis contiguam, et tam ab homine suo Ingelranno scilicet comparatam quam et donum proprium eidem
f. 85 ecclesie de / Bello concessit. Et ut eadem terra omnino libera ab omni seruitute et ab omnium hominum calumpnia in perpetuum eidem ecclesie remaneret, a iamdicto magnifico rege Henrico et a comite Augi Henrico, domino eiusdem Wiðelardi, confirmata est.[2] Cum uero multo iam labore multisque expensis, in domibus, in agriculturis instaurata esset eadem terra, molendino etiam optimo in marisco facto, iamque plurimum commodi expectaretur, precipue cum esset ecclesie contigua, quasi quinque milibus distans,[3] abbate Radulfo huic uite finem faciente, et Warnerio succedente, dominus fundi eundem abbatem Warnerium conuenit, frequenter ab eo plurima exigens tanquam pro beneficii recompensatione. Sed cum abbatem iam tederet eius exactionum, reputans ne forte mala exinde traheretur consequentia, iamque ea que idem fundi dominus frequenter exigebat fructus a iamdicta terra prouenientes uiderentur excedere, abbas manum omnino retraxit, nec se de cetero huiusmodi uexationibus et exactionibus uelle subiacere constanter

[1] See p. 118. Barnhorn is on the coast near Bexhill. The manor's lands extended later into the marsh, but at this period reclamation was just beginning. The edge of the marsh slopes sharply upward to Ingelran's land, an ideal holding for a

strong man. Yet he would spare neither his own weakness nor expenses; rather he took infinite pains to guard the prosperity of his abbey and to advance it. Now that he had finished the affair as he wished, with the exemption and privileges preserved intact, and had nothing to fear from that quarter, he set about recovering what had been badly let go, and getting title, as the right of the church, to what had been alienated in the time of the war. And since we have determined to pass down to our successors some cases as examples, we must briefly refer to an earlier time, in order to elucidate matters fully.

Back in the days of the famous King Henry son of the noble King William, conqueror of the English throne and founder of the church of St. Martin of Battle, Abbot Ralph, of happy memory, had charge of the abbey. For a price he purchased three wists in Barnhorn from Ingelran, called 'beacon-rider', the vassal of Withelard de Baillol, with Withelard's consent, as we have noted above.[1] Indeed Withelard added gratis, from his own land, part of the marsh adjoining the three wists, and made over to Battle abbey both the land bought from his vassal Ingelran and his own gift. And so that the land might remain the church's, free from all service and from the claims of all men in perpetuity, it was confirmed by the noble King Henry and by Henry count of Eu, Withelard's lord.[2] Much labour and expense were then put into land reclamation and building, improving the holding greatly. An excellent mill was built in the marsh, and it was expected to be very profitable, since it lay only five miles from the abbey.[3] After Abbot Ralph died and Warner succeeded, the lord of the estate came to him often, demanding many things as payment for the fief. The abbot wearied of his demands, thinking to himself that evil consequences might perhaps grow out of the affair; and already the lord of the fief was by now demanding more than the yield of the land. Then the abbot retreated, saying that he did not wish to subject himself to constant harassment and demands of this sort. The exactor,

radcnecht. Such a man can be found performing his service in the *Carmen*, ll. 149–67.

[2] The count's charter is extant: HBA charter, vol. 42/1132. Henry I's confirmation is *Regesta*, ii, no. 1061.

[3] The monks of the early twelfth century had little arable land within carting distance. Barnhorn was throughout the Middle Ages a chief supplier of corn. Searle, *Lordship*, p. 455. HBA Accounts: Barnhorn. At such an early date (1107–24) the mill, built in the sea-marsh rather than on the windy coastal upland, would presumably have been a tidal mill.

asseruit. Cernens idem exactor se quesita pro uelle assequi non posse, totam prefatam possessionem, quasi in ius suum redigens, ecclesie de Bello subduxit, eamque cuidam Hastingensium Siwardo nomine Sigari filio, accepta ab eo pecunia, in uadimonium tradidit. Hac itaque uiolentia spoliata est ecclesia non tantum terra ipsa, sed
f. 85v et expensis, et omnibus que tunc temporis in ipsa re/perta sunt. Quod cum satis egre abbas et eius procuratores accepissent, et hinc magnas ac multimodas querimonias mouissent, domino rege Henrico in transmarinis partibus ab hac uita subtracto, nullam iuris sui restitutionem habere potuerunt. Succedente rege Stephano, cuius temporibus, iustitia minus preualente, qui plus poterat plus faciebat, sicque interdum cedebat unicuique pro iure, quod quoquo modo diripuisset, ecclesia sancti Martini de Bello non modo predictum tenementum de Bernehorne, sed et alia perplurima sui iuris uiolenter sublata recuperare nequiuit, licet frequenter inde moueretur calumpnia.

Succedente post decessum regis Stephani inclito rege Henrico, prioris Henrici nepote, qui auita tempora renouaret, cum iam Warnerius abbas cessisset, eique uir uenerabilis abbas Walterus successisset, idem abbas Walterus quo regi familiaris fieret obtinuit, sicque coram eo super iamdicto tenemento de Bernehorne querimoniam mouit. Rex igitur ad abbatis instantiam litteris suis Iohanni tunc comiti Augi precipiendo mandauit, ut abbati super predicto tenemento plenum rectum teneret, aut si non faceret, uicecomes Sussexie hoc faceret, ne rex inde amplius clamorem audiret.[1] Gilebertus uero de Baillol, qui tunc temporis dominus fundi uidebatur, super hoc multis modis conuentus, et per comitem, uicecomitem, abbatem et suos requisitus,[2] per plurimum tempus actum subterfugit, et ne conflictum iniret multipliciter dissimulauit.
f. 86 Vn/de licet plurimum temporis casso labore consumeretur, noluit tamen abbas ceptis desistere, sed dominum regem tum per se, tum per suos sepe conueniens, ut causa ipsa in curiam regiam transferretur tandem obtinuit. Sed domino rege nunc in Normanniam transfretante, nunc in Angliam redeunte, negotiisque propriis insistente, cum causa eadem coram iusticiis qui uice regis in eius

[1] This seems to be the only record of this writ. It is a writ of right or a writ *precipe*, ordering the court of Eu to convene his honorial court of Hastings rape, and threatening the count with a shire-court in the matter if he cannot settle the case. For the writs, and for this case in particular, see Van Caenegem, *Writs*, pp. 206–12, 220–1, 234–5. For a similar writ of Henry II see *Facsimiles of Early Charters from Northamptonshire Collections*, ed. F. M. Stenton, Northampton-

seeing that he was unable to get just what he was demanding, withdrew the entire property from the church of Battle, as if bringing it back under his legal control, and gave it in gage for money to Siward of Hastings, called 'Sigar's son'. By this violence was the church despoiled not only of the land, but of its investment and of everything found on the land at that time. This was most disagreeable to the abbot and his administrators, and they raised many and various complaints. But across the channel King Henry had died, and they were unable to get any restoration of their rights. King Stephen succeeded, and in his time justice seldom prevailed. He who was strongest prevailed. So for some time one yielded to anyone as his right what in fact he had stolen. The church of St. Martin of Battle was unable to recover not only the Barnhorn tenement, but many other of its rightful possessions that had been violently taken, no matter how frequently complaints were made.

After King Stephen's death the famous King Henry succeeded, grandson of the earlier Henry. He brought back the times of his grandfather. By then Abbot Warner had resigned and had been succeeded by the venerable Abbot Walter. This abbot managed to become a friend of the king and thus he took before him a complaint about Barnhorn. At the abbot's request the king sent a writ to John, count of Eu, ordering him to do full right to the abbot concerning the tenement, and warning that if he did not, the sheriff of Sussex would do so, in order that the king might hear no more complaint about the matter.[1] Gilbert de Baillol, at that time titular lord of the estate, was addressed in many ways about this, and summoned by the earl, the sheriff, the abbot, and his men.[2] But for long he did nothing and made all sorts of excuses to avoid the suit. Such proceedings wasted a great deal of time in fruitless effort, but the abbot would not give up. He kept petitioning the king, both personally and through his friends, and at length got the case transferred to the royal court. But the king would now be crossing to Normandy and now returning to England on his own affairs. Therefore, although the case was over a long period brought before the justices who presided over his court in the king's place

shire Record Soc. (London, 1930), no. xx, p. 58. The case is discussed by Warren, *Henry II*, pp. 325–7. Warren supposes that de Baillol had mortgaged the land, but the description can equally apply to a *vif-gage* lease. No payments by the abbey for writs appear on the pipe-rolls of Henry II.

[2] In the return of John, count of Eu, in 1166, Gilbert is shown as holding 'of the old enfeoffment' a fief owing the service of three knights. *Red Book*, i. 203.

curia presidebant diutius uentilaretur, licet rex nunc mandatis nunc preceptis abbati plenitudinem iustitie frequentissime indiceret exhiberi, nunquam tamen res digno potuit fine concludi.

Domino rege tandem apud Clarendonam moram faciente, post multa aduerse partis subterfugia, post dissimulationes plurimas, post abbatis et suorum fatigationes multimodas, utrique parti regia indicitur auctoritate, ut die determinato regio tribunali apud locum prefatum sine omni subterfugio et dissimulatione debeant pariter assistere. Cum igitur excusationi iam locus non esset, assunt utrinque, domino rege pro tribunali residente. Astant in medio unus ex monachis abbatis, Osmundus nomine, et Petrus de Chriel miles,[1] qui ab initio totius cause incipientes, qualiter iamdicta terra de Bernehorne ex parte fuerit ecclesie sancti Martini de Bello data, ex parte comparata, qualiter postmodum ablata, quousque etiam iam per plurimum tempus post litis ingressum transactum processum sit in causa, coram rege et eius assessoribus ex ordine
f. 86v exposuerunt, conqueri etiam adicientes super plurima / et dispendiosa negotii dilatione, et abbatis ac suorum frequenti et inani fatigatione. Cum igitur iam nichil esset in quo recordationi prosecutionis cause possit merito contradici, curia regia in omnibus testimonium perhibente, ex regis permissione leguntur in omnium audientia cyrographa emptionis et donationis, sed et carte confirmationum. Quibus cum quid responderet pars aduersa minus haberet, Gilebertus de Baillol, ne nichil obicere uideretur, se predecessorum suorum cyrographa audisse, sed nulla sigillorum testimonia in eis se appensa causatur uidere.

Quem intuens uir magnificus ac prudens Ricardus de Luci ipsius abbatis frater, tunc domini regis iusticia prima, querit utrum ipse sigillum habeat. Quo asserente se sigillum habere, subridens uir illustris, 'Moris', inquit, 'antiquitus non erat quemlibet militulum sigillum habere, quod regibus et precipuis tantum competit personis,[2] nec antiquorum temporibus homines ut nunc causidicos uel incredulos malitia reddebat.'

Cumque confirmationi Henrici regis senioris calumpniam niteretur inferre idem Gilebertus, asserens abbatem et monachos domino regi non pro equitate sed pro uoluntate posse persuadere, dominus

[1] De Criol held the adjacent manor of Ashburnham and a house in Battle. The family was one of a network of intermarried Kentish–Sussex minor gentry. Searle, *Lordship*, esp. p. 165. Du Boulay, *Canterbury*, s.n.

and, although the king, now by notifications, now by commands very frequently ordered justice to be done to the abbot, never could the issue be satisfactorily settled.

Finally the king settled for some time at Clarendon. After many subterfuges by the opposing party, after many dissimulations, after much plaguing of the abbot and his men, both parties were notified on royal authority that on a fixed day they were to appear before the royal court there without any excuses. Since there was no essoining, both parties were present, the king presiding over the court. One of the abbot's monks, Osmund, and a knight, Peter de Criol,[1] stood up before everybody and explained the whole matter to the king and his justices from the very beginning: how the land at Barnhorn had been acquired by the church of St. Martin of Battle, partly by gift, partly by purchase; how it had afterwards been taken away, and how far progress had been made on the case in the long period since the beginning of the dispute. They also added a complaint about the long and costly delaying of the business and the frequent, vain importunings by the abbot and his men. Since there could be no reasonable contradiction of this description, and since the royal court bore witness to everything, by the king's permission the chirographs of purchase and gift were read before everyone, as were charters of confirmation. The opposing party had little it could say to these, but Gilbert de Baillol, lest he seem to be making no objection, argued that he had heard chirographs of his predecessors read, but that he did not see the evidence of their seals appended to them.

That august and prudent man, Richard de Luci, the abbot's brother, and at that time the lord king's chief justiciar, looking him over, inquired whether *he* had a seal. He answered that he had a seal. The great man smiled. 'It was not the custom in the past', he said, 'for every petty knight to have a seal. They are appropriate for kings and great men only.[2] Nor in old times did malice make men pettifoggers and cavillers, as is true nowadays.'

Then Gilbert tried to challenge the confirmation of King Henry I, arguing that the abbot and monks were attempting to persuade the lord king not out of a sense of justice, but to have their own way.

[2] No one knew better than de Luci the problems of land-transfer. The statement is evidence that the lord's confirmation, not the authentication of the donor's wish, was warranty in a land-transfer of the early twelfth century. See Milsom, *Legal Framework*, ch. 1.

rex propriis manibus cartam et sigillum aui sui regis Henrici apprehendens, et ad eundem Gilebertum conuersus, 'Per oculos', inquit, 'Dei, si cartam hanc falsam comprobare posses, lucrum mille librarum mihi in Anglia conferres.' Illo ad hec aut paruum
f. 87 aut / nichil respondente, rex subintulit uerbum memoriale: 'Si', inquit, 'monachi per similem cartam et confirmationem huiusmodi ius in presenti loco, scilicet Clarendona, quem plurimum diligo, se habere possent ostendere, nichil esset in quo eis iuste possem contradicere, quo minus eis omnino dimitteretur.'

Conuersus igitur rex ad abbatem et suos, 'Ite', inquit, 'et consilio habito, inuicem conferte, si forte sit aliquid cui amplius quam huic carte uelitis inniti. Non tamen uos puto ad presens aliam quesituros probationem.' Abeuntes itaque abbas et sui super hoc consilium endeavouring inituri, cartam suam ad omnem probationem esse sufficientem cognoscentes ex uerbis regis ultimis, quibus dixit, 'Non uos puto ad presens aliam quesituros probationem,' in presentiam regis et assidentium habito iam consilio redeunt, se non alias inniti aut aliam quesituros, extra cartam, probationem asserunt, nil se maius uel minus extra cartam exigere, super hoc autem se iudicium regie curie expectare. Non habente aduersa parte quid responderet, quippe cum cartam falsitatis nec auderet nec posset arguere, quia non posset probare, unanimi consensu totius curie regie adiudicatum est, abbati et ecclesie sancti Martini de Bello omnia debere restitui, que carte sue exigebat testimonio. Cernens igitur Gilebertus de Baillol se tenemento de Bernehorne esse destitutum, in omnium obsecrat audientia, catalla militis sui qui idem tenementum
f. 87v de / eo tenuerat sibi inde tollenda relinqui. Dominus rex ad hanc petitionem respondens, 'Non poteras', inquit, 'manifestius confiteri, quam hoc petendo, te nullum ius in terra illa habere.' Monuitque rex ut[a] catalla eis dimitterentur.[1]

Ad regis igitur imperium fiunt littere regio sigillo signate, ad quatuor milites qui tunc ex eius precepto uicecomitatum Suthsexie

[a] Rex ut: *Add. in marg. and aligned with text by scribe, who evidently missed the two words in changing to a new line*

[1] Presumably Henry is saying that in making the request, Gilbert is admitting that he will not at a later stage be able to establish his better right to the land, and is trying to get at least something, namely his tenant's chattels, out of it. For this and from the king's earlier advice '*For the present*, I do not think you will

The lord king took the charter and the seal of his grandfather, King Henry, into his own hands and, turning to Gilbert, replied, 'By God's eyes, if you could prove this charter false, you would make me a profit of a thousand pounds in England.' Getting little or no answer to this, the king added this memorable statement, 'If by a like charter and confirmation the monks could show this sort of right to this very Clarendon which I dearly love, there would be no way justly for me to deny that it should be given up to them completely.'

Turning to the abbot and his entourage, the king said, 'Go, take counsel, and consider together whether there is anything on which you would rather rely than on this charter. But for the present I do not think you will look for other proof.' The abbot and his friends went out to consult. They realized from the king's final words, 'for the present I do not think you will look for other proof', that their charter was quite sufficient proof, and after their consultation they returned into the presence of the king and his justices to say that they did not place their reliance in anything else besides the charter, that they demanded neither more nor less than what was in the charter, and that they awaited the judgement of the royal court on the matter. Their adversary had nothing to say; he neither dared nor could impugn the genuineness of the charter, because he could prove nothing. Therefore the whole royal court decided unanimously that everything demanded upon the evidence of their charter should be restored to the abbot and church of St. Martin of Battle. Gilbert de Baillol, realizing that the tenement of Barnhorn had been taken away from him, implored in everyone's hearing that the chattels of his knight who had held the tenement from him be resigned to himself, and removed from there. To this petition the king replied, 'You could not confess more plainly that you have no right in the land than by asking that.' And the king ordered that the chattels be given to the monks.[1]

At the king's order letters were drafted, sealed by the royal seal, and quickly sent to the four knights who at that time, by his

look for other proof', and from the wording of the *consensus*, the proceeding sounds more like *novel disseisin* than a final trial of right; the monks are being put back into possession, but the king does not exclude the possibility of Gilbert suing on the issue of *right* later. The right of a twelfth-century lord to the chattels of his tenant, villein or not, is indirectly recognized in the *Dialogue of the Exchequer*: when the lord fails to pay full scutage, not only his chattels, but those of his knights and villeins are to be sold. *Dialogus*, pp. 111, 112.

regebant celerius directe,[1] ut absque dilatione terram quam abbas de Bello in curia sua coram eo dirationauerat, scilicet tres wistas terre in Bernehorne, cum toto marisco, et decimam quandam de Bocholte, ecclesie sancti Martini de Bello restituerent, tam integre et tam plenarie, tam libere et quiete tenendam, sicut temporibus regis Henrici aui sui teste carta sua tenuerant,[2] designata prius terra ipsa et terminis eius peragratis per duodecim uiros fideles de uicinio ipsius tenementi qui metas eius scirent, et obligati sacramento ueritatem dicerent.[3] Quo suscepto mandato, Ricardus de Chaaines[4] qui unus erat ex iiii^{or} militibus uicecomitatum Suthsexie tunc temporis regentibus, sociorum suorum sibi uice commissa, iamdictum tenementum adiit, sumptoque tam ab hominibus eiusdem tenementi quam et ab his qui in eius confinio habitabant sacramento, metisque designatis abbatem et ecclesiam sancti Martini de Bello inde inuestiuit.

Recuperata hoc modo, licet cum labore et difficultate, sepefata terra, iamque ut putabatur sopitis omnibus, cum remota omni calumpnia nullius esse uideretur mali in posterum suspicio, /
f. 88 Robertus quidam de Yclesham cum matre sua Matilde quoddam pratum infra ambitum tenementi illius positum repente inuasit. Cuius fenum cum ui conaretur auferre, abbas premunitus congregatis uiris quampluribus uim ui reppulit, et fenum, parte aduersa confusa, sibi reponi fecit.[5] Iamdictus ergo Robertus curiam domini regis adiens, et quia rex non aderat in audientia iusticiarum eius conquerens, homines qui sacramento prestito metas tenementi de Bernehorne designare debuerant asseruit plus iusto occupasse, et sic cum non traheretur in causam, terram suam sibi sublatam esse. Ad eius itaque instantem querimoniam abbas cum hominibus qui terram peragrauerant ad curiam agitur, super ea quam idem Robertus affirmabat iniustitia satisfacturus. Nec cunctatus abbas mente robustus, licet corpore inualidus, se die determinato in

[1] For local justiciars see H. A. Cronne, 'The office of local justiciar in England under the Norman kings', *Univ. of Birmingham Historical Jnl.* vi (1957), 18–38, and D. M. Stenton, *English Justice between the Norman Conquest and the Great Charter, 1066–1215* (Philadelphia, 1964), pp. 65–8. Evidently local justiciars were acting in place of a sheriff in the county. See D. M. Stenton, in *Cambridge Medieval History*, v (Cambridge, 1926), p. 584 for references to such justiciars at the time.

[2] The singular implied subject, *ecclesia*, combined with the plural verb shows the chronicler incorporating a writ here. It survives in a long quotation in the *Curia Regis Rolls* (HMSO, London) ii. 178–9. In 1203 John of Northeye claimed

command, governed the county of Sussex.[1] Without delay they were to restore to the church of St. Martin of Battle the land to which the abbot of Battle had established title before the king in his court: namely three wists of land in Barnhorn with the whole marsh, and the tithe of Buckholt, to be held as wholly and fully, as free and quit as they had held them in the time of his grandfather King Henry, witness his own charter.[2] But first the land was to be defined and its boundaries walked by twelve faithful men of the locality who would know its boundaries and would tell the truth on oath.[3] Richard de Kaines,[4] one of the four knights then in charge of Sussex, carried it out for the others. He went to the manor and took the oath both of the men of the manor and of the neighbourhood. They agreed on the boundaries and he then invested the abbot and church of St. Martin of Battle with the land.

In this way the land was recovered after much labour and difficulty. It was thought that all was finally quiet and all claims settled. There seemed nothing to worry about in the future, when suddenly Robert of Icklesham and his mother Matilda seized a meadow that lay within the boundary of the manor. They attempted to carry off the hay by force, but the abbot had been warned and, gathering a number of men, met force with force. He put his adversaries to flight and recovered the hay.[5] Therefore Robert went to the king's court and since the king was absent, he complained to his justices that the men whose duty it had been to mark the boundaries of Barnhorn had taken in more than was just. Thus, although he had not been sued, his land had been taken away from him. As a result of his complaint, the abbot was summoned to court, along with the men who had perambulated the land, to answer for what Robert swore was an injustice. The abbot, strong in mind though weak in body, appeared with no delay before the

the tenement as the son of Reinger who had held it from Gilbert de Baillol at the time of this suit, and the descendant of Ingelran (Engerann) who had held it from a de Baillol in the time of Henry I. Reinger, his son claimed, had been a minor at the time of the suit and should not have been sued, nor should de Baillol, for he had no demesne there, being only its *capitalis dominus*. No decision is recorded, but the abbey kept the land.

[3] An example of the perambulation by neighbours on oath. For their place in twelfth-century land-law see Van Caenegem, *Writs*, pp. 77–9, 84–97.

[4] Richard was a tenant of the honour of Mortain, in Sussex. *PR 23 Henry II*, p. 191.

[5] The taking of its harvest is the vital act in establishing seisin of land. Van Caenegem, *Writs*, pp. 306–7, and ibid., n. 1.

presentia iusticiarum apud Wintoniam exhibuit, hominibus secum adductis qui sepenominatum tenementum de Bernehorne peragrauerant et eius metas designauerant. Astante Roberto de Yclesham et super terra sua sibi subdole ut asserebat sublata conquerente, procedunt prefati xii^{cim} uiri ei in faciem resistentes, iterato sacramentum prestare parati, se non quidem amplius, quinimo ne sacramenti prestiti uiderentur transgressores, minus iusto suo ambitu conclusisse. Vnde idem Robertus, false conquestionis reus esse conuictus, omnium iudicio misericordie regi addicitur. Quo comperto, clam se subtrahens fugam iniit, nec calcarium suorum oblitus, aut equo parcens, prius a fuga destitit, quam ad
f. 88^{v} propria tre/mebundus perueniret. Abbas uero cum suis ad sua gratulabundus rediens, quoad uixit iamdictum tenementum pacifice omni sopita calumpnia possedit.[1] De his quidem hactenus dixisse sufficiat, iamque ad cetera sollicitudinis sue transeamus exercitia.

Preerat eius temporibus domini regis forestariis quidam Alanus de Nouauilla uocatus, qui ex concessa sibi potestate satis malitiose innumeris et insolitis questionibus diuersas per Angliam prouincias uexabat. Quia enim nec Deum nec homines uerebatur, nec ecclesiasticis nec secularibus parcebat dignitatibus. Domino itaque rege in transmarinis agente, inter cetera iniquitatis sue opera idem Alanus in maneria ecclesie sancti Martini de Bello infra terminos forestarum sita insurgens, de uno eorum, scilicet Bromham, xx^{ti} solidos, et de quodam membro eiusdem, scilicet Anestia, dimidiam marcam, et tantumdem de manerio de Bricthwoldintune, pro exartis ui exegit. Collecta est hec pecunia per uicecomites prouinciarum et ad scaccarium domini regis delata, ubi a thesaurariis recepta in erario domini regis est reposita. Quo cognito, abbas unum ex monachis suis cum cartis dignitatum et libertatum suarum ad scaccarium transmisit ut in audientia iusticiarum super hac insolita et indebita exactione conquereretur.[2] Monachus uero eo perueniens coram Roberto comite Legacestrie et Ricardo de Luci, qui tunc summam regni iusticiam uice regis exequebantur, et coram
f. 89 aliis baronibus scacca/rii conquerens super illata iniuria rem ex

[1] Despite the contemptuous description of him, Robert was evidently escaping before he could be forced in to a formal quitclaim without compensation before the justices. The motive is clearly described by Van Caenegem, *Writs*, pp. 43–4. As it turned out, Battle abbey only secured Robert's quitclaim after paying eight marks plus a continuing half-mark per annum. The chronicler's evidently disingenuous *quoad vixit* implies that it was Walter's successor who settled with Robert, and the extant chirograph of Abbot Odo (1175–1200) proves it. HBA charter, vol. 42/709.

justices at Winchester on the appointed day, bringing with him the men who had perambulated the Barnhorn tenement and had determined its boundaries. Robert of Icklesham stood up and made his complaint about his land taken from him, as he asserted, by guile. But the twelve men were firm. They denied this to his face, and so that they might not seem untrue to their oath as warrantors, they were prepared to go further and take an oath again, that they had not included in their boundary more, but less, than was just! So Robert, shown to be guilty of a false plea, was given over to the king's mercy by a unanimous judgement. When he heard this, he took flight secretly, sparing neither his spurs nor his horse, nor pausing till he reached home, all a-tremble. The abbot with his entourage returned home rejoicing, and as long as he lived he held the tenement peacefully, quit of all claims.[1] This is all that needs saying about the affair, and we shall pass on to other examples of his solicitude.

In those days Alan de Neville was chief among the king's foresters. By the power given him he most maliciously harried the various counties throughout England with countless and unaccustomed inquisitions. Since he feared neither God nor men, he spared neither ecclesiastical nor secular privileges. The king had gone across the channel, and this Alan, among his other works of iniquity, bestirred himself against those manors of the church of St. Martin of Battle that lay within the forest. By force he demanded from one of them, Bromham, 20*s*., and from its member, Anesty, a half-mark, and as much again from Brightwalton, for assarts. This money was collected by the sheriffs of the counties and taken up to the lord king's Exchequer, where it was received by the treasurers and deposited in the lord king's treasury. When the abbot found this out, he sent one of his monks to the Exchequer with the charters of his privileges and liberties, to complain to the justices about this unwonted and undue exaction.[2] The monk arrived there and took the complaint about the injury to Robert, earl of Leicester, and Richard de Luci, who were at that time acting as the king's chief justiciars in his place, and to the other barons of the Exchequer. He explained the matter thoroughly, offered the

[2] The abbey's forged foundation charters contain general exemption from 'all aids and pleas', from 'all custom of earthly service and all subjection and exaction of any persons whatsoever'. *Regesta*, i, no. 62; ii, no. 348a, p. 401. One refers specifically to assarts: *Regesta*, i, no. 261. A charter was probably forged for this very occasion, however, for it alone contains forest clauses and hunting rights for the abbot. *Regesta*, i, no. 263; ii, p. 397.

ordine pandit, cartas legendas proponit, restitutionem ablatorum expetit. Auditis ex cartarum testimonio ecclesie libertatibus, omnium unanimi iudicio pecunia iamdicta iam per plures dies in thesauro regis reposita extrahitur, coram omnibus monacho redditur, franguntur tallie, omnisque eiusdem pecunie memoria de rotulis eraditur.[1] Domum uero rediens idem monachus abbati rei geste ordinem insinuat, pecuniam sepedictam suo arbitrio relinquit. Quam abbas suscipiens ad prenominata maneria transmisit, hominibus a quibus exacta est restituendam.

Predictus uero Alanus quoad uixit, ut regi thesaurizaret, quaslibet tam ecclesiasticas quam seculares personas uexare non destitit, et ut placeret regi terreno, regem non timuit offendere celestem. Vnde quantum gratiarum a rege, cui sic placere studuit, in fine consecutus sit, rei exitus docuit. Nam cum ad extrema deductus esset, cuiusdam monasterii fratres aliquid de eius substantia, ut credi potest, monasterio suo conferri cupientes, rege adito, tollendi et apud se humandi cadauer illius licentiam quesierunt. Quibus rex affectum suum circa eum hoc modo insinuans, 'Mea', inquit, 'erit eius substantia, uestrum sit eius cadauer, demonum inferni anima ipsius.' Ecce dolenda retributio, ecce tam sui quam substantie sue miserabilis facta distributio. Datur hinc quarumlibet potestatum officialibus sibi precauendi materia, dum hunc de quo sermo est attenderint ex malignitatis sue operibus a rege cui placere studuit nichil gratiarum aut boni affectus con-
f. 89v secutum / esse, sed et celestis regis offensam incurrisse. His igitur, que per digressionem diximus, eo quod ad rem minus spectare uidentur, omissis, ad ea que de uiro uenerabili abbate Waltero restant dicenda redeamus.

Sed quoniam ecclesia sancti Martini de Bello, sicut et quamplures per Angliam ecclesie, hostilitatis tempore sub rege Stephano suo iure multipliciter est spoliata, quod, redeunte postmodum pace sub magnifico rege Henrico secundo, per eiusdem abbatis industriam est consecuta, necesse est in singulis rebus breuiter summatimque iustam in primis possessionem, iniustamque postmodum spoliationem frequenter ad preterita tempora recurrendo insinuare, ut in restitutionis executione possit res plenius elucescere.

[1] The pipe roll for 1166–7 retained the reference, noting that Battle abbey had been given quittance as the result of its liberties as contained in its charters. *PR 13 Henry II*, PR Soc. xi (1889), pp. 8, 132. The chronicler shows that he understood Exchequer procedure and was probably the abbot's agent on the

charters to be read, and sought restitution of what had been taken. Having listened to the liberties of the abbey from the evidence of the charters, all unanimously judged that the money, already several days in the king's treasury, be taken out again. In front of everyone, it was given to the monk, the tallies were broken, and all mention of the money was erased from the rolls.[1] When he returned home the monk explained the whole affair to the abbot and left the money to his judgement. The abbot took the money and sent it to the manors to be restored to the men from whom it had been taken.

This Alan never left off plaguing both ecclesiastics and laymen as long as he lived, in order to enrich the king. To please an earthly king he feared not to offend the king of heaven. But how much gratitude he earned from the king he thus strove to please, the outcome showed in the end. When he was dying, the brothers of a certain monastery, hoping (as one may well believe) to get for their house some of his wealth, went to the king and sought permission to bury his body among them. The king showed his feelings about him in his reply: 'His wealth is going to be mine. You may have his corpse. The devils of hell may have his soul.' Behold the mournful recompense; behold the wretched distribution of him and of his wealth. This should be a warning to officials of whatever powers, that they should consider this man of whom we speak. By his evil deeds he won neither gratitude nor goodwill from the king he strove to please, but he incurred the wrath of the heavenly king. But this has been a digression, for it has little to do with the issue in hand. We shall leave it therefore and return to what remains to be told of Abbot Walter.

Like many churches throughout England in the time of the strife under King Stephen, Battle abbey was despoiled in many ways of its rights. When peace returned under the noble King Henry II, it regained them by the industry of its abbot. It is necessary therefore in each affair to give a brief summary of the original just possession and of the subsequent unjust spoliation, frequently going back over times past, so that the issue in the prosecution of the recovery may be shown clearly.

occasion. His remark that there was an erasure from rolls is significant as very early evidence for the existence of Memoranda Rolls. *The Dialogue of the Exchequer* mentions rolls of this sort in the reign of Henry II, but the earliest surviving roll is 1199–1200. *Dialogus*, pp. 115, 151. *Memoranda Roll 1 John*, ed. H. G. Richardson, PR Soc. N.S. xxi (1943).

Superiori digestum est narratione, Willelmum regem, incliti regis Willelmi Anglie conquisitoris et ecclesie de Bello fundatoris filium, dedicationi eiusdem ecclesie interfuisse, eique in dotem quasdam ecclesias in fundo dominii sui in Norðfolkia, Suðfolkia, et Essexia sitas concessisse, ita quidem ut, personis decedentibus que prius institute erant, de cetero tam personatus earum quam et fructus ex eis prouenientes ecclesie de Bello perpetualiter cederent. Quarum persone cum usque ad hostilitatis que erat sub rege Stephano tempora ex plurima parte superstites fuissent, quidam, quibus territoria in quibus eedem ecclesie site uidentur, postea quam effecte sunt dotales a regibus, concessa sunt, ius patronatus in ipsis ecclesiis querebant. Agentes itaque plus pro uoluntate quam pro ratione, quos uoluerunt institui fecerunt, ecclesia sancti Martini de Bello penitus destituta. /

f. 90 Exempli igitur gratia, sub hac hostilitatis tempestate erat quidam Robertus de Creuequeor, uir quidem secundum idem tempus prepotens et magni nominis, qui quoddam regis predium, Middehale scilicet, ex regis Stephani largitione possidebat.[1] Cuius territorii ecclesia una erat ex dotalibus ecclesiis a rege Willelmo secundo in dedicatione ecclesie sancti Martini de Bello concessis. Decedente uero ipsius ecclesie de Middehale persona, iamdictus Robertus ius patronatus in ea uendicans, de rapina deo uictimas offerens,[2] eam canonicis de Ledes concessit et confirmauit.[3] Quo cognito, uir uenerabilis abbas Walterus, nunc prefatum Robertum super iniusta inuasione, nunc canonicos super uiolenta intrusione et restitutione facienda conuenit, nec impetrauit. Queritur hinc iustitia regalis, inde ecclesiastica, sed habundante iniquitate ad tempus non inuenitur.[4] Rege Stephano decedente, et pacifico rege Henrico secundo succedente, hostilitas expellitur, pax iampridem expulsa reuocatur. Abbas ergo tempus oportunum nactus, quippe cum iustitiam paulatim uigore resumpto reflorere uideret, causam suam nunc in curia regali, nunc in ecclesiastica uentilandam exponit. Canonici uero patrono suo Roberto scilicet iam destituti, nil sibi prosperum in hac parte sperantes, pro uiribus

[1] A Kentish baron. His son Daniel de Crèvecœur is found holding as early as 1155–6. *PR 2–3–4 Henry II* (1844, repr. 1930), p. 66. He had a large holding in Kent in the returns of 1166. *Red Book*, i. 190–1, 203. He also held of the count of Eu in Hastings rape where Battle lay, but by 1166 he did not hold anything for service in Suffolk. For an Anglo-Norman genealogy of the family see

In the above narration, it has been said that King William, son of King William the famous conqueror of England and founder of Battle abbey, was present at the dedication of the church and endowed it with some churches from his own demesne in Norfolk, Suffolk, and Essex. When the parsons already invested with them died, the rectories and the issues of the rectories were to fall to the church of Battle for ever. The parsons for the most part survived into the time of strife under King Stephen, and certain men, who had been given the territories in which these churches are physically located, after the churches had been given by kings as part of the endowment, sought the right of patronage in them. Urged more by will than reason, they caused to be instituted whom they liked, and the church of St. Martin was quite defrauded.

For example: during the disturbances of the anarchy there was one Robert de Crèvecœur, a man of great power and a great name at that time. He held the royal manor of Mildenhall by the gift of King Stephen.[1] The church of the area was one with which King William II had endowed Battle abbey at its dedication. When the parson of Mildenhall church died, this Robert appropriated the right of patronage and, offering to God sacrifices from plunder,[2] he gave it to the canons of Leeds.[3] When Abbot Walter found this out, he brought actions, now against Robert for unjust disseisin, now against the canons for violent intrusion and for restitution. But he could get nowhere. He appealed to royal and to ecclesiastical justice on the matter, but justice was not to be found in the midst of iniquity.[4] When King Stephen died and the peace-loving Henry II succeeded, violence was banished and long-banished peace recalled. The abbot watched justice gradually come to flourish once more with renewed strength, and when he found a suitable time he took his case both to the royal court and to the ecclesiastical. The canons were by now bereft of their patron, Robert, and could hope for no success that way, but nevertheless

Leslie Sherwood, 'The Cartulary of Leeds Priory', *Archaeologia Cantiana*, lxiv (1951), 34.

[2] Augustine, *Sermo*, 113, no. 2: *PL*, xxxviii, cols. 648–9. Gratian, C. 14 q. 5 c. 2. Cf. Prov. 15: 8.

[3] Founded by Robert de Crèvecœur. L. Sherwood, p. 26, notes an agreement in the Leeds cartulary between Abbot Odo of Battle (1175–1200) and the monks of Battle, and Prior Nicholas and the canons of Leeds, regarding reciprocal rites for one another's dead. The agreement probably marks the end of this dispute.

[4] Cf. Matt. 24: 12. Possibly an oblique reference to Prov. 15: 5, 'In abundanti justicia virtus maxima est: cogitationes autem impiorum eradicabuntur.'

tamen restiterunt. Sed cum iam nullum esset diffugium, ad sedem apostolicam utrinque est appellatum. Presidebat tunc temporis Romane ecclesie papa Adrianus, ad cuius audientiam causa uentilanda dirigitur.[1] Ventilata igitur iam aliquandiu causa in curia
f. 90v Romana, tan/dem definito consilio nuntii qui ob id illuc missi fuerant in Angliam remittuntur, duobusque Anglie episcopis, Ricardo scilicet Londoniensi, et Iocelino Saresberiensi, causa eadem audienda et terminanda auctoritate apostolica committitur.[2] Licet enim domino pape de iure ecclesie sancti Martini de Bello, quinetiam toti curie Romane satis constiterit, tum ex clerici cuiusdam Alexandri nomine qui uices eiusdem ecclesie tunc ibidem exequebatur uiua assertione, tum ex domini Cantuariensis archiepiscopi Theobaldi et quarundam aliarum personarum testimonio, que propriis oculis uisa, auribus audita, manibus contrectata, scripto notauerant, et sigillis suis munita ad eandem curiam transmiserant, noluit tamen dominus papa diffinitiuam promulgare sententiam, quinimmo causam ipsam iamdictis episcopis commisit diffiniendam. Rediens in Angliam prefatus clericus Alexander, mandati apostolici baiulus, episcopis illud presentauit, et ut pars aduersa citaretur obtinuit.

Quotiens igitur canonici actum subterfugerint, quotiens dissimulauerint, quotiens mandatum apostolicum plus arte quam ueritate deluserint, quotiens re minus efficaciter procedente iterata conquestio nunc ad regias cis mare, nunc ad apostolicas trans mare delata sit aures, non est qui facile possit explicare. Post multiplices tandem fatigationes, prescriptis iudicibus, tum apostolica tum regia auctoritate, precipitur ut omni occasione remota, partibus conuocatis, res audita et decisa iusto et debito fine terminetur. Igitur dies peremptorius prefigitur partibus apud uillam que
f. 91 dicitur / Stanes, ut illic ueritate rei diligentius ac plenius inquisita iustitie plenitudo hinc inde exhibeatur. Die et loco determinato adest uir uenerabilis Iocelinus episcopus Saresberiensis, assunt et quidam ex clericis uiri uenerabilis Ricardi episcopi Londoniensis, tunc ne illic interesset corporis inualitudine detenti, assunt inquam domino Saresberiensi in iudicio assessuri, commisasque sibi uices domini sui executuri. Abbate ad diem et locum, non in propria persona, sed per procuratorem sufficientem apparente pars aduersa,

they resisted as much as they could. When at last there were no twists left, both sides appealed to the holy see. At that time Pope Adrian presided over the Roman church and the case was directed to him for a hearing.[1] For some time it was aired at the Roman court, which finally decided that the messengers who had been sent there with it should go back to England. The case was referred to two English bishops, Richard of London and Jocelin of Salisbury, to be heard and settled with apostolic authority.[2] Now the rights of Battle abbey should have been clear to the pope and indeed to the whole Roman court, through both the oral explanation of the abbot's current agent, a clerk named Alexander, and the testimony of Archbishop Theobald and others, as to what they had seen with their own eyes, heard with their own ears, felt with their own hands. This evidence they had put into writing, sealed with their seals, and sent to the Roman court. However, the lord pope was unwilling to make a definitive decision and he sent the case to be decided by the bishops. The clerk Alexander returned to England bearing the papal mandate, presented it to the bishops, and got leave to summon the opposing party.

No one could easily explain how often the canons evaded the case, how much they dissimulated, how many times they mocked the papal mandate by relying upon cunning rather than truth, nor, as the procedure proved ineffective, how often complaints were sent both to the king on this side of the sea and to the pope beyond it. Finally, after many exertions, the judges were ordered by both papal and royal authority to accept no further excuses and to call the parties together, hear the case, and bring it to a just and proper conclusion. A day was set without possibility of essoin for the parties at the town of Staines, where, after very careful and thorough investigation as to the truth of the affair, justice might be fully done. On the set day and at the set place the venerable Jocelin, bishop of Salisbury, was present. The venerable Richard, bishop of London, could not be there because of sickness, and he was represented by several of his clerks who were to assist the lord bishop of Salisbury in judging. The abbot appeared on the day and at the place, not himself, but by a satisfactory attorney. The opposing party, suspecting that they had only the slightest, or indeed no

[1] Adrian IV, 1154–9.

[2] Richard de Belmeis II, bishop of London 1152–62; Jocelin, bishop of Salisbury, 1142–84.

de minimo immo de nullo iure suo plurimum diffisa, nec per se nec per responsalem comparuit. Iudicibus manifestam partis aduerse contumatiam attendentibus, iam nulla poterat intercedere dilatio, quin mox in causa procederent, de iure abbatis et monasterii de Bello certissimi. Data ergo sententia auctoritate apostolica, sequestrata est iamdicta ecclesia de Middehale, et abbati causa rei seruande commissa, data quidem conditione, ut si canonici super eadem causa infra annum ducerent litigandum, abbas prefatam ecclesiam resignaret in manus iudicum. Canonici autem, iusta se iudicii ratione ab iniusta possessione uidentes esse amotos, ad tempus quieuerunt a lite, domino scilicet rege Henrico et abbate Waltero superstitibus. Susceptis iudicum litteris patentibus ad Norwicensem episcopum de inducendo abbate in possessionem ecclesie de Middehale causa rei seruande, abbas mox possessione suscepta ecclesiam cuidam clerico, Roberto philosopho nomine,
f. 91v cuius labore et industria / res ex plurima parte ad hunc finem perducta est, de ecclesia sancti Martini de Bello sub certa pensione tenendam concessit. Quam idem Robertus quoad uixit pacifice possedit, nec erat de cetero qui eum super eadem in causam traheret.[1]

His ita licet cum labore et difficultate consummatis, abbas ad cetera iniuste alienata pro uiribus reuocanda animosior redditur et promtior. Igitur ecclesiam de Trilawe, que una esse dinoscitur ex his quas in dotem ecclesie sancti Martini de Bello a rege Willelmo secundo concessas memorauimus, quidam Rogerus presbiter sub certa pensione ecclesie de Bello annuatim soluenda retroactis temporibus tenuerat. Qui cum postmodum, fidei et religionis oblitus, a debite pensionis cessaret solutione, ipsamque ecclesiam a iure ecclesie sancti Martini de Bello niteretur abalienare, ubi res ad abbatis et conuentus de Bello qui tunc temporis erant peruenit noticiam, eum super hoc instantius traxerunt in causam. Tandem conuictus, cum se resistendi impotem iamque ecclesiastica censura ab ipsius ecclesie possessione cognosceret expellendum, Bellum adiit, super transgressione ueniam petiit, se nil tale de cetero attempturum sacramento in capitulo monachorum coram omnibus prestito promisit, se etiam in plena sinodo prouincie sue asserens

[1] The patronage of Mildenhall church was in fact a more complicated problem than this would indicate, for Bury St. Edmunds also claimed it, as the gift of Edward the Confessor. Battle and St. Edmunds were forced to compose their differences after a long lawsuit. *The Letters of Pope Innocent III*, ed. C. R. and

right at all, did not appear or send an attorney. The judges could not fail to observe this obvious contumaciouness. There could be no delay now; rather, they could proceed in the case, quite certain that the abbot and abbey of Battle were in the right. The opinion was given by apostolic authority that the church of Mildenhall be taken into trusteeship and committed to the keeping of the abbot with the condition that if within the year the canons should institute litigation about it the abbot should resign the church into the hands of the judges. The canons, seeing themselves removed from an unjust possession by a just judgement, kept out of litigation for the time, namely during the lifetimes of King Henry and Abbot Walter. The judges' letters patent authorizing the abbot's custody of the church of Mildenhall were taken to the bishop of Norwich, and the abbot quickly took possession. He granted the church away from Battle abbey on a fixed pension to one Robert, called 'the philosopher', a clerk whose labour and industry were in large measure responsible for this ending. Robert held it peacefully as long as he lived; nor was there henceforward anyone to drag him to law about it.[1]

Though it had been with much labour and difficulty that this success had been won, it made the abbot bolder and more willing to attempt the recovery of other unjustly seized properties. Now, in times past, one Roger, a priest, had held the church of Thurlow for a fixed pension paid yearly to Battle abbey. As we have recorded, it was one of those with which King William II had endowed the church of St. Martin of Battle. After some time this priest, forgetful of fealty and religion, had stopped payment of the pension he owed, and tried to deprive the church of St. Martin of its rights over the church. When this came to the notice of the then abbot and convent of Battle they immediately began a lawsuit against him. His guilt was plain and when at length he recognized that he was powerless to resist and would be ejected from the possession of the church by ecclesiastical judgement, he came to Battle and sought forgiveness. In the chapter house before all the monks he promised on oath that he would in future not try anything of the sort. He declared that he would make it public in a full synod of his diocese that no one had any right in the church of

M. G. Cheney (Oxford, 1967), nos. 408, 436, 694, 750, 1069. Thereafter Battle received a fixed annual pension from Mildenhall, but did not hold the advowson. Searle, *Lordship*, p. 252, n. 9.

omnibus palam facturum, neminem in ecclesia de Trilawe preter abbatem et monachos de Bello ius aliquod habere, ad nullius nisi ad eorum presentionem quempiam illic institui debere. Hac con-
f. 92 ditione ueniam optinuit, / et ex abbatis et conuentus gratia in eadem ecclesia ministrans, et debitam pensionem integre persoluens, quoad uixit, ut datur intelligi, fidelis permansit.

Post cuius decssum, cum iam regnante rege pacifico Henrico secundo uir uenerabilis abbas Walterus ecclesie sancti Martini de Bello preesset, miles quidam Haymo Peccatum dictus, fundi dominus, ius patronatus in ipsa ecclesia de Trilawe uendicans, eam cuidam clerico, Willelmo scilicet de Orbec, abbate et conuentu de Bello inconsultis concessit.[1] Sed cum iam omnibus constaret omne ius ipsius ecclesie ad abbatem et monachos de Bello pertinere, sciens idem miles prefatum clericum ad presentationem suam extra conscientiam abbatis et monachorum per episcopum non facile instituendum, a domino rege litteras quasdam ad episcopum Norwicensem subdole impetrauit, ut antefatum clericum ad ipsius tanquam domini fundi presentationem institueret.[2] Quod et factum est. Sciens uero clericus se minus canonice institutum, et in futurum precauens, abbatem de Bello Walterum adiit, multisque precibus et obsequiorum promissionibus agere cepit, quo per eum in eadem ecclesia confirmaretur, nec tamen optinuit. Abbas itaque non iam equanimiter sustinens commissam sibi ecclesiam iure suo aliquatenus priuari, nunc a regia, nunc ab ecclesiastica curia iustitie plenitudinem sibi petit exhiberi, hinc super militis uiolentia conquerens, inde super clerici intrusione.

Aliquanto tempore per dissimulationes et subterfugia partis
f. 92v aduerse frustra consumpto, cernens abbas cause sue / dispendium generari litteras ad uirum uenerabilem Gilebertum episcopum Lundoniensem[3] a sede apostolica per prefatum Robertum philosophum impetrauit, ut si iudici super clerici in ecclesiam intrusione constaret, eum omni occasione remota amoueret, ipsamque ecclesiam abbati et monachis de Bello auctoritate apostolica restitueret. Citatus clericus semel et iterum, nec comparens, ad

[1] Hamo Peche was an important baron in Suffolk and Norfolk. He held a barony in chief in Suffolk, and held various fiefs of Roger Peverel, of the abbey of Bury St. Edmunds and the honor of Clare. *Red Book*, i. 48, 363, 364, 366–7, 393, 403. He served as sheriff of Cambridgeshire and Huntingdonshire in 1163.

Thurlow save the abbot and monks of Battle, and that no one should be instituted there save at their presentation. On this condition he obtained pardon, serving in that church by grace of the abbot and monks, and paying fully the pension he owed, he remained faithful the rest of his life, as tradition has it.

After his death, when Henry II the peace-lover was already king, and the venerable Walter was abbot of Battle, a knight named Hamo Peche, lord of the manor, laid claim to the right of patronage in the church of Thurlow, and, without consulting the abbot and convent of Battle, he granted it to a clerk, William of Orbec.[1] But since it was known to everyone that the entire right to that church belonged to the abbot and monks of Battle, this knight knew that the clerk would have difficulty in being instituted by the bishop on his own presentation and without the knowledge of the abbot and monks. Therefore he craftily got a mandate from the lord king to the bishop of Norwich to institute the clerk at his presentation as lord of the manor.[2] And so it was done. But the clerk knew that his institution was not canonical, and fearing for the future, he came to Walter, abbot of Battle, and made him many prayers and promises of obedience if only he might be confirmed by him in the church. But he was not successful. The abbot did not take calmly that the church committed to him should be at all deprived of its rights. First from the royal, then from the ecclesiastical courts he sought that full justice be done him, complaining in the former about the violence of the knight, in the latter about the intrusion of the clerk.

After some time had been spent in vain, because of the dissimulations and subterfuges of the opposing party, the abbot, seeing that the case was becoming costly, used Robert 'the philosopher' to obtain a mandate from the apostolic see to the venerable Gilbert, bishop of London,[3] to the effect that if it were judged that the clerk had been intruded into the church, he should remove him without any claim remaining, and should restore the church to the abbot and monks of St. Martin with apostolic authority. The clerk was summoned a first and a second time, and

PR 10 Henry II, PR Soc. vii, p. 16. Of William of Orbec nothing is known; Orbec is in Calvados, whence many of the lay lords and ecclesiastics of the area originated.

[2] Perhaps the king was represented as being ultimate lord of a manor in ancient demesne, and himself presented the clerk as a favour to Hamo.

[3] Gilbert Foliot, bishop of London 1163–87. For Robert 'the philosopher' see *Letters of Gilbert Foliot*, pp. 514–15.

diem tandem peremptorium apud sanctum Paulum Lundoniis uenire compellitur. Conueniunt partes et litem ineunt, episcopo illic presidente iudice. Agit abbas ueritatis, rationis, et cartarum fultus testimonio; renititur clericus pro uiribus, ecclesie licet minus canonice adquisite nolens sponte renuntiare. Demum iudicis arbitrio relinquitur diffinitiua sententia. Qui cum assessoribus suis de omnibus conferens, habito cum eis consilio, ratione sic exigente, clericum tanquam intrusum ab ipsa ecclesia de Trilawe auctoritate apostolica omnino amouit, eandemque abbati et ecclesie sancti Martini de Bello restituit. Addidit autem abbas hanc eandem ecclesiam de Trilawe prefato Roberto philosopho concedere, quam idem Robertus dum uixit sub certa pensione ecclesie sancti Martini de Bello annuatim soluenda possedit pacifice.

Post aliquantum tempus cum huic uite finem fecisset idem Robertus philosophus, abbas ipsam ecclesiam de Trilawe cuidam clerico Thome nomine de se et commissa sibi ecclesia de Bello pensionaliter tenendam concessit. Verum prefatus clericus Willelmus de Orbec, priusquam Thomas clericus in corporalem
f. 93 mitteretur possessionem, predicti / Haymonis Peccati fultus patrocinio, memoratam ecclesiam non timuit iterato illicite occupare. Quo cognito, abbas non iam clericum, qui auctoritate apostolica iampridem inde omnino amotus fuerat, sed militem scilicet Haymonem Peccatum qui ius patronatus uendicabat, in causam trahendum esse decreuit. Igitur in audientia magnatorum qui in curia regia uices domini regis exequebantur, super huiusmodi fatigationibus conquerens, ipsum Haymonem accusat ut illate uiolentie auctorem. Regia ergo auctoritate dies prefigitur, quo pariter apud Lundonias abbas et idem Haymo conueniant, hic conquestionem suam prosecuturus, ille responsurus. Die et loco determinato adest abbas cum suis, nec adest Haymo, sed excusatorem mittens se ne illic interesset finxit corporis inualitudine detineri. Hi uero qui curie regie preerant, super abbatis inani fatigatione et aduerse partis subterfugio indigne ferentes, omne ius ecclesie de Trilawe in manus domni regis iudicauerunt sequestrandum.[1] De cetero alium diem peremptorium apud Norðhamtonam

[1] The cases concerning advowsons appear to have been undertaken between 1164 and *c.* 1170. They portray vividly the problem that is the background of the assizes *utrum* and *darrein presentment*. In the Constitutions of Clarendon in 1164 (cap. 1), Henry II had declared litigation concerning advowsons to be within the competence of his court. Stubbs, *Charters*, p. 164. The assize of *darrein present-*

did not appear. Finally he was forced to come on a fixed date at St. Paul's, London. The parties met and commenced their suit before the bishop as the presiding judge. The abbot pleaded his case, appealing for witness to truth, reason, and charters. The clerk argued with all his might, unwilling to renounce the church, though acquired uncanonically. Finally the time came for the judge to make the final decision. He went over everything with his assistants and listened to their counsel. Reason pointing in this direction, he altogether removed the clerk from Thurlow church by apostolic authority as an intruder, and restored it to the abbot and church of St. Martin of Battle. But the abbot went on to grant the church of Thurlow to Robert 'the philosopher'. As long as he lived he held it peacefully for a fixed annual pension paid to the church of St. Martin of Battle.

Some time after, Robert 'the philosopher' died and the abbot gave Thurlow church to a clerk named Thomas to hold for a pension from himself and from Battle abbey, entrusted to his care. But before Thomas the clerk could be put physically into possession, the clerk William of Orbec, aided by the patronage of Hamo Peche, was bold enough to occupy the church again illegally. When the abbot heard this he decided to implead not the clerk, who had already long since been totally removed from the church by apostolic authority, but the knight Hamo Peche who was claiming the right of patronage. Therefore he complained about this harassment before the magnates who were in the king's court in his place, accusing this Hamo as responsible for the violence. By royal authority a day was given for the appearance of both the abbot and Hamo in London, the one to prosecute his complaint, the other to answer. On the day and at the place set the abbot was there with his entourage, but Hamo did not come, sending instead a fictitious excuse of sickness. Those who were presiding over the king's court were displeased at the useless vexation of the abbot and at the subterfuge of the opposing party, and they adjudged all right of patronage in the church of Thurlow to be taken into the king's hand.[1] Furthermore they decided to set another day, without

ment, which is not relied upon in these cases, was, in Van Caenegem's opinion, not available until 1179–80 (Van Caenegem, *Writs*, 332–3). In Battle's litigation we have a very early example of *curia regis* procedure. After 1180 immediate seisin would be awarded the claimant who, in time of peace, had presented the last parson whose death left the church vacant, without prejudicing the question of right.

prefigi decreuerunt ut prefatus Haymo eo ueniens, quid iuris in ipsa ecclesia sibi uendicauerit publice manifestaret. Abbas uero, cum se ad diem et locum denominatum ueniendo fatigare aut nollet aut non posset, unum ex monachis suis, Osmundum nomine, sufficienter in ipso negotio instructum, cum testimonio cartarum uices suas executurum illuc direxit. Haymo etiam Peccatum, presentiam suam illic minime exhibens, filium suum Gaufridum Peccatum illuc transmisit, patrem de absentia excusaturum, et /
f. 93v de cetero uices eius illic executurum. Conuenientibus hinc inde partibus, monachoque ius ecclesie sue tum uiua uoce, tum cartarum que illic recitabantur testimonio in audientia presidentium exponente, et de illata iniuria conquerente, cum iam ab aduersa parte aliquid in contrarium putaretur obiciendum, repente prenominatus Gaufridus, pro patre suo et se, qui heres eius uidebatur, liti et iuri quod in sepedicta ecclesia de Trilawe hactenus uendicauerant omnino renuntiauit, asserens se contra huismodi cartarum testimonia nil in posterum presumpturum, quippe cum rex, qui ecclesie sancti Martini de Bello iamdictam contulit ecclesiam, posset si uoluisset nullo resistente contulisse et fundum. His contra spem auditis, totum ius ecclesie de Trilawe monasterio sancti Martini de Bello adiudicatur, sicque omnis controuersia quiescens sopitur.

Detinebat tamen adhuc ipsam ecclesiam minus canonice eam adeptus, ut dictum est, Willelmus de Orbec, cuius se tanquam personam gerens quoslibet ex ea prouenientes fructus percipiebat. Aduersus quem restabat agendum, ut de cetero totius querele tolleretur occasio. Sed iam eorum quos antea protectores habere uidebatur patrocinio destitutus, tanto erat discrimini uicinior, quanto a ratione remotior. Ex sola itaque institutione sua per episcopum facta partem suam tueri nitebatur, sed frustra, quippe cum constaret omnibus eam minus esse canonicam. Artatus ergo plurimum, cernens se hinc gratia possidendi, illinc ratione resistendi destitutum, nec ultra inueniens diffugium, toti iuri quod in
f. 94 ipsa ecclesia / uidebatur habere cogitur renuntiare. Veniens igitur in presentiam domini Norwicensis episcopi, ecclesiam cum omni iure suo in manus eius resignauit, sicque eo destituto episcopus prefatum Thomam clericum ad presentationem abbatis et conuentus sancti Martini de Bello instituit. Possedit eam de cetero idem Thomas clericus pacifice sub annua pensione, undique quiescente qualibet aduersariorum inquietatione.

A primis dedicationis monasterii sancti Martini de Bello tempori-

possibility of essoin, at Northampton, when Hamo might come and show publicly what right he claimed for himself in the church. The abbot, either unwilling or unable to tire himself by attending on the day and at the place fixed, sent in his place one of his monks, Osmund, well briefed in the affair, who took with him the evidence of charters. Hamo Peche did not show up, but sent his son Geoffrey Peche to make his excuses and otherwise to act in his place. When the parties were met, the monk complained of the injury and enlarged before the bench upon the right of his church, both orally and by the evidence of the charters that were read aloud. It was thought that something would be said in opposition by the opposing party, but suddenly Geoffrey, on behalf of his father and of himself as heir apparent, wholly renounced the litigation and the right that they had up to then claimed in Thurlow church. He swore that in the future he would undertake nothing against the evidence of charters of this sort, since the king who gave the church to St. Martin's of Battle, could, had he wished, have given the manor too without impediment. These unhoped-for words assured that all right to Thurlow church was awarded to Battle abbey; and thus all the controversy ended.

However, William of Orbec still remained in possession of the church he had taken uncanonically, as we have told. He acted as if he were the parson and received all its profits. It remained to sue him to remove all cause of dispute in future. But now that he was without the patronage of his former protectors, he was as far from reason as he was close to danger. He tried to defend his side of the dispute merely on the grounds that he had been instituted by the bishop. This was useless, since it was apparent to all that it had been uncanonical. He was quite hemmed in: on the one side he saw that he was without the goodwill necessary to possess it; on the other without means of resistance. Finding no other line of escape, he was forced to renounce all right he seemed to have in the church. In the presence of the lord bishop of Norwich he resigned into his hand the church together with any right he had there, and when he had thus been deprived, the bishop instituted Thomas the clerk at the presentation of the abbot and monks of St. Martin's, Battle. After that, this Thomas the clerk held it peacefully for a yearly pension, and all harassment by adversaries was everywhere quieted.

From the earliest times of the dedication of the monastery of St.

bus usque ad uiri uenerabilis Walterii fere nouissima tempora, ex ecclesiis dotalibus eidem monasterio in eius dedicatione a rege Willelmo secundo assignatis pauci et rari prouenere fructus. In earum siquidem assignatione tam regis eiusdem et episcoporum, quam et aliarum personarum que simul dedicationi intererant actum est consilio, ut superstitibus earundem ecclesiarum personis, que ante monasterii dedicationem et earum eidem factam assignationem institute uidebantur, de qualibet earundem nouem ecclesiarum pensio decem solidorum monasterio de Bello annuatim solueretur, et personis decedentibus de cetero tam ecclesiarum quam et fructuum ex eis peruenientium abbati et monachis de Bello dispositio libera relinqueretur. Prudenti etiam actum est discretione, ut abbati singulis annis semel partes illas in quibus ipse ecclesie site uidentur uisitationis gratia adeunti, in singularum ecclesiarum possessionibus ab earum personis, duarum noctium hospitia preter iamdictas pensiones officiosissime prepararentur,
f. 94v ne / si in omni uisitationis ipsius itinere abbas sibi et suis ex propriis omnino prouideret, plus fortassis in expensis quam in fructibus ab ecclesiis prouenientibus esse uideretur.

Igitur personis iamdictis diu superstitibus, cum nil ultra decem solidos abbas et monachi de Bello de singulis ecclesiis per plurimum tempus perciperent, pensiones ipsas, eo quod omnes ex denario numero constarent, 'decimas' appellauerunt. Nemo itaque de nomine 'decimarum' estimet contendendum, tanquam alique portiones decimarum in prefatis ecclesiis, et non magis ipse ecclesie monasterio de Bello sint assignate; cum satis constet, ex regis Willelmi secundi, qui dedicationi interfuit, et fratris eius ac successoris regis Henrici confirmationibus, ipsas ecclesias cum decimis et fructibus ex eis prouenientibus monasterio sancti Martini de Bello integre esse concessas.

De his igitur nouem ecclesiis dotalibus, personis earum adhuc superstitibus, plus abbati et monachis de Bello prouenit laboris quam utilitatis. Quia enim in remotis partibus site non nisi cum difficultate frequenter adiri poterant, abbate et monachis pro negotiorum diuersitate alia procurantibus, et ab earum frequenti uisitatione cessantibus, debite pensiones nunc egre, nunc nullatenus soluebantur. Quo cognito, bone memorie abbas Radulfus, conuentus sui usus consilio, omnium simul ecclesiarum curam cuidam Ricardo de Bellafago Norwicensi archidiacono commisit, sumpto ab eo sacramento apud Bellum, in capitulo monachorum, in

Martin of Battle until almost the very last days of the venerable Walter, the churches with which King William had endowed the monastery at its dedication had provided small and infrequent profits. By the decision of the king and bishops, as well as others who were present at the dedication, a provision of the grant was that the parsons of those churches, if they had been instituted before the dedication of the monastery and the grant of the nine churches to it, should, while they lived, each pay annually to Battle abbey a pension of 10*s*. When the parsons should die, both the churches and their profits should be left to the free disposal of the abbot and monks of Battle thereafter. It was also prudently stipulated that, besides these pensions, two nights' hospitality once every year should be most courteously provided for the abbot by their parsons on the property of each of the churches, should he visit the areas in which they are situated. Otherwise, if on every journey of visitation the abbot had to draw on his own goods for himself and his entourage, the expense might perhaps prove more than the churches provided in profits.

The parsons lived for a long time. And since for a long time the abbot and monks of Battle received nothing beyond 10*s*. a year for each church, and since all these pensions were alike in having the number ten attached to them, they called them 'tenths'. No one should imagine it can be argued from the name 'tenths' that some part of the tithes of the churches had been assigned to Battle abbey, and not the churches completely. For it is fully evident from the confirmations of King William II, who was present at the dedication, and of his brother and successor King Henry, that the churches themselves, with their tithes and their profits, were given in entirety to St. Martin of Battle.

While the parsons of these nine dower churches still survived they were more trouble than use to the abbot and monks of Battle. Since they were situated in far-off parts, they could not be reached often except with great difficulty. The abbot and monks, having a variety of other responsibilities, left off visiting them frequently, and the pensions were paid sometimes reluctantly, sometimes not at all. Abbot Ralph, of happy memory, realized this, and following the counsel of his convent he committed the care of all the churches at once to Richard de *Bello Fago*, archdeacon of Norwich, receiving his oath at Battle in the chapter house, in the presence of all, that he

f. 95 omnium presentia, quod debitas pen/siones annuatim integre solueret, et in conseruatione iuris eorum se ubique omnino fidelem exhiberet.[1]

Sed ut postmodum contigit experiri, et sacramenti neglecta est religio, et multiplex exinde rerum facta est perplexio. Ipso namque Ricardo de Bellafago post aliquantum tempus ad episcopatum promoto, quidam ipsius filius Alanus de Bellafago ecclesiam de Brantham, que una est ex dotalibus ecclesiis, occupauit. Presumpsit hoc sola patris sui minus canonica auctoritate, qui sacramenti et religionis oblitus eandem sibi paulo ante in possessionem redegerat, seque eius tanquam personam gerebat. Cui temerarie filius eius succedens hereditate uidebatur possidere sanctuarium Dei. Succedente post modicum abbati Radulfo iam defuncto abbate Warnerio, defuncto etiam rege Henrico primo, cum rex Stephanus se regni successorem ingereret, pace temporibus suis a regno exclusa, direptioni patebant omnia. Summe tunc temporis uidebatur esse prudentie, cum quis rebus suis iam direptis, siqua forte post direptionem supererant, ne et ipsa diriperentur poterat conseruare, quia iam direpta reuocare omnino erat impossibile. Percipiebat, hac hostilitatis tempestate, fructus et beneficia ecclesie de Brantham Alanus de Bellafago, se ipsius tanquam personam gerens, et licet frequenter commonitus ad satisfaciendum minime consensit. Quoniam igitur nulla erat uirtus cogendi, dilata est pro necessitate temporis omnis aduersus eum actio, si forte succedentia tempora expulsa hostilitate aliquid pacis secum deferrent atque
f. 95v iustitie. Renuntiauit sponte, sub hac patrie turbatione, regimi/ni abbatie de Bello abbas Warnerius, cui post modicum successit uir uenerabilis abbas Walterius. Defuncto interea rege Stephano, et rege Henrico secundo substituto, cum iam in regno pax aliquatenus esset reformata, abbas Walterius commisse sibi ecclesie cepit sollicitius curam agere.

Post aliquantum uero institutionis sue tempus, pro consuetudine eorum qui nouas suscipiunt administrationes, predia et possessiones in diuersis et remotis partibus positas gratia uisitationis aditurus, presbyteris et clericis dotalium ecclesiarum quas in Essexia, Norðfolkia, et Suthfolkia sitas memorauimus dedit in mandatis, ut sibi suisque, pro debita consuetudine, duarum prepararent in ecclesiarum possessionibus hospitia noctium. Perueniens

[1] Richard, perhaps from Beaufour in Calvados, occurs as archdeacon between *c.* 1115 and 1135, in which year he was consecrated bishop of Avranches. He

would pay the pensions owing in full annually, and would be wholly and in all cases faithful in the protection of their rights.[1]

As it afterwards proved, the fulfilment of the oath was neglected, and a tangle of ambiguity was thereby created. After some time Richard de *Bello Fago* was raised to a bishopric, and his son, Alan de *Bello Fago*, appropriated the church of Brantham, one of the dower churches. He dared to do so on the sole and uncanonical authority of his father, who, having forgotten his oath and duty, had a little earlier taken it into his own possession, and was acting as if he were the parson. His son boldly succeeded him and was clearly in possession of a sanctuary of God by inheritance. After a while, Abbot Ralph died and Abbot Warner succeeded. King Henry I died too, and afterwards King Stephen forced himself upon the realm as successor. Peace was driven out during his days, and everything lay open to plunder. In those days it seemed to be the highest prudence for anyone whose possessions had been plundered, if by chance anything remained after the plunder, to guard that as best he might, lest it too be taken, for it was quite impossible to recover what had been plundered. During this anarchy, Alan de *Bello Fago* received the fruits and profits of Brantham church, going on as if he were its parson. Though often reminded, he would not agree to pay anything. Therefore, since there was no power to force him, any action against him was put off by force of circumstances, till, in a new epoch, the anarchy might be brought under control and an element of peace and justice restored. During the country's disturbance, Warner, abbot of Battle, resigned his rule and shortly thereafter the venerable Abbot Walter succeeded him. King Stephen died meanwhile, and Henry II became king, and when peace had been somewhat restored in the realm, Abbot Walter began most actively to exert himself in the administration of the abbey committed to him.

Some little time after his institution, he planned to make a visitation to the manors and possessions in various distant parts, as is the custom of those who undertake new administrations. He therefore gave notice to the priests and clerks of the dower churches in Essex, Norfolk, and Suffolk to prepare for himself and his retinue two nights' lodging on their churches' property, as

was probably related to William de *Bello Fago*, bishop of Norwich, 1085–91, and to Ralph de *Bello Fago*, the Domesday tenant. Le Neve, ed. Greenway, ii. 67.

usque Brantham nuntii baiulus, Alano de Bellafago mandatum abbatis porrexit, sed ille ad eum nec ut dominum nec ut hospitem suscipiendum ullatenus consensit, se nullo huiusmodi circa eum asserens obligari debito. Distulit abbas ad tempus tante iniurie tantique contemptus ultionem querere, si forte idem Alanus in se rediens uellet resipiscere. Cernens Alanus se rem tam presumptuosam impune transisse, nec sic contentus, malo peius studuit adicere.

Abbate namque partes illas, in quibus memorate dotales ecclesie site uidentur, iterato adeunte, contigit eum in festiuitate transitus beati Martini[1] usque Mendelsham, cuius territorii ecclesia una est ex dotalibus, peruenire, et in ecclesie possessione prout decebat a persona eiusdem ecclesie antiquitus instituta Withgaro nomine susceptum, solennitatem patroni sui ibidem
f. 96 celebrem agere. / Volens idem Withgarus suis post se prouidere, abbatem conuenit, ut quendam filium eius, Nicholaum nomine, in ipsam ecclesiam de Mendlesham admittendum consentiret, ipsius abbatis presentatione per episcopum instituendum. Consensit tandem abbas ad petentis instantiam, mediante tamen conditione, ut scilicet idem Withgarus, qui eatenus nomine eiusdem ecclesie decem tantum solidos annuatim soluerat, de cetero solueret xl[a]. Facto utrimque consensu, dies statuitur quo consensus firmius roboraretur. Adest die determinato abbas cum suis apud Colecestriam, adest et cum filio suo Nicholao Withgarus. Firmatur tam a patre quam et filio fidei et sacramenti interpositione de soluenda pensione xl solidorum prememorata conuentio, presentibus illic cum abbate monachis suis, militibus etiam, clericis et laicis quampluribus audientibus. Statuitur postmodum ab abbate dies alius, quo pariter Withgarus et filius eius Nicholaus apud Bellum conueniant, conuentus consensum cum carta confirmationis suscepturi. Assunt pariter apud Bellum die condicto, scilicet in purificatione beate Marie, ubi in abbatis et totius conuentus presentia predictus Nicholaus fidem et sacramentum iterato prestitit de xl[a] solidorum annuatim soluenda pensione, et fidei non ficte circa abbatem et monasterium sancti Martini de Bello fideli conseruatione. Fit ad ista conuentus communis assensus, data sibi carta confirmationis.

Cum igitur per aliquantum tempus prenominate pensionis scilicet xl solidorum facta esset integra solutio, predictus Alanus de Bellafago Withgarum et filium eius Nicholaum callide cir-
f. 96v cumueniens tandem persuasit, ut fidei sacramentique / religione postposita a iamdicte pensionis xl[a] solidorum solutione cessarent.

was due by custom. When the messenger reached Brantham, he presented the abbot's mandate to Alan de *Bello Fago*, but he would not consent to receive him either as lord or as guest, stating that he was bound to him by no duty of this sort. The abbot bided his time in revenging himself for such an injury and such an insult, in case Alan might come to himself and wish to think again. But Alan, finding that he had got away with so presumptuous a thing unscathed, was not content with it, and took care to go from bad to worse.

Now when the abbot came again into those parts in which the dower churches are located, he happened to arrive, on the feast of the death of St. Martin,[1] at Mendlesham, whose church is one of the dower gifts. He was received on the property of the church honourably by one Withgar, long the parson there, and said the solemn mass of his patron saint there. This Withgar, wishing to provide for his children after him, requested the abbot to agree to present his son Nicholas to the bishop to be instituted into Mendlesham church. Finally the abbot agreed to the earnest petition, but on condition that Withgar, who up to then had paid but 10*s*. annually in his church's name, should from then on pay 40*s*. Both sides agreed to this, and a day was set when the agreement would be formally ratified. On the day, the abbot and his retinue appeared at Colchester, and Withgar was there with his son Nicholas. The agreement concerning the pension of 40*s*. was confirmed by both the father and the son, on their fealty and oath. His monks were present there with the abbot, and many knights, clerks, and laymen heard it. Afterwards the abbot set another day, when both Withgar and his son Nicholas should come to Battle to receive the convent's assent and a charter of confirmation. On the day, 2 February, both appeared at Battle and there in the presence of the abbot and the whole convent Nicholas again swore fealty and took an oath to pay the annual pension of 40*s*., and faithfully to maintain true fealty to the abbot and monastery of St. Martin of Battle. The convent consented unanimously to this, and the confirmation charter was given him.

The 40*s*. pension had been fully paid for some time when Alan de *Bello Fago*, craftily deceiving Withgar and his son Nicholas, finally persuaded them that the duty of fealty and oath might be set aside and that they might stop payment of the 40*s*. pension. Stating that

[1] 11 Nov.

Ecclesiam siquidem de Mendlesham sui iuris esse asserens, irritam esse causabatur extra eum factam pensionis augmentationem. Ad huius assertionis sue munitionem, cartas quasdam Warnerii abbatis nomine prenotatas, que quidem surrepticie et falsitatis notam habere diligenter intuentibus uidebantur, proponebat, quarum auctoritate ecclesiam de Mendlesham, ecclesiam de Brantham, sed et ecclesiam de Branford, que et ipsa una est ex dotalibus, tanquam ex abbatis Warnerii donatione, sui iuris esse ausus est constanter affirmare. Cuius persuasioni fidem accommodantes Withgarus et filius eius Nicholaus consenserunt, et a solutione pensionis xl^{a} solidorum cessantes se ecclesiam de Mendlesham non nomine monasterii sancti Martini de Bello, sed nomine Alani de Bellafago tenere asseruerunt.

Quibus cognitis abbas, iterato prouinciam adiens, utrique dedit in mandatis, ut secum habituri colloquium sibi apud Sanctum Edmundum occurrerent. Assunt itaque secum uenientis Alani de Bellafago armati aduocatione. Conueniente abbate utrumque super conuentionis inter eos habite transgressionem, super fidei et sacramenti preuaricatione, Alanus medium se opponens ecclesiam de Mendlesham sui iuris esse, et Withgarum nomine uicarie eam de se tenere, nec conuentionem de augenda pensione extra eum factam alicuius momenti esse debere proclamauit. Acclamantibus in hec Withgaro et filio eius Nicholao, abbas utrumque seorsum conuo-
f. 97 cans eos a tanti sceleris temeraria / presumptione studuit reuocare, nec tamen optinuit. In sua namque pertinatia nichilominus perdurantes, Alanum omnia tanquam ex eorum ore locutum esse palam clamitabant. Incurrerunt igitur ambo infidelitatis et periurii notam, filiusque ipsius Withgari Nicholaus ab omnibus ut proditor arguebatur, quem constabat super fide circa abbatem cui iam in faciem resistebat integre conseruanda nuper sacramentum prestitisse. Licet tanti criminis notam incurrentes infamie multipliciter subiacere uiderentur, nullatenus tamen a malignitate concepta resipiscere uoluerunt, Alano in eorum defensione pertinaciter persistente. Dicebat enim Withgarus Alanum omnia quasi suo ore proferre, Nicholaus uero se nullatenus a patris sui affirmabat consilio recedere. Videns abbas eos in rebellionis tante obstinatia perdurare, noluit cum eis in nichil utile contendere, commodum iudicans tempus oportunius expectare. Domino itaque rege in transmarinis tunc temporis agente, cum eum abbas in propria persona non posset adire, aliquos ex suis cum litterarum suarum testimonio ad eum transmisit, qui ei uiua uoce rei geste

the church of Mendlesham was his by right, he argued that an increase in the pension was void without his consent. As evidence of his assertion he brought out some charters we have already mentioned, done in the name of Abbot Warner, but seeming, to those who examined them closely, to bear marks of tampering and forgery. By their authority he dared stubbornly to affirm that the churches of Mendlesham, Brantham, and even of Bramford—for this, too, is one of the dower churches—were his by right, allegedly by grant of Abbot Warner. Putting their faith in his persuasions, Withgar and his son Nicholas agreed, and stopping payment of the 40*s*. pension they claimed to hold Mendlesham church not from St. Martin of Battle, but from Alan de *Bello Fago*.

When this became known to the abbot, he went to that district again, and sent to both his mandate to come to St. Edmund's to discuss it with him. They came, armed with the advocacy of Alan de *Bello Fago* who accompanied them. The abbot addressed them both on the breaking of the agreement between them, and on the violation of their fealty and oath. But Alan stepped between them and proclaimed that Mendlesham church was his by right, that Withgar held it as vicar from him, and that the agreement to increase the pension meant nothing since it was done without him. Withgar and his son Nicholas acclaimed all this. The abbot, calling the pair aside, tried hard to recall them from such a rash, presumptuous crime. But he did not succeed, for they remained obstinate and bawled out publicly that everything Alan said was as if from their own mouths. Therefore both were branded as unfaithful and lying, and Nicholas, the son of Withgar, was censured by all as a traitor. For it was evident that though he had earlier taken an oath of fealty to the abbot, he was now resisting him to his face. Yet though they were marked by so great a crime and were seen to be dishonoured in so many ways, nevertheless they did not at all wish to save themselves from their evil course, with Alan tenaciously defending them. Withgar said that Alan spoke for him, and Nicholas affirmed that he by no means disagreed with his father's counsel. The abbot, seeing that they remained obstinate in so great a rebellion, was unwilling to argue with them fruitlessly, and judged it more profitable to await an opportune moment. At that time the lord king was busy across the channel, and since it was not possible for the abbot himself to go to him, he sent him several of his men, with the credentials of his own letters, to explain the whole

ordinem panderent, suumque super hoc consilium et auxilium quererent. Occupauit interea, Withgaro defuncto, Alanus de Bellafago ecclesiam de Mendlesham tanquam uacantem, eamque abbate et conuentu de Bello inconsultis sibi redegit in possessionem, Nicholao periuro Withgari filio penitus eliminato. Quo cognito abbas domino Norwicensi episcopo ecclesiam de Mendlesham sui iuris esse, tum litteris, tum uiua loquentis nuntii uoce /
f. 97v studuit signare, prudenti procurans instantia, ne sepedictus Alanus seu quis alius extra consensum suum in eandem ecclesiam admitteretur per episcopum instituendus. Vtebatur ergo Alanus institutione propria, nec ad renuntiandum iniuste possessioni aliquatenus consensit.

Redeunt interea de transmarinis nuntii abbatis, preceptum regium ad regni iusticias deferentes, quo super ecclesia de Mendlesham abbati de Bello iustitie plenitudo exhibeatur. Dies locusque apud Wintoniam regia auctoritate abbati et Alano statuitur, ut ad unius actionem alteriusque obiectionem ueritatis plenior fieret inquisitio. Actum est hoc auctoritate regia, ad nullius tamen ecclesiastici iuris dignitatisue detrimentum, quippe cum hoc solum curia regia duceret inquirendum, cuius presentatione idem Alanus in ecclesiam de Mendlesham in fundo regio sitam, a predecessoribus ipsius domini regis et se monasterio de Bello concessam et confirmatam, fuerit institutus.[1] Constabat enim eum nullius nisi aut domini regis, tanquam domini fundi, aut monachorum de Bello, quibus ipsa ecclesia regia largitione assignata esse dinoscitur, institui debere presentatione. Adest die et loco determinato superstes adhuc, cuius superius facta est mentio, Robertus philosophus uices abbatis illic aduersus Alanum ibidem tunc etiam presentem executurus. Quo in presentia iusticiarum ius monasterii sancti Martini de Bello exponente et super Alani inuasionem conquerente, Alanus renitens cartas quas abbatis Warnerii nomine prenotatas memorauimus pretendit, seque ex ipsius abbatis dum adhuc uiueret consensu illic admissum esse asseruit. Licet igitur diligenter intu/-
f. 98 entibus palam esset cartas ipsas notam falsitatis habere, erat tamen omnium qui aderant unanime consilium et persuasio, ut hinc inde potius ducerent componendum quam litigandum. Consilio et uoluntati persuadentium pars utraque consentit, sicque ab arbitris

[1] The action of *darrein presentment* in an early form. See Van Caenegem, *Writs*, pp. 330–5.

matter to him by word of mouth and request his advice and help. While he was taking these steps, Withgar died and Alan de *Bello Fago* appropriated Mendlesham church as if it were vacant, without consulting the abbot and monks of Battle, and turning the perjured Nicholas completely out of doors. When the abbot learned this he took the precaution of informing the lord bishop of Norwich by letter and verbally by a messenger that the church of Mendlesham was his by right, in case Alan or someone else should be instituted by the bishop without the abbot's consent and so be admitted into the church. Alan therefore used his own power of institution and would not agree to renounce his unjust possession in the slightest.

In the mean time the abbot's messengers returned from beyond the sea, bringing a royal mandate to the justices of the realm, ordering that full justice be done to the abbot of Battle in the matter of Mendlesham church. By royal authority a day and place were set at Winchester for the abbot and Alan, so that a fuller inquiry into the truth might be made at the one's prosecution and the other's defence. This was done by the royal authority but nevertheless it was not to the detriment of any ecclesiastical right or privilege, since the royal court regarded its inquiry as touching on one point only: at whose presentation this Alan had been instituted into Mendlesham church, located in a royal manor, given and confirmed to Battle abbey by the predecessors of the lord king and by the king himself.[1] For it was clear that he ought not have been instituted at the presentation of anyone save either the lord king as lord of the manor or the monks of Battle, to whom the church had been assigned by the royal generosity, as was well known. Robert 'the philosopher', whom we have mentioned earlier, was still alive then; on that day he represented the abbot in court against Alan who again came in person. He argued the right of Battle abbey before the justices and entered a complaint against the intrusion of Alan. Alan replied, offering charters which, as we have mentioned, had the name of Abbot Warner on them, and he claimed to have been admitted there with the consent of the abbot while he was still living. Now although it was plain to those who studied them carefully that those charters bore the mark of forgery, none the less it was the unanimous counsel and opinion of all present that the thing would be better done by compromise than by litigation. Both parties assented to the advice and wishes of these prompters

datur huiusmodi forma compositionis, quatinus scilicet Alanus, toti iuri quod in ecclesia de Mendlesham se habere fatebatur sponte renuntians, cartas memoratas quibus partem suam tueri nitebatur in manus abbatis resignaret. Cuius sic gratiam adeptus, solam ecclesiam de Brantham quam, ut prediximus, minus canonice assecutus est, ex qua pensio x solidorum pro antiqua consuetudine soluebatur, sub annua pensione unius aurei monasterio sancti Martini de Bello soluenda, nomine ipsius monasterii quoad uiueret teneret,[1] et sic lis omnis et controuersia conquiesceret.

Omnibus hanc compositionis formam probantibus, partibusque hinc inde consentientibus, dies locusque apud Cantuariam statuitur, quo coram iusticiis abbas in persona propria et Alanus confirmande compositionis formate gratia conueniant. Abbate die et loco denominato coram iusticiis apparente, Alanus nec comparens nec excusatorem dirigens omnium iudicio misericordie regis addicitur, postmodum uero dies locusque apud Londonias conueniendi remque confirmandi utrique parti iterato prefigitur. Assunt denique hinc inde ad diem et locum, ubi totius rei serie et compositionis forma in iusticiarum domini regis et aliorum quamplurium audientia plenius exposita, Alanus cartas memoratas in manus abbatis resignauit, sicque cartam abbatis de sola ecclesia de Brantham nomine monasterii de Bello tenenda sub pensione unius aurei annuatim soluenda suscepit. /

f. 98v His ita gestis, cum hinc inde sopita esse putaretur omnis controuersia, repente idem Alanus, tanquam litem nouam initurus, super ecclesiam de Branford, quam sui iuris esse asseruit, uelato tamen sermone agere cepit, sic, ni fallor, cupiens experiri, si quem forte in eam aditum posset inuenire. Sed neminem in hac parte fautorem inueniens, tantam totius curie regie aduersum se excitauit indignationem, ut iam omnium uideretur esse sententia, in nullo tenendam esse paulo ante factam compositionem, sed restitutis ei memoratis cartis suis, ab initio cause repetendum, et in ea non iam pace et concordia, sed lite et iudicio procedendum. Artatus ergo plurimum, quippe cum rem sibi pro uoto

[1] There were no English gold coins at this time. The gold coin most in circulation was the bezant or nomisma of Byzantium. R. S. Lopez, 'The Dollar of the Middle Ages', *Journal of Economic History*, xi (1951), 212–13. Any gold coin seems to have been called a bezant, but generally under Henry II the Exchequer accepted twenty or twenty-four silver pence for one bezant. P. D. A. Harvey, 'The English Inflation of 1180–1220', *Past and Present*, lxi (1973), 28–9,

and the compromise was worked out by arbitrators in this form: Alan was freely to renounce all right he claimed in the church of Mendlesham and was to resign the charters from which he had argued his defence into the abbot's hands. For this he was to have the abbot's favour. He was to hold, from Battle abbey and for life, only the church of Brantham, which, as we have said above, he had acquired uncanonically, and for which the pension under the old custom was 10*s*. But he was to pay annually to Battle the pension of one gold piece.[1] And thus the entire quarrel and disagreement would settle down.

Everyone approved this form of compromise, and since the parties assented to it, a day and place were fixed at Canterbury in which the abbot, in person, and Alan were to meet before the justices to confirm the agreement. On the day and at the place fixed the abbot appeared before the justices, but Alan neither appeared nor sent an excuse. He was therefore unanimously adjudged in the king's mercy; and later a day and place were again set in London for the parties to meet and confirm the compromise. Finally they came on the day and to the place set. The course of the quarrel and the form of the compromise were fully explained before the justices of the lord king and many other witnesses. Alan resigned the charters into the abbot's hand and so received the abbot's charter giving the single church of Brantham to him to hold from the monastery of Battle for the payment of one gold piece annually.

When all this was done and the whole quarrel was thought settled thereby, unexpectedly this Alan, beginning what seemed a new dispute, maintained that the church of Bramford was his by right. But he began his process with veiled language, wishing (unless I am mistaken) to test whether he could find some way into the church. But he found that no one would take up his cause. Indeed he roused indignation against himself in the whole royal court, to the point that it seemed to be everyone's opinion that the recent compromise should not at all be held to: instead, he should be given back his charters, and the case should be started again from scratch, with proceedings not by peaceful compromise, but by lawsuit and judgement. He was therefore considerably hemmed in, and when he realized that the affair had turned out hardly

and G. C. Brooke, *English Coins* (3rd edn., London, 1950), pp. 68, 107, 110. Such an exchange rate implies that the payment was very likely little more than a token of lordship and not the old rent of 10*s*.

minime cessisse conspiceret, abbatem per Ricardum Pictauiensem archidiaconum[1] adiit, toti se iuri quod in quibuslibet ecclesiis monasterio de Bello dotaliter assignatis fatebatur habere pollicens omnino renuntiaturum, si quendam fratrem eius Rogerum de Bellafago nomine in solam ecclesiam de Brantham consentiret instituendum, sub eadem pensione qua paulo ante inter abbatem et ipsum compositum est, nomine sepefati monasterii de Bello, quoad uiueret tenendam. Porro abbas suorum usus consilio peticioni Alani decreuit in hac parte satisfaciendum, tempus ut putabatur oportunum nactus, quo ipse Alanus ab omnibus que sunt monasterii sancti Martini de Bello omnino redderetur alienus. Consensit igitur, prudenter tamen, non quasi ad hoc omnino uoluntate ductus, sed tanquam id interuenientis archidiaconi dilectioni prestiturus. In omnium itaque tam iusticiarum scilicet domini regis, quam et baronum et aliorum quamplurium qui scaccario
f. 99 intererant presentia et audientia, Alanus / publice procedens ecclesie de Brantham, ecclesie de Mendlesham, ecclesie de Branford, ceterisque omnibus ecclesiis dotalibus in perpetuum renuntiauit, sicque abbas solam ecclesiam de Brantham Rogero de Bellafago sub pensione unius aurei monasterio de Bello annuatim soluenda tenendam concessit. Sed ne extra consensum conuentus sui aliquid in hac parte facere uideretur, diem statuit quo idem Rogerus Bellum ueniens eandem ecclesiam cum carta confirmationis ex consensu conuentus susciperet, prestitoque sacramento de fidelitate seruanda et pensione integre soluenda, postmodum ad episcopum Norwicensem mitteretur, ad presentationem abbatis et conuentus instituendus.

Omnibus uero ut res ipsa exigebat rite peractis, cum iam omnia pacifico fine conclusa putarentur, repente idem Rogerus huic uite finem faciens ipsam ecclesiam uacantem reliquit. Sed prefatus Alanus de Bellafago, defuncti Rogeri frater, eam diu uacare non permittens, abbate et conuentu de Bello inconsultis illicite occupare presumpsit. Quod abbas audiens, nec equanimiter accipiens, in curia domini regis super huiusmodi inuasione iterato conqueri statuit. Sed Alanus hoc cognito plurimum ueritus per quosdam magni nominis uiros abbatem adiit, sibique indulgeri et parci suppliciter postulauit. Magnis uiris illis diligenti cum instantia pro eo interuenientibus et dignam de presumptione satisfactionem

according to his wishes, he approached the abbot through Richard, archdeacon of Poitiers.[1] He offered to renounce all rights whatever in all the churches assigned to Battle abbey as its dower, if the abbot would agree to the institution of his brother Roger de *Bello Fago* in the single church of Brantham, to hold for life from Battle for the same pension he and the abbot had recently agreed upon. The abbot, once more guided by the counsel of his friends, decided to yield to Alan's petition in this respect, this being, as was thought, an opportunity to separate Alan totally from everything belonging to St. Martin's of Battle. Therefore he consented, but he did it prudently, not as one who did it entirely of his own volition, but as one who would do it as a favour to the mediating archdeacon. In the presence and hearing of all the lord king's justices, as well as the barons and many others there in the Exchequer, Alan publicly gave up the churches of Brantham, Mendlesham, Bramford, and all the other dower churches for ever. On his side the abbot granted the single church of Brantham to Roger de *Bello Fago* for a pension of one gold piece payable to Battle annually. But lest he should seem to have done anything in this without his convent's consent, he set a day for Roger to come to Battle and receive the church and a charter of confirmation with the convent's consent. After taking an oath to serve faithfully and to pay the pension fully, he would then be sent to the bishop of Norwich to be instituted at the presentation of the abbot and convent.

Everything was properly completed as required, and it was thought that everything had been peacefully concluded, when suddenly Roger died, leaving the church vacant. Alan, the dead man's brother, did not long leave it vacant; without consulting the abbot and convent of Battle he dared to appropriate it illicitly. When the abbot heard this, he could not take it calmly. He determined to complain again in the king's court about this sort of intrusion. This frightened Alan a good deal, and he approached the abbot through certain men of influential name, praying pardon and forbearance. These great men intervened pressingly for him, and promised a fitting satisfaction for his presumption. They overcame

[1] Richard of Ilchester, one of Henry II's household administrators and close advisers, appears from 1163 as archdeacon of Poitiers. He was consecrated bishop of Winchester in 1174. C. Duggan, 'Richard of Ilchester, royal servant and bishop', *TRHS* 5th Ser. xvi (1966), 1–21.

promittentibus, abbas uictus eorum precibus importunis ad tempus conqueri distulit, uolens interuenientium peticionibus aliquatenus satisfacere, et Alani promissam satisfactionem certius probare. f. 99v Verum / iam imminente uocationis sue tempore quo uite presenti tenebatur renuntiare, nullatenus in hoc negotio ultra processit, unde et Alanus in nullo satisfaciens ipsam ecclesiam de Brantham, abbate defuncto, per aliquot annos propria fretus auctoritate cum fructibus ex ea prouenientibus possedit.

Hucusque de laboribus et sollicitudinibus uiri uenerabilis abbatis Walterii, quibus tam ecclesias quam et terras iniuste alienatas studuit reuocare, sufficiat summatim pauca dixisse, quippe cum omnia ut erant plenius exprimere magni uideretur operis et laboris esse. Decet tamen hoc omnimodis breuiter inserere, quod nisi in ecclesiarum dotalium uirilius prudentiusque institisset reuocationem, profecto ius omne monasterii sancti Martini de Bello, quod in ipsis ab antiquo habebat, absque spe recuperationis penitus deperisset. Milites namque, qui largitione regum qui Willelmo regi secundo in regnum successerant uillas et maneria in quorum territoriis ipse ecclesie site uidentur sunt adepti, ius sibi patronatus in ipsis ecclesiis uendicantes, uille cuiuslibet caput ecclesiam inibi sitam esse dicebant, sicque, eo ipso quo caput totius corporis pars est dignior, amplioris se iuris plenitudinem in ecclesiis quam in territoriis in quibus site sunt habere affirmabant. Sed abbas se in omnibus pro domo Domini scutum uiriliter opponens singulas de singulorum unguibus magna tamen cum difficultate extorsit, et iuri monasterii sancti Martini de Bello restituit. Prouidit itaque in omnibus honori et utilitati commisse sibi ecclesie, licet a quibusdam modernioribus putetur eum in ipsarum ecclesiarum reuocatione prudentius egisse potuisse. Dicitur enim quia si tunc temporis omnimodis institisset, ipsas ecclesias cum fructibus
f. 100 omnibus / ex eis prouenientibus in usus monasterii sui transferre potuisset, institutis per eum uicariis, qui in ipsis sub annua et honesta mercede ministrarent. Putatur autem tunc temporis id potuisse, quippe cum dominum regum haberet admodum beniuolum, per quem et hec et ampliora a summo pontifice poterat impetrasse, obtentu etiam uiri uenerabilis Ricardi de Luci fratris ipsius abbatis, qui secundus a rege summe tunc temporis in regno iusticie nomen officiumque tenebat. Egit igitur abbas ut dicitur in hac parte minus circumspecte dum ipsas ecclesias clericis concessit pensionaliter tenendas, portiones comparatione fructuum ex

the abbot with their importunities and he dropped his complaint for the time, wishing to satisfy in part the prayers of the intermediaries, and to test Alan's promised satisfaction. However, since the time of his calling was imminent, when he must give up the present life, he proceeded no further in the business. As a result Alan made no satisfaction. For many years after the abbot's death he held Brantham church under his independent authority and took all its profits.

For our purposes, it must suffice to have given this brief summary of Abbot Walter's labours and anxieties in attempting to recover both churches and lands unjustly alienated, since indeed it would be a great and laborious task to relate everything fully. But it should be added briefly that unless he had courageously and wisely demanded the restitution of the dower churches, there can be no question that all Battle abbey's old rights in them would have quite perished, without hope of recovery. For the knights who, by the bounty of the kings who followed William II, received the townships and manors in whose districts these churches lay, sought for themselves the right of patronage in them. They maintained that the church was the head of any township in which it was located, and so, in so far as the head is the worthier part of the whole body, they claimed that they had an even fuller right to the churches than to the districts in which they lay. But in all contests the abbot manfully made himself a shield in defence of the house of the Lord, and, though with great difficulty, he wrested every one from their clutches and restored them to Battle abbey as its right. In all things he acted for the honour and the good of the church committed into his keeping, though it is the opinion of some moderns that he could have acted more prudently in getting the churches back again. For it is said that if he had in those days pursued every means, he would have been able to appropriate those churches with all their profits to his monastery, instituting vicars himself who would serve in them for a decent annual wage. It is thought that in those days he could have done this, since he had the lord king's complete goodwill, and through the king he could have got this and more from the pope, especially with the patronage of his brother Richard de Luci, who in those days had the title and office of chief justiciar of the realm, second only to the king. This being so, the abbot acted, it is said, without consideration when he granted those churches to be held by clerks for pensions,

eis habunde prouenientium admodicas suscipiens, cum omnia de facili si institisset posset suscepisse. Verumtamen licet hoc moderniori consilio minime usus fuerit, plurimum tamen in ipsarum ecclesiarum reuocatione constat eum monasterio suo contulisse, dum ius amissum et pene irreuocabile uiriliter reuocare studuit, et iure restituto, cum antea ab aliquibus earum ut predictum est paucos fructus, ab aliquibus uero propter hostilitatis tempora omnino nullos susciperet, de simul omnibus supra uiginti duas marcas argenti singulis annis pensionaliter solui fecit. Ex his autem pensionibus septem libras ad opera monasterii assignauit, centum scilicet solidos de ecclesia de Eillesham, et quadraginta solidos de ecclesia de Middehale, perpetuo anathemati subiciens omnes qui eas in alios usus transferrent, aut quauis ex causa auferrent, aut ut transferrentur auferrenturue consilio uel auxilio essent. Egit autem hoc ex uoluntate et consensu conuentus sui, bonum boni operis successoribus suis relinquens exemplum. /

f. 100v Vsque ad uenerabilis huius uiri tempora, medietas decime de dominio de Wi bouariis curie eiusdem manerii erat assignata, fuitque hereditas domini merces mercenarii.[1] Videns abbas hoc omnino non esse canonicum, bubulcis alias, hoc est de terra dominii de Wi, prouidit,[2] ipsamque medietatem decime, ipsis eatenus assignatam, sacristarie monasterii sui de Bello ex consensu conuentus sui assignauit, statuens ut ex ipsa decima duo nominatim cerei inuenirentur, in choro coram conuentu quotiens illic presens indigeret lumine lucerne arsuri. Statuit preterea singulis annis caritatem quandam albi uini conuentui fieri cum singulis guastellis piperatis singulis monachis, exceptis simenellis debitis ex communi cellario appositis,[3] cum duobus etiam ferculis optimis, exceptis ferculis debitis de coquina, ita quidem ut, si fieri aliquatenus possit, unum semper de ferculis esse debeat de recenti salmone, et in mensura uini cuilibet fratrum apponenda nil sit minus galone. Hanc caritatem fieri uoluit dum in hac uita superfuit in decollatione beati Iohannis Baptiste;[4] post decessum uero suum, in die anniuersario obitus sui. Ne quis uero successorum eius in posterum hanc ipsius constitutionem imminuere uel eam immutando ei

[1] Cf. Lam. 5: 2.

[2] Cf. Luke 15: 17. The granting of tithes to laymen had long been forbidden. See Constable, *Tithes*, pp. 84 ff. This may, however, have been Abbot Walter's interpretation of the canon of the Council of Tours in 1163. See Will. Newburgh, i. 138. If the interpretation was common, it was of great importance

accepting by comparison a small proportion of their considerable revenues when he could easily have had everything, had he persisted. Nevertheless, though he did not follow this modern plan, it is certain that he conferred a great benefit on his monastery by recovering the churches. He worked courageously to regain a right that was lost and well-nigh irrecoverable. Previously he had received from some, as we have said, few profits, and from others, because of the anarchy, none at all. But once his rights were restored, he made them, as a whole, pay over 22 marks of silver annually as pensions. From these pensions he assigned £7 to the upkeep of the monastery: namely, 100*s*. from Aylesham church and 40*s*. from Mildenhall, putting a perpetual anathema on any who transferred them to other uses or took them away for whatever reason, and on any who might aid or counsel such a transfer or withdrawal. And he acted in this by the will and consent of his convent, leaving his successors a good example of good works.

Until the abbacy of this venerable man, half of the tithes of the demesne of Wye had been assigned to the oxherds of that manor, and the Lord's inheritance was the wage of hirelings.[1] The abbot, seeing that this was not at all canonical, provided differently for the oxherds, out of the demesne land of Wye,[2] while the half of the tithes up to that time assigned to them he now assigned to the sacristy of his monastery of Battle with the consent of his convent. He specified that with these tithes two candles should be bought, to burn in the choir before the monks whenever they needed lamplight there. He specified moreover that once a year an allowance of white wine be given the convent, with a pepper-cake for each monk, beyond the regular simnel-bread of the communal store.[3] There were also to be two cooked dishes of the best quality, beyond the ordinary dishes from the kitchen. They should be such that, if at all possible, one of them should always be fresh salmon, and the measure of wine for each brother should be not less than a gallon. This allowance he wished to be made, while he lived, on the feast of the beheading of John the Baptist.[4] After his death it was to be on the anniversary of his death. And lest any of his successors should dare in the future to lessen his decree, or to oppose him by

in the little-documented transformation of the *bovarius* from slave, or dependent and landless ploughman, to dependent landholder. Cf. M. M. Postan, 'The Famulus', *Econ.Hist.Rev. Supplements*, no. 2 (1954), pp. 5–14.

[3] Wastel is a finer flour than simnel, producing a cake, here a spice-cake.

[4] 29 Aug.

aliquatenus presumeret contraire, ipse stola assumpta in capitulo fratrum cum candela accensa singulos etiam fratres qui seu sacerdotii seu diaconii fungebantur officio singulas stolas et
f. 101 candelas accensas sumere ius/sit, sicque etiam subdiaconibus manipulos cum candelis accensis, his uero qui inferioris erant ordinis cum conuersis solas candelas accensas habentibus, omnium ore et consensu omnes ipsius institutionis sue uiolatores perpetuo et inexorabili subiecit anathemati.

Huius uenerande memorie uiri temporibus, duo milites in uicinio monasterii sancti Martini de Bello habitantes, scilicet Ingelrannus de Scoteni, et Robertus Bos, eidem monasterio pro sua suorumque salute duas terras de dominio suo sibi inuicem contiguas iuxta nemus quod dicitur Bodeherste contulerunt, ab omni consuetudine terrene seruitutis immunes.[1] Eratque militum ipsorum eo laudabilior deuotio, quo id eidem monasterio conferendum decreuerunt, quod quanto erat uicinius, tanto uidebatur commodius. Dicitur autem ab incolis terra illa, quam Ingelrannus de Scoteni contulit, 'wista Smewini' usque in presens.

Superior edidit narratio abbatem Gausbertum incliti regis Willelmi primi temporibus a quodam milite Osberno scilicet Hugonis filio xxx[ta] acras prati apud Bodeham, datis ei quinquaginta solidis, comparasse. Quia uero idem pratum aliquantulum a monasterio est remotum, expedire uisum est ut alicui fidelium qui in uicinio mansionem haberet ipsius prati committeretur custodia. Sed quia tutum minime uidebatur hanc curam alicui committere qui de monasterii non esset possessione, nec quia pratum illud totum in udo est locus aliquis patebat ubi competens mansio ad habitandum in ipsa possessione fieri posset, processu temporis cum
f. 101v milite quo/dam Roberto scilicet Borne, in uicinio prati ipsius habitante, actum est ut quandam partem terre prato contiguam de dominio suo Deo et beato Martino in liberam et perpetuam concederet monasterii possessionem.[2] Facta est ergo illic custodi prati mansio competens ad inhabitandum. Rogatus nihilominus idem Robertus Borne a fratribus, uiam a predicto prato quousque feudum suum uersus Bellum extenditur concessit, a patre suo pridem concessam, per quam fenum et alia necessaria ab eodem prato usque Bellum carris et uehiculis pertraherentur, omnino quidem liberam, et ab omni fratrum, heredum ac successorum suorum calumnia perpetuo quietam. Dederunt autem ei fratres

any change in it, before the brothers in chapter he put on his stole and took a lighted candle, and commanded each of the brothers who were priests or deacons to take up stoles and lighted candles. The subdeacons had their maniples and lighted candles, while those who were of inferior grade, and the lay brothers, had lighted candles only. Then in the presence, and with the consent, of all, he pronounced a perpetual and irrevocable anathema on all violators of his decree.

In this venerable man's day, there two knights who were neighbours of the monastery of St. Martin of Battle, namely Ingelran de Scotney and Robert le Bœuf. For the salvation of themselves and their families they gave the monastery two adjoining holdings from their demesnes, next to Bathurst wood, free from all customary earthly services.[1] The piety of these knights was the more laudable since they decided to give the monastery what was particularly useful, since it was particularly near. The holding that Ingelran gave is still called 'Smewin's wist' by the peasants.

We have seen above that in the time of the famous King William I Abbot Gausbert had purchased thirty acres of meadow at Bodiam from the knight Osbern, son of Hugh, for 50*s*. Now because the meadow lies some little distance from the monastery it seemed advantageous to put it in the custody of some one of the faithful who might have a house near it. But it did not seem at all safe to commit its care to someone who was not a tenant of the monastery, and there was no place where a habitable house could be built on the property because the meadow is so wet. Eventually an agreement was reached with a knight, Robert Borne, who lived near the meadow, to give a piece of his demesne land next to the meadow to God and St. Martin in free and perpetual possession.[2] A habitable house was built for the meadow's keeper there. At the brothers' request this Robert Borne, like his father before him, granted a right of way from the meadow towards Battle through his fief, so that hay and other goods could be carried in wagons and carts from the meadow to Battle, and he conveyed this wholly free, and for ever quit of all claims of his brothers, his heirs, and successors.

[1] Scotney, a tenant of the count of Eu in Crowhurst near Battle, was a member of a widespread Kentish-Sussex gentry family. Du Boulay, *Canterbury*, p. 337. Robert le Bœuf's lands were eventually all bought out by Battle Abbey in the thirteenth century. Searle, *Lordship*, p. 159.

[2] *Regesta*, ii, nos. 782, 1225, pp. 391, 407. Bodiam meadow borders the Rother at a point about five miles from Battle. See above, pp. 86, 122.

tum pro mutua beneficii recompensatione, tum testimonii futuri gratia sex solidos, et caligas ferreas quas quidam proprie ocreas dicunt, auxilium scilicet quo unum ex fratribus suis militie ascriberet.[1]

Cum uero modicum terre inter sepedictum pratum et prefatam mansionem custodie ipsius prati adquisitam restaret interiacens, quod agendis fratrum, ut ea scilicet que illuc in usus eorum nauigio aduehebantur in sicco collocanda reciperentur, uidebatur accommodum, uir uenerabilis abbas Walterius, antedictum Robertum Borne et filium eius Radulfum tum per se tum per suos conueniens, cum eis egit et obtinuit, ut quemadmodum dictam mansionem, ita et modicum illud terre quod eidem adiacebat, quia de dominio suo erat, Deo et beato Martino pro sua suorumque salute libere quiete et perpetuo possidendum concederent. Cum igitur ambo consentientes in monasterio beati Martini coram eius altari ipsum terre
f. 102 eiusdem iam fecissent heredem, decreuit ab/bas eam non omnino gratis suscipere, quinimmo tum pro mutua uicissitudine, tum pro testimonio in futurum, patri x solidos, filio uero aureum unum dari fecit. Que de terrulis his licet modicis meminimus, hic iccirco memorie committenda inseruimus quia priusquam sic adquisite monasterii iungerentur possessionibus, tam fratres quam eorum ministri, preter rerum suarum dispendia plurima, multarum molestiarum subiacebant uexationibus. Non enim ad sepedictum pratum accessum uel inde recessum nisi per terras non suas habere poterant, terrarum circumiacentium possessoribus eis calumniam inferentibus, nec sibi per terminos suos liberum transitum habere permittentibus. Verum ipsius uenerabilis abbatis sollicita procuratione, tum he tum alie res monasterii perplurime meliorem statum sunt adepte.

In diebus eius commissum sibi monasterium sancti Martini de Bello uisitare dignatus est Dominus, cum ad declaranda beati confessoris sui Martini merita, locum ipsum miraculorum choruscare fecit frequentia. Conuenit itaque eo tum penitentie et remissionis peccatorum, tum sanitatis adipiscende gratia, sexus utriusque plurima multitudo. Verum cum ex eo uenientibus nonnulli repente corruentes in terra uolutarentur, et nescio quo occulto Dei iudicio miserabiliter cruciarentur, alii ex his qui aderant nec simili pene ac ludibrio subiacebant diuinitatis operibus,

[1] This is an indication of the extremely high value of armour for the class of

The monks gave him, both as payment for the kindness and as future evidence, 6*s*. and iron leg-pieces, by some properly called 'greaves', so that he might get a place for one of his brothers in the army.[1]

There remained a bit of land lying between the meadow and the keeper's house. This was ideal for the brothers' dealings, providing a dry landing-place for goods shipped up for their use by boat. The venerable Abbot Walter, both personally and through friends, approached Robert Borne and his son Ralph, and convinced them to give the bit of land, since it was part of their demesne, just as they had the adjoining house, free, quit, and in perpetual possession, to God and St. Martin for the good of their souls and those of their family. When they both, with full consent, had made him heir to the land before the altar in St. Martin's monastery, the abbot determined not to take it wholly without payment. Both to have an exchange between them and as evidence for the future, he gave the father 10*s*. and the son one gold piece. Though these are tiny bits of land to have talked about at some length, we have recorded the facts because, before they were acquired in this way as part of the monastery's properties, both the brothers and their servants were subjected to considerable harassment, quite apart from the considerable loss to their goods. For they had no way in or out of the meadow except through lands not their own, and the holders of the surrounding lands challenged them and would not permit them to cross their lands freely. But by the abbot's solicitous management in this as well as in so many other affairs, he improved the condition of the monastery.

In his day the monastery entrusted to him was deemed worthy to be visited by the Lord, for He made the abbey glitter with frequent miracles, so that the merits of St. Martin, His confessor, might be declared abroad. A great multitude, men and women alike, came both for penance and the remission of sins, and for healing. But a few of the pilgrims, suddenly falling to the ground, rolled about and were pitiably tortured by some hidden judgement of God. Other pilgrims who were present and were not subjected to a similarly ludicrous punishment, chose unreasonably to

'country knights' in Henry II's reign. Robert Borne was providing for his brother a career as a professional paid soldier: one of the 'agrarii milites' turning into one of the 'solidarii milites' on whom Henry II was coming to rely. Stubbs, *Charters*, p. 152. Cf. Sally Harvey, 'The Knight and the Knight's Fee in England', *Past and Present*, xlix (1970), 35.

tanquam non ex deo fuerint, minus sana mente ceperunt detrahere, f. 102v nullaque in se pietatis seu compas/sionis uiscera habentes, proximos in angustiis positos, quibus ex communi fragilitatis humane conditione compati debuerant, insolenter irridere.[1] Prouocatus Dominus tum ex his, tum ex quorundam inhabitantium non digna coram se conuersatione, indignari cepit aduersus ingratos, gratiamque concessam subtraxit indignis, cuidam fidelium suorum reuelans in uisione, propositi quidem sui fuisse locum ipsum coram hominibus clarificare,[2] sed inhabitantium quorundam habundante malitia se a proposito declinasse, gratiamque concessam subtraxisse. Quid igitur ad ista dicendum est? Plangere in his magis decet quam aliquid dicere. Heu, heu, quanta est infelicitas hominum qui diuinitatis operibus ingrati existunt, creatorique suo famulatum debite seruitutis impendere negligunt. De quibus proculdubio constat, quod sicut multa sunt que immeriti a Deo accipiunt, sic innumera sunt que ingrati amittunt. Veruntamen cum sit suauis Dominus, benignus et multae miserationis,[3] gratiam concessam non omnino abstulit, sed ut uoluit transtulit. Transtulit siquidem eam de matre ad filiam, de ecclesia scilicet beati Martini de Bello ad ecclesiam beati Nicholai in ciuitate Exoniensi sitam, quam ipsius ecclesie de Bello constat esse cellam, loci ipsius uisitans deiectionem. Nondum enim ecclesia illa a primis fundamentis plenam acceperat consummationem, cum iam secundo ex repentino urbis incendio redacta esset in desolationem.[4] Apparuit igitur illic in miraculorum signis gloria Domini,[5] nec tantum locum ipsum, uerum f. 103 etiam diuersas regni / partes ad quas seu monachi seu clerici loci ipsius nomine directi predicationis gratia peruenerunt mirifice illustrauit. Crebrescentibus miraculis, circumquaque dilatatum est nomen beati Nicholai, cepitque locus ipse ab utriusque sexus, a diuerse etatis, religionis et ordinis fidelibus cum tanta beneficiorum comportatione frequentari, ut ex ipsorum beneficiorum copia non solum ecclesia pridem incendio dissipata reedificaretur, uerum etiam fratribus illic conuersantibus satis honesta ad inhabitandum edificia pro loci capacitate construerentur. Non usquequaque in his ecclesia sancti Martini de Bello frustrata est, gratia Dei, quia honor filie gloria est matris eius.[6] O beata loca et tempora, que sic Dei uisitauit clementia!

1 Cf. 2 John 3: 17. 2 Cf. Matt. 5: 16.
3 Cf. Pss. 100: 4; 109: 20.
4 For the foundation see above, p. 82 There it is said that St. Nicholas's had

disparage the divine manifestations as if they were not from God. Havings hearts with neither piety nor compassion, they haughtily laughed at the distress of the neighbours whom they should have pitied out of a sense of common human frailty.[1] Exasperated by these pilgrims and too by the unworthy life of some of the inhabitants, the Lord grew angry against the ungrateful, and withdrew the grace bestowed upon the unworthy. He revealed in a vision to one of His faithful that He had intended to make this abbey shine before men,[2] but the malice of some of its indwellers had turned Him from His intention and He had withdrawn the grace He had bestowed. What should be said of this? Mourning is more fitting than anything one might say. Alas, alas, how unfortunate are men who are ungrateful for the actions of the divine and who refuse the submissiveness that is owed their creator. One lesson is clear. Just as the undeserving receive much from God, so without doubt the ungrateful lose immeasurably. However, as the Lord is gentle, kind and of great mercy,[3] He did not wholly take away His given gift, but transferred it as He would. Thus He transferred it from the mother to the daughter, from the church of St. Martin of Battle to the church of St. Nicholas in the town of Exeter, succouring the dejection of that cell of Battle abbey. For that church had not yet been fully built up from its first foundations when it was reduced to desolation a second time by a fire that swept through the town.[4] Wherefore the glory of the Lord showed forth there in miracles,[5] and not only there, but it shone forth wonderfully in the various parts of the realm where monks or clerks of the church were sent to preach in its name. The miracles were reported abroad, and everywhere the name of St. Nicholas was repeated. The place began to be visited by the faithful of both sexes, of various ages, orders, and ranks, bringing such gifts that out of the abundance of offerings not only could the destroyed church be rebuilt, but buildings as handsome as the place afforded could be built for the brothers' residences. In this way the church of St. Martin of Battle was not entirely disappointed, by the grace of God, for the honour of the daughter is the glory of her mother.[6] Oh happy places and times which the mercy of God has visited thus!

been completed and that services were being held there. The fire is not mentioned elsewhere.

[5] Cf. Deut. 29: 2–4; Ps. 135: 9; Dan. 3: 32–3; John 4: 48.

[6] Cf. Walther, no. 9505a: *Filius est patris sapiens et gloria matris*, a thirteenth-century proverb.

Multa quidem sunt que a uiro uenerabili abbate Walterio et per ipsum magnifice gesta cognouimus. Sed ne lectores auditoresue nimia prolixitate uideamur onerare, libet de cetero breuitati insistere, et prudenti lectori facile cognoscenda plura paucis explicare. Exequendi pastoralis officii modus ei talis inerat, ut inobedientibus et indisciplinatis rigidum se et seuerum exhiberet, mansuetis uero et obedientibus placabilem se et beniuolum ostenderet. Misericordiam plurimam circa pauperes habens, esuriem eorum datis reprimebat alimentis et nuditatem protegebat indumentis. Leprosorum maxime et elephantiosorum ab hominibus eiectioni compatiens, eos non solum non abhorrebat, uerum etiam in persona propria eis frequenter ministrans, eorum manus pedesque abluendo
f. 103v fouebat, et inti/mo caritatis pietatisque affectu blanda oscula imprimebat. Dignitates libertatesque commisse sibi ecclesie nullatenus passus est imminui, nec res possessionesue eius negligentia distrahi uel dissipari. Curam possessionum ecclesie sic aliis committebat, ut tamen omnium ipse curam gereret. Ecclesiam ipsam, quam hostilitatis tempore regendam susceperat, cum omnibus suis ab hostium incursione pro uiribus protexit, et que direpta fuerant postmodum pacis tempore uiriliter reuocauit. Primis promotionis sue temporibus hospitalitati non usquequaque potuit uacare, quippe cum sibi rerum facultas uideretur deesse. Sic enim pene cuncta que monasterii erant manus hostilis inuaserat, ut modicum illud quod uidebatur superesse ad qualemcumque sustentationem fratrum uix posset sufficere. Pacis postmodum tempore, cum iam plurima ex parte licet cum nimiis laboribus et expensis distracta reuocasset, domus sue statum in melius commutans, antiquas debitasque consuetudines restituit, ita quidem ut omni pulsanti aperiretur,[1] hospitalitatis beneficium postulans nemo repulsam pateretur, omnibus pro dignitate seu conditione personarum officium humanitatis exhiberetur. Visitationis gratia ecclesie sue maneria frequenter adiit, non plus aliis credens de rebus sibi commissis quam sibi, et in ipsis edificia quorumlibet potentum ac nobilium receptui apta construi fecit. Maneriis ipsis in diuersis et remotis partibus positis, cum uicecomites aliique prouinciarum potentes eum super libertatibus et dignitatibus suis, tam ab eo, quam ab hominibus ecclesie, indebita

[1] Cf. Matt. 7: 7.

Many and noble are the deeds we know that were done by Abbot Walter and in his name. But lest we seem to burden our readers and hearers with excessive prolixity, we shall be brief henceforward, and in a few words explain much that the prudent reader may easily understand. His way of doing his duty as shepherd was to show himself inflexible and harsh to the disobedient and indisciplined, while to the gentle and obedient he showed himself easily appeased and kindly. He had a great deal of pity for the poor, alleviating their hunger with gifts of food and covering their nakedness with garments. Above all he had compassion for those afflicted with leprosy and elephantiasis and therefore cast out by mankind. Not only did he not shrink from them; on the contrary, frequently ministering to them himself, he would wash their hands and feet and kiss them gently in the deep sympathy of his charity and piety. The privileges and liberties of the church committed to him he did not allow to be lessened a jot, nor did he suffer its possessions and properties to be broken up or dissipated by his negligence. He committed the care of the church's properties to others in such a way that nevertheless he himself had the ultimate responsibility. He had undertaken to govern the church in the time of strife, and with all his might he protected it and all its people from the inroads of its enemies. Things that were stolen he afterwards manfully regained when peace came. In the early days of his elevation he was unable to devote anything to hospitality, since the wherewithal seemed to be lacking. Hostile hands had seized nearly everything belonging to the monastery, till the little that was left was barely sufficient for the sustenance of the brothers. Afterwards, in peacetime, when he had, to a large extent, though with exceeding labour and expense, recovered what had been stolen, he bettered the state of his abbey, and restored the old and proper customs, so that to everyone who knocked the door was opened,[1] and no one requesting the gift of hospitality was refused. Everyone had good manners shown him according to his rank or station. For the sake of visitation he went often to the manors of his church, being unready to believe others rather than himself in matters entrusted to his care, and he had constructed on them buildings where any magnates and nobles could be received. As to the manors situated in various and remote parts, the sheriffs and other county magnates tried to harass him in connection with his liberties and privileges, making undue demands of him and the church's men.

f. 104 exigendo uexare / niterentur, putantes se sic ab eo tanquam pro redemptione rerum et libertatum suarum munera accepturos, ipse quidem, omnium eorum timore nudus, nullius eorum cupiditati satisfacere uoluit. Sic quippe de domini regis beniuolentia confidebat, per quem de omnibus que uoluit impetrauit, seque uexare uolentes potestate uexandi et spe muneris ab eo percipiendi frustratos compescuit. Decore preterea domus Dei delectatus, monasterium suum tot tantisque palliis, casulis, cappis, albis, dalmaticis, tunicis, tapetis, signis, uariisque ornamentorum uarietatibus adornauit, quot et quantis nemo predecessorum suorum illud dinoscitur adornasse. Claustrum fratrum a primis ecclesie fundamentis minus decenter extructum funditus diruit, aliudque ex tabulatis ac columnis marmoreis opere polito et plano construxit. Quo consummato, lauatorium ex simili materia et opere facere intendens, artifices quidem conduxit, sed morte preuentus, cum consummare non posset, substantiam qua consummaretur assignauit.

Florente sic in omnibus statu ecclesie, cum iam in hoc esse uideretur ut ex flore fructus uberior procederet, repente spes omnis absciditur, dum idem uir uenerabilis de medio tollitur. Extrema namque sui corporis parte semimortua, cum per plures annos egritudine continua laborasset, sibi in nullo indulgens, quominus seipsum pro domo sibi commissa in quibuslibet aduersis scutum opponeret, tandem cum quoddam monasterii manerium Wi nomine uisitandi gratia adisset, cepit repente solito molestius
f. 104v sentire. Ingrauescente / per dies infirmitate, satis uicini monasterii de Fauresham abbatem Clarenbaldum, uirum quidem uenerabilem et in partibus suis religiosi nomen habentem, euocauit, cum eo de salute anime sue conferens, et de excessibus quos in presenti uita contraxerat penitentiam agens. Non est enim homo qui uiuat, et non peccet.[1] Sacramenta nichilominus corporis et sanguinis Domini frequenter suscipiens, priori monasterii sui dedit in mandatis, ut ad se cum quibusdam fratribus postposita ueniret dilatione. Veniente secundum mandatum ipsius priore cum fratribus, cepit diligenter etiam cum eo de salute anime sue agere, et tam ab ipso, quam a fratribus qui cum eo erant, de omnibus quibus eos seu merito seu immerito contristauerat indulgentiam petere, prius eis similia remittens. Prior uero cum fratribus totius conuentus uices agens ei de omnibus pro omnibus indulsit, omni-

[1] 3 Kgs. 8: 46

They thought that in this way they would get bribes from him to redeem his goods and privileges. But quite without fear of anyone he refused to satisfy their cupidity. He relied indeed upon the goodwill of the king, through whom he got what he wished in all matters, and by it he checked those who wished to harass him, and robbed them of their power of harassment and of their hope of being bribed by him. He delighted, furthermore, in beautifying the house of God. He adorned his monastery with pallia, chasubles, copes, albs, dalmatics, tunics, tapestries, armorial hangings, and various kinds of ornaments. They were more and better than any of his predecessors is known to have provided. He levelled the brothers' cloister, which had been unprepossessing since the abbey was first built. He constructed another, with pavement and columns of marble, polished and smooth. When that was completed, he had plans to construct a place to wash, of the same material and workmanship, and had hired the artisans. He was outdone by death, but though he could not complete it, he earmarked money for its completion.

The church was thus flowering, and just as it seemed that from the flower would come a most plentiful harvest, all hope was suddenly cut off and the venerable man was taken from our midst. The extremities of his body were half dead, since for many years he had laboured under continual bad health, never indulging himself, but making of himself in every adversity a shield to protect the abbey entrusted to his care. At last, while he was at the manor of Wye on a visitation, he began to suffer more grievously than usual. He grew worse daily until finally he called Abbot Clarembald of the near-by monastery of Faversham, a venerable man and one with a reputation for piety in his area. He consulted with him about the health of his soul and did penance for excesses he had committed in the present life. For there is no man who lives and does not sin.[1] He frequently partook of the sacraments of the body and blood of the Lord. He sent the prior of his monastery orders that without delay he should come to him with certain brothers. The prior came with the brothers as commanded; he deligently undertook to work with him for his soul's salvation. Both from the prior and from the brothers with him, he prayed indulgence for everything with which, rightly or wrongly, he had afflicted them, pardoning them first for the same. The prior and the brothers, acting for the whole convent, forgave him everything in everyone's name, and blessed

umque ore benedixit. Benedicens omnes[a] ipse paterno affectu, sententias quauis occasione in quoslibet fratrum precipitatas relaxauit, [et][b] omnes ex officio pastorali quo fungebatur absoluit.

Cum uero per singulos dies uiribus corporis destitueretur, uisitaturus eum uir illustris Ricardus de Luci frater eius aduenit, uisoque eo fretusque colloquio, cum super eo sanitati restituendo spem nullam conciperet quatinus celeriter ad monasterium suum deportaretur admonuit. Ne quid eorum que tenet institutio ecclesiastica properanti ad transitum deesse uideretur, sana mente sanoque intellectu semper deum inuocans tandem inungitur, sicque
f. 105 feretro impositus equis deportantibus usque Bellum trans/uehitur. Quo perueniens iam omnino erat sine uoce, solo spiritu in pectore palpitante. Accurrunt cum gemitu filii, patrem plusquam seminecem iamque migrantem uisuri, non tamen eius colloquio fruituri. Accedunt singuli sic iacentem deosculantes, et decetero quia dies illucescere uidebatur, horam incognitam expectantes exitumque suum orationum deuotione munientes.[1]

Iam noctem cum die subsequente sic solo spiritu palpitans transegerat, noxque secunda tenebris suis terras obtexerat, cum iam a cunctis qui aderant putaretur sine mora migraturus, cum omni uelocitate in fratrum delatus est capitulum, illic pro loci consuetudine emissurus spiritum. Vbi cinere et cilicio substrato depositus, repente omnia corporis membra que pridem premortua uidebantur cepit mouere, et motu labiorum gestum loquentis exprimere. Excitatis fratribus omnibus, ori eius qui propius assistebant aures adhibuerunt, sed cum solus esset sibilus sine uoce, nichil eorum que dicere intendebat potuerunt discernere. Nocte transcurrente cum iam mane diluxisset, animam in manus uoluntatemque creatoris sui reddidit, fratribus circumstantibus et proficiscentem cum orationum deuotione Domino commendantibus. Exequiis ut decebat per biduum celebratis, demum terra terre ex qua sumpta est redditur, et coram maiori crucifixo et altari crucis

[a] omnibus *MS.*: *the scribe has marked the incorrect form, but has not changed it* [b] *Winterbottom. MS. has* et *after* benedicens

him for all of them. Blessing everyone with a father's love, he in turn relaxed any hasty sentences imposed on any brothers on whatever occasion, and absolved all by his pastoral power.

Since he was growing weaker day by day, his distinguished brother, Richard de Luci, came to him. After he had seen and talked with him, it was his opinion that there was no hope of recovery and he advised that he be moved without delay to his monastery. Lest anything ordained by ecclesiastical custom should seem to have been neglected as he hastened to his end, he was finally anointed, being of sound mind and clear understanding, and calling ever upon God. He was thus placed on a horse-drawn litter and carried to Battle. By the time he arrived, he was already completely speechless and only breathing. His sons ran to him groaning; they were to see their father more dead than alive and already departing, but they were not to enjoy converse with him. They approached one by one, and kissed him as he lay. Since dawn seemed about to break, they settled to await the unknown hour, supporting his departure by fervent prayers.[1]

Yet he lived through the night, and then the following day, struggling merely to breathe. A second night had darkened the earth when all those about him thought him about to die shortly. They carried him with all haste into the chapter house, that he might give up his soul there as was the custom of the abbey. When he was laid on ashes and a haircloth, suddenly all the members of his body, that had for long seemed dead, began to move, and his lips' motion had the look of speech. All the brothers were excited and those nearest put their ears to his mouth, but it was only a hiss, not a voice, and they could make out nothing of what he meant to say. The night passed, and when dawn had just come, he rendered his soul into the hands and will of his creator. The brothers stood around him and commended the departing one to the Lord with their fervent prayers. The funeral rites having been celebrated for two days as was fitting, the dust was returned to the dust whence it came and he was buried before the large cross and the altar of the

[1] In the *Regularis Concordia* the whole convent is to assemble to assist the departure of a brother with a cycle of prayers. *Regularis Concordia*, p. 65. For the ceremony of death see also Lanfranc, *Constitutions*, pp. 122–131: when the senses fail, the psalter is recited without ceasing as long as he lives, by two monks at a time, in rotation.

Crucifixi sepelitur.[1] Appositus est igitur ad patres suos anno incarnationis dominice millesimo centesimo septuagesimo primo, pro-
f. 105v motionis sue anno / tricesimo tertio, undecimo kalendas Iulii.

Qui cum in multis operibus suis bonis merito sit laudandus, in hoc tamen precipue est admirandus, quod cum res possessionesque ecclesie hostilitatis tempore plurima ex parte distractas multo labore et expensis innumeris reuocauerit, domum statui pristino restituerit, ecclesiam ornamentorum plurima uarietate decorauerit, domum tamen ipsam nullo penitus debito intus uel extra obligatam reliquit. Ministris nihilominus tam suis qui sibi familiarius adherebant, quam his qui in communi fratrum administratione erant sic in omnibus prouidit, ut nemo eorum de his que sibi recompensandi laboris sui gratia debebantur, quicquam deesse merito posset causari. Super hec omnia, argentea quedam uasa moriens ecclesie dereliquit, ex quibus ad honorem Dei et ipsius memoriam fabrefacta est super maius altare dependens corona, auro ad ipsius inaurationem addito, simili materia fabrefactam habens in medio columbam, Corpus Dominicum continentem.[2] Igitur ex tanta beneficiorum eius recordatione, memoria ipsius uiget in multiplici benedictione.

Rebus humanis sic exempto uiro uenerabili abbate Walterio, uir illustris Ricardus de Luci frater eius curam domus destitute cepit diligenter agere, fratrumque desolatorum quieti et consolationi prouidere. Nemini uero fratribus minus cognito uel suspecto uoluit domus committere procurationem, qui eorum quauis occasione posset perturbare quietem. Erant autem duo fidelis prudentie uiri in burgo de Bello pre foribus monasterii mansionem
f. 106 haben/tes, Petrus scilicet de Criel miles et Hugo de Beche, qui ex habitationum suarum uicinitate ab ipsis fere cunabulis frequentes habebant ad fratres accessus, in multis agendis ecclesie fideles inuenti, et ideo inter amicos fratrum amici familiarissimi.[3] Virum illustrem Ricardum de Luci super his non latuit, quippe cum

[1] The *Regularis Concordia* specifies that if a brother dies during the dark hours he is to be buried after mass and before the dinner-hour. If he dies during daylight, brothers are to watch beside the body by turns, chanting psalms throughout the day and the following night. The body is to be buried when dawn has broken. Lanfranc, *Constitutions*, pp. 127–8, advises that whenever a monk dies, if it happens at, or after, daybreak, the burial is to be put off till after the Chapter on the following day. It is clear that within a similar, general tradition Benedictine houses had their own burial customs, but that the distinction

Crucifixion.[1] He was gathered to his fathers in 1171, in the thirty-third year of his abbacy, on 21 June.

He was one who deserves praise for his many good works, but in this above all he should be admired: that after the goods and properties of the church had in very large measure been lost in the time of the anarchy, with much labour and expense he regained them; he restored the abbey to its original state; he decorated the church with a great variety of ornaments; yet for all this, he left the abbey with no debt within or without. He made such provision for the officials, both those of his own private household and those who administered for the community as a whole, that none of them could complain in the slightest that he had not been paid what was owing to him for his work. Beyond this, he left the church a bequest of siver vessels, out of which, to the honour of God and in his memory, was cast the crown hanging above the high altar. Gold was put on to gild it, and it has in the centre a dove made of the same materials, containing the Lord's body.[2] From such a remembrance of his favours, his memory thrives and is greatly blessed.

After Abbot Walter was removed from worldly affairs, his distinguished brother Richard de Luci undertook to care for the bereft abbey, and to provide for the peace and consolation of the abandoned brothers. He wished to appoint as custodian no one little known to or suspected by the brothers, for such a one could disturb their peace. There were two men of the borough of Battle, faithful and wise, whose houses were just by the gates of the monastery. These were the knight, Peter de Criol, and Hugh de *Beche*, men who, living so close, had, almost from their cradles, had constant admittance to the brothers. In many business matters of the church they had proved faithful, and were thus, among the brothers' friends, the most trusted.[3] The distinguished Richard de Luci knew of them; indeed he had long been acquainted with

between death during the dark and during the light was the centrally important fact determining the time of burial.

[2] The pyx was not uncommonly suspended above the altar, and sometimes inside a metal dove, in the Middle Ages. A pyx, so suspended, fell while King Stephen was hearing mass before the battle of Lincoln in 1141, and the event was taken as an evil omen. Rog. Howden, i. 201.

[3] For Criol see above, p. 214. Hugh de *Beche* held the three-virgate 'manor' of *Beche*. See above, pp. 48, 60. His family had held the messuage near the abbey gates as early as the first rental. Above, p. 52. It continued to be an important local family until *c.* 1400. For both see Searle, *Lordship*, 165–6, 185–7, 333–6.

amborum noticiam iampridem habuisset, quoniam fratre suo Walterio abbate superstite, inter primos sibi ministrantium habebantur primi. His itaque de mandato suo ad se uenientibus, totius monasterii curam in secularibus commisit, precipiens ut fratribus in necessariis uictus et uestitus honeste prouiderent, reparationi domorum, in quibus fratres ex regulari consuetudine cotidie conueniunt, cum officinis aliis fratrum usibus necessariis intenderent, seruientibus quoque qui in eorum communi administratione erant, et sine quibus esse non poterant, congrue prospicerent.[1] Suscipientes hi duo uiri procurationis officium, cum tanta diligentia per iiii^or annos quibus uacabat ecclesia fratribus ministrauerunt, ut nullum penitus defectum seu penuriam in his que ad uictum ipsorum atque uestitum regulariter et consuetudinaliter pertinebant ex contemptu uel negligentia procurantium sustinerent. Nullam ecclesia his diebus dignitatis libertatisue sue sustinuit diminutionem, nullam aduersariorum impugnationem, scientibus omnibus uirum illustrem Ricardum de Luci ipsius esse protectorem, qui ex summa qua post dominum regem fungebatur potestate, quoslibet
f. 106v in ipsam insurgere molientes poterat / reprimere. Inerat namque ei ad expedienda ipsius ecclesie negotia emergentia uoluntas tam promta, tanta diligentia, ut in ipsis expediendis omnem abscideret dilationem, sciens quoniam sepe mora trahat periculum. Vnde quia, propter regni ardua negotia quibus maxime prospicere tenebatur ex officio iusticiario, quibuslibet negotiis minoribus audiendis semper uacare non poterat, notariis suis sigillique sui custodibus precepit, ut quotiens aliquos ad ipsum pro quibuslibet eiusdem ecclesie agendis interpellandum uenire cognoscerent, mox sententia eius non expectata nisi in arduis, nomine suo cuncta pro quibus uenissent expedirent.[2]

Sub hoc tempore presbyterum ecclesie de Wi, Willelmum nomine, decedere contigit, qui eiusdem ecclesie medietatem ex concessione abbatis defuncti et fratrum possederat. Quod cum ad uiri illustris Ricardi de Luci peruenisset noticiam, litteras deprecatorias pro filio suo Godefrido de Luci priori et conuentui direxit, ut ei ecclesiam ipsam sicut Willelmus tenuerat tenendam concederent. Lectis in omnium audientia litteris, decreuerunt tanti uiri peticionibus non deesse, quem sibi in omnibus agendis senserant gratanter

[1] Thus the two custodians were given no responsibility for managing the abbey estates. Their orders are indeed to maintain only a minimum household at the abbey. De Luci himself evidently kept the management, and the profits, of

both, for while his brother Abbot Walter lived, among his leading officials they were the foremost. Now he sent for them and gave them the custody of the whole monastery, in secular affairs. He commanded that they provide the brothers honourably with their needs in food and clothing, that they see to the upkeep of the buildings in which the brothers assemble daily by the rule's custom, together with the other workshops needed by the brothers, and that they properly oversee the servants who managed the common household and whom they could not do without.[1] The two men agreed; they served as stewards during the four years of the vacancy with such diligence that the brothers suffered neither a lack nor a stinginess in the customary food and clothing, owing to any disregard or negligence on their part. During that time the church suffered no diminution of its privileges and liberties, and no lawsuits, for everyone knew that the illustrious Richard de Luci was its protector—he who after the king wielded the greatest power—and could put down any of its adversaries. There was in him a will so prompt to deal with the affairs of the church, and such diligence, that in dealing with them he would brook no delay, for he knew that delay often brings danger. Since as chief justiciar he had to oversee the most serious affairs of the realm, he had not always time to listen to all sorts of minor matters. Therefore he ordered his scribes and keepers of his seal, that whenever they heard of people coming to speak to him about any business of the abbey, they were in his name to see to the affairs on which they came, without consulting him except on difficult matters.[2]

About this time, William, priest of Wye church, died. He had held half the church by grant of the late abbot and brothers. When news of this reached the distinguished Richard de Luci, he sent a letter to the prior and convent, asking that they grant his son Godfrey de Luci the church on the terms on which William had held it. The letter was read in the presence of everyone, and they decided not to refuse the requests of such a man, for they realized that he was their willing patron in all their affairs. They therefore

the abbey's estates for himself. Though custodians accounted to the Exchequer for the abbey's income, the amounts reported by de Luci are unbelievably small in comparison with the vacancy accounts during the Interdict. See Searle, *Lordship*, p. 92, n. 12. It is a nice example of Henry II's patronage to a loyal servant.

[2] The Angevin justiciar would normally govern in his own name and under his own seal. West, *Justiciar*, p. 76.

adesse. Igitur unanimi consilio prebentes assensum postulanti, rescripto significauerunt se quod petebantur prestare, Willelmum quidem presbyterum medietatem tantum ipsius ecclesie possedisse, seque eamdem medietatem Godefrido de Luci filio suo peticionis sue gratia concedere. Cognoscens Godefridus concessam sibi non integre ecclesiam sed tantum ecclesie medietatem, mox
f. 107 ingratus pro bonis stu/duit mala rependere, totis uiribus agens, quo medietatem non concessam de fratrum manibus extorqueret, sicque totam simul ecclesiam sibi in possessionem redigeret. Festinus itaque dominum regem seu per se seu per suos adiit eique ecclesiam de Wi defuncto presbytero uacare, seque succedendi defuncto prioris et conuentus de Bello assensum habere suggessit, postulans ut quoniam abbate defuncto ipse rex uices abbatis uidebatur agere, ecclesiam ipsam confirmato eorum assensu sibi regia auctoritate dignaretur concedere. Videtur in hac sua suggestione regi facta quod de concessa sibi sola dumtaxat ecclesie medietate meminimus suppressisse, aut eum quouis alio modo tacita ueritate circumuenisse. Annuens namque rex postulanti, totam ecclesiam de Wi non solum sibi concessit, uerum etiam confirmauit, necnon uiro uenerabili Ricardo tunc Cantuariensi electo ut per eum institueretur litteras direxit. Idem uero electus, licet minoris adhuc esset dignitatis ac potestatis, electione sua nondum per dominum papam confirmata, quantula tamen potuit illum auctoritate instituit, quali etiam carta potuit institutionem confirmauit.[1] Postmodum cum sedem apostolicam sacrandus adisset, expeditisque omnibus pro quibus ierat, denuo in Angliam redisset, eidem Godefrido ad se uenienti iam archiepiscopus, iam totius Anglie primas, iam apostolice sedis legatus, omnia ut pridem concessit et episcopali auctoritate confirmauit. Dicitur tamen eum conditionaliter instituisse, saluo scilicet omnium hominum iure. Erat itaque toto tempore quo uacabat ecclesia inter fratres et ipsum Godefridum plurima dissensio, dum
f. 107v ipse / Godefridus totam ecclesiam sibi niteretur in possessionem redigere, fratres solam ipsius medietatem ei non concessam sibi ipsis conarentur retinere.

Multas per Angliam ecclesias multaque sub hoc tempore contigit

[1] Richard of Dover was elected in June 1173. He was confirmed and consecrated by the pope in April 1174. *Letters of Gilbert Foliot*, no. 20, pp. 292–3. Our author is anticipating the argument presented by Gerard Pucelle when pleading Battle's case in the 1170s. The canonical requirement that confirmation must

unanimously agreed, and in their reply they notified him that they assented to his request: that William the priest had held only half of the church and that at his petition they granted his son Godfrey de Luci that half. Godfrey knew he had not been granted the full church, but half only. Yet soon, ungrateful, he repaid evil for good, trying with all his strength to swindle the brothers of their half, and so to have the whole church himself. In haste he went to the lord king, either personally or through friends, and told him that, its priest having died, the church of Wye was vacant, and that he had the consent of the prior and convent of Battle to succeed him. He petitioned that, since the abbot was dead and the king himself was the one to act in place of an abbot, he deign to grant him the church by royal authority since he had their assent. It would seem obvious that in his notification to the king he had suppressed what we have mentioned about only half the church having been granted him, or that he had in some other way got round the king, while the truth was passed over in silence. For the king assented to the petition and not only granted him the whole church of Wye, but even confirmed the grant, and then sent a written directive to the venerable Richard, archbishop elect of Canterbury to institute him. Though the elect had as yet little privilege or power, since his election had not yet been confirmed by the lord pope, nevertheless he instituted him with what little authority he could, and confirmed the institution as far as his charter might.[1] Afterwards, when he had gone to the holy see for consecration, and had done everything he had gone for, and had returned to England, he was approached by Godfrey, and, now as archbishop, primate of all England and legate of the apostolic see, he granted all as he had done before, and confirmed it by episcopal authority. But it is said that he confirmed him conditionally, namely, saving the rights of all men. So there was much discord between the brothers and Godfrey throughout the vacancy, as Godfrey strove to gain possession of the whole church and the brothers tried to keep for themselves the half not granted to him.

It happened that at this epoch many churches and monasteries

precede the bishop's exercise of his jurisdictional powers is a late twelfth-century one, developed in the 1160s. Benson, *Bishop-Elect*, esp. pp. 91–4, 368–74. Henry II's actions in 1173–4, as here described, show clearly that he did not recognize such a limitation on the archbishop's powers. Probably in this very year, however, Pope Alexander III, in an instruction concerning the bishop elect of Hereford, linked confirmation with the power to grant benefices. Ibid., p. 109.

uacare monasteria. Vacandi causam, licet aliquantulum uideatur ab re, indignum tamen putauimus penitus silendo pretermittere. Apposito ad patres suos in senectute bona Theobaldo Cantuariensi archiepiscopo, successit ei nomen officiumque suscipiens archiepiscopi Thomas Cantuariensis archidiaconus, domini regis cancellarius quem superior edidit narratio cum bone memorie abbate Walterio aduersus Cicestrensem episcopum Hylarium uiriliter stetisse, seque pro defensione libertatis ecclesie sancti Martini de Bello aduocatum exhibuisse. Cuius meritorum memoria tanto debet apud eiusdem ecclesie fratres esse celebrior, quanto ad eorum tuendas libertates dinoscitur fuisse sollicitior.[1] Erat quidem dum cancellarii fungeretur officio inter quoslibet post dominum regem nominatos in regno nominatissimus, inter quoslibet potentiores potentissimus, inter quoslibet regis familiares familiarissimus. Procurauit itaque rex omni cum instantia quatinus archiepiscopatus Cantuariensis apicem consequeretur, cuius dignitas inter ecclesiasticos honores prima in regno esse dinoscitur. Putabat namque eum ex antiqua familiaritate in omnibus que uellet assensum prebiturum, nec sibi quauis occasione in aliquo contradicturum. Verum eo talia proponente, Deus longe aliter dignatus est disponere.[2] Adeptus siquidem tante dignitatis apicem, uir uenerabilis Thomas plus
f. 108 cogitabat de onere / quam de honore, plus de cure pastoralis grauitate quam de temporali dignitate. Honores in eo secundum uulgare prouerbium mutabant mores,[3] non ut fere omnium mos est, in deterius, sed per singulos dies in melius. Veterem namque hominem qui secundum seculum erat exuens, nouum hominem qui secundum deum creatus est, satagebat induere.[4]

Cepit interea rex uelle opprimere dignitates ecclesiasticas, archiepiscopi et suffraganeorum eius assensum exigens. Consentientibus episcopis, non consensit archiepiscopus, defensorem se exhibens ecclesie, non impugnatorem. Exarsit igitur aduersus eum rex cum episcopis et regni optimatibus in tanta indignatione, ut iam nichil esse uideretur antiqua dilectio, concepti circa ipsum odii comparatione. Stetit nichilominus tamen ipse pro ecclesia, sed solus.[5]

[1] Theobald died in April 1161. Thomas Becket was consecrated 3 June 1162. Our author is referring to Becket's advocacy of Abbot Walter in 1157. Above, pp. 198–204. For Becket's later version of the affair see above, p. 208, n. 1.

[2] Cf. Prov. 11: 9.

[3] Cf. Walther, no. 11125: 'Honores mutant mores, sed raro in meliores.'

[4] Eph. 4: 22–4.

[5] According to Gilbert Foliot, himself undoubtedly partial, the bishops stood

throughout England were vacant. Though the cause of these vacancies may seem to be somewhat off the subject, yet we have considered it unworthy to pass over it wholly in silence. Theobald, archbishop of Canterbury, having been gathered to his fathers at a ripe old age, Thomas, archdeacon of Canterbury and the lord king's chancellor, received the title and office of archbishop in his stead. We have written of him earlier in our tale, for it was he who acted as advocate in defence of the exemption of the church of St. Martin of Battle, and manfully stood alongside Abbot Walter, of happy memory, against Hilary, bishop of Chichester. The memory of his merits deserves to be the more honoured among the brothers of this church as he is known to have been so solicitous in defending their privileges.[1] While he was chancellor, he was, after the lord king, the most famous of the famed, the mightiest of the mighty, the most intimate of the king's confidants. The king was insistent that he be raised to the archbishopric of Canterbury, acknowledged first in rank among the ecclesiastical benefices of the realm. He thought that because of their old friendship he would agree to anything he wanted and would never disagree with him. So he proposed, but God saw fit to dispose things very differently.[2] Raised to the height of honour, the venerable Thomas thought more of duty than honour, more of the seriousness of pastoral care than of worldly privilege. In him, as the common proverb has it, honours changed conduct,[3] but not, as with the conduct of nearly all men, for the worse, but day by day for the better. For he put off the old man who is according to the world, and strove to put on the new man, who is created according to God.[4]

Meanwhile, the king began to wish to suppress ecclesiastical privileges, demanding the assent of the archbishop and his suffragans. Though the bishops consented, the archbishop did not, standing forth as the defender of the church, not its attacker. The king, along with the bishops and magnates of the realm, was so enraged against him that the old fondness was nothing in comparison with the hatred he now conceived against him. None the less he stood firm for the church; but he stood alone.[5] All were

unanimous in 1164 in their opposition to the king's demand that they assent to the document known later as the Constitutions of Clarendon. There, in 1164, as Foliot bitterly wrote him, Becket suddenly gave way. *Letters of Gilbert Foliot*, no. 170, esp. pp. 233–4. For the developing relations between the archbishop and his suffragans see D. Knowles, *The Episcopal Colleagues of Archbishop Thomas Becket* (Cambridge, 1951), pp. 60 ff.

Aduersantibus sibi cunctis, cum nemo secum ageret solusque agens parum aut nichil proficeret, uidens periculis pericula succedere, elegit potius spontaneum subire exilium quam dignitatis ecclesiastice presentialiter uidere dispendium. Transferens itaque se ipsum de medio iniquitatis, Francorum regnum adiit, pacem querens in solo alieno, quam non habebat in proprio.[1] Exulabat ergo pauper et egenus, rerum ac possessionum suarum fructuumque ex eis prouenientium potestate mox spoliatus. Quot passionibus sex exilii sui annis subiacuerit, per neminem preter ipsum potuit exprimi, quia nemo preter ipsum habuit experiri. Inter innumera flagitia sibi enormiter illata, hoc uidetur flagitiosissimum, quod cum ipse in persona propria deesset ad iniuriam, exarsit indignatio
f. 108v in uniuersam eius cognationem. / Addicti sunt siquidem prescriptioni quotquot uidebatur habere propinquos et beniuolos, cum exule exules, et que deesse uidebantur passionum eius passionibus suis adimplentes. Erat uisu nimium miserabile, dum non etati, non sexui, non conditioni pepercit tanta crudelitas, compulsis egredi pregnantibus cum paruulis pendentibus ad ubera, iuuenibus etiam cum ueteranis baculo regentibus membra debilia.[2]

Exilii anno septimo iam inchoato uisus est eum rex recepisse in gratiam, reformataque specietenus pace permisisse, quatinus exilium patria commutans pacifice remearet in Angliam. Repatrians itaque patriarchatus sui adiit ecclesiam, promissa pace frui cupiens, nec tamen promissam inueniens. Vix enim per mensem in ecclesia sua resederat, et ecce insurgentibus in eum iiii^or militibus a curia regia uenientibus, non dico missis, in ecclesia pro ecclesia perimitur, pastor ecclesie, a regeneratis in Christo et ecclesia, iam tamen tanto commisso flagitio alienatis ab ecclesia.[3] Terras celerius percurrit, maria pertransit fama tam enormis sceleris, et clamore de terris ad celos ascendente, mox ostenditur de morte presulis quod sit martyrium, ubique terrarum choruscante frequentia miraculorum. Videbatur interea martyr Domini, immo pro martyre suo Dominus innoxii sanguinis ultionem querere, cum rex regis filius,[4] in regem patrem suum insurgens, eum, quampluribus procerum regni consentientibus, multis etiam opem prestantibus,

[1] He was given asylum at the Cistercian abbey of Pontigny. Becket fled from England in November 1164.

[2] A contemporary story, very likely accurate. *Materials*, v. 151–2.

[3] Becket was murdered 29 Dec. 1170 by four barons. Two eyewitnesses wrote accounts of the event: William FitzStephen, *Materials*, iii, esp. 132–9, and

against him; none acted with him, and acting alone he could accomplish little or nothing. Seeing dangers following dangers, he chose rather to undergo a voluntary exile than to stay and see the wasting of ecclesiastical privilege. Removing himself from the midst of evil, he went to France, seeking the peace on alien soil that he did not have at home.[1] He went into exile a pauper, soon despoiled of control over his goods and possessions, and the income from them. How many sufferings he endured during the six years of his exile, none besides himself could relate, for none besides himself had to experience them. Among the innumerable outrages done to him, this seems the most disgraceful: that since he had escaped injury to himself, the hatred was turned against all his kindred. As many were added to the decree as seemed to be kindred or kindly to him, exiles with the exile, completing in their sufferings anything he escaped in his. The sight was pitiful, for such cruelty spared neither age, nor sex, nor rank, and turned to wanderers pregnant women with babies at the breast, children, and old people supporting their feebleness with a staff.[2]

At the beginning of the seventh year of his exile it seemed that the king had taken him back into favour, and had re-established peace. But it was in name only. He was allowed to end his exile and come back peaceably to England; and home he came to the church of his archdiocese, wishing to enjoy the promised peace. Yet he found not what was promised. For he had been home in his church hardly a month when suddenly four knights who came (I do not say were sent) from the royal court, attacked him, and he died in the church, for the church, as the shepherd of the church, at the hands of men sanctified in Christ and the church, but now, after such an outrage, cast off from the church.[3] The news of such a crime spread swiftly over land and sea, and the cry rose from earth to heaven. Immediately everywhere on earth miracles began, to show that the death of the priest was in fact a martyrdom. Meanwhile the Lord's martyr, or rather the Lord, for His martyr, seemed to seek vengeance for the innocent blood. For the king, the king's son,[4] rebelled against his father, bent on expelling him from the throne, and many of the magnates sided with him, and helped him.

Edward Grim, *Materials*, ii, esp. 430–8. John of Salisbury witnessed all but the dénouement and wrote the earliest account. *Letters of John of Salisbury*, ii, no. 305.

[4] Henry the 'young king' had been crowned on 14 June 1170.

regno conatus est expellere. Erat igitur pater omni destitutus
f. 109 consilio atque solatio hinc / eum seua memorati flagitii redarguente conscientia, inde ineuitabili imminente periculo, quippe cum filius eius, parata nauium multitudine in transmarino littore, cum intolerabili exercitu armatorum regnum iam uideretur occupaturus.[1] Sic in arto positus didicit humiliari, et iam feritatis oblitus Cantuariam celerius adiit, discalciatisque pedibus cum appropinquaret ciuitati, sepulchrum beati martyris petiit se reum confitens, ueniam postulans, dignum penitentie fructum promittens.[2] Memor Dominus cum martyre suo solite misericordie, non distulit humiliato misericordiam prestare, subitum quendum timorem hostibus eius immittens, ut mox mutato consilio ceptis desisterent, et a mari quod transnauigare parauerant pedes retraherent.[3]

Hostibus eius uniuersis in breui uirtute diuina triumphatis, regno quoque pacificato, agere cepit quatinus ecclesia Cantuariensis regni sui metropolis pastorem susciperet. Electus est itaque iamdictus Ricardus Cantuariensis ecclesie monachus, a summo Romane sedis pontifice ut supra meminimus post modicum consecratus. De quo pretermittendum minime uidetur, quippe cum sequenti narrationi sit necessarium, quod cum mox post electionem suam, consecratione sua non expectata, quedam publice statuenda decreuisset, dominus papa in ipsius consecratione cuncta que a die electionis sue statuisse uisus est in irritum redegit.[4] A primis igitur diebus exilii beati Martyris Thome usque ad succedentis sibi archiepiscopi
f. 109v Ricardi reditum a sede apostolica / multas ut prediximus per Angliam ecclesias multaque contigit uacare monasteria. Vacantibus namque sedibus episcopalibus, episcoporum electio nulla fieri potuit uel debuit, cum archiepiscopus non adesset qui eorum electionem confirmaret et electos consecraret, nec minus otiosa uidebatur quorumlibet ad monasteriorum regimen uocatio, dum per dioceses minus essent pontifices, per quos uocatorum fieret

[1] Henry the 'young king', his brothers, and a large following rebelled against Henry II in 1173–4. The king was concerned about invasion, and one was in fact planned for the summer of 1174. Our author seems to be the only English chronicler to speak of naval forces. Cf. Warren, *Henry II*, pp. 125 and ibid., n. 2, 134–5. The awareness was probably the result of Battle's proximity to the Cinque Ports.

[2] Matt. 3: 8.

Wherefore was the father bereft of all advice and comfort. On the one hand the memory of the outrage tortured his conscience, while on the other an inevitable danger seemed imminent, since his son, with a large fleet prepared on the opposite shore, and with an invincible army, seemed about to invade the realm.[1] Between them he learned humility. Forgetting his fierceness he went swiftly to Canterbury. Entering the city barefoot, he sought the tomb of the blessed martyr, confessing his sin, praying forgiveness, and promising worthy fruits of penance.[2] The Lord and His martyr were, as ever, compassionate and did not delay mercy to the humbled. He visited his enemies with a sudden fear, so that they suddenly changed their minds and, leaving off what they had undertaken, they withdrew from the sea they had planned to cross.[3]

Quickly he triumphed over his enemies through the divine power, and when peace was restored to the realm he undertook to secure a shepherd for the metropolitan see of Canterbury. Richard, formerly a monk of Canterbury, was elected and after a little time, as we have said, he was consecrated by the pope. It seems that this should be mentioned, since it is especially necessary to what follows. For immediately after his election, when his consecration was not anticipated, he had publicly promulgated some regulations, and at his consecration the lord pope declared all his decrees invalid from the day of his election.[4] Therefore from the beginning of the exile of the blessed martyr Thomas to the return of his successor Archbishop Richard from the apostolic see, many churches, as we have said, and many monasteries, became vacant throughout England. For when bishoprics became vacant, no elections could be made, nor would it have been right, while the archbishop was not present to confirm the election and consecrate the elect. It was equally pointless to appoint abbots while the bishoprics had few incumbents who could institute the

[3] Henry sailed from Normandy in early July 1174, to aid his forces against the rebels in England. His departure from Normandy led his enemies to abandon the proposed invasion of England and to attack Rouen instead. Upon arrival, Henry made the dramatic gesture of hastening to Canterbury for forgiveness, as his recent biographer says, 'to separate St. Thomas from the rebels' cause'. Warren, *Henry II*, p. 135. By the end of the summer the rebellion had collapsed, and the Battle monks were not alone in seeing in this the sign of the saint's forgiveness.

[4] See *Letters of Gilbert Foliot*, p. 293. *Letters of John of Salisbury*, ii, p. xlv. As far as England was concerned, Alexander III's pontificate was the turning-point in the doctrine that an *electus* cannot administer church property until he has been confirmed. Benson, *Bishop-Elect*, pp. 108–11.

institutio.[1] Preterea cum rex omnibus interesse uolens nichil preter se fieri permitteret, orta post martyrium beati Thome mox inter ipsum et filium eius de qua diximus dissensione, ex multa circa alia occupatione, minori circa ecclesias utebatur sollicitudine. His, licet aliquantulum uideantur ab re, non tamen hic sine causa breuiter insertis, quippe cum quedam sequentium ex ipsis habeant pendere, iam nunc ad exequendam propositi nostri seriem reuertamur.

Anno incarnationis uerbi Dei millesimo centesimo septuagesimo quinto, regni uero domini regis Henrici secundi anno uicesimo primo, ordinatus, ut iam dictum est, et in sede sua confirmatus uir uenerabilis Ricardus Cantuariensis archiepiscopus singulos episcopos qui sedibus pontificalibus eatenus uacantibus presiderent ordinauit, paulo ante electos.[2] Ordinatus est tunc temporis ecclesie Cicestrensi episcopus beate recordationis Iohannes,[3] ipsius ecclesie decanus, Hylario episcopo, cuius superius frequens facta est mentio, huic uite pridem subtracto, dum adhuc beatus martyr Thomas esset in exilio. Consummatis itaque omnibus que circa pontificum ordinationem facienda uidebantur, agere ceperunt tam /
f. 110 rex quam ipse archiepiscopus super eligendis monasteriorum prelatis et instituendis. Communicatoque inuicem consilio uacantium monasteriorum uniformiter scribendum decreuerunt congregationibus, quatinus singuli singulorum monasteriorum priores, sociatis sibi iiii^or aut quinque congregationum suarum fratribus, se eorum conspectibus apud Wedestoche omni occasione postposita presentarent, ut illic in eorum presentia abbates sibi ipsis, Deo procurante, digne preficiendos eligerent. Quorum ut electio a remorante in monasteriis uniuersitate omnino rata haberetur, litteras de communi consilio et consensu conuentuum suorum secum deferrent. Ad agendum huiusmodi negotium, duo mox clerici sunt directi, qui diuersas prouintias percurrentes commissamque legationem in monasteriis que uiciniora uidebantur expedientes Bellum usque peruenerunt. Quorum aduentu cognito, mox priore uocante conuenit in capitulum tota simul congregatio. Introducti clerici regis et archiepiscopi mandata porrexerunt, que ilico in omnium audientia lecta sunt.

1 The diocese of Chichester, in which Battle lay, was indeed without a bishop from Hilary's death in July 1169 to the consecration of John of Greenford in Oct. 1174. A number of other sees had fallen vacant as well and were filled in

appointees.[1] And since the king wished to be concerned in every decision, he would permit nothing to be done without him. Now when, after the martyrdom of St. Thomas, the dispute of which we have spoken arose between the king and his son, he was much taken up with other matters and little with churches. This may seem somewhat off the subject, but it has not been put in idly, since it has significance for part of what follows. We can now therefore return to the events we are in the course of explaining.

In the year 1175, in the twenty-first year of the reign of the lord King Henry II, the venerable Richard, archbishop of Canterbury, consecrated and confirmed in his see, himself consecrated individual bishops who had been elected for some little while, to administer the hitherto vacant bishoprics.[2] At that time the see of Chichester received John, of blessed memory,[3] dean of the cathedral, to replace Hilary, of whom we have made frequent mention, and who had died some while before, when the blessed martyr Thomas was still in exile. When the ordination of the bishops was finished, both the king and the archbishop took up the election and institution of abbots. Having taken counsel together, they decided that the vacant monasteries should all receive written instructions to this effect: that the prior of each monastery, accompanied by four or five brothers of the community, should present themselves to them for inspection at Woodstock without excuses, so that they might, with God's help, elect worthy abbots there in their presence. In order to be sure of the consent of the whole monastery, they were to bring with them letters of the general opinion and consent of their convents. To get this business done, two clerks were immediately sent through the various counties. These men carried out their commission in the nearer monasteries, and eventually came to Battle. When their arrival was announced, the whole convent gathered together in the chapter house at the summons of the prior. The clerks were brought in and handed over the mandate of the king and archbishop. It was immediately read aloud before all.

1173–4: Bath, Ely, Hereford, Lincoln, and Winchester, besides Chichester. For the king's interests in the elections see C. Duggan in *TRHS*, 5th ser. xvi (1966), 12–14.

[2] The chronicler is a year out. Richard of Dover was consecrated archbishop in April 1174. In June he consecrated the bishop of Bath, and on 6 Oct. 1174 he consecrated the bishops of Chichester, Ely, Hereford, and Winchester.

[3] John of Greenford, bishop of Chichester. He died in late April 1180. See above, p. 278, n. 1.

Expeditis omnibus que per clericos ipsos illic agenda uidebantur, cum iam abscedendum putarent, repente nuntius alius aduenit, qui litteras inopinatas priori et conuentui nomine regis porrigendas detulit, continentes quidem quatinus prior et fratres, qui curiam regiam eligendi gratia pastoris adituri erant, cartas dignitatum ac libertatum suarum a rege Willelmo monasterii ipsius inclito fundatore successoribusque eius regibus sibi concessas secum deferrent. Stupefacta ad hoc mandatum uniuersa congregatio,
f. 110v cepit ex ipso amplius timere, quam de priori / sollicita esse. Monasterii namque sui dignitatibus multos inuidere certum habentes, plurimum uerebantur, ne forte rex, cuiuslibet maligna suggestione, cartas iamdictas uellet surripere ne abbas nouiter monasterio preficiendus ad monasterii ipsius protectionem earum frui posset auctoritate. Non enim a memoria exciderat qualiter, ut superior edidit narratio, aduersus easdem libertates fuerit aliquando a pluribus conclamatum, ipsas minus rationabiles esse, nec nisi prius mutatas atque correctas obseruari debere.[1] Plus itaque ex hoc mandato sinistrum quam prosperum suspicantes, mentibus per diuersa et incerta rapiebantur, attentius tamen orantes euenire sibi prospera. Igitur communicato consilio tractabant de preficiendi sibi pastoris electione, cupientes eum omnimodis sibi secundum cartarum suarum tenorem prefici de propria congregatione.[2] Consenserunt itaque in duas capituli sui personas, ut si forte una non admitteretur, altera reciperetur.

Imminente iam die qua coram rege et archiepiscopo erat conueniendum, prior sociatis sibi iiii^or fratribus iter eo ueniendi arripuit, interminante eis uniuersa congregatione, ne quemquam preter personas in quas communiter consenserant admittendum presumerent. Venientes usque Wedestoche die determinato, multitudinem priorum similiter cum monachis suis illuc uocatorum inuenerunt congregatam. Expectantibus omnibus uocationem suam, ecce primi adesse iussi sunt, abbatem electuri, prior et monachi sancti Martini de Bello, procedentesque primi intra portas regias, ceteris foris expectantibus, sunt introducti, ac in presentiam
f. 111 Gilberti Londoni episcopi, et quarundam / aliarum personarum, quas ad eorum animos indagandos, uel potius ad eos ad regie uoluntatis consensum inducendos, rex et archiepiscopus

[1] At the Lambeth meeting. Above, p. 158.

[2] This is contained in the Battle forgery BL Add. Ch. 70980, first shown in 1157. See above, p. 196. Prior Odo had come, as we shall see, to ask for charters

The clerks had completed their mission and were about to leave when suddenly another messenger arrived. He brought an unexpected letter for the prior and convent in the king's name. It stated that the prior and brothers who were to go to court to elect an abbot were to bring with them the charters of privileges and exemptions granted them by King William, the renowned founder of the monastery, and by the kings his successors. The whole congregation was stupefied at this command. They began to be more afraid over this one than anxious to obey the earlier. For, knowing with certainty that many were prejudiced against their monastery's privileges, they were much afraid that the king, at some malicious suggestion, might wish to confiscate the charters so that the newly appointed abbot might not be able to protect his abbey by their authority. For the memory of what we have earlier told had not been forgotten: how, once, many men had cried out in unison against these privileges, saying that they were unreasonable, and ought not to be observed save in a changed and corrected form.[1] Suspecting more misfortune than favour from this mandate, they imagined all sorts of possibilities, but prayed most intently that it would turn out well. They considered the question of electing an abbot, wishing with all their hearts that he might be appointed from their own congregation, according to the tenor of their charters.[2] They agreed on two members of their chapter, so that if by chance one were not acceptable, the other would be allowed them.

When the day drew near on which they were to go before the king and the archbishop, the prior set out with four of the brothers and the whole convent forbade them to dare consent to the appointment of anyone besides the persons they had chosen in common. Arriving at Woodstock on the day fixed, they found gathered a multitude of priors, alike summoned there with their brothers. Everyone waited to be called, and behold! the first ordered in to elect an abbot were the priors and monks of St. Martin of Battle. Advancing first through the royal doors, with the rest left waiting outside, they were brought into the presence of Gilbert, bishop of London, and some other personages who had been sent by the king and archbishop to explore what was in their minds, or rather, to bring their minds round to accepting the royal

based upon the earlier forgeries of Battle, which would have given Christ Church an uncustomary exemption from the archbishop. The struggle between the archbishop and his cathedral monks was clearly far from over.

direxerant, sunt perducti. Sciscitati sunt illic presidentes, si secundum susceptum regis et archiepiscopi mandatum instructi uenissent, si litteras de consensu uniuersitatis sue, quo quicquid illic per presentes fieret, a non presentibus ratum haberetur, detulissent; si in aliquam personam consensissent. Respondentibus illis ad singula, cum quidem sciscitantibus esset in ceteris satisfactum, personarum in quas conuenerant electioni regem non consentire dicebant, quippe cum una earum sibi omnino esset incognita, altera minus accepta, nec uelle regem regni sui honores cuiquam tribuere, quem seu minus notum seu suspectum uideretur habere. Alias itaque personas quarum promotioni rex assensum preberet eos nominare monebant, utque eos de uoluntate regis plenius instruerent, plures eis nominetenus proponebant, nunc minarum asperitatibus ad consentiendum urgentes, nunc uerborum blanditiis persuadentes. Stabant in sua pro uiribus fixi sententia prior et fratres, seque extra ea in quibus monasterii sui uniuersitas consenserat sibique facienda iniunxerat nichil posse presumere asseruerunt, maxime autem electioni personarum ab eis nominatarum se nullatenus adquiescere, quippe cum earum noticiam non habentes, de laudabili ipsarum uita et digna coram Deo et hominibus conuersatione possent dubitare. Instanter urgentibus regie uoluntatis fautoribus, prior et fratres regis uoluntatem uniuersitati sue renuntiaturi indutias petebant, nec impetrabant. Igitur quo se
f. 111v uerterent nescie/bant in anxietate plurima positi, dum neminem preter eos, quibus sibi preficiendis unanimis monasterii sui congregatio assenserat, auderent eligere; illis econtrario qui pro regia uoluntate agebant pertinaciter insistentibus, quatinus incontinenti alium eligerent.

Cum autem in huiusmodi conflictu plurimum diei tempus casso labore consumeretur, repente rex, quem cum archiepiscopo expectantem donec de assensu prioris et fratrum cum uoluntate sua sibi nuntiaretur iam tedebat morarum, indignantis uultum preferens accurrit, cur moras necterent inquisiuit. Vrgentibus eo acrius his qui ab ipso missi fuerant satis aduertebant prior et fratres non se posse secundum propositum procedere, aliud sibi consilium necessario querendum fore.

Aduenerat tunc forte illuc pro negotiis ecclesie Cantuariensis, nuper incendio dissipate, uir eximie religionis, Odo, ipsius ecclesie prior,[1] cui, preter cetera quibus pollebat uirtutum insignia, nomen

[1] Odo is thought probably to have been subprior previously. Le Neve, ed. Greenway, ii, 10. He was elected prior before 1169, but was not recognized by Becket. *Materials*, vi, nos. 351, 412, 502. The church of Canterbury was burned 5 Sept. 1174. Gervase of Canterbury i. 1–29.

pleasure. There they were asked by those presiding to say whether they had come instructed according to the mandate of the king and archbishop: if they had brought a letter of consent from their community, by which whatever was done by those present there would have the ratification of those not present: and if they had agreed upon any person. They answered each question, and while their interrogators found them satisfactory otherwise, they said that the king did not assent to the election of the persons on whom they had agreed. One was totally unknown to him and the other not welcome, and the king did not wish to bestow the honours in his realm on any who were little known or suspect. They warned the monks to name other persons, whose promotion the king would be pleased to accept. In order to instruct them thoroughly in the king's wishes, they proposed many possible names to them, pressing them to consent, now with threats, now with blandishments. The prior and brothers with all their might remained firm in their opinion. They said that they dared to arrogate to themselves no powers of acting beyond the instructions agreed by their monastery's congregation. In particular they could not assent to the election of the persons proposed to them; indeed, having no knowledge of them, they must be left in doubt about the worthiness of their life and conversation before God and men. But the agents of the royal will kept on, vehemently pressing, and the prior and brothers begged for a delay to report the king's will back to their community. They prayed in vain. They knew not where to turn in their great anxiety. They dared not elect any except one of those whom their monastery had selected unanimously to rule them, yet the agents of the royal will were firmly insisting that they elect another forthwith.

Much of the day had been spent in the fruitless labour of this disagreement, when the king, who with the archbishop was waiting for the news of the compliance of the prior and his brothers with his wishes, grew tired of the delay. He suddenly strode in with an angry look and asked why they were holding things up. At this his agents pressed yet harder, and the prior and brothers saw quite sufficiently that they were not going to be able to proceed according to their plan, and that they had better look for another.

By chance the affairs of the church of Canterbury, recently destroyed by fire, had brought there its prior, Odo, a man of exceptional holiness.[1] Besides his other great virtues, he was

celebre fecerat insignis eloquentia, qua cum esset doctus lege diuina oportune nouerat proferre noua et uetera. Hic quidem, quoniam carte dignitatum ac libertatum Cantuariensis ecclesie in ipsius repentino incendio erant ex plurima parte absumpte, regem conuenerat, ut eas auctoritate regia innouaret. Visus est rex postulanti uelle satisfacere, spem sibi multam ponens promissionibus, in fine tamen effectu carentem. Credens sic promittenti uir simplicis ac recti animi, adiecerat postulare, ut cartis ipsis formam cartarum monasterii sancti Martini de Bello dignaretur apponere. Rex petenti non tantum non contradixerat, quinimmo ad optemperan-
f. 112 dum tam deuotum tamque promptum se specietenus / exhibuerat, ut mox priori et conuentui de Bello litteras supramemoratas transmitteret, sibique cartas dignitatum ac libertatum monasterii deferri iuberet. Venerat igitur usque Wedestoche prior ille uenerabilis, spe maxima regie promissionis adductus.

Prior uero et fratres sancti Martini de Bello hunc maxime opinionis uirum esse cognoscentes, communicato consilio eligendum eum preficiendumque sibi decreuerunt, Gileberto Londonie episcopo ceterisque in quorum stabant presentia idipsum omnimodis persuadentibus.[1] Quem quidem eo affectuosius pre ceteris sibi ad eligendum propositis fratres admittendum censuerunt, quo cum alios omnino nescirent, ipsum ex parte cognouerunt. Si quid uero eis notitie ipsius in morum inexperta deerat honestate, spe bona supplebant et nimia sue opinionis dilatatione. Sperabant namque sibi et ecclesie sue non inutilem futurum, quem ecclesie Cantuariensi in qua prioratus fungebatur officio didicerant fuisse necessarium. Nuntiatur regi et archiepiscopo per episcopum Londonie quod super ipso eligendo inierant consilium; probat uterque prebens assensum. Mittuntur ergo ad ipsum uenerabilem priorem uocandum duo episcopi, qui eum cum honore perducant in presentiam regis et archiepiscopi. Mirabatur uir prudens tantam sibi inopinate exhiberi honoris reuerentiam, credens sibi ad honorem temporalem posse sufficere, si modo per quemlibet inferioris dignitatis et ordinis ministrum in eorum presentiam iuberetur adesse. Venientem susceperunt cum honore rex et archiepiscopus, et cum simul sederent eum inter se medium sedere fecerunt. Introducti sunt interea prior et fratres sancti Martini de

[1] In the election of archbishop in 1173 the Canterbury monks had wanted Odo as archbishop. *Materials*, iv. 177. According to Ralph de Diceto, it was Gilbert Foliot himself who had thwarted Odo's election and had been the

renowned for his eloquence, with which, as one learned in divine studies, he knew how to bring forth at the right moment new teachings as well as old. Canterbury's charters of privileges and exemptions had been for the most part destroyed in the sudden fire, and he had come to the king hoping that he would renew them with the royal authority. The king seemed willing to accede to his petition, giving him, by his promises, great hopes that were not in the end fulfilled. This guileless and open-hearted man, believing the king, added the request that he would deign to model the charters on the formulae of those of St. Martin of Battle. Not only had the king not refused the petition; indeed on the surface he had shown such a devout and ready intention to comply that he had sent that letter to the prior and convent of Battle ordering them to bring him their charters of privileges and exemptions. Therefore the venerable prior had come to Woodstock, lured by the greatest faith in the royal promise.

The prior and brothers of St. Martin of Battle knew of him as a man with a very high reputation. Consulting together, they decided to elect him to rule them, Gilbert, bishop of London and the others before whom they stood having used every kind of persuasion to this end.[1] The brothers were the more willing to agree to his admission than to that of the others proposed to them for election, because they knew nothing at all of them, but had heard something of him. So although there were gaps in their information as to the probity of his behaviour, yet they made do with hope and with the size of his reputation. For they hoped that they would find useful to themselves and their church a man whom they had heard was a necessity to Canterbury where he was prior. The bishop of London announced to the king and the archbishop that they were considering this choice, and they both agreed. Two bishops were sent to summon the venerable prior, and to escort him ceremoniously into the presence of the king and the archbishop. The wise man marvelled that so much reverential honour should be shown him so unexpectedly, thinking that it would have been quite in keeping with his temporal rank to have been ordered into their presence by someone of a lower rank and order. When he came, the king and archbishop received him with honour, and, seated as they were together, they made him sit between them. In the mean time the

determining voice in that of Richard of Dover. Ralph de Diceto, i, 369. Cf. Gervase of Canterbury i. 239–40; *Letters of Gilbert Foliot*, no. 220 and n.

f. 112v Bello, de preficiendi sibi pastoris electio/ne palam pronuntiaturi. Ad quorum ingressum, ceperunt cogitationes in uiri illius uenerabilis cor, ut ipse postmodum asserere solitus erat, ascendere, iamque mente uaticinabatur suspectum habens quod incontinenti contigit experiri. Processerunt itaque introducti, et quia prior impeditioris erat lingue, paulo ante paralysi percussus, uni ex fratribus qui secum aderant uices suas commisit in electionis publicande pronuntiatione.

Quas ille suscipiens, coram rege astitit, et in huiusmodi uerba erupit, 'Gratias agit, excellentissime domine, in monasterio nostro commorans congregatio nostra, gratias agimus et nos qui congregationis hic uices exequimur, gratias inquam communiter uestre referimus serenitati, quod cum nos et ecclesiam nostram, immo uestram a principatus uestri initio dilexeritis, dilectionem ipsam operis semper exhibitione probare dignati estis. Experti namque loquimur. Felicis etenim recordationis domini Walteri de Luci quondam abbatis nostri temporibus, humilitati nostre uestra nunquam defuit sullimitas, que monasterii nostri negotia tanquam propria fuerint semper promouenda decreuit, nec libertates dignitatesque ipsius regia sibi auctoritate a primis fundamentis concessas aliquatenus imminui permisit. Nec post eiusdem patris nostri decessum circa nos licet immeritos conceptus pietatis uestre tepuit affectus, cum quidem, uacante iam per annos iiii^or ecclesia nostra, pii pastoris uices nobis impenderitis, necessariis uictus et uestitus sufficienter et honeste nobis exhibitis, prescriptis etiam dignitatibus et libertatibus nostris in sua integritate conseruatis. In his uero
f. 113 plurimum honoris uir il/lustris dominus Ricardus de Luci uestre celsitudini dinoscitur contulisse, qui commissum sibi procurationis officium tum per se, tum per ministros suos tam sollicita deuotione studuit circa nos adimplere, ut nemo nostrum merito possit causari, sibi quicquam eorum, que ratio dictabat administranda, defuisse. Nostre igitur exiguitati sic hactenus in omnibus uestra condescendere dignata est excellentia, ut desiderii quidem nostri fuerit, nemini in posterum nisi uobis subesse, si idipsum ratio ecclesiastici usus et ordinis uellet admittere. Quis enim bene in bonis expertum non satis experto uelit sponte commutare? Verum quoniam ab ecclesiasticis procedit institutis, singulis ecclesiis singulos pastores prefici debere, qui subditorum moribus informandis prouida sollicitudine possint inuigilare, huc uestra dominique archiepiscopi uocati auctoritate en assumus, ut pastorem nobis Deo auctore digne

prior and brothers of St. Martin of Battle were brought in to announce publicly their election of a shepherd to rule them. At their entrance the venerable man began to have suspicions, as he used later to tell, and he foresaw what was going to happen to him forthwith. Once brought in, they advanced, and since the prior had a speech impediment, having recently suffered a paralytic stroke, he asked one of the brothers with him to make the public announcement of the election for him.

Accepting the responsibility, the brother stood before the king and spoke words of this sort: 'Most excellent lord, our congregation in our monastery thanks you, and we who represent the congregation here thank you. Communally, I say, we give your serenity thanks that, since you have loved us and our—or rather your—church from the beginning of your reign, you have always deigned to show that love in your works. For we speak who are experienced. Indeed in the time of our late abbot, Walter de Luci of happy memory, your highness never failed our humility, and decreed that the affairs of our monastery were to be forwarded as your own. Nor would your highness permit its liberties and exemptions, granted from its first foundation by royal authority, to be in any way diminished. Nor has the affection conceived towards us through your piety, not our merits, cooled since the death of our father. While our church has been vacant now for four years, you have acted the part of a good shepherd to us, you have provided sufficiently and honourably for us the necessities of food and clothing, and you have protected our liberties and privileges in their integrity. In this that illustrious man Richard de Luci is known to have brought much honour to your highness. He has striven with such anxious devotion to perform his office of steward, both in person and through his officials, that none of us can justly complain that any reasonable assistance has been lacking. Thus up to this moment your excellency has deigned so to condescend in everything to our inconsequence, that it would be our wish to be ruled by no one save yourself in future, if ecclesiastical usage and rules allowed it. For who, after much experience of the good, would willingly change it for what he has not experienced? But our ecclesiastical ordinances provide that every church should be ruled by its own pastor, who will be on hand to watch anxiously over the moral growth of those in his care. Therefore we are here in answer to the summons of yourself and the archbishop to elect, with God

preficiendum secundum instituta canonum eligamus. Est enim omnino temerarium, transgredi decreta maiorum. Virum itaque uenerabilem Cantuariensis ecclesie priorem dominum Odonem in nomine sancte Trinitatis eligimus, nostreque electioni a uestra sullimitate assensum dari postulamus.'

Vix electi nomen in omnium audientia publicauerat, cum idem electus in uocem contradictionis erupit, dicens, 'Nominari me audiens, et inopinata electione ad regimen monasterii de Bello uocari, non illo, non alias, extra nostram Cantuariensem ecclesiam, consentio transferri. Meipsum uero summi pontificis protectioni subicio, et ne uos fratres qui huc pastoris eligendi gratia uenistis
f. 113v me eligatis, uosque domine rex / et domine archiepiscope ne eis in electione assensum prebeatis, omnimodis inhibeo, et ne quid aduersum me in hac parte possit attemptari, sedem apostolicam appello.'

Stupentibus ad hec omnibus qui aderant, cum unus eorum ipsum in hoc responso nimis festinasse diceret, 'Festino', respondit, 'quia festinare compellor.' Et adiciens, 'Ego', inquit, 'ad huc ueniendum nulla quidem tractus sum curiositate, nulla cuiuslibet honoris dignitatisue temporalis impulsus sum cupiditate, sed sola negotiorum Cantuariensis ecclesie sum perductus occasione. Que si per me possunt expediri, gaudeo; sin autem, domum licet inactus redeo. Sed cur mihi inuito et ingrato suscipiendum proponitur, quod plures ex his forte qui assunt nec inuitos nec ingratos uelle suscipere non dubitatur? Si uero id agitur ut sic amouear a prioratus officio, prioratui libentissime cedo, et in ecclesia Cantuariensi simpliciter conuersaturus, cum prioratu cuilibet prelationi sponte renuntio. Prioratum namque ipsum mihi semper plus sensi fuisse oneri quam honori, quem proculdubio inuitus suscepi, inuitus et coactus hactenus tenui.'

Hec eo dicente, mirabantur omnes eum cum tanta constantia respuere, quod solent plurimi etiam religiosorum summo desiderio affectare. Nec sine causa se sponte prioratui suo uelle renuntiare dixisse putabatur, dicentibus archiepiscopum ipsius constantiam et morum perfectionem nimium formidare, tanquam non facile nisi ex ratione posset ad uoluntatum suarum consensum inclinari, ideoque ipsum archiepiscopum uelle illum cum quadam astutia a
f. 114 prioratus officio amouere, et sub quadam specie maioris ho/noris conferendi alias transferre. Hoc autem tanquam cauendum licet prior ipse uenerabilis frequenter audierit, persuaderi tamen sibi ut

as our guide and according to the canons, a pastor to rule us. For it is entirely rash to transgress the decrees of the elders. In the name of the Holy Trinity, we choose the venerable Odo, lord prior of Canterbury, and we pray your highness' assent to our election.'

Scarcely had the name of the elect been pronounced before all, when he broke out in opposition, crying, 'I hear myself named and by this unexpected election called to rule the monastery of Battle. I do not consent to be transferred there or anywhere outside our church of Canterbury. I throw myself on the protection of the pope. I forbid in every way possible to me that you brothers, who have come here to elect a pastor, should elect me, or that you, lord king and lord archbishop, should assent to such an election. I appeal to the holy see, that no attempt may be made against me in this respect.'

Everyone there was amazed at the outburst. Someone said that in his reply he was too hasty. 'I am hasty because I am forced to be hasty', he answered, and added, 'I was not attracted here out of curiosity, nor tempted by greed for any honours or temporal dignities. I was brought only by the need to do the business of the church of Canterbury. If I can get that finished, I shall rejoice. If not, I shall simply return home. But why is an abbacy offered to me? I do not wish it, nor am I grateful for it. There are doubtless many who have come here, who would accept it without unwillingness nor ingratitude. If this is being done to remove me from the office of prior, I give it up most gladly, and will return to being a simple monk in Canterbury cathedral. And along with my priorate, I am glad to renounce any preferment whatever. For me, being prior has always been more a burden than an honour. I certainly undertook it unwillingly and have held it to this moment unwillingly and under compulsion.'

His way of saying this caused everyone to marvel at such firmness in refusing what most men, even monks, are wont to aspire to as their highest ambition. Rumour had it that not without reason was he willing to give up the office of prior. Some said that the archbishop very greatly feared the firmness and perfection of his behaviour, as one who could not easily, save by reason, be got to consent to his will. Therefore the wily archbishop wished to remove him from the office of prior, and, under the guise of a greater honour, to transfer him elsewhere. And although the venerable prior had often heard that he should beware of this, he could not be

crederet non potuit, quousque rei euentus experimentum dedit.[1] Instabant itaque rex et archiepiscopus cum aliis qui aderant persuadentes ad consentiendum, sed ille inflexibilis permanens non adquiescebat. Petebat inducias deliberationis, ut Cantuariam rediens illic fratrum suorum colloquio frueretur et consilio, sed non impetrabat, scientibus omnibus eum nullatenus denuo rediturum, si semel liberum posset habere recessum. Precipiebat rex quatinus prior et fratres sancti Martini de Bello electum suum acciperent, sed appropinquantibus illis electus ipse eos repellebat, et ne se contingerent interposita appellatione inhibebat. Repulsi abibant retrorsum, eum tamen eo magis sibi preferri cupientes, quo amplius recusabat.

Igitur cum ad consentiendum nullatenus flecteretur, quidam episcoporum qui aderant archiepiscopum monuit, ut in ipsum excommunicationis sententiam promulgaret. Sed uir ille uenerabilis oculos in eum indignantis more dirigens, 'Non tuam', inquit, 'non illius formido sententiam, cum quidem me summi pontificis protectioni supposuerim, sedemque apostolicam appellauerim.'

Monebat rex regem filium suum qui tunc forte aderat, pace inter eos paulo ante post prescriptas inimicitias reformata, monebat et omnes quos apud ipsum electum quicquam posse putabat ut eum ad consentiendum satagerent inducere. Stabat solus contra omnes, secularium negotiorum se, inter cetera quibus excusationi insistebat, asserens ignarum, res monasterii posse pati dispendium, si
f. 114v regendi nescius rectoris susciperet officium. / Causabatur preterea se corpore nimis esse inualidum, laboris impatientem, oportere monasteriorum rectores esse robustos, et cum sint multi rerum ecclesiasticarum impugnatores, earumdem protectores necessario tam in secularibus studiis quam in diuinis debere esse exercitatos. Audiens eum rex huiusmodi excusationes pretendere, quem precibus non potuit uel persuasionibus, flectere studuit promissionibus. Dignitates ergo libertatesque monasterii sancti Martini de Bello, quas pre ceteris regni sui ecclesiis ac monasteriis habere dinoscitur, ei proposuit, affectumque suum et deuotionem, quam circa eas in sua integritate conseruandas eatenus habuerit, asserens eidem affectui ac deuotioni sue plurimum fore adiciendum, si ipse ad id quod sibi proponebatur consentiret suscipiendum. Ipso namque

1 Our author writes as if Odo were himself the origin of this conjecture, and it is not unlikely that the archbishop would have felt more comfortable with prior Odo raised to an abbacy at some distance from Canterbury, since Odo's attempt

persuaded to believe it until the event proved it.[1] The king and the archbishop urged him to accept, and some others there added their persuasions, but he remained inflexible in his refusal. He asked for a delay for consultation, so that he might return to Canterbury and be advised by his brothers there. This was not allowed, since everyone knew that if he were once free to leave, he would not come back. The king ordered the prior and brothers of St. Martin to receive him as their abbot elect, but when they approached him, he repelled them and, shielded by his appeal, did not allow them to touch him. Rejected, they drew back, but none the less they wanted him the more for his refusal.

Since nothing could move him to consent, one of the bishops present advised the archbishop to pronounce a sentence of excommunication against him. But the venerable prior turned a disdainful eye upon him. 'I fear neither your sentence, nor his', he said, 'since I have placed myself under the protection of the pope and I have appealed to the apostolic see.'

The king asked the king his son who happened to be present, and with whom he had lately made peace after their quarrel, and he asked all whom he thought had weight with the abbot elect, to try to induce him to consent. He stood alone against all, saying, among other excuses, that he was ignorant of worldly business. He maintained that the properties of the monastery could suffer if a man took over the rule who was ignorant of ruling. Furthermore, he argued that he was too unwell, unable to bear strain, that abbots should be robust, and that since there are many aggressors against the properties of churches, their defenders should of necessity be experienced in secular studies as well as divine. The king, listening to these excuses, tried to influence by his promises one he could not move by prayers and persuadings. He told him of the privileges and exemptions of the monastery of St. Martin of Battle, which it is famed for possessing above all the churches and monasteries of his realm. He told him of his own affection and of his devotion in preserving them in their entirety to the very moment. He stated that he would be even more loving and devoted if he would consent to undertake what was being suggested to him. He promised that

to secure charters modelled upon Battle's was clearly a serious challenge to the archbishop's authority.

pacifice et quiete in monasterio degente, se aduersus omnes in ipsum uel res sibi commissas insurgere molientes protectioni et defensioni omnimodis affuturum pollicebatur, indempnitati sue et suorum se in omnibus prouisurum, dummodo de negotiis suis in eorum emersionibus per quemlibet monasterii fratrem aut seruientem sibi nuntiaretur. Manebat ille inflexibilis ad omnia, in nullo amplius cedens promissionibus quam antea persuasionibus. Supplicabat autem obnixius ut sibi liceret patria egredi sine ulla in posterum spe remeandi, malle se dicens in solo alieno quietum uiuere sub lege claustrali, quam in proprio curis secularibus implicari. Sic uicissim rex cum suis instabat, ille supplicabat, neuter tamen alteri pro uoto cedebat, sicque dies ad occasum, re
f. 115 nullum capiente effectum, propera/bat. Rex tamen nolens ceptis desistere, tam erat instando infatigabilis, quam ille non adquiescendo inflexibilis.

Cum igitur tempus casso labore consumeretur, iam omnino circa eum inclinandum humani studii defecisse uidebatur consilium, nisi superuenisset diuinum. Sed quem ad uoluntatis sue arbitrium pertrahere non potuit potestas terrena, repente cum uoluit de facili flexit uirtus diuina. Occurrerunt namque subito menti eius Theophili actus qui Christum negauit,[1] qui cum ante negationem tante opinionis fuisset, ut eum clerus et populus ecclesie Dei in ordine pontificali preficiendum eligeret, uocanti se ecclesie pertinaciter resistendo curam pastoralem temere refugit, uoluntatemque propriam communi preponens utilitati, in ecclesie offensione Christum ecclesie sponsum offendit. Quem indignatus indignatione Dominus dimisit secundum desideria cordis sui que contra Dominum elegerat, ut iret in adinuentionibus suis, manum sue protectionis subtrahens, et ipsum proprie fragilitati relinquens. Qui diuina protectione destitutus, et post modicum per alium episcopum quem eo recusante sibi ecclesia prefecerat, a uicedominatus honore et officio quod eatenus habuerat amotus, primo quidem de sua deiectione doluit, dolens absque remedio diuine consolationis; tristitiam postmodum incurrit, tristis desperauit, desperans, diabolo professus seruitutem sub cyrographo, Christum negauit. Hec inquam menti sue, haud dubium quin Deo immittente occurrentia, uir uenerabilis prior Cantuariensis Odo uoluebat in pectore,[2] iamque in anxietate spiritus sui positus cepit sibi
f. 115v ipsi metuere, ne si forte ultra / resistere sue uocationi presumeret,

[1] The story is also found in *The South English Legendary*, i, ed. C. D'Evelyn and A. J. Mill, EETS (London, 1956), 221–37. [2] Cf. Luke 2: 19.

he himself would be in all ways the patron and defender against all who might attempt anything against Odo or the possessions committed to him, leaving him to live peacefully and quietly in the monastery. He would provide complete security for him and his, if he would but send him word of problems in their affairs through some brother or servant of the monastery. But Odo remained unmoved by all this, giving way to promises no more than he had to persuadings. He implored with all his might that he be allowed to leave his homeland with no hope ever of returning, saying that he would prefer to live a monastic life quietly on foreign soil, than to be involved in secular cares in his own land. Thus in turn the king and his retinue were urging, and he was imploring, and neither would give way. The day was drawing to a close with no settlement made. But the king was unwilling to give up what he had undertaken, and was as indefatigable in pressing as the prior was stubborn in not yielding.

Time and effort were being wasted. It looked as though all that man could do to sway him was in vain, without help from God. But one whom earthly power was not able to subdue to its will, divine goodness easily and suddenly directed when it wished. For suddenly there came into his mind the story of Theophilus who denied Christ.[1] Before this denial he had had such a reputation that the clerks and people of God's church had elected him to preside as bishop. But he stubbornly spurned the church that called him; rashly rejecting pastoral care, he put his own will before the general interest. In offending the church he offended Christ the bridegroom of the church. The disdained Lord in disdain abandoned him to the desires of his heart which he had chosen against the Lord. He withdrew His protection and left him to his own weakness, to wander in paths of his own contriving. Bereft of divine protection, he was shortly removed by the bishop who after his refusal had been put over itself by the church, from the honour and office of deputy which he had held. At first he grieved over his outcast state, grieving without the comfort of divine consolation. Then he was overcome by a melancholy; melancholy, he came to despair, and in his despair he made a written contract to serve the devil and denied Christ. This tale, I say, came into his mind, without doubt by God's inspiration. Odo, prior of Canterbury, that venerable man, considered it in his heart,[2] and in his anxiety began to fear for himself, lest if he presume longer to resist his call,

quicquam Theophili actibus simile uel deterius aliquid sibi contingeret.

Recordabatur nichilominus et beati Anselmi Cantuariensis archiepiscopi, qui suscepto dudum religionis habitu in monasterio Beccensi, cum se in omnibus ab ipso conuersionis sue initio tam honeste, tam discrete, tam digne et laudabiliter habuisset, ut eum sibi monasterii ipsius uniuersitas processu temporis, priore suo defuncto, nomine et officio prioris prefici desideraret, desideriis quidem eorum satisfacere distulit, se tanquam indignum et tanto oneri imparem arbitratus, alium digniorem eligi, sibique indulgeri postulauit. Sed cum uniuersa congregatio sic in eius fixa maneret electione, ut eam in neminem preter ipsum uellet transferre, ipse uirum uenerabilem Maurilium tunc temporis Rothomagensem archiepiscopum adiit, ut eum tanquam uirum discretum super re huiuscemodi quid expedire uideretur consuleret.[1] Archiepiscopus, audito uniuersitatis in eum consensu, ut adquiesceret in uirtute obedientie sibi iniunxit, et si forte in posterum ad altiora promouendus canonice uocaretur, ne resisteret omni qua potuit auctoritate precepit. Accidere namque frequenter asseruit ut dum aliquis sciens et potens aliis preesse atque prodesse uocante eum ecclesia non acquiescit, offensus Dominus gratiam sibi concessam subtrahit, et eum in aliquod crimen coram Deo et hominibus detestabile ruere permittit. Vnde cuilibet sanum sapienti magis attendenda est multorum communis utilitas quam propria, licet sibi ipsi uideatur utilis, uoluntas.

Pulsatus huiusmodi cogitationibus, uir prudens et discretus Odo prior Cantuariensis plurimum anxiabatur, cum quidem tam so-
f. 116 lenni electioni sue / non consentire perpenderet esse periculosum, consentire autem uoluntati et proposito suo esset omnino contrarium. Mouebatur eo amplius quod in electione sua uidebatur regnum et sacerdotium conuenisse, procurante scilicet eam rege patre cum rege filio et regni magnatibus, archiepiscopo metropolitano cum suffraganeis, priore etiam monasterii sancti Martini de Bello cum fratribus eo secum perductis. Quid igitur faceret? Importunis omnium precibus, immo potius diuini timoris

[1] Maurilius, archbishop of Rouen, 1055–67. Anselm had been a monk for only three years, and was asked to replace his mentor Lanfranc, who had not died, as our author believes; he had been made prior of Caen. Eadmer, *The Life of St. Anselm Archbishop of Canterbury*, ed. R. W. Southern (NMT, 1962; OMT,

something like the fate of Theophilus or worse might happen to him.

He remembered no less the blessed Anselm, archbishop of Canterbury, who was formerly a monk in the monastery of Bec. From the very beginning of his conversion he had conducted himself in everything so honourably, so discreetly, so worthily and so praiseworthily, that when in the passage of time the prior died, the congregation of the monastery desired him to become prior. He put off agreeing to their desires, thinking himself unworthy and unequal to such a burden, and begged them to excuse him and elect another more worthy. But since the whole congregation remained firm about his election and would give it to none save himself, he went to the blessed Maurilius, then archbishop of Rouen, to consult him as a man of judgement about what should be done in a matter of this kind.[1] The archbishop, when he heard that the congregation was agreed about him, ordered him to acquiesce, as a matter of obedience. And he commanded with all his authority, that if he should in the future be called canonically to a yet higher post he must not resist. For, he said, it frequently happens that when someone with the knowledge and ability to rule and benefit others does not acquiesce when the church calls him, the Lord, affronted, withdraws His grace, and permits him to fall into some crime detestable before God and man. Wherefore it is well for every wise man to attend more to the general good of the many than to his own will, even if that is where his own good seems to lie.

Agitated by reflections of this sort, the prudent and discerning Odo, prior of Canterbury, worried greatly. For while he considered that not to consent to so solemn an election was dangerous, yet to consent was totally against his will and his plans. He was the more moved because in his election it seemed that the temporal and sacred powers were agreed: that the old king, the father, and the young king, his son, were promoting it together, joined by the magnates of the realm, the metropolitan archbishop with his suffragans and lastly the prior of the monastery of St. Martin of Battle with the brothers he had brought with him. What therefore was he to do? He was conquered at last by the importunate prayers of all,

1972), pp. 11–12, 21–2. The tale of seeking Maurilius's advice concerning monastic office appears to have been transferred from Anselm's earlier indecision about undertaking the monastic life, where Eadmer has it, to this period, more appropriate to Odo's situation.

correptione tandem deuictus, non quidem quod electioni adquieuerit publice pronuntiauit, sed tantum a solita cessans contradictione, tacendo se eorum uoluntati et arbitrio dimisit. Mox archiepiscopus altissona modulatione ymnum 'Te deum laudamus' incipiens, quod in abbatum electione minus fieri solet, demum data oratione solita, eius electionem confirmauit.[1] Electus est itaque hoc modo vi° idus Iulii, dolentibus et flentibus tam monachis quam ceteris omnibus quotquot illuc a Cantuaria contigerat secum aduenisse.

Vtrum ex diuina prudentia an ex humani consilii processerit prudentia quod illuc sic eligendus aduenerit, incertum habemus, cum tamen non incongrue, seu ex Deo seu ex hominibus fuerit, procuratum esse uideamus, ut qui formam cartarum monasterii sancti Martini de Bello se accepturum putauerat, monasterium ipsum cum cartis eius et dignitatibus omnibus regendum disponendumque susciperet. Verum ecclesie Cantuariensi ex cartis monasterii de Bello illo delatis nichil prouenit utilitatis, quippe cum nec prolate fuerint illic nec interrogate, immo nulla super ipsis, an illic
f. 116v ad manum / haberentur, uel a rege uel ab archiepiscopo facta mentione. Reportate sunt igitur in monasterium cum omni integritate, fratribus omnibus plurimum exultantibus in earum satis desiderata receptione. Culpam quidem nullam uir uenerabilis iam electus ex eo contraxit quod Cantuariensi ecclesie negotium ibidem per eum minus expeditum fuerit, quia quisquis pro persona propria cogitur agere, his que extra personam suam sunt poterit minus intendere. Venit illo ut pro negotiis eiusdem ecclesie pro uiribus instaret, sed eadem necessitate proprie persone compulsus intermisit. Auditus est postmodum frequenter asseruisse, quod nisi occasione eorum que sibi animo meminimus occurrisse summi regis indignationem incurrere expauisset, nullius unquam terrene potestatis fauore aut gratia, uel etiam terrore, ad consentiendum electioni sue animum accommodasset.

Consummatis omnibus que circa electionem facienda uidebantur, rex ab eo sacramentum seruande fidelitatis pro consuetudine non exegit, sciens eum nullatenus prestiturum, immo magis si ab eo exigeretur, renuntiandi electioni inde occasionem quesiturum.[2] Prior et fratres sancti Martini de Bello, peractis omnibus pro quibus illo uenerant, ipsum utpote sibi iam electione prelatum

[1] The *Te Deum* was sung immediately following the election of a bishop. Benson, *Bishop-Elect*, p. 114, citing Egidius of Bologna and William Naso.

or rather by the warning of a divinely sent fear. He did not publicly declare that he acquiesced in the election; he but ceased to argue, and by his silence he gave himself up to their will and judgement. Immediately the archbishop began loudly to chant the hymn '*Te Deum laudamus*', something not usually done at the election of an abbot, and when at last the usual prayer had been said, he confirmed the election.[1] He was elected in this manner on 10 July, while both the monks and all the others who had come with him from Canterbury grieved and wept.

Whether it was divine wisdom or human counsel that caused him to come to be elected in this way, we do not know. Yet we think it not unsuitably managed, whether thanks to God or men, that one who hoped to receive the formula of the charters of the monastery of St. Martin of Battle, should receive the monastery itself, with its charters and all its privileges, to rule and control. No advantage accrued to the church of Canterbury from bringing the charters of Battle thither. Indeed they were neither offered nor inquired about; no mention was made of them or whether they were there at hand, either by the king or the archbishop. Therefore they were carried back to the monastery quite undiminished, and all the brothers rejoiced exceedingly to get them back. The venerable abbot elect was not blamed for the fact that Canterbury's business there was not successfully concluded, for anyone forced to act on his own account will be less able to exert himself for things outside himself. He came there to use all his powers on behalf of the affairs of his church, but, driven by personal necessity, he neglected it. Afterwards he frequently said that had he not, thanks to the intervention of the thoughts we have mentioned, feared incurring the wrath of the Highest King, neither the favour, grace, nor even fear of any earthly power would have made him consent to his election.

When everything that had to be done at an election was completed, the king did not require from him the customary oath of fealty, knowing that he would never take an oath, and further that, if it were demanded of him, he would use it as an opportunity of renouncing the election.[2] The prior and brothers of St. Martin of Battle, having accomplished their task, consulted him as their

[2] Clause 12 of the Constitutions of Clarendon required that after election the elect 'should swear homage and fealty to the lord king as his liege lord . . . saving his order', before his consecration. Stubbs, *Charters*, p. 166. Henry is being depicted as particularly tactful.

quid faciendum decerneret conuenerunt, mestum consolari cupientes, omnimodamque cum reuerentia sibi obedientiam promittentes. Precepit ille omnes pariter domum remeare, dicens se Cantuariam aditurum, ibique communicato cum ecclesie sue fratribus consilio, de quorum sincero circa se non dubitabat affectu, se ad eorum arbitrium electioni sue uel penitus renunti-
f. 117 aturum, uel omnino / assensum prebiturum, quippe cum necdum usquequaque penes se deliberasset, in quam se partem pronior inclinare uellet. Ad eius iussionem prior et fratres ad monasterium redeunt, uniuersitati monasterii que gesta fuerant nuntiant, et cum non ut sibi de electione iniunctum fuerat fecerint, se de impossibilitate excusant. Nutu diuino, cunctis que per eos gesta nuntiabantur, tanquam a Deo ordinatis, mox uniuersa congregatio consensum prebuit, gaudens quidem et exultans, ac spem plurimam concipiens, quod bono initio bona deberet succedere finalis conclusio. Erat omnium unanimis exultatio, talem tantumque sibi prefici uirum, quem ad consentiendum nulla precipitasset ambitio, sed quem canonica procreasset electio.

Electus uero ipse Cantuariam ueniens, cum quidem eorum que circa eum gesta fuerant fama precessisset, uniuersam Cantuariensis ecclesie congregationem nimio merore ac luctu repperit deficientem, tantum uirum sibi auferri aliasque transferri unanimiter deplorantem. Communicare cepit cum omnibus consilium, maxime tamen cum fratribus discretioribus sibique amplius familiaribus, in quam se partem, consentiendi scilicet aut renuntiandi, pronior inclinaret, aliis sic pro ratione, aliis uero sic pro uoluntate, persuadentibus. Summum tamen erat precipuumque consilium, electioni que ex Dei uoluntate processisse uidebatur non resistere, immo magis ut presens tristitia uerteretur in gaudium Deum obnixius obsecrare.

Veniente post aliquot dies Cantuariam archiepiscopo, directi sunt eo a conuentu monasterii sancti Martini de Bello quidam ex fratribus, qui electioni interfuerant, electum suum ab omnimoda
f. 117v subiectione Cantuariensis ecclesie libe/rum postulaturi. Introducti sunt illuc uenientes in monasteriale capitulum, ubi uniuersa congregatione presente, et archiepiscopo presidente, cum de electi sui exemptione agerent, eumque a professione quam illic in monachatu confirmatus fecerat absolui specialiter exposcerent, ipse electus in medium processit, seque nullatenus sic uelle absolui asseruit.

abbot elect as to what they were to do, trying to console the mourner, and promising him all obedience and reverence. He ordered them all to return home together, saying that he would go to Canterbury. There he would consult the brothers of his church, of whose sincere affection towards himself he was in no doubt, and he would follow their advice about his election, whether to renounce it wholly, or wholly assent. For he was not yet entirely decided to which side he was the more inclined. At his command the prior and brothers returned to the monastery and told the congregation what had happened. They excused themselves for not having accomplished what had been enjoined upon them in the matter of the election, on the grounds of its impossibility. Divinely inspired, the whole congregation gave consent to everything they heard had been done, as ordained by God, even rejoicing, exulting, and hoping greatly that a good beginning should be rounded off by a happy ending. The rejoicing was unanimous that a man of this character and importance was to rule them, one whom no ambition had hurried to his acceptance, but whom a canonical election had produced.

The abbot elect himself, arriving at Canterbury, where the news of what had happened to him had already arrived, found the whole congregation of Canterbury abandoned to grief and mourning, all bewailing that such a man was to be taken from them and taken elsewhere. He began to consult with them all, but especially with the more discerning brothers, and those closest to him, as to what side he should lean, towards acceptance or refusal. Of course, some argued from the stand of reason, some from will. Nevertheless, the best and most compelling advice was not to resist an election that seemed to have been the will of God, but rather to pray God earnestly that his present melancholy be turned into joy.

When the archbishop arrived in Canterbury a few days later, the convent of St. Martin of Battle sent there certain of the brothers who had attended the election, to request that their abbot elect be free from any sort of subjection to the church of Canterbury. They were introduced and taken to the monks' chapter house, where the entire congregation was present and the archbishop was presiding. When they brought up the exemption of their abbot elect and asked particularly that he be absolved from the profession he had made there when he became a monk, the abbot elect himself walked to the centre and stated that he did not in the

Huiusmodi namque exemptione se ab ecclesia Cantuariensi omnino alienum fieri timebat, quam cum pre ceteris ecclesiis omnibus tanquam in ea sumpto religionis habitu, ab adolescentia conuersatus, specialiter diligeret, plus honorem dignitatemque suam diminui arbitrabatur quam augeri, si se quauis exemptione ab ea contingeret alienum fieri. Porro archiepiscopus eius pium circa eandem ecclesiam laudans affectum, eum ab omni illius subiectione ad predictorum fratrum instantiam nichilominus absoluit, monens de cetero ut a prelibato affectu suo non tepesceret, sed siquando ecclesia Cantuariensis eius consilio et auxilio indigeret, deuoti sibi filii obsequium et beneficium impenderet. Sic demum facta oratione, dataque benedictione, diu multumque coram omnibus commendatum sepedictis fratribus omnino emancipatum dimittens, precepit ut tanquam deuoti filii dignum patrem debito affectu diligerent, honorem et reuerentiam impenderent, precepta eius uel monita non neglegerent, eius exemplo uiuere contenderent, ex quibus omnibus coram Deo gratiam, et coram hominibus honorem proculdubio inuenirent. Susceperunt illi sibi dimissum tanquam diuinitus datum, iam tanto letiores, quanto de ipso certiores, dantes Deo gloriam ipsique omnimodam dilectionem promittentes et obedientiam.

f. 118 Paucis diebus postmodum decursis, ipse / omnibus uale dicens non sine dolore omnium, tam monachorum scilicet quam et ciuium, quos mellitis sermonibus ad celestium mandatorum custodiam frequenter solitus erat informare, iter ueniendi Bellum arripuit, atque eo pridie nonas Augusti peruenit, occurrente ei uniuersa monasterii congregatione, eumque cum solenni et letabunda processione suscipiente. Introductus in monasterium, facta oratione uniuersam congregationem suscepit in pacis osculum, sicque in capitulum est perductus, regulam beati Benedicti de ordinando abbate illic auditurus.[1] Sed cum plurima populi multitudo, que ad famam tanti uiri concurrerat, post eum sequens tanto impetu irrueret, ut facile arceri non posset, ipse fratri qui lecturus coram eo processerat innuit, ut omnino ab ipsa lectione cessaret, ruptoque ex regulari consuetudine silentio, in huiusmodi uerba erupit; erat enim uniuersitas fratrum ibi congregata.

'Satis', inquit, 'perpendo, fratres karissimi, ex officio quod mihi extrinsecus exhibetis, quam pium circa me intrinsecus affectum

[1] *Regula*, c. 2, 3, 64. For the ceremony to be followed at an abbot's reception and first attendance at chapter see Lanfranc, *Constitutions*, p. 72. The monks of Battle were receiving Odo as if he had already been blessed.

least wish so to be absolved. For by an exemption of this kind he feared becoming a total stranger to the church of Canterbury. Since he particularly loved it above all other churches, as the place where he donned the habit of the religious life, and his home since youth, he would judge his honour and dignity diminished rather than enlarged, if he were made a stranger to it by any exemption. Then the archbishop, praising his dutiful affection towards the church, and despite the brothers' request, did not absolve him at all from such subjection. He warned him besides not to let his affection cool: that if ever the church of Canterbury should be in need of his counsel and aid, he should give it the allegiance and service of a devoted son. Thus at last when prayer had been said and the benediction given, he released him to the brothers, commending him highly and lengthily before all. He ordered the brothers to love their worthy father with the affection due from devoted sons, to load him with honour and reverence, not to neglect his commands and admonishments, to try to live by his example. If they did all this, they would without doubt find grace before God and, before men, honour. They received him who was released to them, as a divine gift. Now they were happy in that they were certain of him; and they gave glory to God, and promised him love and obedience in every way.

A few days later he said farewell to all. To the sadness of everyone, both monks and burgesses, whom in sweet sermons he had been wont frequently to instruct in the keeping of the heavenly commands, he set off on his journey to Battle. He arrived there on 4 August, and the whole congregation of the monastery came out to him and received him in a ceremonial and joyous procession. Brought into the monastery, he said a prayer and received the whole congregation with the kiss of peace. And so he was led into the chapter house, to hear there the reading of the rule of St. Benedict on the ordaining of an abbot.[1] But a great crowd of people drawn by the fame of so great a man had followed him and rushed in with such a crush that it could not easily be kept out. He therefore motioned to the brother who had stepped forth to read before him, to give up the reading. Since the customary silence had been broken, he spoke out in words of this sort (for the congregation of brothers were all present there):

'Dearest brothers, I am assured of the dutiful affection you have for me inwardly by the ceremonial kindness you show me

habeatis. Nullis namque meis precedentibus meritis, me uobis non satis cognitum uestrique notitiam minus habentem tanti habendum censuistis, ut licet minus idoneum, immo, ut uerius fatear, omnino indignum, uobis tamen nomine et officio pastoris omnimodis prefici uolueritis, renitentem nec adquiescere uolentem compuleritis, inuitum et coactum ad qualemcumque tandem consensum perduxeritis. Fateor me tamen, adhuc nutante uoluntate, de ipso consensu nondum plene deliberasse. Iam uero ad uos uenientem cum tanta solennitate suscepistis, cum quanta si quemlibet eorum suscepis-
f. 118v setis qui solent honoribus / temporalibus delectari, in nullo sibi minus in hac parte fuisse satisfactum posset merito causari. Verum licet uestram circa me beniuolentiam satis attendam, ad Cantuariensem tamen ecclesiam, a cuius dulcissimis mihi uberibus me per uos auulsum doleo, semper mente recurrens, dubitare me fateor utrum uobis pro pio affectu gratias debeam an pro mea quam per uos incurri perturbatione maliuolentiam. Honorem uero mee indignitati impensum non tam mihi quam summo pastori Deo reputo exhibitum, quia ipsum in mea humilitate suscepistis, cuius me uices in uobis agere desideratis.[1] Ipse namque se in suis seu recipi seu sperni asserit, et prophetam uel iustum in nomine prophete uel iusti suscipientibus mercedem prophete et iusti promittit.[2] Dignetur ipse si me uobis preesse decreuit talem efficere, qui uos in pascuis gregum eius possim digne deducere, sibique de uobis sine meo periculo lucra multiplicia comportare.'[3]

Hec et his similia perplura non sine lacrimis dixit, fratrumque omnium animos in sui amorem amplius excitauit. Delectabantur nihilominus et turbe que irruerant super his que in ipso attendebant, quia morum uenustatem, quam intrinsecus in mente habebat, extrinsecus in uultu representabat. Ne uero circa hec prolixius exequenda diutius immoremur, consummatis omnibus que in eius susceptione agenda uidebantur, dimissisque omnibus in propria, tam his scilicet qui uenienti occurrerant, quam his qui eum a Cantuaria uenientem non sine graui merore deduxerant, ipse decetero in medio fratrum conuersari cepit, seque omnibus formam bene uiuendi uerbo et exemplo exhibuit, studens omnimodis amplius ab omnibus amari quam timeri./

f. 119 Sic electo, sic in monasterio suscepto, sola restabat adhuc, ut

[1] *Regula*, c. 64.
[2] Cf. Matt. 10: 40–1.
[3] *Regula*, c. 2. Since the ceremony and the reading, presumably of his duties

outwardly. For none of my merits have gone before me. Without sufficiently knowing me, you have resolved to honour me, who myself have little knowledge of you. Though I am little suitable, or, to put it more correctly, am wholly unworthy, you wished me to be set to rule over you in the name and office of shepherd. You compelled me, resisting and not wishing to acquiesce. You finally brought me, reluctant and forced, to a sort of consent. But I confess that my will wavers still, that I am still in some doubt about this consent. But you have received me upon my arrival among you with such ceremony that had you been receiving someone of the station of those used to the delights of worldly honours, he would have had nothing to complain of in its propriety. But though I appreciate your goodwill towards me, nevertheless I keep returning in thought to Canterbury church, from whose sweetest breast I have, to my grief, been torn by you. I confess that I doubt whether I owe you thanks for the dutiful affection or ill will for the uprooting I have suffered through you. But I reflect that the honour heaped upon my unworthiness is not really given to me but to God, the highest shepherd, for in my lowliness you have received Him whose place you wish me to fill among you.[1] For He declares that in His own He is received or spurned, and to those who receive a prophet or a righteous man in the name of a prophet or a righteous man, He promises the reward of such.[2] If He has decreed that I lead you, may He deign to make me such as can worthily lead you in the pastures of His flocks and without danger to myself bring Him back an increased profit from you.'[3]

This he said, with much more along the same lines, and not without tears, and he made all the brothers love him the more. The mob that had burst in was no less enraptured by what it saw in him. For the inward sweetness of his mind shone outwardly in his face. Yet I must not be prolix: everything was done that was necessary for his reception, and everyone was sent off home, both those who had met him at his coming and those who had sorrowfully conducted him from Canterbury. From then on he began to live amongst the brothers. In word and example he showed himself to all a pattern of living well, doing his utmost to be loved by all rather than feared.

Having been elected and received in the monastery in this

and desired qualities, had been interrupted, Odo gave his first sermon on those paragraphs in the Rule.

sic consummarentur omnia, benedictio ab episcopo percipienda. Verum quoniam ad eius noticiam iam uenerat predecessoribus suis abbatibus ab episcopis Cicestrensibus frequens et multiplex illata uexatio, cauendum sibi omnimodis decreuit, ne in benedictionis susceptione uel obedientie professione quicquam prepropere fieret, quo sibi simile aliquid uel deterius contingeret. Aduenit illuc interea, a Cicestrensi episcopo Iohanne directus, Cicestrensis ecclesie decanus Iordanus cum quibusdam concanonicis suis, ut electum abbatem super benedictione percipienda conuenirent, eiusque animi propositum indagarent. Quorum aduentus causa plenius audita et cognita, electus ipse electionis sue per regnum et sacerdotium facte modum et ordinem eis exposuit, seque extra regis et archiepsicopi conscientiam nichil inde facturum esse asseruit, maxime cum id in se habere uiderentur monasterii libertates, quod electus abbas in suo monasterio deberet benedici, sicut primum abbatem Gausbertum Cicestrensis episcopus benedixit. Et ut maiorem assertioni sue faceret fidem, cartas monasterii id ipsum continentes in eorum presentia fecit exhiberi.

Dimissis itaque clericis post modicum idem electus regem et archiepiscopum adiit, rem totam eis exposuit, nolle se asserens aliquid per se temere attemptare, quo monasterii dignitates uideretur imminuere. Persuasum est itaque domino regi ab his qui erant a latere, ut a quolibet episcoporum suorum electum ipsum in sua faceret benedici presentia, ne si alias extra regis presentiam benediceretur, aliqua forte aduersus eum per episcopum et cano-
f. 119v nicos Cicestrenses controuersia excitaretur, qua / postmodum uexationi subiceretur. Quod cum nemo in presentia regis presumeret attemptare, possent omnia cum pace consummari, relicta posteris memoria pii affectus et regie protectionis ad monasterium quod est corone regie signum.

Videbatur sic persuadentibus rex assensum uelle prebere, cum Cantuariensis archiepiscopus Ricardus ipsum electum benedicendi a domino rege licentiam petiit et impetrauit, nulla se asserens hoc appetere consuetudinis uel subiectionis occasione sed ex pio dilectionis affectu quo se deuinctum fatebatur electi persone.[1] Data ergo die dominica, cuius diem crastinum celebrem reddebat sancti Michaelis solennitas, uenit electus abbas abbatis nomen et officium iam plenius suscepturus usque Mallingam, manerium scilicet

manner, he lacked but one thing before everything could be complete: the blessing of a bishop. But since he already knew of the frequent and multifold vexations inflicted upon his predecessors by bishops of Chichester, he resolved to be most wary, lest in receiving the blessing or making profession, he might do something over-hastily that would bring down similar or worse trouble upon himself. In the mean time, John, bishop of Chichester, sent Jordan the dean with several other canons to come to an understanding with the abbot elect about the blessing, and explore his intentions. When he had listened to a full explanation of their visit, the abbot elect explained to them the mode and course of his election, one involving church and realm. He assured them that he would do nothing in the matter without the joint knowledge of the king and archbishop, particularly since the monastery's exemptions seemed to include the blessing of the abbot elect in his own monastery, as the bishop of Chichester had blessed Gausbert the first abbot. To increase their faith in his assertions, he had the monastery's charters containing this shown to them.

The abbot elect dismissed the clerks with this, and after a little he went to the king and archbishop and told them all about it, saying that he did not wish by himself to do anything rash, by which he might seem to be diminishing the privileges of the monastery. Those around the king urged him to have the abbot elect blessed in his own presence by any of his bishops, lest if he were blessed elsewhere, out of the king's presence, the bishop and canons of Chichester might raise a dispute against him that would one day subject him to harassment. Since no one would dare to try this in the king's presence, everything could be settled in peace, and a testimonial left to posterity of the pious affection and of royal protection enjoyed by the monastery that is the emblem of the royal crown.

The king seemed willing to approve these promptings when archbishop Richard sought and obtained the king's permission to bless the abbot elect, declaring that he sought this not to establish a custom or a subjection, but out of the pious love by which he confessed himself bound to the abbot elect.[1] A Sunday was set, the day before Michaelmas. To receive in full the name and office, the abbot elect went to Malling, a manor of the archbishop near

[1] Ralph de Diceto, i. 403, mentions the quarrel with the bishop of Chichester over Odo's blessing.

archiepiscopi iuxta Lewes situm, ubi ab archiepiscopo et a suis cum honore susceptus, solenniter omni amota professione, uel etiam professionis interrogatione, est benedictus.[1] Vnde in crastino, quo ut diximus beati Michaelis solennis agebatur memoria, cum ad monasterium suum reuerteretur, occurrente sibi processionaliter ac festiue omni congregatione, cum magna omnium susceptus est exultatione, cognita eius ad secum commanendum confirmatione.

Cepit iam tunc esse in orationibus deuotior, in diuinis meditationibus ardentior, in uigiliis crebrior, in exhortationibus et exemplorum bonorum operibus studiosior, in lectionibus frequentior, uerbo et opere omnibus bene uiuendi forma factus.[2] Misericordie uisceribus affluens omni se petenti tribuebat, omnibus sine discretione personarum hospitalis, omnibus pretereuntibus ad ingrediendum monasterii portis apertis, tam ad reficiendum quam
f. 120 ad pernoctandum. Per/sonis quas monasterii regula intra ipsius septa non permittit pernoctare, extra murorum ambitum fecit hospitalitatis humanitatem impendere. Obsequiis diuinis in monasterio, lectioni et meditationi simul cum fratribus uacabat in claustro, cibum sumebat in refectorio, ubique in omnibus unus, hoc solo excepto, quod in communi fratrum non quiescebat dormitorio. Patiebatur enim assiduam stomachi indigeriem, qua supra modum ab annis iuuenilibus uexatus nunquam facile nisi medicinarum usu, et tunc quidem cum difficultate, soluebatur. In cuius solutione cum esset uerecundissimus, neminem admittebat consortem, neminem uel ad uisum uel ad auditum proximum. Hac ergo de causa, extra commune fratrum quiescebat dormitorium, alias per omnia conuersatus in illis quasi unus ex illis. In gestu, actu, et habitu, nichil tumidum, nichil quod leuitatis notam pretenderet ostendebat, bona prouidens semper et in omnibus, non tantum coram Deo sed etiam coram hominibus. Inerat ei discreta modestia et modesta discretio, communi fragilitati condescendere, omnibus omnia fieri, nolens a malo uinci sed magis studens in bono uincere. In expositionibus scripturarum diuinarum, et in tractatibus, quos undecumque sumens materiam uel in scriptum redigebat uel ad edificationem audientium nunc Latine nunc Gallico sermone, frequenter uero ad edificationem rudis uulgi lingua materna

[1] The archbishop's manor of South Malling in East Sussex was conveniently close to Battle, and was within the diocese of Chichester; yet since it was an

Lewes, where he was honourably received by the archbishop and his retinue, and, with all profession and even questioning about his vows solemnly waived, he was blessed.[1] The following day, Michaelmas, as we said, when he returned to his monastery, the whole congregation came to meet him in solemn, joyous procession, and all who received him rejoiced, for they were now sure that he was to stay with them.

From that time, he began to be more devout in prayer, more ardent in meditation, more frequent in vigils, more assiduous in exhortations and in works that set good examples, more regular in reading lessons. In word and deed he became to all a pattern for living well.[2] Rich in inward pity, he gave to all who asked of him, welcoming all without distinction of persons. The monastery's gates stood open for all passers-by to enter, to refresh themselves, or to stay the night. For those whom the monastery's rule does not permit to stay the night within its enclosure, he philanthropically provided hospitality outside the walls. He found time for divine services in the monastery, and readings and meditation along with the brothers in the cloister. He ate his meals in the refectory and in everything he was one of them, with the single exception that he did not sleep in the common dormitory. For he suffered from a constant stomach complaint that had tormented him terribly since childhood, and from which he was never relieved easily without using medicines, and even then with some difficulty. Since he was exceedingly ashamed at these eliminations, he suffered no companion, no one even near enough to see or hear. Because of this, he slept outside the common dormitory of the brothers. In all else he dwelt with them as if one of them. In gesture, act, and appearance he showed no haughtiness, nor anything that betrayed a sign of shallowness. He cared for the good always and in all things, and that not only before God, but before men too. There was in him a discerning forbearance and a forbearing discernment that made him sympathetic to ordinary frailty. He was all things to all men, unwilling to be defeated by evil, but striving rather to win by goodness. In explaining divine scripture and in his treatises—whatever the matter he took up, whether he was writing or preaching in Latin or French or often, for the instruction of the ignorant

archiepiscopal peculiar, the abbot was outside the jurisdiction of the bishop. I. J. Churchill, *Canterbury Administration* (1933), i. 76–8.

[2] The abbot's first duty, according to St. Benedict. *Regula*, c. 2.

publice pronuntiabat, tam euidens, tam facundus, tam gratus omnibus apparebat, ut que obscura uidebantur, et ab antiquis doctoribus minus explanata, lucida redderet et euidentissima,[1]
f. 120v nec fastidirent audientes, licet quandoque / diffusius loqueretur, loquentis prolixitatem, tum persone tum sermonis ab eo prolati delectati dulcedine. Excitabatur eo amplius ad eum audiendum fidelium deuotio, dum ipsum non attenderent aliud loquentem et aliud operantem, quia se secundum quod ore proferebat, operum executione exhibebat. Interiorem uitam eius, et intimum circa Deum et proximum deuotionis affectum diuino examini iam decetero dimittentes, qualiter in rerum sibi commissarum regimine se habuerit perstringamus.

Cum post susceptam ab archiepiscopo benedictionem, et in pastorali regimine confirmationem, per aliquot dies in monasterio suo resedisset, a iam substituto sibi successore in Cantuariensis ecclesie Christi prioratu Benedicto, postmodum Burgensi abbate, rogatus Cantuariam adiit,[2] ubi cum tanta solennitate a monachorum uniuersitate, et ciuium ac promiscui sexus multitudine processionaliter est susceptus, ac si adesse nuntiaretur celestis angelus. Paucis ibi moratus diebus, curiam domini regis postmodum adiit, ubi a rege tanti habitus est, ut quendam Rogerum, Cantuariensis ecclesie monachum regi omnino incognitum, in monasterio sancti Augustini Cantuarie abbatem fieri permitteret, eo solo contentus, quod abbas de Bello ipsius commendauit personam.[3] Licet enim predictus Rogerus alios ab initio mediatores apud regem habuerit et intercessores, non potuit tamen rex ad consensum pertrahi, nisi prius constaret sibi de honestate persone ex abbatis de Bello cui fidem habuit commendaticia assertione, sciens eum morum ipsius per experimentum habere noticiam, quem sue nouerat subditum discipline cum prioratu fungeretur
f. 121 Cantuariensis ecclesie. Sic illo / promoto, contigit predictum Cantuariensis ecclesie priorem Benedictum regis indignationem incurrere. Sed abbate interueniente qui mediator intercessit, rex eundem priorem in tantam gratiam recepit, ut eum processu temporis ad abbatiam Burgi promoueret. Hec ideo inseruimus, ut quante apud ipsum regni principem seu quaslibet diuerse conditionis personas habitus sit reuerentie, quante opinionis, quante honorificentie, liquido possit aduerti.

Vnam ex cartis regis Willelmi fundatoris monasterii de Bello

mass, in the mother tongue—he was so lucid, so eloquent, and so agreeable to all, that what seemed obscure and not clarified by the doctors of old, he made clear and very plain.[1] Nor did his hearers scorn any prolixity on the part of the preacher—though sometimes he spoke rather wordily—for they were charmed with the sweetness both of his person and his words. The faithful were the more willing to listen to him because they knew he did not say one thing and do another; he practised what he preached. For the rest, we will leave to divine judgement his interior life and his innermost and deep devotion to God, for we must narrate briefly how he managed the temporal responsibilities committed to him.

After he had been blessed by the archbishop and confirmed in his pastoral office, he stayed for some days in his own monastery. When he had been replaced at Canterbury and Benedict, afterwards abbot of Peterborough, had succeeded him as prior, he went at Benedict's request to Canterbury.[2] There he was received in procession by the whole monastery and a crowd of burgesses, both men and women, with as much ceremony as if an angel from heaven had been announced. He remained a few days there and afterwards went to the king's court where he was so esteemed by the king that he allowed Roger, a monk of Canterbury, totally unknown to the king, to be made abbot of St. Augustine's, Canterbury, on the sole recommendation of the abbot of Battle.[3] It is true that Roger had from the outset go-betweens and negotiators at court, but still the king could not be got to consent until he had first satisfied himself as to the suitability of his person by the recommendation of the abbot of Battle, in whom he had faith. For he knew that the abbot could speak from experience of the man, having been his prior at Canterbury. After this preferment, Benedict, prior of Canterbury, happened to incur the king's displeasure. But at the abbot's intervention as a mediator, the king took back the prior into favour to such an extent that in the passage of time he promoted him to the abbacy of Peterborough. We have put this in so that it can be seen plainly with how much reverence, esteem, and honour he was valued by the king himself and by persons of divers conditions.

About this time it happened that one of the monastery's

[1] Few of Odo's writings can be positively identified. See *DNB* s.n., and J. Leland, *De Rebus Britannicis Collectanea*, iv (London, 1774), 68–9.

[2] Benedict followed Odo as prior in 1175 and became abbot of Peterborough 1177–93. *Heads*, pp. 34, 61.

[3] Abbot of St. Augustine's 1175–1213. Ibid., p. 36.

contigit tunc temporis in ipso monasterio uetustate dissolui. Quam cum abbas regi porrexisset, 'Hec', inquit rex, 'renouatione indigeret.' Abbate ad hoc respondente, 'Et nos ut eam si placet auctoritate regia renouando confirmetis supplicamus.' 'Non hoc', inquit rex, 'nisi ex iudicio curie mee facturus sum.'

Diuertit ad hec abbas a rege, et uirum illustrem Ricardum de Luci adiens, regis sibi exposuit responsum. Ad quod uir illustris Ricardus respondens, 'Si nostrum', inquit, 'super hoc expectatur iudicium, ad effectum peticionis tue unanimem inuenies totius curie consensum.' Loco et tempore ex consilio uiri illustris Ricardi expectato, cum post modicum rex in medio procerum suorum resideret,[1] abbas procedens cartam suam uetustate dissipatam in conspectu omnium proposuit, et ut regia auctoritate renouaretur expetiit. Rege super hoc si faciendum esset necne iudicium procerum requirente, 'Decet', inquit Ricardus de Luci, 'decet uos, si placet domine, cartam ecclesie de Bello renouare, cuius etiam si omnes carte perissent, nos omnes carte eius esse debemus, qui
f. 121v de conquisitione apud Bellum facta feodati sumus. / Et quoniam iudicium nostrum utrum faciendum sit necne exigitis, ut cartam predictam auctoritate uestra confirmando renouetis adiudicamus.'

Rex ad hec, uocato Waltero de Constanciis, tunc cancellario suo, postmodum Lincolniensi episcopo, et post modicum Rothomagensi archiepiscopo,[2] iussit cartam nouam nominis et sigilli regii secundum formam carte ueteris fieri, precipiens carte noue imponi, se confirmationem illam fecisse pro amore Dei et peticione Odonis abbatis, nomen et meritum eiusdem abbatis uolens esse in recordatione.

Et quoniam in cartis et munimentis, a diuersis personis diuerso tempore super eodem negotio datis, solet in posterioribus priorum mentio fieri, ita ut quod posterius est uideatur precedentium exigere testimonium huiusmodi uerbis, 'sicut carta illa, uel illius N., testatur', iussit rex ne clausula illa inseretur, sed aliam antea inusitatam ipse dictauit, et super his que uiderat in persona propria testimonium perhibens, carte precepit imponi, hoc modo: 'Quoniam inspexi cartam Willelmi proaui mei, in qua prescripte

[1] To judge from his prominent role in what follows, Richard seems to have advised waiting for one of the Exchequer sessions or a specialized session *coram rege*.

[2] Walter of Coutances, archdeacon of Oxford, though not formally chancellor, was acting in that capacity and as keeper of the seal from 1173–89. He was

charters, of King William, the founder of the monastery of Battle, had deteriorated from age. The abbot showed it to the king, who said, 'This could do with renewing.' To this the abbot replied, 'And we pray that, if it please you, you will renew it and confirm it by your royal authority.' The king said, 'I will not do it except by a judgement of my court.'

At this the abbot took his leave of the king, and going to the illustrious Richard de Luci he told him of the king's reply. The great man said, 'If our judgement is required in the matter, you will find the whole court in unanimous agreement that your petition be granted.' On the great man's advice, the abbot waited a bit for a place and time when the king would shortly be sitting in the midst of his barons.[1] Then he advanced and in view of all presented his charter, decayed with age, and requested that it be renewed by royal authority. The king asked a judgement of the barons about it, whether it should be done or not. 'It is proper', said Richard de Luci. 'It is proper for you, if it please you, my lord, to renew the charter of the church of Battle. Even if all its charters perished, all of us should be its charters, for by the conquest at Battle we were all enfeoffed. And since you require our judgement whether or not it should be done, we adjudge that you renew the charter and confirm it with your royal authority.'

The king listened, and then called over Walter of Coutances, then his chancellor, afterwards bishop of Lincoln, and shortly after that archbishop of Rouen.[2] He ordered that a new charter be made in the royal name and sealed with his seal, following the form of the old charter, and specifying that in the new charter it be stated that he had confirmed it for the love of God and at the petition of Abbot Odo, wishing the name and merit of the abbot to be recorded.

Now in the charters and muniments given by various persons at different times concerning the same matter, it is the custom that the later documents mention the earlier ones, so that the later seem to require the evidence of the earlier, for example in such words: 'as is asserted in the charter, or in the charter of N.' But the king would put in no such phrase. He himself dictated another never before employed and, bearing witness in his own person concerning what he had seen, he ordered it to be alluded to in the charter as follows: 'Since I have inspected the charter of William my

elected bishop of Lincoln in May 1183 and translated to Rouen in Nov. 1184. He died in 1207.

libertates et quietantie, et libere consuetudines ab eo prefate ecclesie concesse continebantur.'

Nec dedignatus est inclitus princeps super predicta clausula reddere rationem: 'Si', inquit, 'clausula que suppressa est inserta fuisset, carta posterior sine priore modicum conferret. Nunc uero nulla in posteriori de precedentibus originalibus facta mentione, hec carta sola sufficeret, etiam si omnes alie carte de Bello deperissent.'[1] His a rege dictis, exegit abbas a cancellario et obtinuit ut sibi tres cartas unam eandemque formam secundum preceptum regis continentes scribi, regisque sigillum singulis faceret apponi.
f. 122 Commisse sibi ecclesie diligenter in hoc et prudenter / prospexit, ut quoniam possessiones monasterii sunt a monasterio plurimum remote, siquando quauis ex causa quamlibet trium cartarum contingeret, uel etiam duas, extra monasterium alias deferri, una saltem earum ad manum semper haberetur in monasterio.

Infra quadriennium quo, ut superius expressum est, post decessum abbatis Walterii destituta pastore uacauit ecclesia, contigit Humfridum quendam presbiterum et personam ecclesie beate Marie de Bello, que contigua muro monasterii parrochialis habetur, huic uite finem facere.[2] Prior et conuentus, licet orbati pastore, ipsam ecclesiam in usus proprios auctoritate propria redegerunt, omnes ex ea prouenientes fructus nemine contradicente percipientes, capellano quodam in ea uicarii officium exequente, sed nichil in ea perpetuitatis habente. Institerunt plures precibus ut eis ecclesia a conuentu concederetur, nec obtinuerunt. Inter quos Ricardus, tunc Pictauensis archidiaconus, postmodum uero Wintoniensis episcopus, scripsit eis diligentius supplicans, tanto de impetrando securior, quanto uidebatur esse potentior.[3] Sed prior et conuentus inito communi consilio scribenti rescripserunt, predictam ecclesiam monasterii esse capellam, adeo ut ipsius capelle altare quasi unum ex altaribus monasterii habeatur, capellanum inibi ministrantem consiliorum monasterii tanquam unum ex monachis debere esse conscium et ob hoc fidelissimum, huiusmodique ac similibus de causis se nemini memoratam ecclesiam concessuros, nisi qui in ea in propria persona ministraret. Memorato
f. 122v archidiacono a / peticione sua ad huiusmodi responsum cessante,

[1] Henry's charter exists. It is BL Add. Ch. 70981. It is closely related to the forged charter BL Cotton Ch. xvi. 28, and to the statements of abbey liberties given by the chronicler, above, pp. 70, 84. But, significantly, this *inspeximus* does *not* include the clause exempting the abbey from episcopal 'domination'. It appears,

ancestor, in which were contained the aforesaid liberties and exemptions and free customs given the church by him . . .'

The famous prince even deigned to explain the point of the clause. He said, 'If the clause we avoid were to have been put in, the later charter would confer little without the presence of the earlier. But now, since in the later one no mention has been made of the original prototypes, this charter alone would be enough, even if all the other charters of Battle had been lost.'[1] After the king had explained this, the abbot asked the chancellor, and received his permission, for three charters to be written for him, all containing exactly the formula that the king had ordered, and for each to be sealed with the royal seal. He provided for his church carefully and prudently in this. For the monastery's estates lie at some distance from the monastery, and if ever for some reason one, or even two, of the three charters were therefore taken elsewhere, one of them at least would now always be at hand in the monastery.

During the four-year vacancy after the death of Abbot Walter, the death occurred of Humphrey, priest and parson of St. Mary's of Battle, the parish church close to the monastery wall.[2] The prior and convent, though without an abbot, appropriated the church on their own authority, and received all its profits. No one obstructed them in this. A chaplain undertook the duties of vicar there, with no permanent rights in it. Many prayed the convent to grant them the church, but they were unsuccessful. Among them, Richard, then archdeacon of Poitou and afterwards bishop of Winchester, wrote asking for it most seriously, very sure of his demand since he was so powerful.[3] But the prior and convent took counsel together and replied to his letter that the church was a chapel of the monastery, so much so, that its altar is considered as one of the altars of the monastery, that the chaplain serving it should be as intimate in the counsels of the monastery as one of the monks, and therefore most faithful. For these among similar reasons they would grant the church to no one who could not serve there in person. In the face of this sort of answer the archdeacon

therefore, that Abbot Odo took a genuine charter of William I to Henry II, and thus secured royal confirmation of liberties less compromised by scandal. This suggestion was first made by V. H. Galbraith, 'A New Charter of Henry II to Battle Abbey', *EHR*, lii (1937), 67–73, where both charters are printed.

[2] The early twelfth-century rental above, p. 56, lists a priest, Humphrey. He would be in his seventies or eighties if he is the same man.

[3] Richard of Ilchester: see above, p. 249, n. 1.

quidam Aluredus de sancto Martino, qui in finibus Hastingensium sub comite Augi uicecomitis exequebatur officium, a domino rege tunc temporis trans mare moram faciente litteras ad priorem et conuentum impetrauit deprecatorias, ut ecclesiam predictam cuidam capellano Thome nomine, ipsi Aluredo tunc adherenti, concederent.[1] Sed fratrum uniuersitas huiusmodi mandatum egre suscipiens, habito unanimi consilio monasterii sacristam Robertum de Chaam nomine, ipsi Aluredo notum et familiarem, ad eum trans mare direxit, cum eo omnimodis acturum, ut a peticionis sue recedens instantia super prefata ecclesia eos minime uexaret, clericoque suo alias prouideret. Prosperatum est iter fratris transfretantis, expeditoque per eum negotio, memoratus Aluredus a sua peticione quieuit quam uniuersitati fratrum onerosam esse cognouit. His ita quiescentibus, quieuerunt et ceteri, posseditque extunc pacifice ecclesiam uniuersitas monasterii, toto postmodum tempore quo monasterium abbate caruit, usque ad Odonis abbatis aduentum, eam ad luminaria monasterii assignans, maxime autem ad cereum coram maiori altari et corpore Christi, reliquiis quoque sanctorum inibi repositis iugiter arsurum. A prima enim fundatione monasterii usque ad tempus illud, lampades oleo immundo et fetido infuse coram Christi corpore accendebantur.

Suscepto apud Bellum Odone abbate, post paucos susceptionis
f. 123 sue dies scripsit ei Ricardus Cantuariensis / archiepiscopus, totius Anglie primas, et apostolice sedis legatus, se auctoritate legati illo esse uenturum.[2] Sciens itaque abbas clericorum archiepiscopi cupiditatem, qui si forte sepe nominatam ecclesiam parrochialem uacantem inuenirent, eam importunis precibus archiepiscopi mediantibus de manibus suis extorquerent, decreuit aduentum archiepiscopi preuenire, ex consensu conuentus licet egre sustinentis, cuidam cognato suo Iohanni nomine capellano ecclesie de Heriatesham eam concedens, mediante tamen conditione ut scilicet in propria persona in ea deseruiret.[3] Et ne moleste ferret conuentus assignationem suam super ecclesia irritam fieri, luminaria quoque que ad decus et decorem monasterii constituerant crederent debere extingui, satisfecit eis abbas super luminaribus

[1] Alured of St. Martin is listed by the count of Eu in 1166 as holding a knight's fee from the count's demesne. *Red Book*, i. 203. He may also have held from the bishop of Chichester. Ibid., p. 199, and Mayr-Harting, *Acta*, pp. 97–8.

gave up his request. Then one Alured of St. Martin, who was acting as a sheriff of the count of Eu for Hastings, begged the king, then overseas, for an intercessory letter to the prior and convent to the effect that they should grant the church to a chaplain Thomas, at that time a hanger-on of Alured.[1] But the convent received such a mandate with displeasure, and by a unanimous decision sent the monastery's sacristan, Robert de Chaam, a friend and companion of Alured, to him across the sea to use every means with him to withdraw his petition, not to harass them about the church, and to provide elsewhere for his clerk. The brother's crossing was prosperous. He settled the matter, and Alured gave up his petition, which he saw to be a burden upon the corporation of brothers. When these gave up, the others too gave up, and from then on the corporation of the monastery was in peaceful possession of the church during the rest of the vacancy, until the coming of Abbot Odo. It applied the revenue to the lighting of the monastery, mostly for candles to burn perpetually before the high altar and the Body of Christ, and the relics of the saints resting thereon. From the earliest beginnings of the monastery until then, lamps filled with an impure and stinking oil had burned before the Body of Christ.

Only a few days after Odo became abbot of Battle, Richard, bishop of Canterbury, primate of all England and legate of the apostolic see, wrote to say that he would visit the abbey in his capacity as legate.[2] The abbot, aware of the cupidity of the archbishop's clerks, knew that if they found the parish church vacant, they would snatch it from his hands by their importunate requests to the archbishop. He determined to act before the archbishop's arrival. With the consent, though unwilling, of the convent, he granted it to one of his kindred, John, chaplain of Harrietsham, but only on condition that he serve there in his own person.[3] And lest the convent take it ill that its assignment of the church revenues was being annulled, and believe that the lights they had put up to the honour and beauty of the monastery would be extinguished,

[2] Archbishop Richard made a legatine visitation in 1174–5. C. R. Cheney, *From Becket to Langton: English Church Government 1170–1213* (Manchester, 1956), pp. 139–40. However much the monks of such exempt houses as Battle might escape episcopal visitation, legatine visitation was necessarily accepted, and must have done much towards a solution of the problems of exemption and discipline.

[3] Harrietsham, in east Kent, a manor of Canterbury.

non extinguendis, promittens se alias satis habunde prouisurum, quo sic continuarentur, ne super ipsis quicquam subtraheretur.

Admissus in ecclesiam prefatus Iohannes solo iure aduocationis, iamque nimium securus, cepit de institutione sibi per episcopum facienda minus esse sollicitus, trahebaturque animo ad uicariam ecclesie de Heriatesham in qua ex multo tempore ministrauerat, dicens se persone illius ecclesie fidei et sacramenti interpositione obligatum, ministerii sui termino nondum preterito. Cumque hec in Augusto mense gererentur, indutias seipsum expediendi usque ad festum sancti Michaelis petiit, et impetrauit, ministrante interim in concessa sibi ecclesia capellano quodam circa regimen animarum minus idoneo, quod quidem abbas moleste accipiebat.
f. 123v Veniente atque / elabente indutiarum termino, uenire distulit qui expectabatur, mandans se nondum plene expeditum, petensque iterato indutias usque ad natale Domini subsequens, et super petitis impetrans. Sed nec tunc ueniens, rursus indutias usque ad Pascha expetiit, et egre optinuit. Cumque iam Pascha pertransisset, et nec etiam tunc ipse ueniret, satis intellexit abbas eum frustratoria dilatione moras nectere, quo possit in propria persona in predicta uicaria de Heriatesham ministrare, et per uicarii administrationem fructus parrochialis ecclesie de Bello percipere. Dicebatur etiam aliud aliquid esse in causa, quare abbatis subterfugeret presentiam. Nam cum minus continens esse diceretur, abbatis uerebatur honestatem, sciens quod ab abbatis amicitia alienus redderetur, si inhoneste ac turpiter uiuens incesti notaretur infamia. Dedit ergo ei abbas in mandatis, ut infra natiuitatem sancti Iohannis Baptiste sese expediens omni excusatione postposita ueniret; sin autem, alium in memoratam ecclesiam instituendum ipso penitus excluso prouideret. Cum autem nec tunc adquiesceret, immo magis habita secum deliberatione responderet, se malle alienum fieri a personatu parrochialis ecclesie de Bello, quam a uicaria ecclesie de Heriatesham, cepit iam tunc abbas de alio instituendo esse sollicitus, beate Dei Genitrici, in cuius memoriam constructa est ecclesia, humiliter supplicans, ut in ecclesia sua ministrum prouideret
f. 124 idoneum. Sacerdotes quos bone opinionis et fame esse di/dicit tam ex remotis partibus quam ex finitimis plures ad se uenire faciens, eis sepedicte ecclesie ministerium obtulit, et ex ea proueniens beneficium. Sed in locis oportunis congruas ad ministrandum mansiones habentes, nota pro ignotis noluerunt commutare.

Suggestum est interea abbati de quodam diacono, Waltero

the abbot made reparations, so that the lights need not be extinguished, promising to provide abundantly from other sources: they would be maintained unimpaired.

This John, admitted into the church by mere right of advowson, and now exceedingly secure, began to be less than eager to be instituted by the bishop. His heart belonged to the vicarage at Harrietsham where he had been priest for a long time. He said he was bound to the parson of that church by an oath of fealty, since the term of his ministry had not yet expired. This was in August, and he asked for, and was allowed, a delay until Michaelmas to settle his affairs. In the mean time the church granted to him was being served by a chaplain not really capable of the care of souls, and this troubled the abbot. The time-limit was reached and passed, and the awaited chaplain still put off coming, reporting that he was not yet fully disencumbered. Again he asked for a delay, till Christmas next, and this was granted. But he did not come then either; instead he sought a further delay, until Easter. This was granted unwillingly. And when Easter had gone by and he had not come even then, the abbot realized that he was inventing delays so that he might himself continue in person as vicar of Harrietsham, and receive the profits of the parish church of Battle while a vicar served there. It was said too that there was another reason why he avoided the abbot. It was said that he was unchaste and therefore feared the probity of the abbot, knowing that he would lose the abbot's friendship if through his impure and shameful life he should be marked by the disgrace of unchastity. So the abbot gave orders that he must be free before midsummer, and must come with no excuses, or else he would pass him over and present someone else to the church. However, he would not acquiesce even then, but instead, having thought about it, replied that he would prefer to lose the rectory of the parish church of Battle than the vicarage of Harrietsham church. Therefore the abbot began to be anxious to institute someone else, praying the Holy Mother of God, to whom the church was dedicated, to provide a suitable minister for her church. He contacted priests he learned to be of good reputation, bringing many to him from far and near, and offering them the ministry of the church and its revenues. But having agreeable houses in locations convenient for their ministries, they did not wish to change the known for the unknown.

At last a certain deacon, Walter, was recommended to the abbot.

nomine, qui in Bercsire in episcopatu Saresberiensi moram faciens, et inde trahens originem, immunis quoque ab omni ecclesiastico beneficio, in gestu et actu inter scolarum exercitia morum pretenderet honestatem. Dicebatur a quibusdam, diuinitus de eo fuisse reuelatum, ut ad prenominate ecclesie ministerium uocaretur, loco manifeste in quo esset inueniendus declarato. Abbas ergo, litteris ad eum directis, ut secum locuturus ueniret mandauit, uenitque uocatus, in loco super quo reuelatum fuisse dicebatur inuentus. Cui licet antea incognito abbas regendam obtulit ecclesiam, et ut in ea ministraturus proximo ordinationis tempore susciperet presbiteratus officium. Diaconus nulla cupiditate illectus, seseque humiliter excusans, respondit, propositi sui nondum esse ut regendarum animarum curam susciperet, ad quam se minus idoneum asserebat, summo sibi esse desiderio scolasticis adhuc exerceri studiis, nichil super re tam ardua se posse repente presumere, nisi prius inquisito amicorum suorum assensu atque consilio. Has et huiusmodi pretendens excusationes, nitebatur omnimodis subter-
f. 124v fugere quod solent multi summo desiderio affectare. In/stabat abbas ut quod offerebatur susciperet, dicens hoc magis ex diuino quam ex humano prouenisse consilio, ut ad sepedicte ecclesie regimen uocaretur, ipsum Dei et beate uirginis Matris incursurum offensam, si subterfugeret uocationem quam constabat omnino esse canonicam. Hesitabat inter hec diaconus cui se parti potissimum inclinaret, suscipiendi scilicet aut recusandi, quia suscipiendo scolastici exercitii disciplinam relinquere penitus erat proposito suo contrarium, et recusando Dei offensam incurrere erat periculosum. Paucorum ergo dierum habita deliberatione, magnorumque ac prudentum uirorum usus consilio, licet non sponte consensit, suscepitque ecclesiam sepedictam ab abbate et conuentu in capitulo Belli, ex iure patronatus, Iohanni tunc Cicestrensi episcopo qui iam successerat Hylario post modicum presentatus.[1] A quo personatum ecclesie curamque animarum suscipiens, proximo ordinationis tempore ad sacerdotii gradum est promotus. Ministrauit extunc in commissa sibi ecclesia, uerbo et exemplo populum sibi creditum diligenter instruens, factusque forma gregis, sic omnes ad uirtutum prouectum informare studuit, ut liquido possit aduerti, uocationem ipsius a Deo fuisse, qui eum ecclesie sue preuiderat necessarium et utilem fore.

[1] John of Greenford, d. 1180.

He was living in Berkshire, in the diocese of Salisbury where he had been born. He had no ecclesiastical benefice but amid his activities as a student his bearing and behaviour seemed to show a probity of morals. It was said by some that there had been a divine revelation that he would be called to the ministry of this church, and the place disclosed where he might be found. The abbot wrote, inviting him to come and speak with him, and he came at the invitation, having been found in the very place indicated by the revelation. Although the abbot had not known him before, he offered him the church, and, so that he might take up the ministry there, suggested that he receive the priestly office at the next ordination. The deacon, not moved by cupidity, humbly excused himself, saying that it was not yet his plan to undertake the cure of souls, for which, he said, he was not fit, since it was still his highest desire to continue his scholastic studies. He said he could not rashly decide anything about so difficult a matter without seeking the advice and agreement of his friends. Offering these and like excuses, he endeavoured in all possible ways to avoid what many are wont to snatch at with the greatest desire. The abbot was firm that he should accept what was offered, saying that it had come about rather by divine than human will that he was called to the ministry of this church, that he would offend God and the Blessed Virgin if he avoided a calling that was beyond question wholly canonical. The deacon was at a loss as to whether he most favoured accepting the offer or refusing it. For by accepting it he must give up his scholastic studies, quite contrary to what he had planned. Yet by refusing, he must incur the dangerous displeasure of God. But having thought about it for a few days, and following the advice of great and prudent men, though it went against his will, he gave in and received the church from the abbot and convent in the chapter house of Battle, by their right of advowson. Shortly thereafter he was presented to John, then bishop of Chichester, Hilary's successor.[1] Receiving from him the parsonage of the church and the cure of souls, he was raised to the priesthood at the next ordination. From then on he served in the church committed to him, earnestly instructing by word and example the people entrusted to him. He became the model for the flock; so industriously did he teach all how to make progress in virtues that it is clear that his call came from God, who had foreseen that he would be useful and necessary to His church.

Tunc temporis accidit quendam Hugonem Romane ecclesie diaconum cardinalem, a latere domini pape Alexandri missum,
f. 125 legationis gratia uenire in Angliam. Qui conuoca/tis archiepiscopis, episcopis, abbatibus, et tocius regni clero, concilium generale apud Westmonasterium concitauit, tum de negociis pro quibus uenerat tractaturus, tum de statu Anglicane ecclesie et causis ecclesiasticis cogniturus.[1] Abbate de Bello generali edicto inter ceteros ad concilium uocato, scripsit ei predictus auctoritate apostolica, speciale sibi dirigens mandatum, ut omni excusatione remota in presentia sua appareret, Godefrido de Luci super ecclesia de Wi responsurus, et iuri pariturus. Abbas suscepto hoc mandato plurimum turbatus est animo, sciens dominum regem predictam ecclesiam de Wi prefato Godefrido de Luci uacante ecclesia de Bello absque omni exceptione dedisse et confirmasse, ipsum quoque Godefridum ad presentationem domini regis a Ricardo Cantuariensi electo fuisse susceptum, et auctoritate qua electus potuit in ecclesia institutum, carta nichilominus sibi a prefato electo super ipsius institutione prestita, quam idem electus postmodum ab apostolica sede rediens, et a papa Alexandro consecratus, iam archiepiscopus, iam primas, iam apostolice sedis legatus, omni qua fungebatur auctoritate confirmauerat. Metuebat ergo cernens undique imminens periculum, quoniam si aduersus Godefridum litem iniret, contra regie auctoritatis donationem, et archiepiscopi institutionem, ac utrorumque confirmationem, contraque dominum Ricardum de Luci sepedicti Godefridi patrem, totius Anglie post dominum regem iusticiam capitalem, irreuerenter agere
f. 125v uideretur. / Si uero liti renuntians a causa deficeret, mox ecclesia de Wi Godefrido absque ulla exceptione tota adiudicaretur, monasteriumque de Bello annis singulis amissioni decem marcarum subiaceret.

Recurrens igitur abbas ad nota et consueta deuotionis et orationis presidia, seseque fratrum commendans orationibus, dominum regem adiit, quomodo in causam traheretur exposuit, prudenter principis animum, cui se parti potius inclinaret, cupiens indagare. Supplicabat regi ut se uerbo simplici certum redderet, si ecclesiam

[1] Hugo Pierleone came to England in 1176 to conclude an agreement in direct discussion with Henry II that would regularize the king's relations with the

About this time a certain Hugh, cardinal deacon of the church of Rome, was sent from the staff of the lord Pope Alexander to England as legate. He summoned the archbishops, bishops, abbots, and clergy of the whole realm to a general council at Westminster, both to take up the business for which he had come and to hear about the state of the English church and to hear ecclesiastical cases.[1] Among the others the abbot of Battle was called to the council by the general edict. The legate as well wrote him a special mandate with apostolic authority, directing him to appear before him, with no excuses, to answer Godfrey de Luci concerning the church of Wye and to settle the matter justly. When he received this mandate, the abbot was much disquieted, knowing that the lord king had unconditionally granted and confirmed the church to Godfrey de Luci during the vacancy of Battle abbey. He knew that at the king's presentation Godfrey had been received by Richard, archbishop elect of Canterbury, and instituted to that church with the authority possible to a bishop elect. Moreover, he knew that a charter had been given him by the bishop elect concerning his induction, which when he returned from the apostolic see, now consecrated by Pope Alexander, archbishop, primate, and legate of the apostolic see, he had confirmed with all the authority he now wielded. Therefore he was apprehensive, seeing imminent danger all around. For if he entered into a lawsuit against Godfrey, he would seem to be disrespectful of a gift made by royal authority, of the archbishop's institution to a benefice, of the confirmation of both, and of Richard de Luci, Godfrey's father, the chief justiciar of all England after the lord king. Yet if he should give up the dispute and withdraw from the case, the whole church of Wye would at once and unconditionally be awarded to Godfrey and he would lose for the monastery of Battle an annual payment of ten marks.

The abbot resorted to the known and customary protection of devotions and prayer, and commending himself to the prayers of the brothers, he went to the lord king. He explained how he had been drawn into the case, hoping carefully to search the heart of the prince and find which side he favoured the more. He begged the king to tell him simply whether or not he had granted the church

papacy, a reconciliation begun with the Compromise of Avranches four years earlier. Ralph of Diceto, i. 410, gives the agreement they worked out. See Warren, *Henry II*, pp. 537–8 and 538, n. 1.

de Wi Godefrido de Luci concessisset, necne, asserens se nullatenus aduersus ipsum Godefridum litem initurum, si sibi de regis donatione posset certius innotescere. Rex donationem per se factam sciens non esse canonicam, cepit dissimulare, dicens non se habere in memoria quod sepedictam ecclesiam Godefrido concesserit uel confirmauerit. Abbas, ab eo nichil certum ualens extorquere, diuertit ad archiepiscopum, sciscitans ab eo si Godefridum ad presentationem domini regis in ecclesia de Wi personam instituisset et institutionem auctoritate qua fungebatur confirmasset. Archiepiscopo magna cum assertione protestante se Godefridum non nisi ad portionem ecclesie quam Willelmus presbiter, de quo superius facta est mentio, die qua in fata concessit possederat instituisse, nichilque super his que archiepiscopum contingebant esse uerendum, abbas, quasi iam secure litem ingressurus, iam de solo aduocato, cui causam suam committeret defendendam, cepit
f. 126 esse / sollicitus.

Conueniens itaque quendam clericorum archiepiscopi, magistrum scilicet Gerardum cognomento Puellam, uirum quidem eruditissimum et litteratisssimum, postmodum uero Cestrensem episcopum, causam suam sibi exposuit, rogans ut antique familiaritatis gratia sub mutue uicissitudinis obtentu eam fouendam susciperet.[1] Clericus ille, audita et plenius cognita cause serie, respondit, causam illam dominum suum archiepiscopum contingere, nec se partem aliquam posse tueri, quia domini sui actus uelut minus rationabiles uideretur improbare. Illo sic excusante, abbas magistrum Bartholomeum Exoniensem episcopum sibi olim familiarem expetiit, ut una cum clericis suis secum in causa sua staret.[2] Episcopus cognoscens quod aduersus Godefridum de Luci esset agendum, respondit eundem Godefridum Exoniensis ecclesie esse canonicum, nec se causam alienam, ad se non pertinentem, contra canonicum suum posse fouere.[3] Pretendente episcopo huiusmodi excusationem, declinauit abbas ad magistrum Iohannem Saresberiensem, postmodum Carnotensem episcopum, eum de causa sua consulens, et auxilium postulans.[4] Sed idem Iohannes se excusans, 'Canonicus', inquit, 'sum Exoniensis ecclesie, nec Godefrido cum eiusdem ecclesie socii et concanonici

[1] Gerard Pucelle was in Archbishop Richard's service from 1174 until he was consecrated bishop of Coventry in Sept. 1183. The see had been moved from Chester in 1102. For Gerard's career see S. Kuttner and E. Rathbone, 'Anglo-Norman Canonists of the Twelfth Century', *Traditio*, vii (1951), 296–303.

of Wye to Godfrey, saying that he would begin no lawsuit against Godfrey if he could know for certain that it was by the king's gift. The king, knowing that a gift made by himself was not canonical, began to dissemble, saying that he did not remember having granted or confirmed the church to Godfrey. The abbot, unable to get a straight answer from him, turned to the archbishop, asking him if, at the king's presentation, he had instituted Godfrey parson of the church of Wye and had confirmed the institution with the authority he exercised. With a strong declaration the archbishop protested that he had instituted Godfrey only to the part of the church held by William the priest (of whom mention is made above) on the day of his death, and that nothing was to be feared as far as it touched the archbishop. The abbot, therefore, now able to enter upon the suit without worries, became anxious only about the advocate to whom he might commit his case for defence.

Thus it was, that meeting one of the archbishop's clerks, Master Gerard Pucelle, a most experienced and educated man, afterwards bishop of Chester, he explained his case to him, praying that he undertake it for the sake of their old affiliation and mutual patronage.[1] The clerk, having listened and fully understood the case, answered that it touched his lord the archbishop, and that he could not take any part, since he would seem to disapprove his lord's actions as unreasonable. Since this man excused himself thus, the abbot asked a former friend, Master Bartholomew, bishop of Exeter, to stand by him in his case, along with his clerks.[2] When the bishop realized that the case was to be against Godfrey de Luci, he answered that Godfrey was a canon of the church of Exeter and that he was unable to help another's case, not pertaining to himself, against his own canon.[3] Thus the bishop excused himself. The abbot turned now to Master John of Salisbury, afterwards bishop of Chartres, consulting him about the case and asking help.[4] But John excused himself. 'I am a canon of the church of Exeter', he said, 'and I cannot be an adversary of Godfrey since we are associates

[2] Consecrated 1161. Died Dec. 1184. For his career see A. Morey, *Bartholomew of Exeter, Bishop and Canonist* (Cambridge, 1937).

[3] In the 1170s Godfrey de Luci was archdeacon of Richmond (York dioc.) and Derby (Lichfield dioc.), dean of St. Martin le Grand, London, and prebendary of Exeter, Lincoln, and London. Le Neve, ed. Greenway, i. 47, ii. 85–6; A. Morey and C. N. L. Brooke, *Gilbert Foliot and his Letters* (Cambridge, 1965), p. 279. See above, p. 9, n. 6.

[4] For John's connection with Exeter, where he was canon and treasurer, see *Letters of John of Salisbury*, ii, xxv–xxvi, xlvi. He was bishop of Chartres 1176–80.

simus possum aduersari.' In hunc modum se excusabant omnes, quotquot habere credebat amicos et familiares. Clerici domini regis et archiepiscopi causam illam dominos suos dicebant contingere, nec se dominorum suorum diffinitionibus posse contradicere. Episcoporum et clericorum alii dicebant Godefridum esse cano-/
f. 126v nicum suum, alii concanonicum. Communis omnium et generalis erat excusatio, se indignationem domini Ricardi de Luci, patris sepedicti Godefridi, nolle incurrere.

Abbate in angustia posito, persuasit ei quidam, ut cum quodam clerico legis perito qui cum legato de Italia uenerat loqueretur, sicque cum eo ageret, ut cause sue susciperet aduocationem, quia terrarum domini regis nec indigena nec incola, nec beneficio seu quauis familiaritate cisalpinis obnoxius, non regem, non principem, non archiepiscopum, non episcopum, non quamlibet ecclesiasticam secularemue regni personam[a] in qualibet aduocatione uerebatur. Adquieuit abbas persuadenti, clericumque conueniens causam suam sibi exposuit, cuius aduocationem clericus suscepit ab abbate marcam argenti recepturus. Iam securus abbas sese recepit hospitio, litem ingressurus in crastino. Nocte superueniente cum iam hora quietis instaret, affuerunt quidam a predicto clerico ad abbatem transmissi, mandatum ipsius abbati uiua uoce exponentes, quod scilicet causam, super qua inter eos conuenerat, fouere non poterat, quia domini regis et magnatum terre indignationi subiacere nolebat. His auditis, nuntiisque qui uenerant dimissis, iam omni spe consolationis succisa, anxiatus est in abbate spiritus eius, sui quoque plurimum anxiabantur. Et quemadmodum inter mestos solet frequenter accidere qui, cum mestitudinis sue remedium non habeant, aliquid sepe loquuntur aut faciunt, per quod mestitudini sue amplius adiciunt, sic unus eorum qui cum abbate erant, /
f. 127 propinquus ei et ceteris familiarior, ad abbatem conuersus dixit, 'Si mihi, domine, ceterisque qui uos contingunt propinquis impensas sufficientes contulissetis quibus scolas frequentare possemus, in lege et decretis iampridem exercitati, uobis in instanti et in aliis necessitatibus possemus esse presidio. Nunc uero in scripturis bruti et hebetes, a nobisipsis consilium non habemus, nec ab aliis prece uel pretio consequi ualemus.' Ad hec abbas, 'Iam me', inquit, 'fere penitet, quod studio legum animum non apposuerim.'

Omnibus qui aderant tum ex nature necessitate, tum ex nocturna

[a] *MS*: personam regni, *marked for transposition*

and fellow canons of that church.' In this way they all excused themselves: as many friends and allies as he thought he had. Clerks of the lord king and the archbishop said that the case touched their lords and they were not able to speak against the decisions of the lords. Of the bishops and clerks some said that Godfrey was their canon, some their fellow canon. The common and general excuse of all was that they were unwilling to incur the displeasure of Richard de Luci, Godfrey's father.

The abbot was reduced to these straits when someone suggested to him that he speak to a clerk, learned in law, who had accompanied the legate from Italy. He might be persuaded to take the case, for he was neither a native nor a resident in the lord king's lands; he was not beholden for a benefice or for any sort of ties of friendship this side of the Alps. He feared neither king, prince, archbishop, bishop, nor anyone ecclesiastical or secular in the realm, whatever advocacy he took up. The abbot acquiesced to his persuader, and meeting the clerk he explained his case. The man undertook its advocacy, agreeing to take a silver mark from the abbot. Feeling secure at last, the abbot took himself off to his lodgings to await the lawsuit on the morrow. Night was falling and the hour of rest was at hand when a delegation came to the abbot from the clerk. They explained their charge orally to the abbot: the clerk would not be able to defend the case they had agreed upon since he did not wish to expose himself to the wrath of the lord king and the magnates of the realm. The abbot listened and then dismissed the messengers. Now all hope of comfort was cut off; the abbot was distressed in spirit, and his entourage exceedingly so. Among mourners it frequently happens that there are those who, having no remedy for their affliction, say or do something that merely adds to that affliction. So now one of those who were with the abbot, a kinsman and more familiar with him than the rest, turned to him and said, 'My lord, if you had only spent enough on me and your other relatives so that we could have attended the schools, we would long since have been knowledgeable in the law and the decretals, and could have been your defence in this and in other necessities. But now, being raw and stupid about writings, we cannot give you counsel, nor can we get it from others, for prayer or price.' The abbot said, 'It is a judgement on me for not having studied the law myself.'

All who were with him then, by the necessity of nature and out of

consuetudine quiescentibus, abbas parum aut nichil repausans noctem totam aut noctis partem maiorem peruigil in oratione transegit insomnem, se causamque suam Deo commendans, sanctoque Martino ut sibi aduocatus fieret humiliter supplicans. Celebratis in crastino diuinis officiis, simpliciter cum suis ad locum decisioni cause prefixum processit, parte aduersa ex opposito ueniente cum aduocatorum multitudine. Procurator et aduocatus principalis in causa partis aduerse erat quidam magister Iuo Cornubiensis,[1] qui procedens in medium, litterasque patentes Godefridi de Luci tunc in transmarinis scolas frequentantis in publicum proferens, commissam sibi manifestauit cause procurationem, et Godefridi ratihabitionem. Erat autem tunc ibi, utpote ad concilium uocati, cleri conuentus maximus, non tamen presidente legato, sed quibusdam suorum quibus cause commiserat decisionem.

Prefatus ergo magister Iuo sic exorsus ait. 'Satis uobis, domini
f. 127v iu/dices, ex patenti testimonio litterarum domini mei Godefridi de Luci credimus constare, ipsum utpote in remotis extra hoc regnum partibus scolarum studia frequentantem huic cause sue interesse non posse, mihique causam eandem procurandam commisisse. Cuius ego aduocatione suscepta, non minorem mihi quam si dominus meus presens adesset postulo dari audientiam, sed tanto diligentiorem, quanto causam quam fouendam suscepi constat esse iustiorem. Cum iam huic uite finem fecisset uir uenerabilis Walterus abbas de Bello, domini mei Godefridi patruus, totius monasterii dispositio in regie sullimitatis deuenit potestatem, adeo ut in domini regis fuerit arbitrio monasterii ipsius regimen cui uellet committere, cum tamen in uoluntate non habuerit aliquem in eo nisi canonice electum substitui. Nondum penes se deliberauerat maiestas regia, cui monasterialis prelationis conferret honorem, cum presbiterum quendam Willelmum personam ecclesie de Wi contigit huic uite renuntiare. Dominus rex, ratione qua potuit de totius monasterii corpore pro uoluntate disponere, predictam ecclesiam de Wi in fundo monasterii sitam domino meo Godefrido de Luci pietatis et caritatis concessit intuitu, et carta sua quam ad manum habemus confirmauit, ut rex, ut fundi dominus, ut monasterii illius, preter cetera regni monasteria,

nightly custom, lay down to rest. But the abbot rested little or not at all; he passed the whole night, or its greatest part, in wakeful, prayerful vigil, committing himself and his case to God, and humbly begging St. Martin to become his advocate. In the morning after divine service, he and his people went unpretentiously to the place set for deciding the case, while the opposing side came against him with a crowd of advocates. The proctor and chief advocate in the case for the opposing side was a Master Ivo of Cornwall.[1] He stepped to the centre and publicly produced letters patent from Godfrey de Luci, who was at that time studying abroad, showing that the case had been put in his hands with Godfrey's approval. There was present a very large gathering of clergy since they had been summoned for a council. The legate was not presiding; he had committed the decision in the case to certain of his legation.

Master Ivo began thus. 'My lord justices, I believe the evidence of my lord Godfrey de Luci's letters makes it clear that it is not possible for him to be here himself, since he is studying at the schools, far away beyond this realm, and that he has appointed me his attorney in this case. Having undertaken his advocacy, I ask that no less a hearing be given me than if my lord were here in person. Indeed, the hearing should be the more attentive as the cause I have undertaken to plead is so clearly the more just. When the venerable Walter, abbot of Battle, my lord's uncle, died, the management of the entire monastery fell to the power of the royal highness to the degree that it was for the king to decide whom he wished to administer the monastery. Of course he did not wish anyone as abbot who was not canonically elected. The royal majesty had not yet decided on whom he would confer the honour of this monastic perferment, when the priest William, parson of the church of Wye, happened to die. The lord king, who had the right to dispose as he wished of the whole monastery, for the sake of piety and charity granted this church of Wye, situated on a manor of the monastery, to my lord Godfrey de Luci. He confirmed it by his charter, which we have at hand, as king, as lord of the manor, as particular patron of this monastery beyond the other monasteries

[1] Ivo of Cornwall occurs as *magister* in 1187 (*Early Yorkshire Charters*, v, ed. C. T. Clay, Yorks. Archaeological Soc. Record Ser. Extra Ser. ii, 1936, no. 190) and as archdeacon of Derby by 1191 (*The Register of St. Osmund*, ed. W. H. Rich Jones (RS), i. 221, 264; cf. 243, 252). I am grateful to Professor C. N. L. Brooke for this identification.

specialis patronus. Nec quidem incongruum fuit domino regi de membris disponere, cui totum corpus erat in potestate.' Et hec
f. 128 dicens cartam domini regis super donatione et confirmatione / in medium protulit. Et adiciens: 'Facta', inquit, 'iure patronatus huiusmodi donatione, uir uenerabilis dominus Ricardus, tunc Cantuariensis electus, dominum meum Godefridum auctoritate qua potuit ad presentationem domini regis suscipiens personam absque omni exceptione instituit, datis sibi in testimonii munimentum institutionis sue litteris, sigillo quod tunc habere uidebatur apposito, licet nondum in plena potestate uideretur constitutus.'

Proferensque in publicum litteras, 'En', inquit, 'ipsius electi testimonium. Sedem apostolicam postmodum adiens, ibique a domino papa solenniter consecratus, ac inde cum plena potestate archiepiscopi, primatis et legati denuo rediens, quod electus minus antea facere poterat, iam confirmatus plena auctoritate instituendo et confirmando roborauit.' Et hec dicendo, cartam archiepiscopi, ipso etiam archiepiscopo presente, in omnium oculis ostendit, ita subinferens: 'Cum igitur', inquit, 'huius ecclesie de Wi non qualemcunque portionem, sed ecclesiam totam cum omni iuris sui integritate dominus meus Godefridus tam excellenti auctoritate obtinuerit, dominus abbas et monachi de Bello ipsius ecclesie medietatem contra regiam episcopalemque dignitatem detinent occupatam. Ergo secundum plenam domini regis donationem et domini archiepiscopi plenam institutionem, plenam petimus possessionem, ad maiorem parati probationem, si forte iam edita uideatur minus sufficiens; abbati et monachis, plena possessione suscepta siquid questionis aduersum nos habuerint responsuri, et
f. 128v secundum iuris ordinem satisfa/cturi.'

Stupefactus ad hec abbas plurimum, stabat expers humani consilii, confisus tamen de diuino, responsurus ad proposita. Cum eos quos credebat amicos ut ad consilium suum uenirent benigne rogaret, omnes se modo quo predictum est excusauerunt, adeo ut nec unus omnium qui aderant preter suos qui secum illo uenerant consilium sibi uel auxilium prestiturus procederet. Nemo enim omnium, timore domini regis et archiepiscopi et Ricardi de Luci, secum stare presumpsit, cognito quod eos causa contingeret.

Aderat illic inter ceteros magister Walerannus Baiocensis archidiaconus, postmodum Roffensis episcopus, qui tunc temporis Cantuariensi archiepiscopo adherens,[1] illic collateralis magistri

[1] Consecrated Dec. 1182. Waleran was a clerk of Archbishop Richard. Le Neve, ed. Greenway, ii. 76.

of the realm. Indeed it was not unwarranted for the king to arrange for the members, when the whole body was in his power.' Saying this, he produced the lord king's charter of grant and confirmation, and added, 'This sort of grant having been made by right of advowson, the venerable lord, Richard, then archbishop elect of Canterbury, received my lord Godfrey as parson at the king's presentation by such authority as he had, and instituted him unconditionally. As evidence of his institution he gave him a letter sealed with the seal he then used, though he had not yet received his full power.'

He produced the letter and went on, 'You see the evidence of the bishop elect. Afterwards, he went to the apostolic see and was there consecrated formally by the pope and returned again with the full power of archbishop, primate and legate. Now that he had himself been confirmed, he reinstituted and reconfirmed the grant with full authority, in a way that he had been unable to do before when elect.' And as he said this he showed the archbishop's charter before the eyes of all, including the archbishop who was present. He then continued, 'Although on such excellent authority my lord Godfrey obtained not merely some part, but all of the church of Wye, with all its rights in full, the lord abbot and the monks of Battle hold back half, which they have seized quite contrary to the royal and episcopal privileges. Therefore we ask for full possession, as the lord king's grant and the lord archbishop's institution were full. We are ready with further proof, if what we have produced seems insufficient. When given full possession, if they have any question against us, we shall answer the abbot and monks and satisfy them at law.'

The abbot, stunned by all this, stood there, destitute of human counsel, but trusting to the divine in replying to all this. When he had begged those whom he thought friends kindly to give him counsel, all had excused themselves in the way we have said. Not one of those present, save his own people who had come with him, would come forward ready to offer him counsel or aid. For none among them all dared to stand with him, for fear of the lord king, the archbishop, and Richard de Luci, for it was known that the case touched them.

There was present there among the rest Master Waleran, archdeacon of Bayeux, afterwards bishop of Rochester, but at that time in the household of the archbishop of Canterbury.[1] He was sitting

Gerardi Puelle residebat. Hic abbatem intuens in angustiis positum, et diuino ut creditur instinctu pietate motus, conuersus ad magistrum Gerardum, 'Magister', inquit, 'Gerarde, sic omnes abbatem de Bello desolatum relinquemus? Dei odium incurrat, qui ei in hac necessitate deerit.' Surgensque et magistrum Gerardum amica uiolentia manu iniecta post se trahens, 'Eamus', inquit, 'et abbatis assistentes consilio ei in causa sua subueniamus.'

Venientibus ex insperato ambobus ad abbatis consilium, abbas iam erat animequior, et de causa sua securior. Non diu protracto, sed maturato expeditoque consilio, redeunt pariter ad iudicum consessum, ubi magister Gerardus, agente magistro Waleranno, immo Deo disponente, procedens in spiritu fortitudinis, non regem
f. 129 ueritus, non archi/episcopum dominum suum, non principes, non quoslibet eorum fautores, libera uoce cepit in hunc modum pro abbate allegare.

'Sicut ea', inquit, 'que canonice sunt inchoata, ut perfectionem obtineant sunt promouenda, sic que contra iuris ordinem perperam sunt attemptata, in irritum sunt reuocanda, aut in statum meliorem transformanda. Allegatum est a parte aduersa, quod monasterio Belli pastore orbato, totius monasterii dispositio in manus domini regis deuenerit, uacantem interim ecclesiam de Wi in fundo monasterii sitam dominus rex domino Godefrido de Luci contulerit, quodque eum regia auctoritate presentatum dominus noster Cantuariensis primum electus, postmodum archiepiscopus, ad eandem ecclesiam susceperit, et personam instituerit. Ad hec imprimis salua pace domini regis respondemus, quod in rebus ecclesiasticis nichil iuris obtinet potestas secularis. Licet ad tempus in rebus monasterii pastore orbati uisa fuerit maiestas regia pro potestate sibi iuris aliquid uendicasse,[1] nichil tamen ad detrimentum monasterii abbatisue futuri de iure potuit uel debuit immutare, alienare, seu aliquatenus disponere, sed abbati futuro resignanda omnia in sua integritate conseruare. Domini igitur regis super ecclesia de Wi in fundo monasterii sita nulla debuit esse donatio, quia uacantis cenobii non tam patronus quam custos, nullam in eo proprii iuris obtinuit possessionem, nec de iure alieno

[1] Gerard's conception of the rights of a patron during vacancy reflects the latest thought of his day among canonists. Between 1175 and *c.* 1180 two influential French treatises dealt with the problem in much the way Gerard presents it here. They were the *Summa Inperatorie Maiestati*, and Peter of Blois's *Distinctiones*. See Benson, *Bishop-Elect*, Appendix 2, pp. 391–6. As

with Master Gerard Pucelle. Thoughtfully he contemplated the abbot in these straits, and he was moved to kindness, as is thought, by a divine impulse. He turned to Master Gerard. 'Master Gerard, shall we all leave the abbot of Battle thus abandoned? He may risk the wrath of God who fails him in this need.' Getting up he seized Gerard with a friendly impetuosity and hauled him along. 'Let us go', he said, 'and give the abbot counsel. Let us help him in the case.'

With both of them coming unexpectedly to counsel him, the abbot felt calmer already, and less anxious about his case. They did not linger; the conference was brief and easy, and they returned together to the judges-delegate, where Master Gerard, advised by Master Waleran—though with God disposing—stepped forward bravely, afraid neither of the king, his lord the archbishop, nor of magnates, nor any of their creatures. In a bold voice he began to argue thus for the abbot.

'Just as affairs which were begun canonically should be advanced to perfect completion, so should affairs which are wrongly attempted against the properly constituted rules of law come to nothing, or be brought into a better state. It has been alleged by their opponents that since Battle abbey was without an abbot, the disposal of the entire monastery lapsed into the king's hand, that the lord king granted to the lord Godfrey de Luci the church of Wye, located on a manor of the monastery and become vacant in the mean time, and that our lord, first the elect and afterwards archbishop of Canterbury, received him into that church as one presented by royal authority, and instituted him as parson. To this we answer, first, saving the peace of the lord king, that in ecclesiastical matters the secular power possesses no right. Maybe for a time, in the case of a monastery bereft of its pastor, the king's majesty seems to have claimed a right where what it had was a power.[1] But it neither could nor should make changes, alienations, or decisions of any kind detrimental to the monastery or the future abbot, but only preserve everything to be turned over in its entirety to the future abbot. Therefore there should have been no grant by the lord king of the church of Wye, located on a monastic manor. For, being not so much patron as custodian of the vacant abbey, he held no possessory rights of his own in it, nor should he

canonical teaching the thought was new perhaps, but St. Anselm had expressed precisely this position during the reign of William II. Eadmer, *Hist. Nov.*, pp. 49–50.

facere debuit donationem. Cum ergo palam sit quod sit irrita donatio,
f. 129v consequens omnino est ut etiam irrita debeat esse presentatio,/ quia qui non potuit dare nec debuit presentare. Presentatus domino Cantuariensi electo per eum dicitur fuisse admissus, sed licet ratione precedentium minus canonica fuerit institutio, et ideo irrita, alia tamen consideratione nulla fuit, nec esse potuit, quoniam electione archiepiscopi per summum pontificem nondum confirmata, electus admittendi uel instituendi non habuit potestatem.[1]

'Consecratus a domino papa archiepiscopus, et a sede apostolica in plenitudine potestatis reuersus, quod minus antea fecerat dicitur solennius fecisse, et episcopali auctoritate confirmasse, sed nulla esse debuit uel potuit ipsius confirmatio, cum in ipsius consecratione sint omnia a summo pontifice cassata, que ante consecrationem eius electionis tempore ab ipso fuerant instituta. Cum igitur electionis tempore facta fuerit presentatio et presentati institutio, dum omnia in consecratione reuocantur in irritum, constat etiam quod quicquid circa presens negotium est attemptatum sub uniuersitate concluditur, unde et in irritum proculdubio reuocatur. Quia enim respectu apostolice auctoritatis modica aut nulla esse dinoscitur potestas episcopalis, que ab excellentiori dissoluuntur, per inferioris ordinis gradum nequeunt accipere firmitatem. Totius itaque rei serie diligentius considerata, dum omnia in iuris ecclesiastici preiudicium perpetrata uidentur, firmitatis sue non immerito robur amittunt, quoniam in ecclesiastice soliditatis radice non subsistunt. Plene institutionis postulat pars
f. 130 aduersa be/neficium cum potius beneficio portionis priuari meruerit, quod in prefata ecclesia de Wi nullo rationis titulo dinoscitur possidere. Spoliatum est iure suo uacans monasterium, nec tenentur iniuste spoliati in iure suo respondere nisi primum restituti,[2] unde et dominus abbas de Bello pro monasterio suo agens iuris sui petit restitutionem, postmodum paratus ad exhibendam iustitie plenitudinem.'

Cum in hunc modum magister Gerardus in omnium audientia perorasset, et allegationem suam legum ac decretorum que hic inserere longum erat auctoritatibus comprobasset, iamque pro allegatione partium ferenda esset sententia, delegati iudices haud dubium quin aduerse parti respectu potestatis deferentes, sententiam

[1] See above, p. 270.

[2] Both lawyers demand possession before a trial of right, the canonical action 'exceptio spolii' being in that respect like the English assize of novel disseisin.

have made a grant of another's right. Therefore since it is evident that the grant is invalid, it follows that the presentation too must be invalid, for he who could not grant should not have presented either. The man presented to the lord elect of Canterbury is said to have been admitted by him, though for the reasons just given the institution was uncanonical and therefore invalid. There is yet another reason why there was not, and could not have been any institution: for the archbishop's election had not yet been confirmed by the pope, and as bishop elect he had no power to admit or institute.[1]

'It is said that after the archbishop had been consecrated by the lord pope and had returned from the apostolic see with full powers, he formally enacted what he had done incompletely before, and confirmed it by his episcopal authority. But his confirmation was illegal and impossible, for at his consecration everything arranged by him between the time of his election and his consecration was quashed by the pope. Therefore since the presentation and institution were made during the time he was bishop elect, since everything is declared invalid upon consecration, it is evident that whatever was attempted in this present business comes under the general rule, and by it is without doubt revoked as invalid. For with respect to the apostolic authority episcopal power is acknowledged as little or nothing; what is nullified by the greater cannot be made durable by the lesser order. When this whole affair is carefully considered step by step, everything done seems to have been prejudicial to canon law. It is not unjust then that it all fall to the ground, for it is not rooted in ecclesiastical solidity. The other party demands the favour of full institution when he rather deserves to be deprived of the favour of a part, for he obviously possesses no title in reason to the church of Wye. A vacant monastery has been deprived of its right, and the unjustly deprived is not bound to answer on the question of right until first restored.[2] And for that reason the abbot of Battle acting for his monastery seeks restitution of his right, and is afterwards prepared to do full justice.'

Master Gerard had addressed the gathering thus, and had established his argument by authorities of the laws and decretals too long to repeat here, and now sentence should have been given on the arguments of the parties. But the judges-delegate (and there is no doubt that they were backing down before the power of the

sub dissimulatione reliquerunt, et partibus ut componerent preceperunt. Abbas cui plus erat desiderio pacis bonum quam lis atque contentio, ex multarum consideratione circumstantiarum decreuit compositionem non respuere, sciens se iam nichil eorum que possederat amissurum, immo magis confisus se amplius adepturum. Formata est illic, uiris discretis hinc inde interuenientibus, huiusmodi compositio, ut scilicet decimis de Bekewelle et Beawerdregge et Holeford ad sacristariam monasterii de Bello ab antiquo assignatis, in eadem assignatione permanentibus, de cetero Godefridus de Luci totam ecclesiam de Wi nomine uicarie perpetue sub pensione xv marcarum monasterio annuatim soluenda possideret.[1] Et quoniam, ut predictum est, Godefridus
f. 130v tunc temporis in transmarinis moram faciebat, in / reditu suo ad monasterium Belli in propria persona accederet, instrumenta omnia que uel regis uel archiepiscopi nomine super prefata ecclesia habere uidebatur monasterio resignaret, munimentumque per quod compositio firmaretur a solo monasterio reciperet. In hunc modum formata et hinc inde approbata compositione, abbas Deo et beato Martino gratias agens in sua rediit, iam tanto hilarior, quanto de causa sua securior. Interrogatus inter gratulandum si iam grauiter ferret, quod decretorum ac legum exercitium non haberet, iocunde respondens, 'Nulla', inquit, 'lex tam bona, nullum adeo efficax decretum, ut est psalmus, "Miserere mei Deus." '[2]

Hec ideo duximus inserenda, ut liquido detur intelligi quantam habuerit in oratione deuotionem, qui iam didicerat in causa sua magis obtinere fusa ad Deum oratione, quam facunda hominum allegatione. Negotium hoc preterea iccirco diffusius texuimus, quia diuine uirtuti abbatisque orationibus ascribendum putauimus, quod cum paulo ante regnum et sacerdotium aut aduersus eum publice staret, aut nullo consilio uel auxilio seu prece seu pretio sibi adesset, inopinatum repente diuinitus intercessit patrocinium, quo partis aduerse deiceretur de qua confidebat potestas, et aduocatorum confunderetur multiplicitas.

Godefridus de Luci his cognitis, licet egre accipiens, non tamen a forma compositionis resilire preualens, in reditu suo a transmarinis monasterium Belli in propria persona adiit, resignatisque omnibus instrumentis suis, cartam confirmationis secundum formam prescriptam ab . . . .[a]

[a] *The text breaks off here: see p. 27*

[1] Cf. above, p. 268. The earlier situation had been that Battle held half the church, from which it received ten marks. It will now receive fifteen, plus the tithes of the three members, the earlier fate of which is not clear.

[2] Pss. 51: 1; 86: 3. It is, of course, an important *oratio* in the Mass.

opposing party) hid their opinion, and ordered the parties to settle by compromise. The abbot, who desired peace much more than argument and contention, considering the many facets of the matter decided not to refuse a compromise, knowing that he would lose nothing that he already held, indeed, trusting rather that he might gain more. Sensible men acted as intermediaries and a compromise of this sort was worked out: the tithes of Buckwell and Bewbridge and *Holeford*, long ago assigned to the sacristy of the monastery of Battle, were to remain permanently assigned. In future Godfrey de Luci was to hold the entire church of Wye as perpetual vicar, paying a pension of fifteen marks annually to the monastery.[1] And since, as we have said, Godfrey at that time was abroad, upon his return he was to come to Battle in person, to resign to the monastery all the documents he seemed to have in the name of the king and archbishop concerning the church, and receive from the monastery alone a record by which the compromise would be guaranteed. The compromise was thus worked out on these lines and accepted on both sides, and the abbot, giving thanks to God and St. Martin, returned home the more joyful that he felt certain of his case. Asked by his congratulators if he still felt annoyed because he had no expertise in the laws and decretals, he happily replied, 'There is no law so good, no decretal so effective as the Psalm, "Lord, have mercy upon me."'[2]

We have added this so that it can be clearly understood what faith he had in prayer, who had learned that he gained more in his case by copious prayer to God than by the eloquent argumentation of men. Moreover, we have written about the affair at length just because we think that one should attribute the outcome to the divine strength and to the abbot's prayers. At one moment both church and realm either publicly opposed him or would give him neither counsel nor aid, neither for prayer nor price. Yet unlooked for and suddenly, a divine patronage intervened. It cast down the power in which the adversary had confided, and confounded the multitude of his advocates.

When Godfrey de Luci heard of this, although he was grudging, he was nevertheless not powerful enough to go back upon the terms of the compromise. On his return from across the sea he came in person to the monastery of Battle, and having resigned all his documents, according to the prescribed terms he [received] a charter of confirmation from . . . .

CONCORDANCES

By Diana E. Greenway

Concordance of Brewer's edition with the present edition

The table shows on which page of the present edition the first word of each page of Brewer's edition is to be found.

Brewer	Present edition	Brewer	Present edition	Brewer	Present edition
1	32	40	94	79	166
2	32	41	96	80	166
3	34	42	98	81	168
4	36	43	100	82	170
5	38	44	102	83	172
6	40	45	104	84	174
7	42	46	104	85	174
8	44	47	106	86	176
9	46	48	108	87	178
10	46	49	112	88	180
11	48	50	112	89	182
12	50	51	114	90	184
13	52	52	116	91	184
14	54	53	118	92	186
15	56	54	120	93	188
16	56	55	122	94	190
17	58	56	124	95	192
18	60	57	126	96	194
19	62	58	128	97	196
20	64	59	130	98	196
21	64	60	132	99	198
22	66	61	134	100	200
23	66	62	136	101	202
24	68	63	138	102	204
25	70	64	138	103	204
26	72	65	140	104	206
27	74	66	142	105	208
28	76	67	144	106	210
29	76	68	146	107	212
30	78	69	148	108	214
31	80	70	150	109	216
32	82	71	150	110	218
33	82	72	152	111	220
34	84	73	154	112	222
35	86	74	156	113	224
36	88	75	158	114	226
37	90	76	160	115	228
38	92	77	162	116	228
39	92	78	164	117	230

Brewer	Present edition	Brewer	Present edition	Brewer	Present edition
118	232	139	266	160	302
119	234	140	268	161	304
120	236	141	270	162	304
121	238	142	272	163	306
122	238	143	274	164	308
123	240	144	276	165	310
124	242	145	278	166	312
125	244	146	278	167	314
126	246	147	280	168	316
127	246	148	282	169	316
128	248	149	284	170	318
129	250	150	286	171	320
130	250	151	286	172	321
131	252	152	288	173	324
132	254	153	290	174	326
133	256	154	292	175	326
134	258	155	294	176	328
135	260	156	296	177	330
136	260	157	296	178	332
137	262	158	298	179	433
138	264	159	300		

II Concordance of the present edition with Brewer's edition

The table shows on which page of Brewer's edition the first word of each page of the present edition is to be found.

Present edition	Brewer	Present edition	Brewer	Present edition	Brewer
32	1	76	27	120	53
34	2	78	29	122	54
36	3	80	30	124	55
38	4	82	31	126	56
40	5	84	33	128	57
42	6	86	34	130	58
44	7	88	35	132	59
46	8	90	36	134	60
48	10	92	37	136	61
50	11	94	39	138	62
52	12	96	40	140	64
54	13	98	41	142	65
56	14	100	42	144	66
58	16	102	43	146	67
60	17	104	44	148	68
62	18	106	46	150	69
64	19	108	47	152	71
66	21	110	48	154	72
68	23	112	48	156	73
70	24	114	50	158	74
72	25	116	51	160	75
74	26	118	52	162	76

Present edition	Brewer	Present edition	Brewer	Present edition	Brewer
164	77	222	111	280	146
166	78	224	112	282	147
168	80	226	113	284	148
170	81	228	114	286	149
172	82	230	116	288	151
174	83	232	117	290	152
176	85	234	118	292	153
178	86	236	119	294	154
180	87	238	120	296	155
182	88	240	122	298	157
184	89	242	123	300	158
186	91	244	124	302	159
188	92	246	125	304	160
190	93	248	127	306	162
192	94	250	128	308	163
194	95	252	130	310	164
196	96	254	131	312	165
198	98	256	132	314	166
200	99	258	133	316	167
202	100	260	134	318	169
204	101	262	136	320	170
206	103	264	137	322	171
208	104	266	138	324	172
210	105	270	140	326	173
212	106	272	141	328	175
214	107	274	142	330	176
216	108	276	143	332	177
218	109	278	144	334	178
220	110				

INDEX